Sexual Politics in Modern Iran

Janet Afary is a native of Iran and a leading historian. Her work focuses on gender and sexuality and draws on her experience of growing up in Iran and her involvement with Iranian women of different ages and social strata. These observations, and a wealth of historical documents, form the kernel of this book, which charts the history of gender and sexuality in Iran from the nineteenth century to today. What comes across is the extraordinary resilience of the Iranian people, who have drawn on a rich social and cultural heritage to defy the repression and hardship of the Islamist state and its predecessors. It is this resilience, the author concludes, which forms the basis of a still unfinished sexual revolution taking place in Iran today, one that is promoting reforms in marriage and family laws, and demanding more egalitarian relations.

JANET AFARY is Professor of History and Women's Studies at Purdue University. Her previous publications include *The Iranian Constitutional Revolution: Grassroots Democracy, Social Democracy, and the Origins of Feminism* (1996) and, with Kevin B. Anderson, the award-winning *Foucault and the Iranian Revolution: Gender and the Seductions of Islamism* (2005).

Sexual Politics in Modern Iran

Janet Afary

CAMBRIDGE
UNIVERSITY PRESS

CAMBRIDGE UNIVERSITY PRESS
Cambridge, New York, Melbourne, Madrid, Cape Town, Singapore,
São Paulo, Delhi

Cambridge University Press
The Edinburgh Building, Cambridge CB2 8RU, UK

Published in the United States of America by Cambridge University Press,
New York

www.cambridge.org
Information on this title: www.cambridge.org/9780521727082

First published 2009

Printed in the United Kingdom at the University Press, Cambridge

A catalogue record for this publication is available from the British Library

ISBN 978-0-521-89846-1 hardback
ISBN 978-0-521-72708-2 paperback

For
The One Million Signatures Campaign

Contents

Illustrations

Acknowledgments

Research for this book was conducted primarily at the Regenstein Library of the University of Chicago, where I have been an Associate Fellow of the Middle East Center since 1991. Many thanks to the Regenstein Library and Center staff for their assistance throughout this period. Larry Mykytiuk at Purdue University's HSSE Library was also immensely supportive and purchased a significant number of relevant journals and books. Azar Ashraf at the Near East Collection at Princeton University Library and David Hirsch at the UCLA Research Library generously guided me through their collections. With introductions from Solmaz Rustamova-Tohidi and Hamlet Isaxanli, I gained access to the Baku Manuscript Institute in Azerbaijan, where I microfilmed many rare titles with the help of Saif al-Din Ma'sum Oghli and especially Aref Ramazanov. In Los Angeles, Laleh Ghahreman from Ketab Corporation and Kikhosro Behrozi from Kolbeh Ketab helped locate other pertinent titles. During and after my visit to Tehran in 2005, I benefited from the help of several dedicated colleagues in that city. Mansoureh Ettehadieh introduced me to her Center, Nashr-e Tarikh-e Iran (Publishing Iranian History). Her student, Elham Malekzadeh, answered numerous queries, found rare materials and illustrations, and provided other access to archives beyond my reach. My old high-school friend and sociologist Shahla Ezazi critically read the final draft and sent a detailed list of corrections and suggestions. Saeid Madani-Ghahfarokhi, editor of *Faslnameh-ye Refah-e Ejtema'i (Social Welfare Quarterly)*, and his colleagues Meroeh Vameghi, Ameneh Sattareh Foroozan, and Mohammad Ali Mohammady, responded in great detail to some issues concerning the last three chapters. Several other people, among them Saeed Damadi, Morteza Dehghani, Farah Ghadernia, Hirmand Hasass, and Hassan Mortazavi, also sent me materials from Tehran.

At Cambridge University Press, I would like to express my profound thanks to my editor Marigold Acland for her encouragement and patience as this manuscript went through various gestations. Her assistant, Sarah Green, diligently worked on resolving glitches in the illustrations; Caroline Diepeveen prepared the index and put up with my many revisions; Monica Kendall deftly edited the manuscript, making it a pleasure to work with her; Phil Treble designed the cover; and Rosina Di Marzo oversaw the whole production and graciously endured my delays. Many thanks also to the anonymous reviewers of the press.

Several fellowships and grants allowed me release time from teaching to complete this book, among them an NEH Fellowship in 2004–2005, a Purdue University Center for Humanistic Studies Fellowship in spring 2003, and a sabbatical leave in spring 2007. My eternal thanks to Ronald Grigor Suny and Gernot Windfuhr, my mentors at the University of Michigan, for believing in me and providing valuable encouragement through the years. I wish Kenneth Allin Luther and Richard P. Mitchell, also from the University of Michigan, had lived to read drafts of this work. Allin had much to say about Shi'i rituals and was a keen follower of the Iranian Revolution. Richard's groundbreaking work on the *Society of Muslim Brothers* (1969) helped to spark my own interest in Islamism.

At Purdue University, I was fortunate to have numerous forms of support from Dean John Contreni, who has opened so many doors. I was equally fortunate to have the support of Berenice Carroll of Women's Studies, who has been a real mentor. Numerous conversations with colleagues in the Department of History and the Women's Studies Program have helped shape this study as well.

Several wonderful friends and colleagues read the whole or large parts of the manuscript and made countless valuable suggestions: Nikki Keddie of UCLA has been an extremely supportive mentor since we first met at a conference on Iran in Washington DC in the 1980s. She read several drafts of this manuscript and made many suggestions. Houchang Chehabi not only read the manuscript carefully, but he also went out of his way to copy and mail hard-to-find materials including memoirs of the Iranian singer Mahvash. Sohrab Behdad patiently corrected statistical errors; Mansour Bonakdarian provided valuable background on the inner circles of Iranian leftists in the 1970s; Thomas M. Ricks aided me with background on the slave economy of the nineteenth century; Erika Friedl and Mary Hegland answered numerous queries; my husband Kevin Anderson read the manuscript several times and helped me find relevant materials from the Frankfurt School of Critical Theory.

A much larger number of people offered helpful critiques of specific chapters or parts of the book: Abbas Amanat, Walter Andrews, Jennifer Ball, Hélène Bellour, Evelyn Blackwood, Jeanne Boydston, Miriam Cooke, Stephanie Coontz, Masserat Amir Ebrahimi, Manoutchehr Eskandari-Qajar, Willem Floor, Ali Gheissari, Shahla Haeri, Azadeh Kian-Thiébaut, Samuel Kinser, Firoozeh Papan-Matin, Arsham Parsi,

John Perry, Nasrin Rahimieh, Everett Rowson, and Houman Sarshar. All have my heartfelt thanks.

Others assisted with source materials, useful suggestions, lively conversations in conferences, or via snail mail or e-mail: John Abromeit, Mahnaz Afkhami, Akbar Aghajanian, Abdollah Aghdasi, Zohreh Arzani Chahla Chafiq, Ken Cuno, Touraj Daryaee Richard Davis, Kianoush Dehghani, Farideh Farhi, Manouchehr Haghighi, Doug Ireland, Meir Javedanfar, Ahmad Karimi-Hakkak, Mehrangiz Kar, Manouchehr Kasheff, Mehdi Khalaji, Jamil Khouri, Lauren Langman, Akbar Mahdi, Fati Masjedi, Rudi Matthee, Behnaz Mirzai, Valentine Moghadam, Majid Mohammadi, David Morgan, Hossein Mohri, Kourosh N. Moradi, Nahid Mozaffari, Majid Naficy, Azar Nafisi, Effat Rahimi-Mohri, Shiri Rotem-Nir, Hadi Salehi-Esfahani Ruth Salvaggio, Farah Shadchehr, Somaya Shahrivari, Mahsa Shekarloo, Margaret Strobel, Sussan Tahmasebi, Kian Tajbakhsh, Mohamad Tavakoli-Targhi, Gholam R. Vatandoust, Paul Vieille, Sohrab Yazdani, Fatemeh Zargari, and Tahereh Zavvarehi. My brother Kamran Afary sent articles on contemporary issues. Shahzad Bashir, Fataneh Farahani, Erika Friedl, Mary Hegland, Hamid Naficy, and Everett Rowson were kind enough to share their unpublished work. For details on the successful family planning program of the Islamic Republic, Muhammad Alizadeh, one of the initiators of the program, proved enormously helpful. I also presented draft chapters of this book at Columbia University, Ohio State University, Osaka University, Pennsylvania State University, Purdue University, UCLA, University of Chicago, University of Illinois Champaign-Urbana, University of Toronto, University of Wisconsin-Madison and various MESA conferences. Throughout, I have benefited from the comments and suggestions of numerous colleagues and students.

I would like to acknowledge the help of the following students at Purdue University, the University of Chicago, Northwestern University, Loyola University, and UCLA who served as my assistants during the writing of this book: Sarah Avery, Sherrema Bower, Laura Eckstein, Haleh Emrani, Li Fei, Lela Gibson, Alex Hanna, Kaveh Hemmat, Brynn Lyerly, Amy Malek, Paul Ong, Robert Oprisko, Khodadad Rezakhani, Stephanie Richardson, Ali G. Scotten, Kaveh Sepehr, Kelly Stalling, Peishan Tan, Tanya Tang, Javid Validashti, Heather Welland, and Mir Yarfitz. For editorial assistance, I cannot thank enough Ahmad Aminpour, Joelle Goldman, Gershon Lewental, Brian Maxson, Melvin Pena, Danny Postel, Rita Sindelar, and especially Nicholas Murray whose remarkable editorial suggestions helped render the work more accessible to the general public. My sister Frieda Afary, a Persian translator, also made numerous corrections, and routinely sent materials for inclusion in the book.

Many of the images and cartoons reprinted here are from Iranian newspapers and magazines of the past century that I have located in various libraries. A few are reprinted from Jane Dieulafoy (1887), Afshar (1992), Filizadeh (2006), and Kiani-Haftlang (2007). Mahdokht Sanati sent several photos from Tehran; Mansoureh Fatoorehchi and Muhammad Eftekhari donated their collection of *Towfiq*; Abbas Towfiq provided a few other graphics from his private collection of *Towfiq*. Some illustrations came from the private collection of Mansore Pirnia and my parents, others were reprinted by the Center for Persian Studies, University of Maryland. Those dealing with the years 2000 often arrived via e-mail from Iran, including photos by Arash Ashoorinia. I am grateful for permission to reprint several images from the Special Collections Research Center of the University of Chicago, the Metropolitan Museum of Art, and www.cartoonstock.com. Whenever possible I have credited the artists and photographers of these illustrations; however, in some cases I was unable to track them down but will be happy to credit them in any future reprint of this volume. I am indebted to artist and photographer Amir Nourmandi of Dlast Studios, Chicago for scanning and editing these images.

More than my earlier books, this study has touched me personally. I owe a debt of gratitude to my grandmothers Rahel Afary and Monir Pirnazar for sharing their life stories with me. Both were married at thirteen in Kermanshah in arranged marriages during World War I. My mother, Anvar (Pirnazar) Afary, married my father Naim Afary in 1950 at age eighteen in Tehran in a semi-arranged marriage. They tried to establish a more companionate marriage at a time when in-laws still ruled the extended family. My sister, Mona Afary, a psychologist in San Francisco, runs the Center for Empowering Refugees and Immigrants (CERI), which caters to women from Asia and the Middle East. My friend Manij Marashi works at Apna Ghar, a shelter for battered women in Chicago with a similar population. My daughter Lena works with an analogous group of women in the legal profession. Many of the Middle Eastern women who have come under their supervision have had arranged or semi-arranged marriages contracted in their native homes. I bounced many of the ideas in this book off of them, as I came to appreciate the vast gulf between the classic patriarchal marriages of our grandmothers, which were restricted but safeguarded by the extended family, and the more individualistic marriages of our time, which aspire to greater intimacy but are often quite fragile.

Unless otherwise mentioned, all translations from Persian are by the author. Translations from the French are by the author, Kevin Anderson, and Gladys M. Francis. Brynn Lyerly and Ashley Passmore translated the materials from German. Translations from the Azeri and the Russian are by Aref Ramazanov. Their help has been indispensable to this project.

I have adopted a modified version of the transliteration system of *Encyclopedia Iranica* (use of vowels o and e in addition to a, i, and u) for Persian words, and a modified version of the transliteration system of the *International Journal of Middle East Studies* (*IJMES*) for Arabic words. I have omitted all diacritical marks except hamzeh or ain. I have also reverted to the *New York Times* style of transliteration for commonly known words (i.e. Ali instead of 'Ali).

Parts of chapters 8 and 9 appeared in an article, "Portraits of Two Islamist Women," *Critique* 19 (Fall): 89–110, and in Afary and Anderson (2005). An early draft of chapter 11 appeared in *Iranian Studies* 42(1) (February 2009).

Map of Iran

Introduction

A few years ago, at a conference on Middle Eastern women in Bellagio, Italy, an anthropologist asked me, "How exactly does a historian of gender go about researching her field?" It was a surprising but valid question, given the relatively recent origin of the field of Middle Eastern gender history. The short answer is that since there are often a small number of historical documents that deal directly with women's issues, much of Middle East gender history is about rereading existing texts, asking how their authors conceptualized masculinity and femininity for their time. The historian must also have a keen eye for silences and gaps in historical records, which can be very revealing. One also needs to adopt an inter-disciplinary approach to capture those subtle transformations in gender roles that are not reflected in historical accounts. Forays into poetry, short stories, novels, cartoons, cinema, as well as works by cultural anthropologists, sociologists, literary critics, and economists of the region can yield great results.

Perhaps the best way to answer the question, and also shed light on the theoretical orientation of this book, is to take the reader through the processes that led to its writing. Initially, I had hoped to explain the underlying gender dynamics of the 1979 Islamic Revolution and its aftermath, here building on the important contributions of Eliz Sanasarian (1982), Parvin Paidar (1995), and more recently Hamideh Sedghi (2007) on women's history and gender policies of the twentieth century. However, my conceptions of the book expanded after conducting a series of seminars at Purdue University on the Critical Theory of the Frankfurt School, the French post-structuralist philosopher Michel Foucault, contemporary feminist theory, and also co-authoring, with Kevin Anderson, *Foucault and the Iranian Revolution* (2005). I gradually concluded that these theoretical writings could provide valuable insights into (1) the exuberance with which women from the *bazaar* and clerical families had embraced the Islamic Revolution and (2) the role of the Islamist state in releasing lower middle-class youth from the grips of their highly patriarchal families.

Historians of the Middle East in the US seldom employ the perspectives of the Frankfurt School with respect to the family and the authoritarian character. Michel Foucault belongs to a different branch of critical theory, but he had also theorized the impact of modernity on the family. As against most members of the Frankfurt School, who had followed Freud's views on sexuality and modernity more or less uncritically, Foucault offered original insights on sexuality by making homosexuality as central as heterosexuality. Once that was done, the attack on homosexuality that accompanied the vaunted sexual liberation of the early twentieth century could be discerned more clearly. Whether or not one agreed with Foucault's overall perspectives on modernity, it was hard not to appreciate his enormous contribution to our understanding of modern sexuality. But what were the consequences of modernity for gender and sexuality in the Middle East, where even talking about the pervasive homoeroticism of the region's premodern culture had been labeled "Orientalism"? Increasingly, I found that sexuality occupied an undeniably crucial place in Iran's history. One could not simply talk about gender and women's rights, particularly rights within marriage, without also addressing the subject of same-sex relations.

The publication of Sirus Shamisa's *Shahedbazi dar Adabiyat-e Farsi* (2002), which deals with same-sex relations in Persian literature, gave me a wonderful excuse to revisit some of the medieval Persian classics from this angle, works that I reread alongside scholarly commentaries on Sufism, most notably those of Annemarie Schimmel (1975) and Julie Scott Meisami (1987). I emerged from this excursion with a new appreciation for the Foucauldian concept of the "ethics of love" as I concentrated on the rituals of male courtship in Persian literature. I also realized that Sufi love, which had always been celebrated for its religious and ethnic tolerance and its break with orthodoxy, might also have embodied a new "ethics of love." This literary-philosophical tradition seemed to break with the conventional status-defined homosexuality of the Middle Eastern/ Muslim world and its rigidly hierarchical social order, aspiring to a new and more reciprocal (homosexual) love.

To pursue the concept of love in modern Persian literature, I also reread many of the literary works of the twentieth century, particularly from the formative period of the 1920s through the 1940s. One of the major preoccupations of the writers of this era had been the ideal of companionate marriage. Some, such as Bozorg 'Alavi, were celebrating companionate marriage with the understanding that it would not necessarily provide greater happiness for women. Others, such as Sadeq Hedayat, lamented the loss of a world where sexualities were more ambivalent, and heterosexuality was not yet normative in the modern sense.

Reading through several new books on homosexuality in the Middle East, including some of the unpublished works of Everett Rowson who was kind enough to share his work with me, reassured me that I was on the right track. Khaled El-Rouayheb (2005), Walter Andrews and Mehmet Kalpakli (2005) had suggested a link between gender segregation and the pervasive homoeroticism of the Muslim Middle East, indicating that these relationships were fueled by a need for companionship rather than lack of sex. Both of these works addressed the idealistic as well as the abusive dimensions of same-sex relations. Afsaneh Najmabadi had adopted a less critical attitude toward status-defined homosexuality in nineteenth-century Iran and also resisted a connection between gender segregation and homoeroticism. But her new work also linked male homosexual practices to women's demands for more companionate marriages (2005, 8).

Late nineteenth-century intellectuals such as Mirza Fath Ali Akhundzadeh and Mirza Aqa Khan Kermani had initiated the debate on *normative heterosexuality* and companionate marriage. In recent theories of sexuality, normative sexuality has come to mean accepting heterosexual relations (and rejecting homosexual ones) as the only proper and healthy sexual behavior. In the twenty-first century, notions of normative heterosexuality are seen as oppressive. However, early twentieth-century advocates of women's rights in Iran and the Middle East saw this problem differently. They regarded normative heterosexuality as an advance because they believed it meant a man would actually love a woman, rather than merely maintain her as an object of procreation.

During the Iranian Constitutional Revolution, liberal and leftist publications campaigned for companionate marriage but not yet normative heterosexuality. The latter gradually impacted Iran from the north and the west. The more modernist Shiʻi Azeri intellectuals of the Russian Caucasus initiated a wide criticism of homosexuality, especially the Tbilisi-based newspaper *Molla Nasreddin*. This illustrated satirical paper, which circulated among Iranian intellectuals and ordinary people alike, was enormously popular in the region because of its graphic cartoons. The paper was also known for its advocacy of companionate marriage and opposition to both pedophilia and pederasty.

For details on the contemporary gay subculture in Iran, I turned to GLBT (Gay-Lesbian-Bisexual-Transgendered) activists inside Iran and abroad. After the public hanging of two teenagers in Mashhad in the summer of 2005 on charges of homosexuality, I began a discussion with editors of *MAHA*, one of the first electronic journals of the Iranian GLBT community, and other members of this community such as Arsham Parsi. I also read through publications such as *Homan*, *Cheragh*, and *Hamjens-e*

Man, which have done much to illuminate the practices of homosexuality and heterosexuality in contemporary Iranian society.

I became aware of a number of other fundamental cultural changes the nation had experienced in the twentieth century, in the process of developing a series of lectures on the evolution of democracy in modern Iran. Iran has undergone not one but several paradigm shifts with respect to gender and sexuality, around the notions of social justice, purity, adulthood, and agency. At the same time it would be an overgeneralization to speak of a complete change of mores in modern Iran, as if earlier notions of justice, purity, and adulthood have been discarded and new ones have taken their place entirely. I began to think about a paradigm shift around the concept of purity, partly under the influence of Mary Douglas's important work, *Purity and Danger* ([1966] 2002). I was interested in the nature of this change – from religious/ritualistic notions of purity to modern concepts of hygiene – and its implications for women's bodies. A second distinct paradigm shift involved age and adulthood. Earlier, girls were married young, often at or before puberty, while status-defined homosexuality involved sex between adolescent and sometimes younger boys and adult men. Social attitudes about the proper age for sex would change, especially by the 1930s. The legal age of marriage for girls would increase to fifteen while adult men's sex with boys would be prohibited.

A third paradigm shift involved notions of social justice. In premodern Iran, as in Greco-Roman or medieval European societies, distributive justice had applied different standards to different social groups in order to maintain a social hierarchy. In contrast, modern justice aspires to treat people of different classes, ethnicities, and genders as formally equal. That (male) Iranian citizens had to be treated equally before the law regardless of their social status or religion, that mutilation constituted cruel and inhuman punishment, that Iran should resolutely adhere to international anti-slavery conventions, and that laws should be uniformly applied in different cities and towns, were all principles that were introduced during the course of the Constitutional Revolution. However, family law, including the rights of women in marriage and divorce, inheritance, and child custody, continued to be defined according to old concepts of justice. The contrast between modern and premodern, *shariʿa*-based,[1] ideals of justice remained a persistent theme in the struggles for women's rights.

These issues alerted me to the category of class, which some of us who have turned to cultural history have tended to play down. The idea that Muslim societies could ban homosexuality but tolerate semi-covert

---

[1] Rules and regulations that are derived in principle from the Qur'an and traditions relating to the words and deeds of the Prophet and the Shiʿi imams that govern the lives of Shiʿi Muslims.

man–boy relationships was corroborated in Iran. However, these relations varied in many ways, and, as in the Greco-Roman world, the degree of class difference between the boy and the man often determined how overt the relationship might be. The same was true of the institution of temporary marriage. As Shahla Haeri has shown in her pioneering study, temporary marriage was more than an outlet for sexual pleasure. It was also a means of circumventing social segregation (Haeri 1989). But an important element in the institution of temporary marriage was also class. Temporary wives provided a lucrative source of income for *bazaar* merchants, who kept these women in their employ. High-status men who kept boy concubines or contracted temporary marriage disapproved of their own daughters becoming temporary wives or their sons becoming boy concubines, unless the prospective male partners were of much higher social status. The institution of slavery also had a profound effect on gender and sexual mores, as master–slave relations transformed all other social relations, particularly those of marriage.

The marriage and divorce certificates and police reports which Mansoureh Ettehadieh and her student Elham Malekzadeh kindly forwarded from Tehran, provided another venue for examining the concept of agency in nineteenth-century Iran. I also pored over numerous harem memoirs, as well as accounts by European travelers written in English, French, and occasionally German. In reading the European memoirs I had expected to find mostly Orientalist perspectives on Iranian women's passivity and submission. To be sure, there was plenty of that. But I also discovered some surprisingly different accounts, especially in the works of women travelers and male court physicians. These narratives, court certificates, and police reports chronicled women's resistance, highlighting the usefulness of the veil in secret sexual encounters, the preponderance of hymen repair and abortion, and women's appeals to police to control unruly husbands.

In a visit to Iran in spring 2005, I noticed some dramatic changes in sexual mores and realized that the nation was quietly moving toward a sexual revolution. It was a revolution that was taking place behind the *hijab* and closed doors, and also working itself out at different stages in rural communities, as Erika Friedl, Mary Hegland, and Soraya Tremayne, who have carried out ethnographic work in villages, have demonstrated. Soon a group of courageous Iranian feminists affiliated with the online journal *Zanestan* began the Million Signatures Campaign, demanding equal rights for women in marriage and the family. The state has tried to bring an end to this campaign and other recent feminist efforts through harassment and intimidation. *Zanestan* has been blocked, forcing the editors to launch the campaign from other Internet sites. In January 2008, the large-circulation feminist magazine *Zanan* was also shut down after sixteen years of publication on the grounds that it showed Iranian women in a "dark light" and was a "threat to the psychological security of society."

This book is dedicated to these courageous feminists in the hope that it might give historical context to their efforts. What follows is the largely untold story of Iran's unfinished sexual revolution, while we listen to the voices of young Iranian women and men who are making history on the ground even as these words are being written.

Most studies of nineteenth-century Iran have painted a chaotic social canvas, focusing on imperialist designs, the intrigues of Qajar rulers, or the poverty, hunger, and ill health of the masses. A focus on the evolution of the institution of marriage offers a different perspective. Qajar Iran had a rigidly hierarchical social order, with a clearly defined class, ethnic, and religious structure and an entrenched pattern of family obligations. Religious beliefs provided the basis for shared values. Many cherished a relative sense of security fostered by communal identities. Marriage was nearly universal, holding families and communities together. Parents found a spouse for their son or daughter and provided the means for their marriage. At or before puberty, the young bride moved in with the groom's family, where the mother-in-law taught her how to be a wife and mother. Reported crimes were low in a world where girls, boys, and women endured or quietly resisted incest, sexual molestation, and rape. Monogamy was the norm for the vast majority of urban, rural, and tribal communities. But among the upper classes, the practices of polygamy and of keeping boy concubines were common.

Three prevalent types of legally sanctioned, heterosexual intimacy existed among the urban elites of this period: *nekah*, or formal marriage; *sigheh*, or temporary marriage; and slave concubinage. *Nekah* was usually contracted between a man and woman of more or less equal social status. A wife in a *nekah* marriage was known as an *'aqdi* wife. *Nekah* was intended to be permanent, but the husband could terminate it by divorce. *Sigheh*, a Shiʿi institution, was a renewable contract of marriage for a defined duration, from a few hours to ninety-nine years. *Sigheh* provided sex for pleasure and was often contracted between a lower-class woman and a man of higher social standing. The wife in a *sigheh* marriage was also known as a *sigheh*. The institution differed from European concubinage in that the recognized children of a *sigheh* marriage were considered legitimate and eligible for inheritance, although the father could easily deny his paternity (Haeri 1989). The third form of recognized heterosexual intimacy involved the purchase or inheritance of a female slave. Having borne a master's child, the slave continued to work as a maid/concubine in the house, though she would normally be manumitted upon the master's death. The children were free and legitimate, provided that the master recognized them. All three of these forms of heterosexual intimacy could be found in the elite harems, together with male slaves and concubines.

The position of an *'aqdi* was relatively stable. By her early thirties, she might be the mother of several grown children and even the matriarch of a family. However, arranged marriage, polygamy, and the extended family often led to weak emotional bonds between an *'aqdi* wife and her husband. While divorce was rare within the rural and urban lower classes, it was more acceptable among the urban middle and upper classes. Strong social ties between the two families, and the financial obligations of a man after divorce, made it difficult, however. The remarriage of a divorced woman from these social strata was justifiable and incurred little stigma.

Strong bonds of love might develop initially in a *nekah* marriage, but sustaining them proved daunting. Family interference and lack of privacy created severe obstacles. Physical intimacy might be confined to the bed, where sex took place quickly and furtively, soon interrupted by children who shared their parents' room. In time, the lack of reliable contraceptives, multiple pregnancies, and high infant mortality rates would exhaust the wife. In addition, social norms encouraged her to minimize her erotic attachment to her husband, and to divert her attention to motherhood and other familial pursuits that earned her more respect and authority.

In elite families, the burdens of physical labor were less onerous, but the impediments to creating and maintaining strong conjugal relations were even more tenacious. A man's rights to divorce and polygamy undermined the couple's emotional investment in one another. The fact that children of all polygamous unions (and any offspring from temporary marriage or a slave concubine) had formal inheritance rights, also weakened the ties between husband and wife (Hodgson 1974, I:341). These male prerogatives reduced the wife's emotional commitment to the husband. Often, romantic feelings for her husband would be transformed over time into a close attachment to her son. Similarly, a husband's easy access to other women and the presence of the mother-in-law in the house reduced his commitment to the happiness of his wife.

However, girls and wives did not always succumb to these pressures. There were no "Great Refusals" in this period, no large-scale public forms of resistance, but in James Scott's apt characterization, numerous smaller and more readily available "weapons of the weak" were deployed in daily life (Scott 1985). Young women resisted their parents' choice of suitors and attempted to exercise some influence over the process. Aided by resourceful midwives and love brokers, women underwent secret hymen repair and abortions, and sought medicinal, magical, and even illicit solutions to a husband's infertility. Wives exercised a measure of control in bed, in the kitchen, and in the general management of the house and the children. Their influence manifested itself in their propensity to withhold or grant favors. A wife could refuse to share in her husband's pleasure in bed, even if she complied with his demand for sexual intimacy. She gained prestige by organizing elaborate dinner parties, keeping her house meticulously clean, and developing extensive information about his relatives. She often called on relatives, neighbors, and even the police in cases of domestic violence. Combined with her skills as a hostess, the decline of erotic bonds with her husband as she grew older might boost her stock in the eyes of her mother-in-law, who had less fear of her daughter-in-law's sway over her son. Often the wife's ties with her mother-in-law and sisters-in-law effectively isolated the husband among the household's most powerful women. Alternatively, the wife could strike a balance in her own house by reinforcing her relationship with the family into which her sister-in-law had married. Should her concerted efforts to control her husband fail, a woman could resist her husband's decision to take another wife and try to wreck his second wedding, sometimes by attempting suicide. Overall, the wife invested less in the emotional relationship with her husband and more in the relationship with her children and his or her kin. As she grew older, the wife could become a powerful matriarch who exercised control over the life of her sons and her daughters-in-law, thereby also asserting increased authority over her husband in his old age.

Nineteenth-century Iranian society did not adhere to modern definitions or sensibilities concerning same-sex relations. Although legally prohibited, homosexual sex was common, and homoerotic passion was accommodated. Falling in love with a youth and celebrating that love were recognized practices, as long as the lovers remained circumspect and observed certain conventions. Elite urban men often flouted these conventions. In the royal court and among government officials, wealthy merchants, and clerics, the practice of keeping boy concubines was widespread and commonly known; close, homosexual relations between free adult men were less often discussed or divulged, however. Among married women, same-sex relations known as sisterhood vows were also culturally recognized practices. Although we have much less information on female homosexuality, we know that such courtships involved an exchange of gifts, travel to a shrine, and cultivation of affection between the partners. Finally, while people were expected to observe rigid social hierarchies, such social orders could be breached in both heterosexual and homosexual unions. The slave who gave birth to a son could become a *sigheh* wife. The favorite *sigheh* often became an '*aqdi*, and the chosen boy concubine could rise to a high post at the royal court.

Gender and sexual conventions changed as a result of protracted encounters with the Ottoman Empire, Russia, and Western Europe, the rise of democratic reforms, and the advent of modern nationalism. By the early twentieth century, the foreign slave trade was restricted, while the Constitutional Revolution dismantled the harems. Several Iranian journals and many women's associations campaigned in favor of greater women's rights although in the course of the revolution, the most vocal advocate of new gender and sexual mores, the journal *Molla Nasreddin*, emerged from outside the country in Tbilisi (modern Georgia). An Azeri-Iranian diaspora publication, the journal advocated companionate marriage and criticized sexual relationships with minor children, including the institution of child marriage. It also suggested a link between men's intransigence toward gender reforms and their reluctance to abandon sex-segregated homosocial spaces. Notably, *Molla Nasreddin* became the first publication in the Shi'i Muslim world to endorse normative heterosexuality. In the decades that followed, other Iranian intellectuals, first in the diaspora and later within Iran, continued to push for the type of agenda initiated by *Molla Nasreddin*.

In the late 1930s, modernization in Iran came to involve the use of the police to enforce new disciplinary practices on women's and men's bodies, a process that accelerated after women were unveiled by state decree. Women's bodies became sites of political and cultural struggle, complicated further by the subjection of unveiled women to an intense public gaze and sexual harassment. Reforms in health and hygiene in this period had an equally important impact. Old rituals of purification, which had marked public and private spaces for men and women, were reinterpreted in light of modern sciences, which featured explanations involving germs and sickness. With religious justifications for gender segregation weakening, and the state encouraging greater public participation by women, social hierarchies loosened. As a new Civil Code raised the legal age of marriage for girls to fifteen and further eroded the hierarchies that had enforced gender segregation, Iranian women began to assert themselves through schools, clubs, and other institutions of civil society.

Leading intellectuals of this era such as Ahmad Kasravi developed new normative discourses on sexuality and marriage. Although marriages were still arranged by parents and required paternal approval, a more companionate form of marriage gained greater approval. Support for formal polygamy (having multiple 'aqdi wives) and status-defined homosexuality sharply declined, while heterosexual monogamy came to be seen as the new norm. Paralleling earlier patterns in the West, the urban communities of Iran became less accepting of pedophilic relationships, regardless of context. Overt bisexuality became less prevalent among men and women of the middle and upper classes. People of the upper classes, including a new generation of men in the Pahlavi dynasty, also abandoned the practice of keeping multiple wives. The old middle classes, composed of those affiliated with the *bazaar*, the clerical families, and the tribal leaders, continued to practice polygamy, although even in these instances the number was usually limited to two wives.

From 1941 to 1953, Iran experienced a period of relative political freedom from the Pahlavi autocracy as the Allies ousted Reza Shah Pahlavi in favor of his young son Muhammad Reza Shah, and a variety of political parties emerged. Subsequently the struggle for the nationalization of oil, led by Prime Minister Muhammad Mosaddeq and the National Front, set Iran against Britain. Gender issues were just beneath the surface of these economic and political conflicts, however. Contemporary periodicals reveal that the struggle over women's suffrage became highly contentious during these years, dividing the National Front. Had the Western powers allowed Mosaddeq to carry out his twin projects of social reform and national independence, these issues might have been resolved peacefully. Instead, the 1953 Anglo-American coup derailed the democratic movement, and Muhammad Reza Shah Pahlavi returned to power.

Although the shah crushed democracy with brutality, he continued to support gender modernization. In the 1950s and 1960s, companionate marriage and the nuclear family began to supplant strictly arranged unions and the remnants of formal polygamy within the new urban middle classes. In addition, the influence of the extended family over the nuclear one was mitigated. Young men took a more assertive part in choosing their spouses, and young urban women gradually followed suit. A rising generation of educated women, among them university professors, lawyers, Members of Parliament, and leaders of the state-sponsored Women's Organization of Iran (WOI), began to cautiously campaign for new laws granting women substantially greater marital rights.

In the 1960s and 1970s, the WOI assisted in reforming the institution of marriage, partially legalizing abortion as well. It also helped enact laws that granted women greater rights in divorce, placing limitations on men's unilateral right to divorce and child custody. Polygamy was legally restricted and subject to the permission of the first wife. The emergence of a modern gay lifestyle in a few sectors of the urban elite also caused social anxiety.

These changes were more dramatic than their counterparts in Europe, in part because they took place over the relatively short period of about seventy years. The triple introduction of normative monogamy, normative heterosexuality, and companionate marriage in the first part of the twentieth century, and the dramatic changes that took place in the status of women and in marriage and divorce laws after 1960, caused severe tremors in the social fabric. This had become quite evident by the 1970s.

The increasingly critical attitudes of Iranian intellectuals in the 1960s and 1970s toward the West are correctly attributed to the CIA-backed coup of 1953, which toppled Mosaddeq's nationalist government. But opposition to Western influences was also rooted in cultural anxiety. Ever since the beginning of the twentieth century, advocates of modernity had pushed for greater women's rights through an implicit social contract. They had promised that if families agreed to greater educational opportunities for their daughters, these new rights would not destroy conventional gender hierarchies. Women tacitly promised to remain attentive wives, mothers, and daughters-in-law, even as they assumed a more public role in society. As Nikki Keddie has pointed out, by the mid-twentieth century, Iran had become a nation of "two cultures," in which the new middle classes hardly comprehended their more religious and conservative compatriots (Keddie 2003, 102). Modern urbanites also assumed that it was only a matter of time before the rest of society joined them. This cultural bifurcation marked the sexual mores of Iranian society, dividing women as well as men.

Women from the educated middle classes followed the dictates of modernity and the consumer society. They went to university, got jobs, played an active role in selecting their mate, and entered into companionate marriages. They petitioned for divorce when their marriages failed and demanded child custody, which the courts were beginning to grant to mothers. Women from the old middle classes continued to observe the veil, seldom went to university, and entered strictly arranged marriages often before finishing high school. Some endured an ʿaqdi or sigheh co-wife, but seldom petitioned for divorce. In their extended families, marriage was still an institution for procreation rather than for emotional intimacy and female sexual fulfillment.

A backlash against the gender reforms of the more modernized sectors of society was underway by the late 1970s. Leftist critics of the Pahlavi autocracy, of Western imperialism, and of consumerism joined forces with conservative Islamists in anti-regime protests. To an extent, these two oppositional factions coalesced, not only on broad political issues, but also in their criticisms of the sexual norms of the modern urban woman. The partial confluence of the two groups' views on cultural issues helped make the Islamic Revolution possible.

Capitalizing on these circumstances, Ayatollah Ruhollah Khomeini, who had lived in exile in Iraq and then briefly in France, managed to assume overall leadership of the revolution and to establish the Islamic Republic in 1979. Retrogressive policies soon followed: the regime attempted to reinstate *shariʿa* law and resegregate public spaces. It also abrogated reforms benefiting women in marriage and divorce, lowered the age of marriage for girls to nine, pursued pronatalist polices, restricted women's employment, and mandated the *hijab* for all women. The very recent toleration of a modern gay lifestyle in elite communities also vanished, sometimes by means of executions.

Post-revolutionary Iran did not experience a wholesale return to the sexual and gender mores of the early twentieth century, however. Parents did not return en masse to the practice of child marriage. The mean age of women at first marriage, which had reached nineteen in 1976, continued to climb. Although they were subject to many restrictions, women were not forced out of public spaces such as mosques, schools, streets, and offices, nor did Iran slide back into illiteracy. In fact, literacy rates increased substantially after the revolution. On the whole, the Islamist regime was not altogether antimodern and it employed various techniques of modernity. It continued the literacy and health campaigns of the Pahlavi era, projects that the public embraced more enthusiastically when offered by an Islamist state that was the product of a popular uprising. The new state even adopted a constitution, one of the characteristic features of a modern nation-state.

The Islamic Republic's constitution granted unparalleled authority to the Shiʿi clergy. The seventy-year struggle among the shah, the Parliament, and the clerics had resulted in a decisive victory for the clerics, who founded a new kind of theocracy that eliminated the position of monarch and gave most of the executive power to the Supreme Leader, at first Ayatollah Khomeini. In addition, the Supreme Leader appropriated many of the former powers of the Parliament. The supervisory bodies of the new state recognized only those people who accepted the principles of the Islamic Republic and expressed devotion to Khomeini. Only groups that did so could participate in the political process. These changes were accelerated by the Iran–Iraq war of 1980–1988.

After 1979 the state gave men more power over women's sexuality and reproductive functions. In the name of protecting the honor of women and the nation, men of all social classes gained easier access to sex through marriage, and sometimes outside of it. Likewise, pederastic relations between adult men and youth were ignored in the newly sex-segregated spaces of the Islamic Republic, while claiming an openly gay or lesbian identity became a capital offense.

The state also attempted to reverse modern trends in love and marriage. Open dating and expressing public affection, even between married couples, could lead to arrest. The morality police punished anyone who violated the *hijab* regulations or any of the other conventions of the sex-segregated order. Unilateral, male-initiated divorce through repudiation was reinstated. During the Iran–Iraq War and in its aftermath, the new theocratic state encouraged polygamy, including temporary marriage, as solutions for war widows and disabled war veterans, and as outlets for those constrained by the strict regulations against dating.

We know from the work of Foucault that in Europe a pervasive discourse about sexuality belied the repressive and puritanical morality associated with Victorian England, where sexuality came under increasing state regulation. The state involved itself in even the most prosaic issues of gender and sexuality, ranging from marriage and fertility to the sexual conduct of partners. As Foucault – who called this state intervention in sexuality a form of "governmentality" – and recent feminist scholars have shown, some of the most radical transformations in gender and marriage relations arose beneath the calls for sexual purity in the Victorian era. Such theoretical perspectives can also help to conceptualize changes in post-revolutionary Iran's economic and sociological indices, including literacy rates, infant mortality, and fertility rates.

To be sure, the Islamic Republic instituted a reversal in women's rights, gay rights, and human rights more broadly. But it also developed policies that have directly affected the sexual conduct of its citizens in ways that are hardly traditional. Indeed, various factions inside the regime have actively deployed what might be called a new sexual economy. The effects of this new economy have proven ambiguous. Its accompanying laws have denied women many basic rights in marriage and divorce, but they have also contributed to numerous state initiatives promoting literacy, health, and infrastructural improvements that benefited the urban and rural poor.

Many of the traditions instituted by the state were in reality "invented traditions," a term coined by the historian Eric Hobsbawm. Here are three examples:

At the turn of the twentieth century, social custom, religion, class, and ethnicity determined a woman's outer clothing. Lower-class and many non-Muslim women wore looser veils, while upper-class urban women were fully veiled. Veiling was thus a class and social marker that more respectable women and their families observed as a way of setting themselves apart from the lower orders. For a short period between 1936 and 1941, the state imposed unveiling. The police ordered all urban women to take off their veils and encouraged then to wear modern dresses and hats. But Iranian society had never experienced what it has endured since 1979 – morality squads dragging respectable women to police stations and flogging them for sporting nail polish or makeup, wearing their *hijab* too loosely, or showing strands of hair.

The practice of honor killings is a second example. Police records and other sources indicate that honor killings were rare in premodern Iran, usually confined to the Kurdish and Arab peripheries of the nation. Most families quietly resolved problems of honor through hymen repair, abortion, or hasty marriage. With regard to married women's extramarital affairs, the husband and family usually handled such matters discreetly, rather than lose honor in the community. Occasionally clerics or the community took action, executing a prostitute or some other low-status transgressor of sexual boundaries. But the post-1979 Islamist state established a new type of "honor killing," one that was adjudicated and enforced by the state, rather than the father, the brother, or the community. The idea that the state would drag an urban, middle-class woman to court and possibly execute her on charges of adultery, even if her family and community vigorously protested, was unprecedented not just in Iran but in the Muslim world.

A third example is the execution of homosexuals. In premodern Iran, discreet homosexual relations were a common practice despite religious prohibitions. The punishment of homosexuality required repeated offenses and the testimony of four adult male witnesses, though even then repentance was possible. Cases actually reported to the police in urban middle-class communities might involve male prostitution in a residential neighborhood and pedophilia but not pederasty. However, the Islamic Republic broke these traditions and also did away with the religious requirement for witnesses. The state continued to ignore homosexual relations in religious seminaries and *bazaars*, but from time to time prosecuted young urban gay men if a single person reported them or simply after a medical examination. After 2005, an official policy of active entrapment via Internet chat rooms was also initiated.

Urban Iranian women reacted in very different ways to the 1979 revolution. On the one hand, modern women from the new urban middle and upper classes resisted the severe restrictions the new regime imposed on their lives. Some fled the country, forming a significant part of the Iranian diaspora in cities such as London, Paris, Vienna, Frankfurt, Toronto, Los Angeles, San Francisco, and Chicago. On the other hand, women from the old middle classes tended to embrace the revolution's culturally conservative ideology and helped to enforce its policies. The regime gained additional recruits through recognizing and subsidizing the families of war veterans and martyrs. Paradoxically, women who joined the regime's Islamist organizations were often able to free themselves from the strictures of the patriarchal family and avoid strictly arranged marriages, or marriage altogether. They joined the literacy and health corps, volunteered for the reconstruction program, enlisted in the auxiliary military organizations that aided the war effort, or signed up for female morality squads that monitored the lives of more modern-oriented women and men.

By the 1990s, a generation of Islamist women that had pursued graduate degrees had risen to prominence. Some were relatives of high-ranking male Islamists; others were related to war veterans and martyrs, or had themselves participated in the war. One might consider them an Islamist "New Class," similar to the Nomenklatura in the Soviet Union (Djilas 1983). Soon, women in these culturally conservative social sectors were marrying later than previously. The number of arranged marriages among them shrank, and that of more companionate marriages grew, reducing the vast cultural gap on gender issues that had existed in the 1970s.

In the 1990s, as the state responded to the increase in fertility by reversing course and encouraging smaller families, the result was even more dramatic. Without relenting on many other women's rights issues, a comprehensive family planning program in both rural and urban communities was established alongside the literacy and health campaigns. Family planning classes offered sex education for prospective couples and encouraged them to limit their offspring to two. By enlisting tens of thousands of female volunteers as counselors, and by providing free contraceptives for married couples, the family planning program contributed to a major decrease in fertility rates.

This birth control campaign showed that the state could adopt a somewhat liberal and tolerant discourse on sexuality in order to achieve its goals – in this case, population control. On most other gender issues, though, the state followed a patriarchal hard line. It stalled, halted, or reversed some previous reforms regarding the legal age of marriage for girls, polygamy, unequal inheritance rights, domestic violence, and divorce. On these issues, the regime often followed a misogynistic reading of Islam, insisting that this was the only proper interpretation of the *shari'a*.

In response to this intransigence, battles for a more tolerant society have been fought in numerous and sometimes unlikely sites since the liberalization of the mid-1990s. Writers, journalists, lawyers, artists, musicians, fashion designers, actors, film directors, college students, and homemakers became activists in the Reform Movement. Reformists came from many different social and religious backgrounds. Some were leftist Islamists who had participated in the revolution, fought in the war, and contributed to subsequent literacy, health, reconstruction, and family-planning campaigns. Many were increasingly dissatisfied with the theocratic state and the losses from the war, in which nearly a million people were injured or killed on both sides. Reformist Islamists and more secular opposition sectors, which were repressed but never extinguished, sometimes reached a provisional agreement to unite for a common cause. The new Reformist organizations were reinforced by the increasing numbers of youth influenced by satellite television and the Internet, who chafed under the restrictions of the theocratic state and its morality police.

By the first decade of the twenty-first century, the institution of marriage had irrevocably changed. Both husband and wife entered marriage with greater expectations about companionship and emotional intimacy, hopes that often remained unfulfilled. These rising expectations contributed in turn to an increase in unhappy marriages and a rising divorce rate, despite limitations on women's right to initiate divorce. In the absence of legal reforms that would have granted women greater rights within the family, and economic reforms that would have provided them with greater financial autonomy from fathers and husbands, social problems among women and girls increased. Since 2000, hundreds of thousands of young women have run away from home, but they have too often ended up in domestic prostitution rings or in the Persian Gulf sex trade. Drug addiction, risky sexual behavior among urban youth, and suicide rates among impoverished rural women were also on the increase.

Today we are witnessing a sexual awakening that builds on the nation's rich religious, cultural, and social repertoire in order to challenge the theocratic regime and to work for a more democratic society. Unlike struggles in the West, where feminist movements emerged out of democratic societies and attempted to expand the limited rights of liberal democratic states, these struggles in Iran are taking place under an authoritarian system. Iranian cinema, women's magazines, secular and Muslim feminists, advocates of women's rights in various government posts, human rights activists, and supporters of modern gay and lesbian lifestyles are all contributing to new discourses on gender, sexuality, and modernity. These new discourses transcend earlier internal religious disputes and ideological divisions between the West and the Middle East. They favor more egalitarian gender relations, sweeping reforms in marriage and family laws, and liberal readings of Islamic law. They also call for a new relationship to the outside world and to the complex phenomenon of modernity itself. Iranian society may be approaching a critical stage in a sexual revolution that began more than a century ago.

This book offers a preliminary study of the evolution of marriage and Iran's sexual revolution since the nineteenth century. The coming years will no doubt see a deluge of publications on this subject, filling in gaps, offering rebuttals, and illustrating variations on these themes according to region, social class, and religious affiliation, all of which I shall welcome. Until then, I hope that my broad sketch will be useful to those who care about gender, sexuality, women's rights, and the rights of sexual minorities.

Part 1

Premodern practices

1   Formal marriage

Iranians view themselves as a romantic people and others seem to concur. In the early 1880s, an American diplomat in Iran fondly recalled that peasants "have a decided taste for poetry, and often fly the heat of midday and find shelter under the great *chenars* [sycamore trees] in the center of the village, where they listen to recitations from the Odes of Hafiz or the *Shah Nameh* of Firdoüsee" (Benjamin 1887, 173). Classical Persian poetry, with its passionate references, is even now on the lips of both intellectuals and ordinary people alike. Sexual pleasure is a common topic of discussion. Lawful heterosexual union is viewed as a form of "pious obligation," and a sacrament approved by the Qur'an (Bouhdiba [1975] 1985, 13), while jokes about the phallus in both sex-segregated spaces and mixed company are routine.

What of marital love? This and the next chapter focus on heterosexual unions in late nineteenth-century Iran in an attempt to explore this question. How many legal forms of intimacy existed in Iran? How did Iranian society perceive marriage? Were marriages stable or rocky? Was romantic love essential to a secure marriage? If not, how did couples cope with the disparity, and where did they turn their attention? I focus on heterosexual unions in Shi'i middle- and upper-class urban communities of Tehran and several other major cities, though Sunni Muslim and non-Muslim urban communities also shared some of these practices. These chapters view the lives of women within a social order that placed strong constraints upon them, a society where *fiqh* (jurisprudence) and custom set the parameters for women's lives. Urban men and women from the *bazaar* and clerical families could not freely determine their marriage partner. Women were largely disenfranchised and lived under the authority of men: fathers, uncles, brothers, husbands, and even adult sons. These are well-known points, documented for centuries in the Western literature on Iran and the Middle East. The above picture presents only one side of the story, however. There was a difference between what *fiqh* or even custom required, and the lived experience of women. Within the above constraints, women worked ceaselessly to carve out spaces for themselves and to turn to their advantage the very constraints imposed upon them. In short, they worked to become agents of their own lives. It is this interplay between constraint and agency that is the focus of these two chapters. Thus throughout the following discussion, after describing *fiqh* and customary practice I proceed with historical examples which often contradict these.

As in records of the eighteenth- and nineteenth-century Ottoman Empire, considerably less information is available on the poorer sectors of Iranian society than on the elites. In addition, Iran lags far behind Egypt and Turkey with regard to the accessibility of records and registers as well as research on the institution of family. For this reason, I have gathered materials for this and the next chapter from social histories of Iran produced since the seventeenth century, while keeping an eye on recent similar writings in the field of Middle East Women's Studies and personal interviews. I have also looked at harem memoirs and various studies on harem life; accounts by European physicians at the court; European travelers' accounts, including memoirs by several women who were keen observers of gender relations despite their Orientalist prejudices, such as Mary Sheil, Carla Serena, Jane Dieulafoy, Gertrude Bell, and Ella Constance Sykes;[1] religious and legal manuals; anthropological studies of Iran since the twentieth century; and Tehran's police records of 1885–1888, which cover many family disputes. In addition, some late nineteenth-century marriage and divorce registers from the office of a leading cleric, Sheikh Fazlollah Nuri, have recently become accessible.[2]

In this chapter I examine *nekah* (the formal institution of marriage). I look briefly at a range of issues, such as the ages of marriage and consent; preoccupations with pollution, purity, and virginity; fertility, hymen repair, and abortion; the mother-in-law; polygamy, matrimonial disputes, divorce and custody; inheritance and economic rights; as well as the practice of veiling, and its use as a method of resistance to imposed sexual norms.

---

[1] Mary Sheil ([1856] 1973), wife of the British Ambassador to Iran, traveled to that country in the 1850s; Carla Serena ([1883] 1983), writer and traveler, was in Iran in 1877–1878; Jane Dieulafoy ([1887] 1983) was an artist and the wife of Marcel Dieulafoy, archeologist and engineer. They traveled to Iran in 1881–1882. Gertrude Bell, the British archeologist who helped fashion the imperial design of the modern state of Iraq after World War I, traveled to Iran in 1892 when her uncle, Sir Frank Lascelles, was appointed British minister in Tehran; Ella Constance Sykes (1898), was a sister of Major Percy Sykes, a British officer in Iran. As Nima Naghibi (2007) has argued, these sources ought to be used with caution, though in the absence of other sources they remain essential.

[2] Throughout the text I refer to these by number as Nuri Documents.

Nekah marriage

In the 1860s marriage was nearly universal in Iran, including for those with physical disabilities. Dr. Jakob Polak (1818–1891), the Austrian Jewish personal physician of Naser al-Din Shah Qajar (r. 1848–1896), who provides us with the most detailed account of urban Iranian sexual practices in the mid-nineteenth century, judges it to be "a simple fact that when a girl reaches a certain age, she must marry and other matters related to wealth and social class are of less concern. In addition, the ease of divorce does not turn marriage into as difficult a task as it was in Europe. We can understand why there are no bachelors and spinsters, which in civilized countries are in abundance" (Polak [1865] 1976, I:205).[3]

In urban *bazaari* and elite families mothers often found the spouses, while fathers and male guardians negotiated the financial details.[4] *Nekah* marriage was contracted through civil law. The bridegroom or his *vali* (guardian) made an offer that the bride or her *vali* accepted. The contract was binding upon payment or promise of payment of *mahriyeh* by the husband to the wife. The *mahriyeh* was a marriage portion payable to the wife at any time after the marriage. Usually the groom's family paid the wife a small amount of *mahriyeh* in advance, and the remainder was paid at the termination of the marriage, whether through divorce or death. The groom's family also paid a small *shir baha* (milk price), another early advance on the *mahriyeh*. Custom dictated that the father use the milk price to purchase his daughter's *jahiziyeh* (trousseau).

The bride or her *vali* could include certain stipulations in the marriage contract, such as the right to domicile and the right to divorce in the event of a husband's taking a second wife. These types of stipulations were

---

[3] Polak was in Iran from 1851 to 1860. He served as obstetrician/gynecologist to many women, both inside and outside the harem. He seems to have been fond of Iranians and intellectually curious about their culture and way of life. He journeyed through the country in the company of the shah, wrote a number of medical treatises about illnesses in Iran, and trained a new generation of Iranian physicians.

[4] The "middling urban strata" included local notables, heads of urban neighborhoods, ordinary landowners and merchants, master artisans, shopkeepers, upper to mid-level clerics, and even some popular preachers who organized religious festivals (Ashraf and Banuazizi, "Class System v. Qajar Period"). At the heart of this strata were the economic and family ties between clerics and *bazaaris* (bazaar merchants). According to Keddie: "Bazaaris are not a class in the Marxist sense, as they have different relations to the means of production; the journeyman artisan or worker in a small *bazaar* factory is in a different position from a banker or moneylender, who may be quite wealthy; nonetheless the expression '*bazaari*' has meaning in its involvement with petty trade, production, and banking of a largely traditional or only slightly modernized nature, as well as its centering on *bazaar* areas and traditional Islamic culture" (2003, 227). As with Keddie and others, I have used the term "old middle classes" to distinguish this strata from the "new middle classes" that emerged in the Pahlavi era.

Figure 1.1 Shirin Khanom, wife of a high-ranking cleric of Isfahan

common. At the time of her marriage in 1888, Safiyeh Khanom made her husband promise that if he ever took her "out of Tehran against her will, whether to the 'Atabat [shrines] or elsewhere, or if he himself lived outside Tehran and left his wife behind, he had to pay 200 *tumans* to her" (Nuri Document 1305 HQ/1888, No. 782). Certain factors were non-negotiable, such as the right of a woman to *mahriyeh* or the right of a man to polygamy (Qur'an 4:3; Haeri 1989, 34–38). Once the contract was signed and the marriage was consummated, the husband had to provide *nafaqeh* (maintenance) for his wife and any children born from the marriage. *Nafaqeh* comprised food, clothing, shelter, and other necessities of life. As elsewhere in the Middle East, the level of a woman's *nafaqeh* depended on her social standing, and her husband was expected to provide for her in the style to which she had been accustomed (Fig. 1.1). The inability or refusal of sexual intimacy on the part of a husband or wife could be grounds for divorce. A woman's refusal could also justify a husband's discontinuation of the *nafaqeh* during a marriage (Qur'an 2:233; Tucker 1998, 43–44).[5]

---

[5] The same requirement held in other Islamic societies. See for example Tucker 1998, 43.

A *nekah* wedding for respectable urban families was expensive. Parents saved and sacrificed their whole married lives in anticipation of the day when their sons and daughters married. The groom's family spent a significant amount of money on clothes, jewelry, and entertainment. The bride's family outfitted her with a *jahiziyeh*, including quilts, beddings, and household items. Elite families supplemented these with additional gifts of silver vases, candelabras, Persian carpets, and slaves of both sexes (Sykes [1910] 2005, 202). The *jahiziyeh* gave a girl an added incentive to marry. An elite girl looked forward to the day when she became mistress of her own house, entertained family and relatives, and thus became an object of respect and envy to her contemporaries. Even Taj al-Saltaneh (1884–1936), a daughter of Naser al-Din Shah, dreamed of having a house of her own and gaining freedom from the confines of the royal harem. In her classic memoir, one of few surviving accounts of Qajar women's lives, she writes, "I reached the age of eight, whereupon I began to hear my nannies and my aunt frequently talk about my wedding – about how I would take a husband and how they would receive clothes and sweets. Such talk gave me immense pleasure, for I thought of unbridled freedom and a house of my own" (Taj al-Saltana 1993, 138).[6]

Age and consent

Both Islamic law and pre-Islamic Sasanian law condoned marriage for girls as early as nine years old (Shaki 1971), though several years often passed between the signing of the marriage contract and the actual wedding. But even before nine, Shi'i and Sunni law gave the father or *vali* of a minor girl the right to arrange a contract on her behalf, though the marriage would be consummated later. When she reached legal majority at the age of nine, her consent in marriage was required.[7] Under certain conditions, a girl could revoke a marriage that her *vali* had arranged for her, but girls were frequently unaware of this provision or lacked the power to do so. The *'ulama* (clerics) differed on whether a father or *vali's* permission was necessary for a girl's first marriage. But all agreed that a divorced or widowed woman could remarry without her *vali's* permission (Stern 1939, 34; Haeri 1989, 39–40; Tucker 1998, 48).

To control the marriage process, and to avoid the complications of having unchaperoned girls around the house, families tended to marry off their daughters at a very young age. In this extended period of

---

[6] Translations of her writings are by Anna Vanzan and Amin Neshati in Amanat 1993.
[7] Nine according to the lunar calendar. This was a few months short of nine in the solar calendar.

engagement the girl stayed with her parents who guarded her chastity, while maids and nannies facilitated secret meetings and the passing of letters. Hence, a certain level of courtship took place after the marriage contract was signed but before it was consummated (Ravandi 1984, VI:250). Moreover, in some rural areas the couple quietly engaged in sexual intercourse with tacit understanding of the parents in this period (Sheikh al-Islami 1925, 3).

Boys gained legal maturity at fifteen, not so far apart from physical maturity as for girls. As Judith Tucker has pointed out in her study of Ottoman Syria and Palestine, a girl's "readiness for intimacy was signaled in large part by her appearance, by whether or not she had become an 'object of desire,' 'fleshy,' (*samina*), or 'buxom' (*dakhma*), physical attributes that signaled that she could now 'endure intercourse'" (Tucker 1998, 44). Thus, a girl might be considered mature enough for intercourse before she began to menstruate. The general rule in Tehran was that girls should marry at puberty, when they had begun to menstruate and developed pubic and underarm hair. The popular classes were less bound by this tradition, and tended to marry off their daughters as soon as they could for financial reasons (Polak [1865] 1976, I:199–200). Among the upper classes, a woman occasionally married much later, at around thirty. There is one documented case of a woman's first marriage in her late forties ('Ayn al-Saltaneh 1999, VI:4910).

The diverse climates, geographies, ethnicities, and social classes of the nation meant that the age of physical maturity differed in each community. In wealthier northern households, marriage was consummated after age twelve or later; in poorer southern families and many tribal communities, around ten or eleven. Northern Tehrani girls were seldom pregnant before fourteen, while southern Shirazi girls could be mothers by twelve (Polak [1865] 1976, I:204; Sykes 1898, 187; Farman Farmaian and Munker 1993, 16).

As a rule, the groom was several years (to a decade or more) older than the bride, but a larger difference in age was also acceptable. Thus a man of fifty or older could marry a pubescent girl (Farman Farmaian and Munker 1993, 16). The opposite happened occasionally. A sixteen-year-old boy could marry an older widow in cases where valid "family, guild, or financial considerations" existed (Polak [1865] 1976, I:206; 'Ayn al-Saltaneh 1995, I:802).

A father or *vali* could promise a minor girl to anyone he wanted, but usually considered the wishes of the mother and the extended family, especially the maternal uncles (*da'is*). Rarely did girls or boys have the opportunity to freely select their spouses or to take part in negotiations over *mahriyeh*. Throughout the Middle East, mothers and other women of the family arranged the children's marriages, subject of course to approval by the father or *vali* (see also Tucker 1998, 42; Taj al-Saltana 1993, 143).

Princesses had the least amount of say over their partners, because their marriages were based on major political and financial considerations; occasionally, however, their opposition to a particular suitor could be taken into account. With her parents' consent, Princess Taj al-Saltaneh rejected one of her suitors who wanted to move her to another city, but she was forced to marry another suitor she also disliked – thirteen-year-old Hassan – whose father headed the royal guard. Taj refused her consent, but like so many other girls was coerced into the wedding. Years later, she complained: "Truly, what greater misfortune could one suffer than to take a husband in childhood, at the age of eight? Especially if it was not her heart and mind that had chosen him, but rather the wishes of her mother and elders who nurtured empty and illusive hopes" (Taj al-Saltana 1993, 146).

Some girls succeeded in rejecting unwanted suitors by showing their displeasure to the boy's family. Once arrangements regarding social position were reached, the mother, grandmother, and aunts of a boy customarily paid a visit to the girl's house. She was supposed to hand them tea and a water pipe and to conduct herself in a polite and submissive manner. But "it sometimes happens that the damsel is perfectly well acquainted by sight with her would-be betrothed and if he has not met with favour in her eyes she now makes a point of behaving rudely to his mother, and the negotiations come to an abrupt conclusion" (Sykes 1898, 188).

A popular form of marriage was between first cousins whose fathers were brothers, or else someone close within the father's lineage. Cousin marriages kept land and property within the family and also offered some protection to women through the tight web of family relationships. In cousin marriages the girl and boy often knew each other since childhood, and felt mutual affection prior to their engagement. In addition, divorce between cousins was less common because of the close ties that bound the extended family (Polak [1865] 1976, I:206; Friedl 2003, 156). The boy or girl could also be married to a more distant relation. In these cases, the two might not meet until their wedding night, though some could find a way around this regulation, especially if servants and family members cooperated (Sykes 1898, 188).

Purity, pollution, and virginity

Islam, especially in its Iranian Shi'i form, is one of many "pollution-conscious" religions of the world, as are Zoroastrianism, Judaism, and Hinduism. Mary Douglas, an anthropologist who coined the term, argues that notions of ritual pollution and purity are often related to a community's need for order and social hierarchy (Douglas [1966] 2002, 1). The orifices from which blood, semen, and urine come represent the vulnerable points of the body, exposing a community to unforeseen dangers. In many societies with patrilineal systems, women are considered to be the "door of entry to the group." These societies exercise a double standard wherein a woman's infidelity (but not a man's) is seen to allow tangible and damaging impurities to infiltrate the family, both physically and morally (Douglas [1966] 2002, 127). In nineteenth-century Shiʿi Iran (as in Orthodox Jewish and Zoroastrian communities), gender behavior was strictly observed, with the fear of transgression always lurking in the air. A woman's sexual and reproductive functions turned her body into a contested site of potential and real ritual contamination. The concept of *namus* (honor) and the need to control women's chastity may be related to this fear of sexual contamination.

Muhammad Baqer Majlesi (d. 1698), a leading Shiʿi theologian who helped spread a new Shiʿi orthodoxy in the late Safavid era, introduced and expanded such notions (Majlesi 1983). According to him, sex with a menstruating woman was a major sin, and a child conceived during menstruation developed deformities (Majlesi 1983, 66–67). A man who looked at another man's wife unrepentantly would go straight to hell, where God would fill his eyes with fire (Majlesi 1983, 307–308); so too with the careless man whose wife wore flimsy clothes while attending "baths, weddings, festive and mourning rituals" (Majlesi 1983, 74). Majlesi's doctrine established sumptuary laws against women dressing like men. The Prophet himself was said to have cursed cross-dressing of proper men and women. "Hats, capes, and turbans," as well as clothing associated with non-Muslims were also strictly forbidden to Muslim women (Majlesi 1983, 8–9), suggesting the existence of such practices in the community. A significant number of Shiʿi purification rituals focused on regulating women's bodies and bodily fluids. Sex was ritually unclean, and every act of intercourse required subsequent ablution before prayer for men. A woman's body was almost always associated with impurity because of her sexual and menstrual secretions.

A family's typical city dwelling was divided into a *biruni* (outer compartment), where male guests were entertained and male servants lived, and an *andaruni* (inner compartment), occupied by wives, female servants, and children. A wife's weekly outing might involve trips to the public baths, visits to saints' shrines, gatherings with neighbors and the extended family, weddings, funerals, and rituals commemorating Shiʿi saints. An elite woman's interactions with the outside world were conducted through slaves, servants, and vendors who came to her house. Respectable women did not attend gatherings in mosques, seminaries, or coffeehouses – institutions frequented by the lower orders, slaves, and prostitutes. Extravagant weddings and other social occasions were held in separate and adjoining halls and gardens.[8] There were some surprising exceptions however. For example, when the royal harem went on holiday, the women would relax unveiled in the Caspian Sea, while the king's retinue watched them from a distance ('Ayn al-Saltaneh 1995, 1:765).

In general, rituals involving purity were observed much more stringently in cities. Until the twentieth century, urban women were not allowed to walk on the same side of the street as men. Like *najes* (polluting) non-Muslims, they often walked alongside the walls (Ostadmalek 1988, 116–117; see also Salami and Najmabadi 2005). However, segregation was not the same as seclusion. Urban women routinely used the anonymity of the veil to move about town, though single women were more restricted than married ones. A girl's seductive behavior caused *fitnah* (serious trouble or even civil war). Purity and honor (*nejabat*) involved more than the expectation of "virginity for girls and fidelity for wives." A woman's conduct should preclude any doubts about her honor (Keddie 1991, 9). And yet, once a woman was legally deflowered, even if she was divorced, she could remarry and move on to a new respectable situation. The remarriage of a divorced or widowed woman was perfectly acceptable and common and involved little stigma, until the third or fourth time – though even this was not uncommon in elite circles.

Fertility, hymen repair, and abortion

Dr. Polak was a great admirer of early universal marriage and felt it benefited Iranian women. In his view early marriage prevented a host of physical ailments that contemporary European society attributed to the womb. Early marriage held the "positive result that hysteria, epilepsy, amenorrhea [absence of menses], dismenorrhea, and masturbation among virgins almost never happens, only here and there among widows and those strongly guarded, and those neglected by their husbands" (Polak [1865] 1976, I:207). Despite his archaic assessments, Polak was correct on one point: mothers did not seem to teach daughters about sex. Most girls were too young at the time of their weddings to know much about the process, and assumed the wedding feast was about finding new relatives and receiving new gifts of clothes, dolls, jewelry, and perhaps a home of one's own.

Early marriage, coupled with malnutrition, had many harsh consequences for women. Women aged prematurely and, according to Polak, seemed

[8] For a more detailed discussion of elite marriage practices, see Nashat 2004, 37–62.

to have reached menopause anywhere from the relatively young age of thirty-two to thirty-five (Polak [1865] 1976, I:195; Sykes [1910] 2005, 218). Multiple pregnancies and childbirths, followed by a host of potential gynecological complications, often made sex difficult after a few years (Javadi *et al.* [1895] 1992, 192–200). High infant mortality rates also had an impact on family size. On average, the fertility rate for an urban nineteenth-century Iranian woman was between six and eight children. Polak and Dr. Ernest Cloquet, Naser al-Din Shah's French physician, believed that in Tehran and urban areas, from half to nearly two-thirds of children died by the age of three, often from seasonal cholera outbreak, linked to contaminated water and food, as well as famine (Polak [1865] 1976, I:195, 217; Sheil [1856] 1973, 149). There were other reasons for multiple pregnancies. Children were seen as "nails" that permanently secured a woman's marriage. As in many other cultures, families assumed that a woman's womb determined the sex of a child. A wife's not giving birth to sons was a valid reason for her husband to take a second wife. Thus women were eager to have many children, preferably boys.

The question of virginity added to the sexual tensions of marriage. A girl's supposed lack of virginity on her wedding night was a "permanent taint" that dishonored her and her entire family (Vieille 1978, 455). Despite ample advice attributed to the Prophet and religious luminaries such as Imam Ghazali and Majlesi, who recommended foreplay in order that men arouse women's desire before coitus, many men were ignorant of these practices. On the wedding night, the groom was under immense pressure to prove his virility, while the wife was terrified that for some reason she would not be found a virgin (Majlesi 1983, 66; see also Mernissi 1987, 41). A cultural emphasis on nuptial defloration often ruined the possibility of sexual intimacy. In such cases, the wedding night could set off a long series of traumas in marital relations (Shahri 1990, I:259).[9]

Freud might have had a point when he stressed the distressing consequences of a girl's first sexual encounter. In a patriarchal order that places paramount value on a woman's virginity, the girl knows that her "loss of virginity brings a diminution of sexual value" (Freud [1910] 1957, 202). A young woman feels great rage at the man who first deflowers her, a feeling that sometimes permanently affects her erotic life. For this reason, Freud thought, "second marriages so often turn out better than first" (Freud [1910] 1957, 208).

[9] Historian Ja'far Shahri is an indispensable but problematic source. His multi-volume study of Tehran at the turn of the twentieth century is replete with prejudices of all sorts and should be used with caution.

Additional anxieties particular to the Middle Eastern culture might arise on the wedding night. Often an older woman was stationed at the door of the wedding chamber to await the auspicious moment and gleefully present the bloodstained sheets to the relatives, proving both the groom's virility and the bride's chastity (Ravandi 1984, VI:250). A groom's avowal that the young bride was not a virgin could cause great turmoil. Polak reports "when a girl marries, she must be a virgin with the hymen intact (*dochtar-e bakere*); if she is without it, it is her fault (see the fifth book of Moses, chapter 22).[10] Often in these cases a woman could be cast out after the first night on a simple statement from her husband. A cruel and unjust practice, often used with evil intent and with the goal of extorting money, is to call the wife defiled" (Polak [1865] 1976, I:213). Resourceful families knew how to deal with these contingencies, however. Before the wedding they took the girl to a midwife who testified to her virginity.

For a girl who had lost her virginity before marriage, one option was to marry her briefly to a low-level cleric (in return for a handsome payment) and then arrange a second marriage with a person of higher status. A divorced woman from a wealthy family could still marry well. Another was to arrange the girl's marriage to an inexperienced youth, oblivious to the markers of virginity. A third common solution was to "stitch her [hymen] with the help of one of several Iranian surgeons who are experts in such matters" (Polak [1865] 1976, I:213).

Likewise, there were solutions to illegitimate pregnancies. As part of its recognition of sexual pleasure, Islam has always recognized certain forms of birth control and contraceptives (Musallam 1983, 13). In the medieval era, contraceptives in the form of vaginal suppositories and tampons were known to some. Jurists often approved these and ruled that a husband's permission was preferable, but not absolutely necessary. Both herbs and opium – which was inserted into the vagina – were routinely used for this purpose, with the unfortunate result that women sometimes became addicted to opium or developed gynecological complications (Shahri 1990, I:269). On the whole, *coitus interruptus* remained the chief method of contraception, however. All schools of Islamic jurists sanctioned it, provided the 'aqdi wife gave her consent (Musallam 1983, 38).

Polak admired the skill of Iranian midwives in delivering babies and performing other minor surgeries on women, but he particularly singled out their skills in performing abortions:

If an unmarried woman, a widow, or a divorced woman gives birth, her death would be assured. This situation is unheard of however. Illegitimate children

---

[10] See Deuteronomy, chapters 13–23.

(*haramzade*) are never found among the Shi'is, and the word exists solely as an insult. All pregnancies outside of marriage end in abortion, in which the placenta is punctured. The midwives perform this operation with skill and experience; at least in Tehran they are well-known and frequently visited. After all, these things were somewhat publicly known and no barriers were placed in the way. Only particularly unlucky creatures attempted to help themselves. Some use large numbers of leeches, some slice veins on their feet, some induce vomiting with Sulfas Cupri, or ingest the sprout of a date pit; failing all of these methods, the stomach is massaged and kicked. Many are killed by these crude practices. (Polak [1865] 1976, I:219)[11]

Illegitimate births among unmarried girls were probably uncommon, since many wed before menarche. But such incidents did occur among married, divorced, or widowed women.[12] Contrary to Polak's observations, reports from the late nineteenth and early twentieth centuries note that "illegitimate children were abandoned on the benches of mosques or in front of shrines" (Shahri 1990, I:469).

Polak claimed never to have performed an abortion, but did not incriminate midwives who did: "How can we blame these women for appealing to a kinder specialist?" (Polak [1865] 1976, I:219). In the Ottoman Empire, elite women used abortion as a method of birth control with their husbands' consent.[13] In Iran, by contrast, '*aqdi* (formal) wives seldom used abortion as birth control because infant mortality rates were so high (Polak [1865] 1976, I:218). The story of Taj al-Saltaneh suggests that some married women did undergo secret abortions, although few divulged it. She chose one after learning her husband had contracted venereal disease and hearing that a favorite niece had died in childbirth. Taj had a botched abortion that left her nerves frail for many years, suggesting a different reality than the more benign one Polak describes (Taj al-Saltana 1993, 300–301; Amanat 1993, 60).

The mother-in-law

The wicked mother-in-law who undermines the relationship between her son and her daughter-in-law, while encouraging that between her daughter and her son-in-law, has been a familiar trope in the folk tales and the modern literature of Iran and indeed the whole Middle East (Fig. 1.2). Fatima Mernissi echoes Philip Slater's classic study of mother–son

[11] Clot Bay, founder of the schools of medicine and midwifery in Ottoman Egypt, was more dubious of Egyptian midwives' ability to deliver babies safely, but he also admired their ability to provide "quick and effective abortions" (Hatem 1997, 70).
[12] Carla Serena ([1883] 1983, 298–299) writes about the rape of a young widow and the birth of her illegitimate child. The woman's brother killed the baby but a cleric spared the mother.
[13] This does not seem to have been practiced in the Ottoman harem (Peirce 1993, 43).

Figure 1.2 Family life, Qajar era

relations in fifth-century Athenian society when she argues, "In Muslim societies not only is the marital bond weakened and love for the wife discouraged, but his mother is the only woman a man is allowed to love at all, and this love is encouraged to take the form of life-long gratitude" (Mernissi 1987, 121).

The powerful mother-in-law was a factor in all Iranian ethnic groups and religious traditions, including the minority Christian, Zoroastrian, and Jewish communities. She was an important presence in every aspect of the young bride's life, more so than her husband. She had often arranged the marriage. After the married couple moved in with the groom's parents, the new bride was expected to work for the mother-in-law by assisting in food preparation and in the other daily requirements of life. A displeased mother-in-law could make the life of her daughter-in-law hell (Fig. 1.3). The mother-in-law could encourage her son to beat her, divorce her, or to take a second wife. The mother-in-law could also have a calming effect on her son, preventing him from using excessive physical or sexual violence in the house. The daughter-in-law had to wait for her own son to marry before she could play a similarly dominant role in his life.

The mother-in-law controlled the financial resources of the home and the social calendar. The daughter-in-law had to obtain her permission to go to the bathhouse, to entertain guests, or even to visit or invite her

Figure 1.3 Mother-in-law and daughter-in-law: fight and make up

own mother. Every family has stories about oppressive mothers-in-law. My maternal grandmother Monir who married Elyahou Pirnazar in Kermanshah in 1924, when she was thirteen and he was twenty-six, recounted an altercation between her mother and her mother-in-law soon after her wedding. Monir's mother was forbidden from coming to their house and was excluded from a large circumcision party for Monir's first child. Elyahou's appeals to his mother on behalf of his young bride were fruitless. My paternal grandmother Rahel who married Faraj Afary in 1915 in Kermanshah, when she was twelve and he was twenty-three, also complained about her mother-in-law. She recalled that in the first years of her marriage her devious mother-in-law slipped handfuls of salt in her food to ruin her cooking. When Faraj came home, his mother complained that Rahel had spoiled the food and encouraged him to give his young wife a sound thrashing. Once the punishment was well underway the mother-in-law intervened, imploring her son to stop, and encouraging the couple to make up.

Mothers-in-law also meddled in the sleeping arrangements of their sons and daughters-in-law. A well-known anecdote describes an extended family sleeping on the cool roof on a hot summer night. The mother-in-law moves to the right side of the roof where her son and daughter-in-law are sleeping, awakens them, and says, "Why are you holding each other so tight? Don't you see it is so hot? Move apart!" After they move apart, she goes to the left side of the roof, awakens her daughter and son-in-law and asks them, "Why are you sleeping so far apart? Don't you see it is so cold? Get closer!" Exasperated, the daughter-in-law retorts, "Praise be to God. One roof and two weathers!"

Although many stories and proverbs focus on the evil deeds of the mother-in-law, in reality, she too was a victim of a social order that discouraged strong conjugal bonds. She of course operated under the patriarchal authority of her husband. In elite Muslim families it was not uncommon for the mother-in-law to move into the home of her son and daughter-in-law if her husband had remarried. In this way, she avoided "the insult of having a younger co-wife in her house in her old age" (Polak [1865] 1976, I:227). By this age, many Middle Eastern women were encouraged to renounce sexual desire for their husbands and view themselves as "asexual" objects (Mernissi 1987, 125). This could result in weak bonds between the mother-in-law and her husband. Her relatively early renunciation of sex and her strong emotional attachment to her son help explain why she threw herself with such zeal into the personal lives of her son and daughter-in-law. By transferring devotion from her husband to her son and by involving herself in his marriage, the mother-in-law filled an emotional void in her life, while also acquiring important "status and power in masculine society" (Vieille 1978, 470).

Formal polygamy

The practice of polygamy in Iran dates back to the Achaemenid elites of the sixth century BCE. During the later Qajar era, it was common among upper-class families, but rare in those of the rural or urban poor (Dandamaev and Lukonin 1989, 121; Ravandi 1984, VI:257).[14] A man was permitted four ʿaqdi wives and an unlimited number of slave girls. In Shiʿi law, he could also have an unlimited number of temporary wives. The Qur'an called for the equal treatment of all wives, but this could be interpreted prosaically as an equal allotment of food, clothing, and space in the house, as well as a system of rotation involving overnight stays with each wife (Qur'an 4:3; Keddie 1991, 8).

For an urban or rural man of modest means, the norm was one wife. A kadkhoda (village elder) might have two wives. Additional instances

---

[14] Sir John Malcolm reports that divorce, polygamy, and temporary marriage were rare among the marginalized Shahsavan and Afshar tribes of Azerbaijan (Malcolm 1829, 447). Nancy Tapper reports the same nearly 150 years later. Divorce and separation were rare even among childless Shahsavan couples (Tapper 1978, 392). Lois Beck notes that Qashqa'i marriages were stable, with divorce and polygamy practiced only when a woman was deemed barren (Beck 1978, 351–373).

of polygamy might result from a man's duty to marry his brother's widow and care for his children. But even in such cases the wife of the *kadkhoda* might protest and do everything in her power to prevent her husband's remarriage ('Ayn al-Saltaneh 1998b, V:3300). If a man's economic and political status significantly improved, he often took a second *'aqdi* wife. Polygamy was also fairly common among the Sunni minority. Even Iranian Jews and Armenians occasionally practiced it (Polak [1865] 1976, I:210). In the 1860s, as Polak reported, "In cities only the lords (*khans*) and government officials have three or four wives. Artisans and merchants cannot afford the expense of several wives. They also hate the commotion and disorder of such practices and therefore live only monogamously. In the plains, and among the nomadic tribes, monogamy is the rule. At most the chief would take two or three wives ... Generally it can be said that monogamy is the rule and polygamy is the exception to the rule" (Polak [1865] 1976, I:209).

A man who had married a royal princess or had received a wife from the shah's harem as a gift was barred from taking a second wife or from divorcing the gift wife. A royal princess, such as Taj – the only *'aqdi* wife of her husband (even if she shared her husband with slave concubines and temporary wives) – was considered happy and fortunate (*khosh bakht*), especially if she had come to her husband's house after a sumptuous wedding (Bell 1928, 78).

Husbands of this sort often chafed under these restrictions. Prince Farman Farma, a respected Qajar aristocrat who had married 'Ezzat al-Dowleh, a daughter of Mozaffar al-Din Shah (r. 1896–1907), dared not take another *'aqdi* wife for the next twenty years, even when she kicked him out of her bedroom. By 1909, Mozaffar al-Din Shah had died, and his son and successor, Muhammad Ali Shah (r. 1907–1909), had also abdicated. Only then did the prince consider himself released from his royal obligation. Although he was a constitutionalist and a major advocate of women's education, Prince Farman Farma quickly took three additional wives (Farman Farmaian 1993, 48–65).

Elite women who could block their husbands from taking a second *'aqdi* did so. In 1853, Polak met a woman who was hitching a ride on the uncomfortable post cart from Tehran to Hamadan in an effort to stop her husband's hasty second marriage. She traveled the 336 kilometers in the astonishingly short period of two days and managed to break off the wedding in time, presumably because she was a former harem wife which prevented her husband from taking a second *'aqdi*. (Polak [1865] 1976, I:226).

Having several wives was a sign of a man's prestige and sexual prowess. It was a way of solidifying one's ties with the upper echelons of society, a way to confirm publicly one's improved economic status. Yet many men felt they needed an excuse for their actions and usually blamed their first wives for their supposed shortcomings. A man would complain that his first wife had given him mostly girls; that his first marriage was strictly arranged and not to his liking; that his first wife had medical problems and avoided sex; or that she was too arrogant and upper class for him. Husbands who took younger second wives of lower social standing usually gave the latter reason.

Often a husband's second formal marriage undermined the first wife psychologically and financially. She might mourn the loss of his physical affection or the fact that her husband was no longer emotionally invested in her well-being and in their relationship. But she particularly resented her loss of prestige in the new arrangement. Polak reports, "the greatest pain in the life of an Iranian woman is when her husband takes a new wife or when he loves another co-wife more. In such situations the women are inconsolable" (Polak [1865] 1976, I:225–226).

A journeyman artisan or worker in a small *bazaar* factory might assume considerable debt (at annual interest rates of 25 percent to 60 percent) to arrange a second *nekah* marriage and throw a week-long wedding reception as a way of showing off to his friends and relatives (Fig. 1.4). Thus the first wife was devastated, not only by loss of intimacy, but also by a loss of authority accompanied by financial loss. Mary Sheil writes, "When

Figure 1.4 Traditional wedding reception: men's quarters

a rival wife is introduced into an establishment [the first wife's] *pin-money* is decreased at *Nowrooz* (New Year's Day); her allowance for new clothes for herself and her establishment is lessened; her children's interests suffer, if she has any; and if not, perhaps her more fortunate rival may have a son; besides a variety of other annoyances" (Sheil [1856] 1973, 144).

A second ʿ*aqdi* in a polygamous relationship was entitled to a separate dwelling. This could be a room in a house, if the husband had only one house, or a separate house and a retinue of servants and maids if he was wealthier. Many elite men acquired several temporary wives and one or two slave concubines, in addition to one or more ʿ*aqdi* wives. In such households with multiple wives and concubines, the senior wife, often his cousin, had more authority. She managed the husband's sleeping arrangements – generally once every four days with each wife, if he had the maximum number of four wives:

> As a rule, the wife who is related to her husband [by blood] takes the highest rank. She leads the house, divides the daily portion of rice, wood, bread, etc.; appoints herself as "*jus noctis*" [in charge of nightly arrangements] and exudes such an authority over the other wives that those in her presence cannot take a seat or smoke without her permission. If any of the other wives bears a child, and has the luck not to lose it to death, she can take the place of the relative as the favored wife. With a princess all the other wives must tend to their places and consider themselves lucky if they and their children receive even a lowly place. (Polak [1865] 1976, I:227)

As elsewhere in the Middle East, the multiplicity of sexual partners, and a man's right to divorce, discouraged the husband from making an emotional investment in his formal wife and instead spread his affection and income among several women, as well as other kin and other pursuits (Sabbah 1984, 107). How did an ʿ*aqdi* cope with the situation? It seems she also invested less in the relationship with the husband and more in the relationship with her or his kin. Elite Iranian women also turned their attention to philanthropic and administrative pursuits which gained them new social contacts. In the city of Ask near the Alborz mountains, Mary Sheil met Khanom, the very capable wife of the governor of Larijan, who ruled the province in her husband's absence. Khanom's husband had moved to Shiraz three years earlier, where his regiment was stationed. He had three wives in Larijan and had taken two others in Shiraz and Tehran. Khanom was torn between, on the one hand, leaving the governance of the town to her co-wives and going to Tehran, hoping to undo the latest marriage, or on the other hand, staying and ruling the province. In the end she decided to stay. "Though the ejection of a rival was something, yet the loss of the keys of the well-filled store-rooms of Ask and Amol, and the transfer of all the power she now possessed to the hands of another wife, were ideas not to be borne; so she determined to remain where she was" (Sheil [1856] 1973, 265).

Polak believed that domestic violence on the part of elite men was rare, but intrigues among wives and their children were common enough. Jealousy among co-wives occasionally gave way to violence and even murder. The most common way of plotting against a co-wife was through the use of herbs and potions, which served a number of purposes. Women of all social classes visited fortune tellers, traveled to saints' shrines, and sought remedies for their psychological ailments. They paid for potions to intensify their husband's devotion to them and decrease his attraction to the co-wife. There were potions that increased a woman's chance of pregnancy, and herbs and poisons that induced miscarriage in a co-wife. For these reasons, many wives avoided the food cooked by a co-wife and did not feed it to their children (Polak [1865] 1976, 1:224).

The institution of polygamy may have broken the hearts and spirits of many young and old women, but it also contributed to the resilience of some. As elsewhere in the Middle East, the acquisition of a second wife initially made a man more valuable, since there were now two women who competed over him, without his having done anything to deserve this extra attention (Mernissi 1987, 115). But on many occasions, wrote Polak, a first wife's conflict with a co-wife could turn into collaboration: "When a woman learns that her husband is considering another marriage, she tries to dissuade him with threats, tears, and begging. If these do not succeed, she then begins to disparage and suspect the chosen one. Finally, however, she gives up her quest and befriends her rival. As a form of compromise, or even friendly competition between the two, they avenge themselves through unfaithfulness to the husband" (Polak [1865] 1976, 1:226). Sheil also comments on the independent spirit of women who lived in polygamous families, and the ways in which they navigated the webs of power and intrigue: "When a woman happens to possess unusual talent, or has a stronger understanding than her husband, she maintains her supremacy to the last, not only over her associate wives, but over her husband, his purse, and property" (Sheil [1856] 1973, 144–145).

Marital disputes

In the 1880s, reported crime rates in Tehran were low among both affluent and middle-class neighborhoods. There were few murders, hardly any major thefts, and missing children were typically located within hours. In a world where women and their families quietly endured sexual transgressions in the private domain, police reports of rape, molestation, incest, or honor killings were also rare. But a significant number of marital conflicts were reported, requiring police intervention. When women called during incidents of domestic violence, husbands could be scolded or taken into custody for such violations. Men had recourse to any number of excuses and tactics to reassert their marital power, however. The primary excuse given by apprehended husbands was that their wives had left the house without their permission to visit relatives, attend mosques, shrines, passion plays, or New Year's picnics (*sizdeh bedar*). Men seeking to retrieve runaway wives commonly claimed that their belongings had also been stolen. Men also complained that their divorced wives had remarried before the *'idda* (waiting period) was over. Occasionally they broke up the wedding ceremonies of their former wives, incidents which led to police intervention (Shaykh Rezaei and Azari 1999, I:385–386, II:465–466, II:508, II:652).

Women called upon the police when their husbands beat them or failed to provide them with maintenance or clothing. Serious altercations might occur if a man took a second wife, either formal or temporary. Hopelessly frustrated by persistent strife in the home, wives sought help through suicide attempts. These seem to have been cries for help to relatives, neighbors, and police. A typical police entry read:

Yesterday the wife of Mashhadi Rahim had a fight with her husband because he took a new wife. The [first wife] ingested some opium. The family found out and took care of her. She was saved. (I:266–267)

Occasionally, desperate husbands in acrimonious polygamous homes also attempted suicide:

Mashhahdi Abbas the Dealer who has several wives, and could not provide for them, has had disturbances. He ate some opium and nearly died. His relatives attempted to save him; so far he has not died. (II:439)

Other police interventions stemmed from fights between co-wives. If the two women became exceptionally raucous and disturbed the neighborhood's peace, the police might advise the husband to divorce one of his wives. Another typical police entry read:

Nazar Ali Khan often has fights with his wife. The reason is that he has taken a young wife. The [first] wife is old and he no longer cares for her. Last night once again they had a fight and a major disturbance. The deputy of the community went there and quieted them down. It was agreed that he should divorce one of them. (I:404)

Adult sons often protested when their father took additional wives. When Sheikh Mohammad Zaki's father, a frail old man, remarried, his son sent him the following message: "What do you need a wife for at this age?

Find a spouse for your sons if you have money" (II:479). This open disrespect infuriated the old man, who contacted the police.

Women also summoned the police to mediate fights over pecuniary maintenance. After a divorce they demanded child support, *mahriyeh*, or back maintenance. Then, as today, the amount of requested maintenance could be quite exorbitant. When the daughter of Zahir al-Molk moved out of her husband's house, she claimed fifteen years of unpaid maintenance (*nafaqeh*) from her husband (II:546). In these police accounts, women often seem assertive and even aggressive. When Akbar the Peddler had a fight with his wife, she beat him instead of the other way around. Akbar attempted suicide with opium, but a neighbor saved him (II:662). When Karbala'i Hassan took a second wife, his first wife contacted the police and claimed her husband had brought a prostitute into their house, thus humiliating him in the neighborhood (II:528). Wives were accused or even convicted of poisoning their husbands. Hussein Ali Haddad ate his wife's porridge, and when he became ill, suspected her of poisoning him. "He took the porridge to the doctor who concluded that it was poisoned." The wife was subsequently arrested (I:342).

Divorce, custody, and remarriage

There were several ways to terminate a marriage, including *talaq*, *khol'*, and *muburat*. *Talaq* (repudiation) was initiated by the husband. It was a revocable divorce, in which the husband pronounced the divorce formula before witnesses, leading to a separation of three months (three menstrual cycles). Usually this type of divorce was also notarized. During this *'idda* the man continued to maintain his wife and had a unilateral right to return to the marriage at his discretion. *'Idda* allowed the husband to change his mind and gave him time to make sure the wife was not carrying his child at the conclusion of the divorce. Some women made it impossible or extremely costly for the husband to return to the marriage during the *'idda*. They stipulated in their divorce contracts that if the husband resumed the marriage, he had to pay a penalty. The amount could be as high as 200 *tumans* (Nuri Document 1305 HQ/1888, No. 736). This form of divorce could only be used twice. Upon a third invocation of *'idda*, the Qur'an legislates that the man "cannot remarry her until she has wedded another man and been divorced by him; in which case it shall be no offense for either of them to return to the other" (Qur'an 2:230). To remedy this situation, one could procure the services of a *mohallel* (temporary husband) who received a fee for his services. However, no respectable man wanted to find himself shamed should the mother of his children marry a *mohallel*. The ignominy of involving a *mohallel* in one's personal life often restrained a husband's behavior. A divorced wife needed strong assurances before she agreed to wed a *mohallel*. An extant *mohallel* contract shows that a regretful husband made the following written promise to his wife:

If my divorced wife named Jahan Khanom takes a *mohallel* and the *mohallel* does not divorce her; or if he divorces her but does not pay her *'idda*; or if she becomes pregnant from the *mohallel* and I decline responsibility for the child; or if after the divorce by the *mohallel* I do not take her as my permanent wife and with a *mahriyeh* of 50 *tumans*; or if I renege on any of these agreements, I promise to pay her 100 *tumans*. In addition, I promise that if after marrying the *mohallel* he inflicts physical injury on her, in addition to the *diyeh* (retribution) I give her 20 *tumans*. (Nuri Document 1305 HQ/1888, No. 781)

The second and third forms of divorce, *khol'* and *muburat*, could be initiated by the wife. In *khol'* a woman renounced her alimony and petitioned a judge for divorce. This method of divorce was irrevocable and the husband paid no maintenance during the *'idda*. *Muburat* was a mutual arrangement, by which husband and wife agreed to end the marriage. A divorce of this kind still required the wife to give up her alimony and observe the *'idda* (Haeri 1989, 44–45). In *khol'* and *muburat*, the wife (or her attorney) usually renounced her alimony in the office of a notary shortly before the divorce. All three types of divorce required the husband to consent and the wife to undergo a period of *'idda*, though not always with pay.

Divorce was therefore difficult but not impossible for an *'aqdi*. Other circumstances existed in which a woman could petition for divorce. A woman could stipulate a right to divorce before marriage in her contract. A husband's impotence and his wife's continuing virginity at the conclusion of the first full year of marriage and cohabitation furnished another valid reason for divorce; so did a husband's disappearance without trace (for four years), or a husband's refusal to provide maintenance and sustenance for his wife according to her social status. Under these conditions, a judge decided whether or not to grant the wife's petition (Mehrpour 2000, 198–199). In the absence of these conditions, an unhappy woman often left her husband and refused to return. At this point relatives, neighbors, and even the police might intercede. To resolve such a dispute, the man might either apologize and reconcile with his wife, or he might agree to divorce her. Elite women used family connections to obtain divorce without losing their alimony ('Ayn al-Saltaneh 1998b, V:3233, V:3747).

I have found no statistics on frequency of divorce in the late nineteenth century. In upper-class circles, a variety of social ties and obligations between the families of the husband and wife hampered the frequency of divorce. The fact that an elite man's divorcing of his *'aqdi* wife was big news in the city and the subject of much gossip suggests that it was not widespread ('Ayn al-Saltaneh 1997, II:1195–1196). In the urban middle classes, a woman's *mahriyeh* (marriage portion) was a deterrent, though here there were more instances of divorce, usually because the husband took a second formal wife (Shaykh Rezaei and Azari 1999, 1:45, 69). Among the rural and urban popular classes, lifelong monogamous marriages were more the rule ('Ayn al-Saltaneh, 1998a, III:1785).

Since marriage united two families, not simply two individuals, relatives on both sides exercised a great deal of authority. The families helped to maintain the marriage, even when relations between the spouses had become strained. Brothers-in-law developed business partnerships as well as close social ties. The wife's mother organized frequent lunches and dinner parties to which the husband's relatives were invited. These social and economic ties discouraged a man from divorcing his wife. A husband was aware of the adverse effects that divorce would have upon him. Not only might he be shamed and ostracized by his friends and by both families, but he could also be left in a state of financial ruin. Some families went as far as to use force or threats of physical punishment to prevent a man from divorcing their sister or daughter. In lower-middle-class neighborhoods, the whole neighborhood and the chief of police might intervene.

A man had the legal right to kill his wife if he caught her at *zina* (*in flagrante delicto*) with another man, but Polak believed such instances were rare because avoiding culpability by actually proving an affair required the testimony of four male witnesses who had seen the sexual penetration, "which was nearly impossible. Hence, husbands preferred divorce more often. Naturally, in such cases the wife cannot claim her alimony" (Polak [1865] 1976, I:215). If a husband killed his wife without proper proof, the state could punish him according to the male/female rules of retribution (*qesas*), which would involve the amputation of one of his limbs ('Ayn al-Saltaneh 1995, I:372). The police records of Tehran contain two incidents of infidelity in the 1880s. In one case, the wife swore that nothing had happened, and her husband relented. In the other case, the woman was called in for questioning by the police, and the male lover and an accomplice received corporal punishment (Shaykh Rezaei and Azari 1999, I:411, II:599). Police records of this period indicate no cases of stoning in Tehran, which seems to have been a practice in Arab and Kurdish peripheries of the nation with tribal connections, where it was also rare (Keddie 2007, 40).

Custody regulations guaranteed that the father paid the costs of raising children and later provided the daughter with a dowry and the son with money to establish himself in a profession. These financial arrangements allowed divorced women to remarry and start new families, making remarriage relatively easy. Even so, Shi'i child-custody laws decidedly privileged the father over the mother. Mothers had physical custody of boys until the age of two and daughters until the age of seven, and they were required to relinquish custody if they remarried (whether after being widowed or divorced), unless the next husband was a close blood relative of the former husband. Otherwise, when the mother remarried, the child was sent to live with the father's family, creating greater hardship for the mother. In cases where a man had wives in different cities, a divorced mother and her child could be separated for years, and this was another reason for women's suicide attempts (Shaykh Rezaei and Azari [1885–1888] 1999, 1:97; Wakin "Family Law").

Despite stringent regulations about virginity at first marriage, women's remarriage was not unusual, with little stigma attached to it. Women of all social classes, including postmenopausal ones, might marry two, three, or four times, as long as they were propositioned by admiring suitors ('Ayn al-Saltaneh 1995, I:345; Shaykh Rezaei and Azari 1999, I:122). The mother of Muhammad Ali Shah, Umm al-Khaqan, was divorced from her royal husband and had remarried two or three times. This became the subject of jokes and innuendo but nevertheless was an acceptable fact ('Ayn al-Saltaneh 1998a, III:1813).

Inheritance and economic rights

At the turn of the twentieth century, married Shi'i women could own property and dispose of it as they wished. These economic rights were rooted in both Islamic and ancient Iranian traditions (Dandamaev and Lukonin 1989, 124). Islamic law recognizes a woman's right to receive an inheritance from her family of origin (parents) as well as brother and sister, or aunts and uncles. However, the Qu'ran specifies that "a male shall inherit twice as much as a female" (4:11). Muslim women could also inherit from their husbands and children. Additionally, they had the right to draw up contracts and to testify in court, although the testimony of two women before a judge counted as that of one man.

A wife was under no obligation to pay for household expenses, even if she was wealthy, and her husband had to provide for her (Mattson 2003, 450–457). In elite Qajar families, as in other elite Middle Eastern families, the *jahiziyeh* (trousseau), the *mahriyeh*, and the inheritance gave women relative autonomy and power. Some women used their wealth to establish charitable *vaqfs* (religious endowments), usually earmarked for religious schools and institutions, or other public welfare projects (Malekzadeh 2006). A woman from an upper-class family could threaten to claim her entire *mahriyeh* if her husband took another wife. Her chances of success were enhanced if her *mahriyeh* was large and beyond the means of the husband to contest. Often a woman who renounced her *mahriyeh* as a gesture of goodwill toward her husband came to regret her decision later in life (Javadi *et al.* 1992, 196–197).

Daughters fared better in Shi'i than in Sunni inheritance law, which favored agnate (paternal) relations (Coulson 1971, 108–134; Charrad 2001). In both Sunni and Shi'i law, a wife inherited a portion of her husband's assets. If she had no children, she inherited one-fourth of his wealth; if she did, she stood to inherit only one-eighth (Qur'an 4:12). While this was not stipulated in the Qur'an, a wife did not inherit her husband's land, only the structures above the land and what was below them (Novin and Khajeh Piri 1999, 114–115). In the Qajar and even the Pahlavi eras, daughters were often disinherited from landownership in rural areas in order to keep property in the patrilineal line of succession (Vieille 1978, 460). This was the case throughout the Middle East (Keddie and Baron 1991, 6).

Although it was possible for an elite woman to receive an inheritance from her parents, siblings, and later from her husband, attaining these rights in practice was difficult. First, many elite urban families left their property in the form of *vaqf* for the sole benefit of the male heirs, and often in order to avoid female inheritance. Indeed, the primary purpose of the institution of *vaqf* might well have been to circumvent Qur'anic requirements on women's inheritance (Keddie 2007, 43). Second, the institutions of polygamy and repudiation made women vulnerable to the vicissitudes of family disputes. There was always a trade-off between quarreling with one's own family of origin over inheritance and the protection one needed from the same relatives if one were to become widowed or divorced. A divorced woman had no financial claims to her husband's wealth, with the exception of the maintenance she received during the *'idda*. Regardless of the length of their marriage and the extent of his wealth, a woman had no share in the property her husband accumulated in the course of their marriage; she was entitled only to the *mahriyeh* and the *jahiziyeh* she brought from her father's house. These assets were usually worth little after twenty years of marriage. Third, women had few personal rights and limited access to public spaces. Gender segregation made it difficult for them to carry out extended public disputes in the office of a notary. As a result, few women petitioned court authorities for their share of inheritance from their fathers without their husband's support. Still, was it wise for a woman to enter a dispute with her brother, even if she had her husband's support? Elite urban women usually settled for partial compensation and chose not to resist their brothers and uncles, on whom they might have to rely in the case of marital problems (Keddie 1991, 8; Kandiyoti 1991, 23–44; Petry 1991). In practice, this meant that the wife, her husband, and their children were all deprived of the woman's inheritance from her family of origin, a fact that further weakened the conjugal unit.

The veil and sexual resistance

Much has been written about the veil and urban women's seclusion. In Iran, as in most Middle East and Mediterranean societies, the code of honor and shame was an inescapable fact of life. Sexual segregation and veiling were the tools that enforced this code in the cities. While tribal women went about their work unveiled, and poor rural women wore a modified form of the veil, elite urban women strictly observed the practice. They might wear fashionable and revealing clothes made from silk, satin, and lace in their homes (Fig. 1.5). From the age of nine, however, many wore a shapeless and loose-fitting cloth known as a *chador* that covered the entire body when outside the home. The *chador* came in a variety of materials (light cotton or silk) and was held tightly below the chin with one hand and without the aid of a pin. Urban Muslim and Jewish women (but not Christian, Zoroastrian, or slave women) also wore a long face covering (*rubandeh*), which revealed the eyes but disguised much of the face (Benjamin 1887, 107; Sykes [1910] 2005, 198) (Fig. 1.6).

Figure 1.5 Women in the private quarters of the house, Qajar era

Figure 1.6 Women in outdoor costumes, Qajar era

There were regional differences in the wearing of the veil. Northern Gilani women, northwestern Kurdish women, and southern Arab women frequented public spaces more freely, often without a *chador* (Fig. 1.7). Central Kashani women observed a stricter dress code, while Tehrani women were somewhere in between. They wore a dark blue or black *chador* and a face covering that was difficult to tolerate during the summer heat, "forcing women to remove it from time to time" (Polak [1865] 1976, I:161). By the mid-nineteenth century, Tehrani women seem to have worn their *chadors* somewhat more casually in public sites such as parks, gardens, and *Ta'ziyeh* passion plays (Azad 1985, 321–322).

Poor urban women lived under fewer constraints and did not need elaborate ruses for leaving the house. They were more physically mobile, often wore a loose veil (and sometimes no face veil), and interacted with men more freely. Impoverished women usually lived in monogamous marriages (serial temporary ones) and worked for a living. Some hawked their merchandise about town. Others served as couriers and matchmakers through whom lovers secretly communicated and lonely widows and divorcées found spouses. Matchmakers did more than find suitable partners. They also worked out the preliminary financial arrangements of a union, leaving the rest to the male guardians (Yonan 1898, 33).

Figure 1.7 Carpet weaving among nomad women

The veil is often regarded as the most oppressive institution of Muslim societies, enforcing gender segregation and restricting women's physical mobility. Mernissi has called it "an expression of the invisibility of women on the street, a male space *par excellence*" (1987, 96). But in a world where a man's *namus* (honor) was defined by the conduct of the women in his family, and gender transgressions of respectable women were severely punished, the full veil also offered some surprising opportunities for resistance to the patriarchal order (Fig. 1.8).

The anonymity of the *chador* and *rubandeh* meant that women could visit public sites incognito and without the knowledge of their husbands. Mary Sheil reported that elite married women used a veil (often that of their lower-class maids) to visit a doctor or to socialize with other women on their own. All classes of women "enjoy abundance of liberty, more so, I think, than among us. The complete envelopment of the face and person disguises them effectually from the nearest relatives, and destroying, when convenient, all distinction of rank, gives unrestrained freedom" (Sheil [1856] 1973, 145). In general, married women used the anonymity of the veil more often than young unmarried girls. Hence, despite its restrictions, marriage also led to a curious freedom. The breaking of the hymen was liberating and occasionally lifted "the barrier to a free sexuality" (Vieille 1978, 456). We should not be surprised, then, to find references in the literature of the period

Figure 1.8 Women in the streets of Tehran, Qajar era

to pimps or love brokers (*dallal-e mohabbat*) and to the secret affairs of married, divorced, or widowed women.

A woman could discreetly signal her availability to men in public in several ways. Women of the upper classes might wear a long lace skirt under their *chadors*, they might slightly open up the front of the veil to reveal part of the face and their figure. In the case of prostitutes, bumping into men on the street indicated their willingness to be propositioned (Shahri 1990, I:470). In the 1880s S. G. W. Benjamin, US Minister in Iran, observed:

The profound disguise worn by the women of Teheran in the street, supposed by foreigners to be a serious inconvenience, is, under existing conditions, of very good advantage, and the women themselves would be the last to advocate a change so long as polygamy exists. No argument is required to show what a power for intrigue exists in such a costume. In her mantle or veil, completely covering her from head to foot, a woman can go wherever she pleases without the slightest possibility of her identity being detected. Not even her husband would dare to raise her veil [in public]; to do so would render him liable to instant death. On the other hand, if a Persian woman wishes to disclose her charms to any one, she generally contrives to find a chance to withdraw her veil for an instant; the rest is arranged by third parties, who are always on hand. (Benjamin 1887, 105–106)

Women also cross-dressed to gain access to forbidden areas. Carla Serena reported that "to secretly enter print shops, cafés or mosques, women dress as men and arrange meetings in such public places" (Serena [1883] 1983, 68). These accounts suggest remarkable agency on the part of urban middle-class women despite enormous social restrictions that hindered their mobility.

Love brokers arranged many of these romantic adventures. They planned clandestine trysts for married, divorced, or widowed women, sometimes known as "single fliers" (*tak parans*), and handsome poor men. Brokers scheduled and arranged illicit relationships and found attractive young men for the occasion. The mourning processions of the months of Muharram and Safar provided occasions for women to spot handsome men in the crowd, sometimes among actors in a passion play or male flagellants in street processions. Like most of the relationships discussed so far, even affairs could involve lengthy negotiations to make sure that the prospective man was not a relative. Often female friends and relatives accompanied the woman on these expeditions, during which they all claimed to be out shopping (Shahri 1990, VI:302–309). Others seem to have searched for lovers on the street. As Shahri points out, "While there were those who made a living from prostitution and sold their body to earn a living, there were also romantic women and girls who followed men and youths and offered themselves without any compensation. Some women even bought gifts for the men, [among them married] women who were deprived and unmarried girls who had to quench their natural desire" (Shahri 1990, I:469).

Love brokers appear also to have been used in more dire situations. Infertility was a great calamity for women, who resorted to a variety of remedies in order to conceive. They tried potions, herbs, and magic, and paid frequent visits to saints' shrines in hopes of a miracle. The problem was more complicated when the husband was too old or impotent. Many amusing popular tales tell of brokers' attempts to solve this problem. I leave it to the reader to judge the veracity of one such story. It is a tale told to Jane Dieulafoy by an old servant named Ali who held a grudge against his pitiless master.

A wealthy landlord in the city of Urumiyeh in Azerbaijan had remained childless after thirty years of marriage to several formal and temporary wives and attempts with innumerable slave concubines. At last, one of his concubines suggested a visit to the shrine of Imam Reza in the province of Khorasan, where he could plead with the saint for a child. The landlord packed all his wives, concubines, and servants for the journey. After fifty days of difficult travel they arrived in the city of Mashhad. As the servant recalled, soon a number of love brokers who knew their way around such problems approached the women:

The master rented a beautiful house, where the wives soon developed very friendly relations with some charming women friends who provided very pleasant company, or so it seemed, because they spent entire days together. During the numerous visits that the new acquaintances of the ladies made to the *andaruni*, and when ladies' slippers placed at the door forbade entry to his own house to my master himself, this admirable man sometimes found the wait to be very long; but he redoubled his fervor and never left the tomb of the Imam except to smoke the water pipe or drink tea with the elderly mullahs, who unanimously promised him numerous progeny as a reward for his devotion. In contrast, the young clerics showed little taste for his company and slipped away as he approached, after having nevertheless assured him of the fervor of the prayers that they were sending skyward on his behalf from morning to night. Soon the master was no longer in doubt concerning his good fortune, and the generosity of the Imam was of such great measure that not only my mistresses, but also all of the female servants, soon informed him of the agreeable success of the pilgrimage.

Consequently, after having thanked God, leaving considerable presents as an offering at the tomb of the Imam, and rewarding his friends the mullahs for their pious services, my master decided, to the great unhappiness of his wives, to make the journey back to Azerbaijan. Seven months after our departure from Mashhad, he experienced the happiness of being a father eight times over. His pride and his joy were unparalleled when the ladies, and especially his favorite, suggested that he should, on account of the miracle, take his numerous progeny to Mashhad.

This wish and this advice originated from a sentiment too pious to be ignored; consequently we set off again, after having made our preparations over several months. This time, I hope, we will count the births by pairs of twins!

Dieulafoy asked the servant why he doubted the magic powers of the shrine. After looking around to make sure no one heard him, Ali replied, "I often saw several young men, disguised in thick *chadors* come to my mistresses while [my master] this son of a dog was wondering about matters of Muslim theology." Dieulafoy persisted, asking, "Don't you think these good clerics could have dressed themselves in female clothes to invite the women to virtue and prayers?" Ali did not think so and believed that all women "be they from Turkey or Persia" used the same scheme "to make their husbands happy" (Dieulafoy 1887, 95–97).

2   Slave concubinage, temporary marriage, and harem wives

Since the primary purpose of *nekah* marriage was procreation and the establishment of a family, men often looked for additional legal forms of sexual gratification in other relations. In the mid-nineteenth century, an ordinary urban man – a butcher or a baker with some discretionary spending – found pleasure in the arms of a *sigheh* (temporary wife). This could be for a few hours or a few days during his visits to provinces and shrines on business or pilgrimage. Sometimes he brought a temporary wife home, where she could become a maid to his *'aqdi* wife. Clerics of all social classes had access to divorced and widowed women, who approached them for legal aid and sometimes became their temporary wives. In addition, the business of contracting temporary marriage for others was an important source of income for low-level clerics. *Bazaar* merchants might keep temporary wives who also served as pieceworkers in their employ. Wealthy men from elite families might have a series of temporary wives, as well as one or two slave concubines. The harems at the royal court contained separate compounds for formal wives, temporary wives, slave concubines of both sexes, and boy concubines, as well as other female relatives. European men, who were denied access to the elite harems (except for medical doctors like Polak and Jean-Baptiste Feuvrier) often fantasized about the polymorphous sexuality of the *andaruni*. To be sure, sex was an important element of harem life, along with procreation and the politics of succession to the throne. But large royal harems also served as symbols of power for the male elite, bearing witness to their superior economic and political positions and were a decisive part of the administration of the state.

The first decade of the twentieth century saw the disbandment of harems. A mid-nineteenth-century ban on the slave trade had drastically reduced the availability of slave concubines from the Caucasus and Africa, and the Constitutional Revolution further weakened the institution of slavery. The number of formal wives in elite homes also decreased for two reasons. First, Iran experienced a significant economic downturn at the turn of the twentieth century. In a weak economy, fewer

men could maintain multiple formal wives. Second, the gradual exposure of elites to modern gender norms, especially monogamous heterosexuality, altered their perception of marriage as an institution. Formal
monogamy became the standard for most wealthy and powerful men,
as it had always been for poor men. On the sidelines, the tradition of
temporary marriage continued, however, mostly among *bazaar* merchants
and clerics.

Slave concubinage

Iran's slave trade dates back at least to the third century CE. Throughout
this period, military and domestic slavery were more common than planta-
tion slavery. Slaves of both sexes worked in the royal court and elite homes
as concubines and domestic servants, harem guards, nannies and tutors,
artists and masons, and performers and entertainers. During the Safavid era
(1501–1722), the slave trade expanded. The number of military royal slaves
who served as the king's bodyguards increased, as did the number of
slaves who worked as artisans and stonemasons in the royal workshops
(Minorsky 1980; Keyvani 1982). As commerce grew, so did the need for
better infrastructure. Slaves were employed in major public works projects,
including construction of buildings, roads, and bridges. The slave trade
continued in the early 1800s to meet the needs of the growing cash-crop
economy. Historian Thomas Ricks has shown that the institution of slavery,
with both male and female slave traders, was deeply incorporated into both
the national and local economies (2002, 78).

Black slaves arrived from the south via the Indian Ocean and the
Persian Gulf and white slaves from the north and east via land and the
Caspian Sea. Iranian pilgrims also brought back slaves from markets in
Mecca and Karbala. Because of their origin, Persians often called black
male slaves *hajji* and female slaves *hajjiyeh*, meaning one who has made
the pilgrimage to Mecca (Fig. 2.1). At Bushire and Shiraz newly arrived
black slaves were stripped naked and inspected by potential buyers in
private homes. For concubinage, customers usually preferred northern
Caucasian and light-skinned Ethiopians to the dark-skinned blacks of East
Africa, who were purchased for use as maids, nannies, and domestics
(Floor, "Barda," 722).[1]

---

[1] Slaves from east Africa (particularly Mogadishu, Zanzibar, and Kilwa) and the Indian
Ocean were imported into the Omani ports of Muscat and Suhar and into the Iranian
Persian Gulf ports of Bandar Abbas, Bandar Lengeh, and Bushire. Turkish, Georgian,
Lesgian, Armenian, and Circassian slaves were brought in from the Caucasus, Uzbekistan,
Afghanistan, and Baluchestan. I am grateful for a personal communication with Thomas

Figure 2.1 Black slave, Qajar era

Iran also had an internal slave trade that fed on the economic plight of indigent families and, at its worst, involved kidnapping. Local traders purchased girls and boys from poor Afghani, Tajik, Khorasani, Kurdish, and Baluchi parents. Border wars, such as the Russo-Iranian wars, tribal wars, and slave raids resulted in the capture of additional youths (Sheil [1856] 1973, 209; Polak [1865] 1976, 248; Floor, "Barda," 770–772). In the south, Arab and Iranian merchants enslaved Baluchis while Sunni Turkomans across the plains of northeast Khorasan came to be called "men stealers" because of their ferocious raids (Sykes [1910] 2005, 69, 109). The Turkomans sold some of their victims to harems inside Iran, sending others to Central Asia. According to Sheil, the despondent relatives of the captured minors often turned to begging to secure their freedom: "I have frequently seen at the gate of the Mission very poor-looking men with long chains suspended from their necks. This was a signal that sons or daughters had been carried off by the Toorkomans, whose release they were endeavoring to purchase by collecting alms" (Sheil [1856] 1973, 210). A different type of kidnapping took place in

M. Ricks on this in July 2006. See also Ricks 1989, 65; Ricks 2002, 77–88; Floor, "Barda," 771; Sykes [1910] 2005, 69. Mirzai suggests the average annual import of black slaves to Arabia, Iran, and India was 6,500 between 1850 and 1873 (2004, 99).

non-Muslim communities. Occasionally Jews, Christians, and other non-Muslim women were stolen from their homes, converted to Islam, and taken as wives (interview with Monir Pirnazar, May 12, 2006). In March 1839, an angry crowd stormed the Jewish quarter of Mashhad, burned down the synagogue, looted homes, and snatched six young girls, two of whom were subsequently married to the *Imam Jom'eh* (Leader of the Friday Prayer). These women were not enslaved so much as forbidden access to their community of origin due to conversion.[2]

Three factors ultimately ended the slave trade and slave concubinage by the twentieth century: (1) Following the 1828 Turkmanchay peace treaty with Iran, Russia banned the sale of Armenians, Georgians, and Circassians from the Caucasus as slaves. While the smuggling of northern slaves into Iran persisted until the late nineteenth century, Caucasian slaves became scarce in harems. (2) In 1807, the English Parliament passed the Slave Act, prohibiting British ships from engaging in slave trade. Thereupon, the British Royal Navy began to patrol the Atlantic Ocean and the Indian Ocean, including the Persian Gulf, with anti-slavery patrols. Between 1848 and 1882, British pressure led to the issuance of several royal decrees by the Iranian court prohibiting the trade. Elite Iranian citizens who had routine dealings with Russian and British diplomatic envoys were also pressed into manumitting their slaves. However, these measures were of limited success, and African slaves remained a visible part of elite household and village life until 1882, when the Iranian government signed a convention to end the slave trade and Naser al-Din Shah (Fig. 2.2) gave British officials the right to inspect Iranian ships for this purpose. This controversial agreement drastically cut the African slave trade but it also gave Britain the right to freely move about the Persian Gulf and expand its political and economic authority. Iran later became a signatory to the anti-slavery Brussels Convention of 1890, the first international agreement to end the African slave trade by land or sea. (3) In the course of the Constitutional Revolution both the foreign slave trade and domestic slavery came under heavy criticism in the Iranian Parliament and in leading newspapers. By the time Iran joined the 1926 Geneva Convention, the trade was limited to the peripheries of the Persian Gulf area.[3]

European travelers routinely commented on what they perceived to be the benign treatment of Iran's urban slaves, which they compared

---

[2] The entire Jewish community of Mashhad converted to Islam to avoid a pogrom, though many secretly maintained their Jewish identity. For details see Pirnazar 2002; Patai 1998.
[3] Information on the slave trade in Iran appears in Ricks 1989; 2002; Floor "Barda," 773; Benjamin 1887, 170; Sheil [1856] 1973, 243–245; Sykes [1910] 2005, 224, 229; Martin 2005, 159–161; and Mirzai 2004.

Figure 2.2 Naser al-Din Shah

favorably to their lot in contemporary America (Polak [1865] 1976, I:249–251; Sheil [1856] 1973, 243–245). Ella Sykes went so far as to call Iran the "paradise" of slaves (Sykes [1910] 2005, 68). Such relatively benign treatment was not universal, especially for agricultural slaves (Floor 2003, 113). Historically, both military and elite households offered opportunities for manumission and integration. Ordinary slaves bought their freedom, while military slaves attained positions of power as generals, ministers, and even kings (Babaie *et al.* 2004, 2–3).

While certainly conscious of color as a matter of aesthetics and social standing, Iranians did not regard it as an insurmountable barrier to the economic and social integration of former slaves (Sykes [1910] 2005, 68). Sheil reports that slaves "are frequently restored to freedom, and when this happens, they take their station in society without any reference to their colour or descent" (Sheil [1856] 1973, 244).

Religious precedents facilitated the greater social mobility afforded to Iranian slaves. The Qur'an recognizes the institution of slavery and recommends (though it does not require) the freeing of Muslim slaves as a sign of devotion to God and penance for one's sins (16:71; 5:89; 4:92; 90:11–13). Muslims viewed slaves both as commodities and as persons with certain limited rights. A male slave (*gholam*) and a female slave (*kaniz*) could be sold, exchanged, rented, inherited, or owned by several masters.[4] Slave owners also had easy sexual access to their *kanizes* or *gholams*. Without the express permission of their masters, slaves did not have the right to own property, testify in legal disputes, or engage in commerce; with permission, however, they could pursue all of these activities.

Masters had certain obligations toward their slaves. Slaves were provided with food and shelter. They were not shackled routinely, could marry, and purchase their freedom. There were even reports of *gholams* marrying freeborn women without a master's consent (Martin 2005, 179). Occasionally, slaves of both sexes learned to read and write ('Ayn al-Saltaneh 1997, II:1752). Non-Muslim slaves who arrived in Iran at a young age converted to Islam, though conversion did not necessarily lead to freedom. They also quickly learned Persian, often speaking in dialects that included words from their homelands. Slave marriages were common, in part because the Qur'an encourages masters to find husbands and wives for their slaves. When a master married his *kaniz* to another man, slave or free, he renounced his concubinage rights over her (Polak [1865] 1976, I:249–251; Taj al-Saltana 1993, 115; Sheil [1856] 1973, 209).

Because slaves were expensive, only well-to-do urban and tribal families tended to own slaves, who served as pages and male concubines (in the case of younger slaves), nannies and servants (older slaves), eunuchs (castrated slaves), or female concubines. One measure of the wealth and influence of an elite man was the number of slaves he owned. While we have no reliable statistics on slaves in the late nineteenth century, it appears that a perpetual imbalance in the ratio of female to male slaves existed from the Safavid to the Qajar period. In the Safavid period the ratio could be as dramatic as 10:1 because of the need for *kanizes* as concubines and as gifts

---

[4] A note on terminology: *barda* or *bardeh* means slave of either sex; *gholam* means page, boy, lad, or male slave. Dehkhoda (1946–) uses the terms *barda* and *gholam* interchangeably for male slaves. See "Gholam," LXXXVI:269–271 and "Gholam va Bandeh az Nazar-e Tarikhi," LXXXVI:271–275.

to dignitaries, visitors, and successful military officers. In the late nine-teenth century, the ratio was 4:1 and the total number of slaves had also dropped (Floor, "Barda," 771; Ricks 2002, 84). By the 1890s, the British Anti-Slavery Society estimated there were "between twenty-five and fifty thousand black slaves still in the country, and eunuchs, not necessarily all of them freed, were still a feature of Iranian upper-class establishments" (Segal 2001, 126–127).

Masters occasionally freed slaves on birthdays or weddings, or other celebratory occasions, or manumitted them in their wills. Once freed, slaves usually lived as servants of the family and saw themselves as members of that family (Polak [1865] 1976, I:251; Algar, "Barda," 776). *Gholams* could purchase their freedom by engaging in trade and retaining a percentage of the transactions. Over time, they could save enough to buy their freedom. Resourceful and intelligent *gholams*, aware that Britain and Russia had banned the slave trade, also appealed to European diplo-mats in Iran and secured their freedom through their intervention (Floor, "Barda," 772; Polak [1865] 1976, I:254–255). However, female *kanizes* who became concubines of their masters had no such option. The masters claimed them as wives and the legations returned them (Mirzai 2004, 244).

Slaves who were severely mistreated had the right to protest. A master's failure to abide by social customs regarding slavery could result in the intervention of a judge and sale of the slave to another owner (Algar, "Barda," 776–779). Polak wrote, "When a slave is badly treated or wounded in her house all the other slaves of the city demonstrate around that house and therefore obligate the court to look into the matter" (Polak [1865] 1976, I:251). However, since a respectable master never sold his slave, and other elite members were reluctant to purchase the slaves of other families, a disgruntled slave owner usually released his *gholam* or *kaniz* without manumission, forcing the slave into prostitution or vagabondage.

Polak reported that life expectancy was short for African slaves in Iran, because they lacked immunity to many local diseases. Frequently suc-cumbing to smallpox, tuberculosis, and measles, few black slaves reached the age of thirty. Most black *kanizes* died soon after childbirth, contracting the same diseases. Slave owners did their best to keep the surviving orphans alive, but few reached puberty. Hence the country's African slave population was small, and after one or two generations the few surviving children of the slaves were integrated into Iranian society (Polak [1865] 1976, I:250–251).

Because of their short life span and the prohibition on the slave trade, black *kanizes* were particularly expensive in the late nineteenth century, and only the very wealthy could afford to own them. Black nannies and eunuchs were viewed as devoted servants with no familial attachments of their own. Some black nannies gained significant authority in notable homes and the royal harem. They developed strong bonds of affection with the children, took the mother's place in their hearts, or even became the youth's first female concubine. Taj wrote with great compassion about the *kanizes* in the Qajar harem who took care of her, many of whom had been imported from East Africa (Taj al-Saltana 1993, 114–115).

But she was also furious with her husband's black nanny and attributed her own unhappy marriage to a possible sexual liaison between her husband and his nanny:

> The seditious intriguer in all this was a black nanny who had raised my husband after his mother's death. She would make the child get into physical fights with slave girls and then kiss them in jest in my presence. She could see this made me very unhappy. Or she would keep him confined to the *birun* [public quarters] and not allow him into the *andarun* [private quarters]. If he had to leave the *birun* out of fear of his father, she would take the child into her own room and put him to sleep while holding him in her bosom. (Taj al-Saltana 1993, 244; see also Amanat 1993, 46)[5]

From our vantage point we can see why a *kaniz*, who had been a boy's first concubine, would resent her master's new bride and make her life miserable. But Qajar society expected total obedience from these discarded women, who took their revenge on young brides like Taj.

Because of their liminal position, *kanizes* were not bound by the conventions of modesty. A *kaniz* could go about in public without a veil. Like a prostitute, she was exempt from many of the gender regulations imposed on women of the upper classes and often accompanied men in public places such as taverns and coffeehouses. If she was accused of fornication, her punishment was also less severe than that of a respectable woman (Marmon 1999, 12; Algar, "Barda," 778; Polak [1865] 1976, I:252). This allowed men other than the master to socialize with a *kaniz* and have easy access to her, with hardly any repercussions (Matthee 2005, 285). Some *kanizes* used this freedom to run away. A few succeeded in finding new homes, where they served as maids. Others were caught by the police and returned to their owners (Shaykh Rezaei and Azari [1885–1888] 1999, I:139, 177, 184).

The most common route to manumission for a *kaniz* was bearing her master's child. A child whose father was free, and who recognized it, was also free and could inherit property. A *kaniz* who gave birth to a master's child was called an *umm walid*, "mother of a child." An *umm walid* would be manumitted upon her master's death. Occasionally she would also receive a separate dwelling and gifts of clothing and jewelry. If the

---

[5] The translation has been slightly revised to reflect current terminology.

master denied paternity, then the slave concubine would not become an *umm walid*, and her child remained a slave (Algar "Barda," 776–779; Marmon 1999, 4; Tucker 1998, 172).

The principle that a man's wife should not be his slave was rooted in both cultural and religious traditions. Husbands had certain sexual obligations toward their wives, but none toward their *kanizes*. A slave had no right to birth control, sexual satisfaction, or children. A master could sleep with several *kanizes* at the same time, an action that would have been reprehensible with regard to his wife (though it did occur commonly in the royal harem). Therefore, a master who wed his *kaniz* also manumitted her, usually because he wanted to elevate the status of a son from that union.

Many *kanizes* who were trained in music and dance became harem tutors. Respectable women sent their slaves to study music with great musicians. In the harem of Naser al-Din Shah, 'Esmat al-Dowleh learned to play the piano through a slave named Tabassom, and in this way became a darling of the shah and the harem (Azad 1985, 405). Each day, the slave returned and taught her mistress what she had learned. Hence *kanizes* facilitated the maintenance of the gender-segregated spaces and allowed elite men to keep their wives and daughters confined, while also providing occasional access for the women to knowledge from the outside world.

Music was not the only art that slaves mastered. Although Persian sources are reticent about this, various texts on harem life indicate that the *kaniz* might also be a sex tutor for adolescent boys and for married women and men. In the sex-segregated world of the elites, it was the *kaniz* who taught elite boys about various techniques of coitus and helped them to learn about women's sexual pleasure. As the Arab Muslim writer Ibn Kamal Pasha (d. 1533) had pointed out three centuries earlier in his treatise on sex and desire in Arab society,

Concubines, because they circulate among various men, sometimes having twenty or thirty consecutive masters, have the opportunity to acquire great knowledge on the subject of copulation. They take advantage of their situation to learn different techniques from each partner. He who wants to make inquiries in this domain must oblige a concubine to communicate to him all the techniques that she has accumulated during her career. Usually they will reveal unsuspected angles to you and cause you to hear sensual sounds and moans never heard before. (Cited in Sabbah 1984, 53)

This high degree of intimacy between the *kaniz* and the future master explains the great influence exercised by royal slaves of both sexes. But proximity did not always protect slaves from the wrath of masters. Although Polak, Sykes, and other Europeans reported that Iranians treated their slaves well, surviving Persian documents suggest that even highly respected slaves of the royal court could suffer brutal treatment (Azad

1985, 413–414). Iranian and Western observers seldom commented on the emotional and sexual violence that slaves endured. The memoirs of Sheil, Taj al-Saltaneh, Carla Serena, and Polak, make brief references to the *kanizes'* tragic lives. They discuss jealous wives who resented their husbands' favorite *kanizes,* or envious *kanizes* who begrudged the good fortunes of their master's wife, suggesting a strong antagonism between wives and *kanizes.* Since having her master's child could free a *kaniz,* she had an incentive to have sex with her master. This in turn angered the mistress of the house, who frequently punished the slave on one or another pretext (Serena [1883] 1983, 66).

Occasionally, slaves were able to retaliate but without gaining much sympathy. Polak recounts the story of a *kaniz* who poisoned the child of her master's formal wife: "A slave who has been caressed by her owner only once, becomes jealous and tries to poison her competition, the formal and authorized wife of her owner. I saw a slave who poisoned the small child of her owner's wife to take her revenge. I was able to save the child but the slave was flailed and kicked out of the house without manumission, making it very difficult for her to get a job" (Polak [1865] 1976, I:252–253). Elsewhere he reported on the execution of such *kanizes* "through untold forms of torture" (Polak [1865] 1976, II:204).

I conclude this section with the story of a young African girl who was purchased in the 1880s and brought to Iran. Although her account reaches us third-hand, it captures some of the routine abuses that slave concubines endured, including *umm walids.*[6] Chaman Andam was a tall, beautiful African woman with olive skin who had been captured from an unknown East African village. Raiders killed the adult members of her family and made off with the children. She was taken to the slave markets of Mecca and sold separately from her siblings. An Iranian merchant she called Hajji (because he was on pilgrimage) purchased her and gave her the name Chaman Andam (Grass Figure). Hajji brought her to Tehran, where she lived in a fetid outhouse with the other slaves and servants. At age ten or twelve he took her to his private bathhouse in the expansive garden:

When at the bathhouse, she was ordered to bathe and wash the old man; in tears and shunned, she did as she was told and resisted little when she was raped by the Hajji. The memory of the incident was as horrific as that bloody day in Africa and wounded her little soul even more. Hajji's sexual adventures with the little slave girl created resentment in the family and turned Hajji's wife and their children against her with increased humiliation and abuse. Hajji continued his sexual

---

[6] The narrator, Massoume Price, conducted an interview with Monir Joon, whose parents sheltered the *kaniz.*

abuses but never treated her like a lover or a favorite concubine or even a person. She got pregnant and gave birth; the newborn girl never received any attention, kindness or money from Hajji. Chaman Andam called her little daughter Jahan and as soon as she turned nine, Jahan was married off to a construction worker who would not want to have anything to do with a black African slave as his mother-in-law. Chaman Andam never saw her daughter again. Soon after her daughter's wedding, just before No Ruz [Nowruz], Hajji died from a heart attack. Right after his death, she was kicked out of the house without a penny or any compensation. Desperate, with nowhere to go, she knocked on neighbors' doors and asked for help ... A patriotic diplomat and an advocate of modern political systems ... took Chaman Andam in and threatened to sue Hajji's family for practicing slavery that was against the new constitution of 1907. (Price 2002)[7]

As the story of Chaman Andam suggests, the progressive atmosphere of the Constitutional Revolution had helped to turn the educated public against slave concubinage. In the late 1920s, as the country became more unified under the new Pahlavi regime, both the slave trade and chattel slavery dwindled to a trickle on the nation's peripheries.[8]

Temporary marriage

Temporary marriage was an arrangement whereby a woman entered into a contract for exclusive sex with a man (on her part) for a definite period of time and for a stipulated sum. Temporary marriage is called *mut'a* in Arabic and *sigheh* in Persian. The woman in a *sigheh* union is also called a *sigheh* wife. The practice was not a Muslim innovation; indeed, pre-Islamic forms can be found with some variations in both Arabia and Iran. Caliph 'Umar (r. 634–644) outlawed *mut'a* marriage as a form of fornication (Smith 1903, 67). Shi'i Muslims maintained the custom viewing it as a legitimate form of marriage, though without the social status of *nekah*. Imam Ja'far Sadeq (d. 765), the sixth Shi'i Imam, is often cited as a proponent of temporary marriage. Since his time, the practice of temporary marriage has divided Sunnis and Shi'is.

Anthropologist Shahla Haeri, who studied the institution of temporary marriage in Qom, Kashan, Mashhad, and Tehran in the late 1970s, points out in her classic study that Shi'i doctrines distinguish ideologically between *nekah* and *mut'a*. "The objective of *mut'a* is enjoyment, whereas that of *nekah* is procreation" (Haeri 1989, 50). With regard to pleasure, the relationship is not on equal footing, however, since "the purpose of a

[7] The constitution of 1906–1907 did not address slavery *per se*. However, according to article 8, "The people of Iran are to enjoy equal rights before the state Law." See Browne 1910, 362–384.
[8] For a discussion of slavery in the Persian Gulf area in 1921–1941 see Behnam 1994, 32–36.

mutʿa marriage is enjoyment, not to both parties, but of the husband only" (Haeri 1989, 57).

Families greatly preferred that their daughter's first marriage be as a *nekah*, unless the suitor came from a much higher social class. As with *nekah*, the *ʿulama* differ on whether a virgin girl needs her *vali*'s permission for a *sigheh* marriage, whereas they are unanimous that a divorced or widowed woman does not. *Sighehs* are usually arranged privately between a man and a woman, though they can be performed by a low-level cleric. In a very simple ceremony, the woman declares her willingness to become a *sigheh* for a specific time and sum, and the man replies: "I accept." The oral contract either expires at a specified time, or is terminated by the husband at will, provided he pays her the stipulated amount (*ajr*). No witnesses are necessary. The woman has no right to remarry before the union expires. A man enjoys many additional rights in a temporary marriage. He may or may not choose to practice *coitus interruptus*. In other words, a *sigheh* cannot prevent a pregnancy unless she chooses a method of birth control that does not interfere with her husband's pleasure. A *sigheh* also has no right to sex or *nafaqeh* (maintenance) during her marriage, though in some cases the husband does provide her daily expenses. While she does not inherit from her husband, the child of such a union is legitimate if the father acknowledges paternity. Given the private nature of most such unions and the frequent poverty of the *sigheh*, proving paternity has always been difficult. However, even a recognized child of a *sigheh* is regarded with less respect than one from a *nekah*. In elite circles, for example, the offspring of a *sigheh* might be regarded as an improper marriage partner ('Ayn al-Saltaneh 1995, I:691).

Upon the end of the marriage a *sigheh* is required to maintain an *ʿidda* period of two months (two menstrual cycles), shorter than that of a formal wife (three months). She also receives no maintenance during this period. She can avoid the *ʿidda* if she claims to be infertile or menopausal. Unlike a *nekah*, a *sigheh* marriage has no limits on the number of renewals. The ease with which a *sigheh* is contracted means that consensual affairs between a (married or unmarried) man and a single woman could hardly ever be labeled fornication, while those between a married woman and any other man could be (Haeri 1989, 53–58; Mehdevi 1953, 144). For all of these reasons, *sigheh* wives generally receive much less respect than *ʿaqdi* wives, and many did not publicize their *sigheh* unions, except in elite harems.

A *sigheh* wife does enjoy certain liberties that *ʿaqdi* wives do not, however. She can live at her own domicile and need not follow her husband to the degree that an *ʿaqdi* wife must. "She has great autonomy to establish relationships, maintain outside interests, leave the household without his permission, or even take a job," so long as these activities do not interfere with the husband's right to sexual enjoyment, as stipulated in the contract (Haeri 1989, 59).

In addition to the above sexual forms of temporary marriage in Iran, there are also nonsexual forms. Nonsexual temporary marriage allows mature women to travel independently. In this type of unconsummated temporary marriage, an adult woman becomes the "wife" of a man (or even young boy) for some days or even hours. The man's acceptance is seen as a gracious act of civility, helping an unchaperoned woman. This form establishes fictive kinship ties between two families, which persist once the "marriage" ends. The woman can now travel with an otherwise unrelated family member to a shrine and stay away from home for months, since she is formally under the protection of a man to whom she is related. In this way, temporary marriage enables divorced or widowed women to circumvent the otherwise rigid constraints of Iranian society. Another common use of nonsexual *sigheh* occurs during a couple's engagement, often a few months or weeks before the wedding. The couple could then go out shopping together and attend to details of the wedding alone (Haeri 1989, 95).

Until modern times, teenage boys in many well-to-do families were given temporary wives before they were considered mature enough to have a *nekah* marriage (Polak [1865] 1976, I:206–207). This arrangement served several purposes. It prevented the boy from commingling with undesirable women and reduced his chances of contracting venereal disease. It also provided the boy's mother with cheap and reliable domestic help, since *sigheh* wives frequently worked as maids in middle- and upper-class homes (Mehdevi 1953, 144–145). An unmarried maid often preferred to become such a *sigheh* in a more prosperous family. The union granted her a modicum of respect and some protection from unwanted sexual advances (see also Haeri 1989, 84). Just as a mother found a *sigheh* for her sons, so a wife who could no longer meet her husband's sexual demands found a *sigheh* for her spouse, a better option than enduring a formal co-wife with equal status (Sheil [1856] 1973, 143).

During travel, war, or government missions to the provinces, urban men rarely took their ʿaqdis along, preferring to marry temporary wives wherever they lingered for a while. Hence the business of providing temporary wives for travelers was brisk. European men in Iran also contracted temporary marriage and found it a convenient way to avoid loneliness. In the early nineteenth century, Horatio Southgate observed that, "The custom is not only prevalent among the Persians, but has been practiced, to a very considerable extent, by foreigners resident in the country, the females, in this case, being generally, if not always, Armenians" (Southgate 1840, 38). As elsewhere in the world where men keep concubines, Iranian (and European) men usually lied to their formal wives about such relationships, keeping their *sigheh* marriages secret. They might also make false promises to the *sighehs*, pledging to turn them into *'aqdis* once certain impediments (a dying wife, a bad financial situation) were resolved. These secretive practices created all sorts of problems and complications that sometimes came to the attention of the police. Occasionally a young provincial man, bearing real or fictitious documents, showed up in the city and demanded recognition as the legitimate son of a respectable family (Polak [1865] 1976, I:208).

Sigheh marriages were also motivated by efforts to have male offspring. Elite men desperate for an heir might take several *sighehs* simultaneously. 'Ayn al-Saltaneh reported that a prince "took four wives two days ago, and plans to take three or four more, hoping to get lucky with one delivering a male child. Whichever woman does so will be very fortunate" (1995, I:340). Later, the same prince terminated his union with twelve such *sighehs* because of financial difficulties ('Ayn al-Saltaneh 1995, I:971). Montazem al-Molk seems to have exceeded acceptable standards by taking forty-seven *sighehs*, making him into a topic of gossip ('Ayn al-Saltaneh 1998b, V:3732). Sometimes abandoned *sighehs* took their complaints to the police. In September 1886, a *sigheh* claimed the substantial sum of 5,000 dinars from her wealthy husband, who had beaten and abandoned her without compensation. Ultimately, she was awarded the full amount (Shaykh Rezaei and Azari 1999, I:119).

The practice of contracting temporary marriages contributed to unhappy *nekah* relationships in elite and urban middle-class circles. The police ledgers of 1886–1887 are filled with accounts of marital conflicts and related suicide attempts, usually by women. Some of these incidents occurred when a husband took a second *'aqdi* or *sigheh* (Shaykh Rezaei and Azari [1885–1888] 1999, I:111). The candid memoir of 'Ayn al-Saltaneh also shows that many elite men made their family lives unbearable by taking multiple *'aqdi* and *sigheh* wives.

Temporary marriage for employment or for pleasure?

Although the Persian term *sigheh* and the Arabic term *mut'a* both mean temporary marriage, Ja'far Shahri suggests that they refer to two slightly different practices in the early twentieth century. Sighehs were young, impoverished women who engaged in temporary marriages as a form of employment. They worked as employees of *bazaari* men in better financial circumstances, or became concubines to several tradesmen. Their incentive was to be "married" and under a man's "protection." According to Shahri:

Some turned to the practice out of sheer destitution. Matchmakers selected most of them for the *bazaaris* – clothes retailers, sock weavers, quilt makers, and others.

The women were a pleasant diversion for the *bazaaris*, someone who took care of their needs, and an employee without wages. For one or two *qaran* daily expenses, the women produced four to five times that amount in *bazaari*-style shirts and pants, also weaving the toes of socks, and stitching quilts. Some *bazaaris* kept twenty to thirty such *sigheh* wives in different corners of the town. (Shahri 1990, I:260)

Other poor women quietly and illegally became concubines to several men and arranged different meeting times with them. They might, for example, see "one before noon, one in the early afternoon, one in the later afternoon, one in the early evening, and one late at night, using the excuse that the landowner or the father, or brother, or other relations were away from the house, and only at that specific time could the women see the men. Sometimes the men bumped into one another and then a calamity ensued" (Shahri 1990, I:260). Most men were well aware of these circumstances. As far as they were concerned, they had complied with their religious duties and contracted a temporary marriage rather than having a simple illegal affair. At this point it was the woman's responsibility to observe the religious requirement (Shahri 1990, I:261).

As noted above, *mutʿa* wives differed slightly from *sigheh* wives. Independently wealthy widows or divorcees who entered *mutʿa* marriages for pleasure, often with theology students and seminarians, "paid the men something in addition, so they could have some fun and also not break the *shariʿa* laws" (Shahri 1990, I:261). *Sigheh* unions had harsh consequences for poor young women who hoped that marriage would provide them with legal rights of maintenance and inheritance. But *mutʿa* unions provided a number of legally and socially acceptable venues for more well-off divorced or widowed women. When a widow became the *mutʿa* wife of a man of a lower class who did not live with her and was often from another province, she did not need the blessings of her family or the detailed property negotiations of a *nekah*.

Shrines were popular venues for contracting *sighehs*. This was a crucial source of income for low-level clerics who lived around the shrines, and landlords in the city who provided this space for such affairs. Horatio Southgate noted, "Many of the inferior sort of Mollahs gain, in good part, their livelihood by negotiating these contracts" (Southgate 1840, 38). The city of Mashhad, site of the Imam Reza Shrine and home to an abundance of matchmakers and love brokers, has a long and storied history in this regard. A married man who came to visit the shrines might contract a *sigheh* for his few days in the city. But many (presumably) divorced and widowed women also took advantage of these religiously sanctioned sexual liaisons (Haeri 1989, 53–81). Here temporary marriage took on an added religious significance. Such a marriage, if contracted with a *seyyed* (descendent of the Prophet), gained a woman *savab* (religious merit) in the next world. Respectable divorced and widowed women quietly vowed that if Imam Reza granted their wishes, they would offer themselves in a *mutʿa* marriage to a *seyyed* for a few hours or days, and in addition give him a monetary gift. Perhaps these arrangements can be seen as a continuation of pre-Islamic practices in Mesopotamia, where ordinary women offered themselves to strangers as part of cultic sexual activities (Westenholz 1989).

British official George Curzon, who visited Mashhad in the late nineteenth century, was stunned by the practice of temporary marriage, which he called "the most extraordinary feature of Meshed life." A large pool of women was available for this purpose, he wrote:

In recognition of the long journeys which they have made, or the hardships which they have sustained, and of the distances by which they are severed from family and home, [the pilgrims] are permitted, with the connivance of the ecclesiastical law and its officers, to contract temporary marriages during their sojourn in the city … In other words, a gigantic system of prostitution, under the sanction of the Church, prevails in Meshed. There is probably not a more immoral city in Asia; and I should be sorry to say how many of the unmurmuring pilgrims who traverse seas and lands to kiss the grating of the Imam's tomb are not also encouraged and consoled upon their march by the prospect of an agreeable holiday and what might be described in the English vernacular as "a good spree." (Curzon [1892] 1966, I:164–165; see also Haeri 1989, 111)

But not all forms of sexual *sigheh* resembled prostitution. Temporary wives of elite men often lived better lives than *ʿaqdi* wives of impoverished men. Fortunate temporary wives might be promoted to the status of formal wives. In more middle-class circumstances, a man who had no sons by his formal wife, but who had one by a temporary wife, might also promote his *sigheh* wife to the position of a formal wife in order to elevate his son's social status. Temporary marriages termed "ninety-nine-year long *sighehs*," meaning ones that lasted a lifetime, were common among wealthier men and suggested (but did not legally require) the greater permanence of *sigheh* unions.

An impoverished temporary wife enjoyed a fragile social status, however. As she aged, her price tumbled in a series of temporary marriages, until in many cases she joined the ranks of common prostitutes. In this next phase of life, she eked out a living on the streets alongside discarded slave concubines, dancers, and musicians. Dr. John Wishard of the American Hospital in Tehran reported that many such women turned to his hospital for help:

The number of legal wives allowed by Mohammedan law is four, but any number of *seegahs*, or concubines, may be taken. These latter are easily cast off, and the result is that many hardships are thus inflicted. Sometimes they are able to find employment in large households as maids, or, as they are called in Persia, *badjees*. Not infrequently they are taken as plural wives of some other man, in order to get their services as maids for the more favoured [wives]. Often, after years of struggle, sickness overtakes them and they are cast out by some wicked master into the street ... These poor women may often be seen sitting by the roadside with no place to go, every door, seemingly, closed against them. They are the result of a terribly distorted social system. (Wishard 1908, 211–212)

Prostitutes often passed as temporary wives to avoid social ostracism. Living in penury, prostitutes quietly entered the seminaries and caravan-saries at dusk, spent the night with a client, and left at dawn. For a few hours they became the *sigheh* of a client, thereby giving a façade of legality to the transaction (Matthee 2000, 121–150; Hejazi 2002, 160; James 1909, 33–47).

Because of their close ties to the police and influential people, sex workers found themselves taking part in the world of politics and intrigue. They serviced so many different kinds and classes of men that if anything happened or anything was in the works, the prostitutes almost certainly heard of it. Polak reported:

Generally, it should be taken into account that the police, *darughe*, and their superiors, *kalanter*, who were responsible for controlling public morality, took advantage of these sorts of women in the form of large sums of money, since the majority of them were in the service of the police, sometimes to extort money, to detect theft, or to carry it out, or research the affairs of a house, or even look into political and diplomatic secrets. ([1861] 1982, 39)

From time to time, at the instigation of the ʿulama, the authorities embarked on moral crusades against the unfortunate prostitutes and called for their expulsion. These events reasserted the moral authority of the ʿulama and provided a form of carnival-like entertainment for the public:

There were several attempts to drive these debauched people out of the city, using some scandal as an excuse. Their heads were shaved and they were paraded in disgrace on a donkey in front of the city. The more desirable ones were able to elude persecution through protection; others paid off the police, and thus the situation remained unchanged. In other cities, such as Tabris [Tabriz], Cazvin [Qazvin], Hamadan, Isphahan, even in the holy city of Kum [Qom], the conditions were the same. (Polak [1861] 1982, 40)

When they were not punishing, taxing, or otherwise harassing prostitutes, law-enforcement officers, politicians, and opportunists had no reservations about turning to them as sexual companions. Targets of both controversy and of pleasure, sex workers served any number of clients and causes.

Harem women

As with slave concubinage and temporary marriage, harems had pre-Islamic roots (Brosius 1996, 84). They were exclusively upper-class institutions belonging to the royalty, sometimes governors of provinces, and urban elites. The term harem referred to the private quarters of a palace where all members of the family, except males of age, resided. The degree of harem women's seclusion varied across different periods. For example, fourteenth-century Timurid harems were less restrictive than seventeenth-century Safavid ones (Babayan 2003, 31). In the early Qajar era, in the period of the founder Aqa Muhammad Khan Qajar (r. 1779–1797) and Fath Ali Shah (r. 1797–1834), harem women lived more restricted lives and occasionally suffered brutal treatment at the hands of the shahs for disobeying their orders. However, by the time of Muhammad Shah Qajar (r. 1834–1848), a Sufi devotee who disapproved of large harems, harem women's transgressions were often ignored. Also, the presence of European diplomats seems to have benefited harem women, who used this outside source of power to their advantage (Amanat 1997, 51).

An important figure of this period was Princess Malek Jahan (1805–1873), wife of Muhammad Shah Qajar. When her son Naser al-Din Mirza was designated crown prince, she became known as the Queen Mother, or Mahd-e 'Olya. Contemporary Iranian historians have portrayed Malek Jahan, who was two years older than her husband, as a highly conniving personality, a morally corrupt figure who cuckolded her ailing husband and abused her powers in her son's court. More recent accounts note her immense intelligence, sagacity, and ability to wield power, through both formal and informal channels (Amanat 1997, 135). It is from the period of Malek Jahan that harem women reappear on the historical scene as assertive players who disobey the stringent regulations of the court, often with few or no repercussions. Near the end of Muhammad Shah's life, when his prime minister and other courtiers complained about Mahd-e 'Olya's multiple extra-marital affairs, the shah divorced her (or by some accounts, demoted her to the position of a temporary wife). This suggests that violent punishment of ʿaqdi and sigheh harem wives had subsided by the mid-nineteenth century. After her husband's death, Malek Jahan assumed a more prominent political role. She controlled government affairs for six weeks, until her son arrived in Tehran and claimed the throne. During this period she also negotiated with the British and Russian governments and received their backing for her son, thus cementing the principle of primogeniture, which the European powers had imposed in 1813, along with the custom that the heir's mother had to be a Qajar *'aqdi*.[9]

Harem segregation was not tantamount to seclusion and isolation. Although sons were preferred over daughters, rulers such as Fath Ali Shah and Naser al-Din Shah were very affectionate toward their daughters and allowed them many privileges (Nashat 2004, 41). The tradition of educating harem women and training them in various physical activities such as horseback riding had continued in the Qajar era. Also it should be noted that the peasant wives who arrived from villages had not lived idle lives. Some, such as Naser al-Din Shah's favorite concubine Jayran, were consummate horseback riders and hunters.

Qajar princesses could conduct their own correspondence without the aid of a secretary (Sheil [1856] 1973, 146). Many could read and write, do calligraphy, and became knowledgeable about literature, mathematics, and history, while also receiving religious instruction. Some also spoke Turkish, Arabic, and French. A few were gifted singers, dancers, painters, musicians, or poets. The harem's private libraries enabled the women to engage in literary activities (Amanat 1993, 37).

We have more detailed information about the second half of the nineteenth century, when Naser al-Din Shah maintained the last large harem. His daughter Taj al-Saltaneh has provided us with some colorful descriptions:

> His Imperial Majesty, my father, had about eighty wives and *kanizes*, each of whom had about ten or twenty maidservants and domestics. The number of women in the harem thus reached some five or six hundred. Moreover, every day the wives, maids, or domestics received numerous relatives and visitors, so that there was a constant flood of about eight or nine hundred women in the harem. In addition, each lady had a residence, a stipend, and the requirements – maidservants, menservants, and all the household necessities – to live outside the harem. Seldom did two ladies share the same house; the exception was when new wives, chosen from villages in the vicinity, were committed to the care of other ladies to be educated in etiquette. Later they were given houses of their own. (Taj al-Saltana [1914] 1982, 14; 1993, 124)[10]

These formal wives, temporary wives, and slave concubines could be loosely divided into four categories, with each wife receiving a salary

---

[9] The tripartite custom that the heir should be (1) the firstborn son of a Qajar ruler, (2) from his *'aqdi*, and (3) born of a Qajar princess, was unsuccessfully contested by Naser al-Din Shah, who acquiesced to it after the death of his favorite, Jayran. See Amanat 1997, 23–25; also e-mail communication with him on October 22, 2006 and e-mail communications with Manoutchehr Eskandari-Qajar, September 2006.

[10] English translation slightly altered on the basis of the original.

depending on her station at the court. This ranged from 750 *tumans* a month for elite wives, to 100 *tumans* for lower-status temporary wives.

Category 1

Formal wives were sometimes princesses or daughters of dignitaries. They each lived in a quarter within the harem complex, had three to four eunuchs, and ten to twenty maids and servants. Their sons were contenders for the throne. Naser al-Din Shah had a total of six formal wives during his lifetime, though at no one time more than the allotted four. One of them was Jayran, who was not a princess, but a singer and dancer in the court of his mother, Malek Jahan. The young shah developed a special bond with Jayran, as his "affection for Jayran was fashioned after a modern romance, individualized and private, in contrast to the collective life of the harem" (Amanat 1997, 317). Naser al-Din Shah showed the same devotion to Amin Qasem, their son, and decided to appoint him heir. In doing so he was breaking two rules, the 1813 one of primogeniture and the older custom that a Qajar *'aqdi* should be mother of the heir. Violating the first rule was easier, and the European powers went along with it, but breaking the second was harder, and the shah faced significant opposition from within the harem, including from his own mother. To solve this problem, Prime Minister Mirza Aqa Khan Nuri arranged to turn Jayran into a respectable *'aqdi*. He commissioned the court historiographer to fabricate a royal genealogy for her, one that connected Jayran's family to ancient Iranian kings and Mongol rulers. Despite continued protests from the harem and ranking clerics, the shah also demoted one of his four *'aqdis* to a temporary wife, allowing him to wed Jayran in a *nekah*. Now Jayran could be his queen, and her sons could become heirs to the throne (Amanat 1997, 319–320). This romantic love story did not have a happy ending, however. Jayran's children died, and she herself passed away and may have been poisoned.[11] After her death, the shah never again challenged the established traditions for selecting heirs.

Category 2

Favorite temporary wives were often peasant girls. 'Ayn al-Saltaneh reports that "it was a custom of the villagers to display their daughters on the roadside so perhaps the shah would be attracted to them and marry them. Most of the wives of the shah are from this group" ('Ayn al-Saltaneh

---

[11] Information from Abbas Amanat, e-mail, December 17, 2006.

1995, I:823). The two most prominent were the rivals Anis al-Dowleh, who had been a handmaid to Jayran, and Amineh Aqdas. Neither of them had children, though Amineh Aqdas had a nephew nicknamed Malijak ("sparrow" in colloquial Kurdish) who became the shah's favorite boy concubine.

The historian Leslie Peirce notes that in Ottoman harems a woman's political power was derived from her age and her status as mother. Postmenopausal women who were mothers of sons therefore gained great authority (Peirce 1993, 23). Age and status as mother were also important factors in Naser al-Din Shah's harem, but not exclusive ones. Here, only seven or eight women had raised children to maturity (Taj al-Saltana 1993, 124). The two favorites, Anis al-Dowleh and Amineh Aqdas, were of humble origins and had no children, yet became powerful women. After the deaths of Jayran in 1860 and the Queen Mother in 1873, Anis al-Dowleh received the wives of European diplomats in her house and functioned ostensibly as the queen (Azad 1985, 397). The shah offered to make her an ʿaqdi, but she refused, not wanting to change the auspicious moment of their wedding, and feeling no need for a change in status in the absence of a son. Amineh Aqdas controlled the harem treasury and was in charge of the shah's sleeping arrangements with his wives and concubines. She and Anis al-Dowleh recruited and trained new concubines of both sexes for the shah. These two influential *sighehs*, together with several others who had produced sons for the shah, wielded more power than some ʿaqdis.

Category 3

Other *sighehs* had much less influence and fewer privileges. Some of them lived in one to three rooms in the harem compound. Others served as handmaids and companions to the more favored wives. The shah treated these lesser *sighehs* and handmaids as disposable merchandise. He invited them to his bedroom once or twice and occasionally gave them in marriage to various political figures in return for services the latter had rendered. With such a marriage, the woman traded her insignificant life in the harem for that of an ʿaqdi in her new house, secure in the knowledge that her husband could neither divorce her nor take another formal wife, as a sign of respect for the shah. (Fig. 2.3).

Category 4

Kanizes were mostly Turkoman and Kurdish in this period, since the slave trade from East Africa and the Caucasus had dwindled. They were servants of the wives, other family members, and *sighehs* of the shah, and

Figure 2.3 Ziba Khanom, former *sigheh* of Naser al-Din Shah and later
'aqdi of a prominent merchant in Isfahan, with her female slave

lived together under the control of an overseer. If they became *umm walid*,
and if the shah recognized the child, the *kaniz* could be elevated to the
status of *sigheh*. In this category we should also include performers, singers,
musicians, and dancers, who were drawn from the ranks of free women and
slaves and became *sighehs* after sleeping with the shah (Fig. 2.4). Jayran had
originally belonged to this category before she made her astonishing leap to
favorite wife (Navaei 1995–1996, 51–55; Azad 1985, 318–431; Feuvrier
[1899] 1947, 116–117; Delrish 1996, 186–216).

Figure 2.4 Female musicians and dancers, Qajar era

Queen Mother Malek Jahan continued to preside over the harem until her death. She had a large retinue composed of private physicians, astrologers, four eunuchs, and many concubines of both sexes, and an elaborate house where sixty to seventy relatives were provided with lunch and dinner each day. She ruled the harem with the aid of about ninety eunuchs. A chief eunuch oversaw the activities of the other eunuchs and the entire harem. Eunuchs worked closely with the *kanizes*, who had easy access to the private quarters of their mistresses and secretly reported on the women's coming and goings (Ghaffari-Fard 2005, 51; Feuvrier [1899] 1947, 117, 373; Bakhtiari-Asl 1996, 25, 52–55; Azad 1985, 240, 329).

Studies of Egyptian, Turkish, and Iranian harems have demonstrated that the women's lives were not idle (Marsot 1978; Delrish 1996). Segregation created a homosocial space with its own "hierarchy of authority" (Peirce 1993, 7). The harem's hundreds of inhabitants and their guests had to be fed several meals a day. The central kitchen functioned somewhat like a huge take-out restaurant. Several hundred slaves and maids gathered by the kitchen at lunchtime in order to carry the dishes back to their ladies' compartments. A few distinguished ladies also had their own private kitchens (Azad 1985, 333). Each wife had a particular responsibility. Some oversaw the kitchen and coffeehouses, others dealt

Figure 2.5 Birthday party in the Qajar court

with religious ceremonies or organized the weekly baths (Delrish 1996, I:86–216). There were numerous birthday parties and family celebrations (Fig. 2.5). National and religious festivities were also staged exclusively for them (Mottahedeh 2002; Ghaffari-Fard 2005).

As in Ottoman society, whenever upper-class men and women appeared in public they rode in carriages escorted by a ceremonial cavalcade and were shielded from the eyes of the pedestrians (Sykes [1910] 2005, 54–55). Paradoxically, the same women so fervently guarded from public eyes in urban areas lounged around unveiled at the Caspian Sea beaches before the eyes of the king's male retinue, some of whom used binoculars to get a good look. 'Ayn al-Saltaneh reports one such incident on a vacation in 1896:

The Bakhtiari tent is below that of Moʿtazed al-Saltaneh. They have good binoculars and are sitting and constantly watching. On the whole, there is no order. Of course when so many good-looking women, whom everyone wants to see, undresses in such proximity, noble and base people have no choice but to gape. When women who are never seen outside even with chador and face covering, now appear naked [unveiled], naturally people watch them and use every trick to do so. People could not but help themselves to observe and they are justified. It is also unfair; one man has so many wives, others none. ('Ayn al-Saltaneh 1997, II:809)

Politics and power

Prominent harem women took part in power politics at the highest levels, which is why royal harems were a crucial part of the administration of the state.[12] Powerful harem women also ruled over the rest of the harem, as this form of patriarchy has always been maintained with the help of senior women and through their control and manipulation. In the court of Naser al-Din Shah, his mother Malek Jahan and his favorites, Jayran and Anis al-Dowleh, functioned as kingmakers and prime-minister breakers. They helped elect ministers, connived against politicians with whom they disagreed, or sent petitions to the shah in support of disgraced politicians. They also maintained regular ties to foreign envoys through the European physicians who visited the court. The women's personal assets gave them access to economic and social power, as well as contact with the ʿulama. Malek Jahan was known for the many mosques, shrines, schools, and gardens she constructed or remodeled. These and other philanthropic projects, such as Khaneqahs (places of worship and congregation of dervishes), religious seminaries, caravansaries, roads, bridges, and hospitals, were maintained as vaqf endowments, turning clerics into influential supporters of their wealthy women patrons (Ghaffari-Fard 2005, 54; Bakhtiari-Asl 1996, 30–31).

Even after the formal establishment of the principle of primogeniture, harem women like Jayran fought to place their sons in the line of succession. Besides working to assure their children's futures, powerful women occasionally poisoned their enemies, and tried to undermine ministers who ignored the traditional privileges of the harem. Malek Jahan helped remove Prime Minister Hajji Mirza Aqasi, a sworn enemy of hers, soon after her husband died. She also instigated the murder of the revered reformist Prime Minister Amir Kabir (in office 1848–1852), who despised Malek Jahan and wished to modernize the monarchy by limiting the harem's authority (Bakhtiari-Asl 1996, 39–44). Jayran, who suspected Prime Minister Mirza Aqa Khan Nuri (in office 1852–1858) in the death of her son, helped oust him from power (Amanat 1997, 330–332). Anis al-Dowleh collaborated in a palace coup against Prime Minister Moshir al-Dowleh in 1873, and established her own superior position in the harem hierarchy. Her motive was revenge for public humiliation. Earlier that year, in the midst of a European trip with the shah, she had abruptly been sent home, presumably at the behest of the prime minister, since the presence of a fully veiled wife who could not be received by European

---

[12] Leslie Peirce has made this argument in the case of royal Ottoman harems (1993).

dignitaries had created complications (Amanat 1993, 30, 74; Yonan 1898, 90).

While acknowledging these women's access to power, we should not succumb to the myth of harem women as the sources of all intrigues. The shah, his ministers, foreign envoys, and the high-status women of the harem all used junior women to cement political alliances. Many young women such as 'Ezzat al-Dowleh, Malek Jahan's daughter, were simply pawns in the system. Her brother Naser al-Din Shah and mother married her twice to candidates of high office, then ended the marriages when they no longer suited their purposes. They also murdered her first husband, Amir Kabir, without any concern for her or her children (Amanat 1997, 373).

Sex and desire

The harem was a site of numerous licit and illicit sexual relationships, with little concern for Islamic prohibitions of any kind. In the twentieth century, the sexual exploits of Qajar kings and harem women appeared in popular historical novels in Iran. Embellished and fantasized accounts of harem lives were sold in serialized form in tabloid magazines. Naser al-Din Shah did not hesitate to take two sisters as temporary wives, or a father and son as male concubines, despite strict Islamic rules against consanguinity and homosexuality (see Azad 1985, 379, 419–420). In his advanced age, the shah continued to *sigheh* a large number of young women, while his courtiers privately joked about his ability to have sex ('Ayn al-Saltaneh 1995, I:738, 802, 828; 1997, II:1019). Older harem women, such as Amineh Aqdas, catered to the shah's sexual whims and trained his future concubines in court etiquette and in the erotic arts (*romuz-e delbari*). Contemporaries compared her to Madame de Pompadour (1721–1764), who recruited concubines for King Louis XV of France after she herself had stopped sharing his bed (Azad 1985, 373).

For most wives and concubines, opportunities to share Naser al-Din Shah's bed were rare. He was not fond of elite wives and preferred village girls. Sometimes he asked for a woman by name. Other times he asked them all to stand in rows, then threw his handkerchief at the ones who took his fancy. Those in the first row had a better chance of being selected than those in the back. Women who had their menses or were pregnant stood in the back. Amineh Aqdas, Anis al-Dowleh, and the harem eunuchs selected those for the first row. Their decisions were based on cronyism – on which women had been more subservient to them, had given them better gifts, or had performed services for them. Others were ordered to stand in the back and were expected to look unattractive and disheveled. If, despite all these precautions, the shah selected a woman from the back row then "woe to the woman who even in such condition could attract his majesty!" (Azad 1985, 391).

The lives of slaves and their children continued to be precarious in the harem, even resulting in their murder on occasion. Hajjiyeh Qadamshah was a beautiful woman of Ethiopian origin who was born to a slave mother in the court. Qadamshah had been a close companion of Malek Jahan and had accompanied the Queen Mother on her pilgrimages to Karbala and Najaf. She may have been a favorite concubine of the queen, since, contrary to prevailing custom, Malek Jahan had refused to grant her permission to marry. Two years after the death of her protector, Qadamshah was tortured to death over a crude joke and gesture she made toward the shah in the midst of court frivolities. Despite the persistent pleas of others, including a ranking cleric, Nasir al-Din Shah refused to budge. He declared her an "ass" and ordered her feet shod like those of a donkey, causing her slow and painful death (Azad 1985, 413–414).

In contrast to Qadamshah, ʿaqdi and sigheh wives were treated more leniently in the court of Naser al-Din Shah than they had been in the Fath Ali Shah era. When a favorite wife, Khanom Bashi, refused to share the shah's bed, he was upset but did not force or punish her (Azad 1985, 381). As with his father Muhammad Shah, Naser al-Din Shah was somewhat indulgent toward harem wives and concubines, even when the women engaged in clandestine affairs behind the high walls (Azad 1985, 385, 409–411; Feuvrier [1899] 1947, 119; Bakhtiari-Asl 1996, 56). Abbas Amanat has written about

lesbian affairs among the royal women, lovers escaping through the roofs of the harem, and royal concubines surprised in the basement with adolescent page boys, or half-castrated but still sexually active eunuchs. Yet, as long as petty scandals did not turn into a common practice or into a public embarrassment, the shah was willing to overlook the royal women's occasional liberties in the hope that his rejuvenated appetite for child concubines ... could be indulged without serious objection by his senior wives. (Amanat 1993, 41–42)

Not everyone broke harem rules as defiantly as Malek Jahan. The less influential and experienced were punished. However, if paid properly, the eunuchs and slaves could provide harem women with handsome male companions. Eunuchs dressed the men in women's clothing, put makeup on their faces, and passed them off as visiting aunts and nieces. The shah and the courtiers might learn about such charades from rival wives, but often chose to ignore them (Azad 1985, 392).

Occasionally we come across stories about half-castrated eunuchs who became involved with harem women. Ten-year-old Abolhassan who had accompanied his mother to the harem of Naser al-Din Shah caught one such couple in bed, while he was playing hide-and-seek with his friends in the harem basement: "There was a mattress on the carpet and beddings, two sheets, a pillow, a fan, and a glass of cold water. From under the sheets I could see the braided hair of a lady. The eunuch Ali Khan poked his head from under the sheets and looked at me so ferociously that I was frightened and ran away" (Bozorg Omid 1957, 41). When the boy insisted on telling his mother what he had seen, she ordered him flogged to make sure he never repeated it. After the death of Naser al-Din Shah, the "eunuch" Ali Khan let his mustache grow and became a manservant in the court of Mozaffar al-Din Shah and "no one asked him, you were a eunuch, how did you become a man?" (Bozorg Omid 1957, 40–41).[13]

The turn of the twentieth century brought the institution of the harem to an end. A week after Naser al-Din Shah's assassination in 1896, Mozaffar al-Din Shah (r. 1896–1907) closed down his father's harem to reduce costs. Four wives with children were moved to a small house; the rest were given small stipends and sent away. Younger favorites such as Khanom Bashi quickly remarried, but older and less significant *sighehs* and concubines endured lonely despondent widowhoods. Mozaffar al-Din Shah kept a small harem composed of seven wives during his short reign ('Ayn al-Saltaneh 1997, II:1030, 1050, 1160). During the Constitutional Revolution, the institution of the harem was dismantled altogether. But even before then, many elite men had started to keep one *'aqdi* and no longer maintained slave concubines, although some kept *sighehs*. Divorced and widowed Qajar princesses lived more independent modern lives, and frequently traveled abroad.

Attitudes about marriage were changing throughout society. Ella Sykes reports that "it is now the fashion in Persia, despite the example set by the Shah, to have only one wife" (Sykes 1898, 189). Sykes attributed this to the great expense of having multiple wives and generalized poverty. A decade later, she reported that the age of marriage of urban girls was gradually rising (Sykes [1910] 2005, 201). Dr. Wishard also noted a move away from multiple *'aqdis*, a change he attributed to the modernist ideals of the Constitutional Revolution:

Polygamy, which formerly was universal, has in a large measure been given up by the better classes, and the wives and families are constantly being given more liberty and freedom. This is especially the case in the larger places, and it is the opinion of those in a position to know that the emancipation of women from the restricted life of the harem is coming in Persia as fast as the women themselves are ready for it. (Wishard 1908, 94)

---

[13] Thanks to Abbas Amanat for bringing this to my attention.

He worried that a "great work of education must first be done before they will be able to discern the difference between license and liberty" (Wishard 1908, 94). Wishard was not alone in fearing women's greater liberty. Whether for economic, social, or political reasons, elite Iranian society was rapidly abandoning polygamous marriages involving multiple ʿaqdis, sighehs, and slave concubines. These changes were accompanied by a reduction in gender segregation and women's entry into the modern public sphere. Yet once the walls separating the private and public realms began to crack, a more anxious discourse on gender propriety emerged. Proper social behavior involved an added ethical and moral dimension, and pressure on women to adhere to a transparent and internalized "veil of chastity" increased.

3   Class, status-defined homosexuality, and rituals of courtship

Although Islamic law prohibits homosexuality, same-sex relationships for men and women in the Mediterranean-Muslim world were implicitly recognized cultural practices, so long as they remained discreet and respected certain conventions. As in many other premodern cultures, Iranians expected male homosexual relations to be asymmetrical, involving people of different ages, classes, or social standings, although other types of same-sex relations were also practiced. Often one partner assumed the "masculine" gender conventions and another the "feminine." As recent scholarship has demonstrated, in most premodern Western societies individuals were not identified by the sex of their object of desire. A man who had sex with other men was not identified as "homosexual," nor was a man who had sex with women called a "heterosexual." Rather, people were identified by their supposed positionality in the sexual relationship. The term *status-defined homosexuality* has been coined to distinguish these earlier norms concerning male homosexuality from those now predominant in the United States and the Western world.[1] Male status-defined homosexuality involved sex between a man and an adolescent boy (*amrad*) – in which the man was assumed to be the active partner, and the *amrad* a passive recipient of his affection. The relationship was defined by rules of courtship and mentorship between the man and the youth and was expected to end when the youth reached adulthood.[2]

These practices were not unique to Iran and the Middle East and found parallels in Greco-Roman antiquity. As Foucault points out, ancient Greek

---

[1] See for example George Chauncey for other asymmetrical patterns in the US before World War II (1994). For earlier discussion of this issue in Iran see Najmabadi (2005).

[2] Throughout this work, I have used the terms *active* (*fa'el*) and *passive* (*maf'ul*) or their Persian near equivalents because these terms were used at the time. The newer terms *top* and *bottom* are more accurate because they describe physical positions, rather than power roles and relationships, which are far too complicated to fit the neat categorizations of *passive* or *active*. Also, when referring to youth, I mean male adolescents. I also note that the term *berdache*, which in French, English, and Native-American communities refers to a transgendered person, has a Persian origin and is derived from the word *barda* which means slave.

society did not define people by their sexual acts as modern society does: "The Greeks did not see love for one's own sex and love for the other sex as opposites, as two exclusive choices, two radically different types of behavior" (Foucault [1984] 1985, 187). However, as in the Middle East, Greco-Roman antiquity assigned gender conventions to the partners and distinguished between the active adult lover, the *erastes*, and the passive adolescent boy, the *paidika* (Foucault [1984] 1985, 47; see also Dover [1978] 1989).

As in much of the Middle Eastern and Mediterranean world, male homoerotic relations in Iran were bound by rules of courtship such as the bestowal of presents, the teaching of literary texts, bodybuilding and military training, mentorship, and the development of social contacts that would help the junior partner's career. Sometimes men also exchanged vows, known as brotherhood *sighehs* (*sigheh-ye baradar khāndegi*) with homosocial or homosexual overtones. These relationships were not only about sex, but also about cultivating affection between the partners, placing certain responsibilities on the man with regard to the future of the boy. Sisterhood *sighehs* (*sigheh-ye khāhar khāndegi*) involving lesbian relations were also common practice in Iran. A long courtship was important in these relationships. The couple traded gifts, traveled together to shrines, and occasionally spent the night together. *Sigheh* sisters might exchange vows on the last few days of the year, a time when the world "turned upside down," and women were granted certain powers over men.

In some mystic circles worldly love was seen as a pedagogical device. Love was the prerequisite for many noble characteristics such as manly virtue, humanity, chivalry, and the ability to avoid worldly pleasures in pursuit of the beloved. Mystical love aspired to reciprocity and the acceptance of certain responsibilities toward each other by both the lover and the beloved. Mystical Persian poetry captures both exploitative and loving same-sex relationships, and in some of its finest examples aspires to an idealized ethics of love.

Recent scholarship on medieval and early modern Muslim societies suggests a possible connection between pervasive homoeroticism and gender segregation in the region. Segregation certainly did not impede all heterosexual relations, since early marriage was the norm. But segregation might have contributed to the widespread existence of homoerotic relations in various ways. Most heterosexual relationships lacked romance since marriages were arranged at a young age and consummated around puberty. In contrast to heterosexual courtships, which were brief and restricted to premarital years, close and affectionate male and female homoerotic relations continued much longer in a world where holding hands, touching, and kissing between men and between women were common practices. The need for love and companionship missing in many marital relationships may have also contributed to the widespread practice of same-sex relations (El-Rouayheb 2005, 30; see also Andrews and Kalpakli 2005, 111).

The Qur'an and homosexuality in the Muslim world

Much like the Jewish and Christian sacred texts, the Qur'an regards male homosexuality as an abomination. The word *lavat* (sodomy) derives from the Arabic Lut, the Qur'anic version of the patriarch Lot, who in the Biblical account was ordered by angels to leave the city of Sodom because of the residents' sexual indiscretions. Since the Qur'an calls the residents of Sodom the "people of Lut," the practice of homosexuality was identified with the name Lut (the man who supposedly resisted the prevalent homosexuality of his community), and hence with the term *lavat*. The condemnation of male homosexuality is explicit: "Of all those in the world will you come to males, abandoning the wives your Lord created for you? Indeed, you are a transgressive people" (Qur'an 26:160–166). But the Qur'an is also compassionate and recognizes the possibility of repentance and forgiveness: "If two among you commit indecency, punish them both. If they repent and mend their ways, let them be. God is forgiving and merciful" (Qur'an 4:16). The punishment of death by stoning did not appear in the Qur'an. Moreover, until the twentieth century the vast majority of religious scholars did not even interpret *sura* 4:16 as addressing punishment for male homosexuality.[3]

Another important consideration is that premodern Muslim societies did not subscribe to contemporary definitions of homosexuality. Islamic law prohibited anal intercourse (*lavat*) but distinguished between expressing passionate love for a youth, which was admissible, and the actual sexual act, which was not. Both the Sunni and Shi'i schools viewed sodomy as an abomination, but falling in love with a youth and expressing this love through verse or prose were acceptable. Various schools of Islam distinguished between kissing, fondling, and sex between the legs (*taf-khiz*), which were generally viewed as minor sins and transgressions, and sodomy, which was deemed a major violation (El-Rouayheb 2005, 1–6).

A few Muslim thinkers held that prohibitions on homosexuality did not apply to the afterlife. The Qur'an promises the company of handsome youths (*ghilman*, Arabic pl. of *gholam*, or page) and beautiful, dark-eyed,

---

[3] Personal communication with Everett Rowson. The death penalty for sex acts, though with virtually impossible witnessing conditions, entered Islamic law only after it was influenced by Jewish law.

virgin maidens (*houris*) as rewards for the faithful in heaven (Qur'an 76:19). The faithful shall wed the *houris* and will be served a magical wine (with no headache or hangover) by the immortal *ghilmans*, boys who are "as fair as virgin pearls" (Qur'an 52:24, 56:15). Standard commentaries on the Qur'an are silent about the possible role of these boys, though such discussions persist in other commentaries and among ordinary people. Two factors worked against homosexual intercourse on earth: the need for procreation and the use of the anus for defecation. Since there was no childbirth and no defecation in paradise, some sources have suggested that *lavat* might be permissible and the boys in descriptions of paradise could be construed as sexual companions (El-Rouayheb 2005, 131–136).

The *shari'a* Islamic law determines what actions of the *umma* (community of believers) are obligatory, recommended, neutral, objectionable, or forbidden. Forbidden actions fall into two categories: (1) those that transgress the limits set by God and are part of *hodud* ordinances such as *zina* (fornication), false accusation of fornication, theft, and drunkenness; and (2) other crimes such as manslaughter or assault that fall outside *hodud* laws and belong to the category of *ta'zir*. While the Qur'an bans homoerotic sex, it does not specifically include it in the category of *zina* punishments, leaving room for ambiguity about how it might be punished. Hence, Muslim jurists have held a range of opinions on homosexuality. Some have asked for the maximum punishment of death, but four factors have prevented such extreme punishment.

First, to prove any type of sexual transgression, the legal system of the *shari'a* demands very solid evidence (four adult Muslim men observing the actual penetration) before imposing punishment, which is often impossible. Second, a false accusation of *lavat* or *zina* is itself a major sin and punishable. Third, the Qur'an includes the possibility of repentance and indicates that one who repents must be forgiven. Fourth, the severity of the punishment and the wide practice of same-sex relations make it very difficult to condemn large numbers of people. Hence, most communities either ignore discreet homosexuality, or revert to customary punishments, less severe than the death penalty (such as flogging). Considerable leeway exists in practice if the sexual lapse does not cause a public scandal. Homoerotic relations between women are also not included in *hodud* violations. Most jurists treat them as minor offenses – certainly not the same as *zina* (El-Rouayheb 2005, 121; Ze'evi 2006, 53–55; Duran 1993, 183).

In the medieval Middle East, religious seminaries and brotherhoods, similar to Greek academies, provided an intellectually engaging and vibrant homosocial environment. It was not unusual for teachers to fall in love with their young students or to act as mediators and arrange the courtship by a male colleague of one of their students (Gazargahi [1502] 1996, 236–237).

Jurists engaged in many debates about the permissibility of sex with one's slave. El-Rouayheb points out that the Hanafi school of Sunni Islam regarded *lavat* with a male or female slave or one's wife a minor sin. In some Sunni schools *lavat* with a male slave was akin to *mutʿa* temporary marriage, not recognized but tolerated (El-Rouayheb 2005, 124). Some Shiʿi theologians quietly tolerated two types of male homosexual relations: sex with one's own male slave, since slaves were not entitled to the same rights as free persons, and sex during travel, when a man did not have access to his wives and slaves (Shamisa 2002, 115–116).

Shiʿi jurisprudence is often assumed to be harsher in its treatment of *lavat* and even non-anal intercourse,[4] but a closer look calls this into question. The first Shiʿi Imam, Ali Ibn Abi Talib (d. 661), opposed homosexuality. So did many others such as the pioneering Shiʿi cleric Muhaqqiq Hilli (d. 1277) and the late Safavid architect of Shiʿism, Muhammad Baqer Majlesi (Majlesi 1983). However, Shiʿi theologians stipulated many conditions before harsh punishment could be carried out. Muhaqqiq Hilli stated that one must confess four times, willingly and freely, to his infraction. Four confessions in one setting were not acceptable; they had to take place in four different settings. In the absence of such confessions, four eyewitnesses were needed and the witnesses must all be men. If the accused repented before the witnesses testified against him, he would be forgiven. If he repented and then confessed, he would also be forgiven. Punishment depended on the number of times the transgression had taken place. In most cases the person was forgiven unless he had violated the law at least three or four times and was caught doing so. (al-Hilli 1974, 1862–1864).

Shiʿi religious manuals known as *Explanations of Problems* (*Towzih al-Masaʿel*), which first appeared in the nineteenth century, define the daily conduct of believers and the mandatory guidelines for purification. These manuals usually state explicitly that same-sex relations are a sin. But many include a brief section outlining the necessary rituals of cleansing and penance for men who have engaged in various forms of same-sex relations, addressing mostly the "active" partner. "Thighing" is treated as a more minor sexual encounter, while sexual penetration requires greater penance. Penitence is achieved through a series of bodily rituals and the giving of alms to the poor. No one need know what transpired, or why someone is fasting or feeding the poor. For the most part, one's thoughts are also exempt. Sexual transgression of any type, unless it has been publicly observed, remains a secret between the individual and God.[5]

---

[4] See for example the argument in the otherwise excellent work by El-Rouayheb 2005, 121–122.
[5] For a compilation of some of these rules by leading ayatollahs of the twentieth century, see *Resaleh-ye Towzih al-Masaʿel* 1993, 100–101.

Sexual inclinations or identities?

In the medieval and early modern Muslim world, sexual inclinations were noted and discussed. However, as with the Greeks, and the premodern West, sexual inclinations were not differentiated so much between homosexual and heterosexual, but between those of adult men who were "inclined toward men" and those of adult men who were "inclined toward women," or between those of men who "took" pleasure and men who "submitted." A man could be inclined toward other men but also married and have a family. A man inclined toward women could have an *amrad* on the side.

Figure 3.1 A princely hawking party, attributed to Mirza Ali, 1570–1580

The adolescent or preadolescent boy in a same-sex relationship was presumed to be the "passive" object of the relationship and might be rewarded with money and gifts for accepting this role (Figs. 3.1 and 3.2). As in classical Athenian society, it was assumed that the boy did not experience pleasure in the activity. In his discussion of Arab literature, Everett Rowson points out that "boys, being not yet men, could be penetrated without losing their potential manliness, so long as they did not register pleasure in the act, which would suggest a pathology liable to continue into adulthood" (Rowson 1991a, 66; see also Dover [1978] 1989, 52). Once labeled "passive," the boy was fair game for others who attempted to seduce him. If the relationship was kept private, he was expected to outgrow this "passive" status, marry, and produce children. If, as an adult, he entered a same-sex relationship, he was assumed to be the "active" partner.

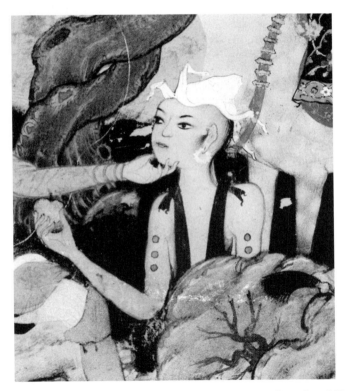

Figure 3.2 A princely hawking party (detail), attributed to Mirza Ali, 1570–1580

Homosexual behavior was also common practice if the man maintained a family and remained discreet. A dominant man who penetrated both women and boys "was just as masculine as those who penetrated women," and could even be regarded as "hyper masculine" (Rowson 1991a, 71). But an adult man who gained a reputation for seeking sexual submission (*ma'bun*) was considered a pervert and was the subject of medical literature. The *ma'bun* did not adopt the demeanor of a woman. Often he married and fathered children. Such a man suffered from a disease, the "loss of manliness," and a loss of "honor." In the male-dominated model of the medieval Muslim world, women were viewed as imperfect men who lacked vital male attributes. A *ma'bun* was viewed as somewhere in the middle. He was a deformed and imperfect man (Ze'evi 2006, 16–47). The term *mukhannath* (pl. *mukhannathun*) referred to an effeminate man who was deemed very close to a woman in his malformation. In modern parlance, we would consider the *mukhannath* to be a transgendered person – a man who resembles a woman in his delicate limbs and soft skin. He might adopt feminine clothing, wear his hair as a woman does, pluck his eyebrows and his beard, use henna on his hands, and in general have attributes of both genders, but without trying to "pass" as a woman. Many became court jesters, entertainers, musicians, and actors and formed platonic friendships with women.[6] Thus the "passive" partner in a homosexual relationship could be labeled in three ways. He could be an *amrad*, an adolescent boy in a covert homosexual relationship. As a mature adult, an *amrad* could become an "active" male, marry, and develop his own string of *amrads*, or he could be a *ma'bun*, an adult man who had not become an "active" male and was thus treated with contempt. Finally, he could be a *mukhannath*, an effeminate man who often became an entertainer.

Homoeroticism in medieval and early modern Iranian society

Like other Muslim cultures, Iranian society fostered a variety of forms of erotic expression, from heterosexual and homosexual to romantic bisexual, and from tender and passionate to frivolous and bawdy. The Mirror for Princes genre of literature (*andarz nameh*) refers to both homosexual and heterosexual relations. Often written by elite fathers for sons, or viziers for sultans, these books contained separate chapter headings on the treatment of male companions and of wives, and sometimes debates

[6] Rowson 1991a, 69–72; see also Rowson 1991b, 671.

on the relative merits and drawbacks of loving a youth rather than a woman. In the *Qabus Nameh* (1082–1083), for example, a father advises his son that both heterosexual and homosexual relations should be part of a man's repertoire of experiences:

As between women and youths, do not confine your inclinations to either sex; thus you may find enjoyment from both kinds without either of the two becoming inimical to you ... During the summer let your desires incline toward youths, and during the winter toward women. (Kaykavus Ibn Iskandar 1951, 77–78)

Classical Persian literature (twelfth to fifteenth centuries), including the poetry of great Sufi masters Sanaʿi (d. 1131), Khaqani (d. 1190), ʿAttar (d. 1220), Rumi (d. 1273), Saʿdi (d. 1291), Hafez (d. 1389), and Jami (d. 1492), overflowed with same-sex themes (such as passionate homoerotic allusions, symbolism, and even explicit references to beautiful young boys), as did the poems of the great twentieth-century poet Iraj Mirza (1874–1926). These allusions are often lost in contemporary editions of these works, which are ornamented with miniature images of heterosexual couples in amorous poses. Many English-language translations purposely confuse the reader. Persian lacks grammatical genders and references clearly meaning *he* are often translated as *she*.

The late scholar of Sufi Islam, Annemarie Schimmel, argues that "the books from the ʿAbbasid period abound with love stories of this kind. The handsome boy of fourteen, radiant like the full moon, soon became the ideal of human beauty, and as such is praised in later Persian and Turkish poetry" (Schimmel 1975, 89). Sometimes, poets divulged their own sexual inclinations in their poems. Often, they followed general trends of the time, since love of a beautiful youth was a common subject of discussion in taverns, seminaries, and at court ("Liwat" 1986, 778). Many poets justified this love by attributing a *hadith* (story) to the Prophet Muhammad in which he saw the Angel Gabriel in human form. The word *shahed*, or "beloved," was thus used in two ways in Sufi poetry. *Shahed* can mean a witness, but it can also mean a male beloved.[7] The beautiful beloved was a "true witness of divine beauty." Simply looking at him from afar could induce "religious ecstasy and worship of the divine" (Schimmel 1975, 290–291).

A recent source for the exploration of homoerotic relations in Iran is Sirus Shamisa's renowned *Shahedbazi* (Amorous Relations with a

---

[7] *Shahid* (martyr) in Arabic is a calque on the Greek word *martyras*, likewise from the verb "to show, to testify," which means "witness [to the faith]." Thanks to John Perry for suggesting this connection.

Shahed). Shamisa states boldly, "Persian lyrical literature is essentially a homosexual literature" (2002, 10).[8] In nearly half of lyric poems, the love object is unquestionably an adolescent boy. In the other half, which is also often homoerotic, the distinction is lost to the reader because the same adjectives can apply to either male or female objects of desire.

The Persian language itself is rich with allusions to homoerotic relations. A wealth of words is used to refer to various stages of courtship, from flirtation (*nazar bazi*), to adoration of the beautiful (*jamal parasti*), to actual homosexual intercourse (*lavat*). As in the Greek tradition, there are different terms for the "active" partner (*fa'el* [the doer], *gholam bareh* or *gholam pareh* [lover of pages], *jamal parast* or *surat parast* [one who loves beautiful faces], *bacheh baz* [pederast], *luti* [from the verb *lavatat*]). There are also terms referring to a "passive" man, such as *ma'bun* or *maf'ul* [the receiver], *amrad* [beardless adolescent], *kudak* [child], *now khatt* [one with a budding mustache], *bi rish* [beardless], and *pesar* [boy] (Shamisa 2002). Some of the terms for the "passive" partner refer to his youth, others to his position in the sexual act. These terms have a more negative connotation when they refer to adult men (*ma'bun* or *maf'ul*). Even allegorical love poems have maintained this bifurcated view of the relationship, where one is a desiring object and another a "passive" recipient of desire. The most enduring symbol of love in Persian poetry is the nightingale, a male courting bird that loves the rose. Drunk with the beauty of the flower, the nightingale serenades his love while the rose remains oblivious to his adorations (Milani 1992).

As in the Greek tradition, the first appearance of hair on the youth's face was talked about, because while the adolescent was considered to be at the height of beauty, his faint mustache (*khatt*) announced that the courtship would soon be over. Persian poets such as Sa'di and Hafez used many metaphors to refer to this stage of a young man's life, typically between the ages of fifteen and eighteen, when the boy's faint mustache was likened to a violet or a budding meadow. His full beard indicated that he was no longer suitable to be the "passive" object of desire. "The public badge of a dominant male was his beard" (Rowson 1991a, 58, 68; see also Najmabadi 2005, 15–17). Hence, a common way of humiliating a man was to shave his beard, placing him in the position of an *amrad*.

Persian literature is full of jokes about a man's beard and his sexual availability. The great satirist 'Obeyd Zakani writes in his *Epistle of the Hundred Precepts*, "Young Turkish slave boys, so long as they are beardless, should be bought at whatever price they are to be had. As soon as

---

[8] Reza Baraheni makes a similar argument (Baraheni 1977, 75).

their beard comes, sell them for what you can get."[9] In poems about military camps, war metaphors are common. The "dagger" of the beloved's eyes, the "bow" of his eyebrow, and the "lasso" of his hair often refer to love affairs involving warriors. Once the meanings behind such terms have been clarified, what seemed at first glance to have been a celebration of heterosexual love has been revealed to be a recognizable paean to same-sex adoration (Shamisa 2002, 52, 13). Ehsan Yarshater argues similarly:

> Unless one is mindful of the fact that the beloved, as a type, is very often a young soldier–cup bearer, who combines the warlike qualities of a warrior with the refinements of a sociable wine server, many aspects of Persian love poetry, and for that matter, much of Ottoman, Urdu, and Islamic Arabic poetry, remain puzzling. We find very often that the image of the *saqi*, as a wine server, mingles with that of the *ma'shuq* or sweetheart. (Yarshater 1960, 52)

Classical poets celebrated homosexual relationships between kings and their pages. From the era of Sultan Mahmoud of Ghazni (r. 998–1030), Iran was ruled by Turkic and Mongol dynasties whose sultans intermarried with Persian elite families. Many of these sultans kept large companies of Turkish soldiers and slaves. Central Asian and Caucasian slaves were especially valued for their fair skin (Brookshaw 2005, 182). They were acquired at great cost and were educated and cultivated with much care. In his study of the erotic arts in Iranian society, Robert Surieu writes:

> From the Middle Ages to the Safavid period, the rulers and the great men of the [Persian] kingdom possessed, in addition to their harems, greater or lesser numbers of male slaves, the *ghelman* (plural *gholam*) boys acquired at a tenderest age from the Turkish tribes of Central Asia, and later from the Caucasus. The prices paid for these boys were often very high ... [in some cases around] 2000 pieces of gold ... They were undoubtedly a costly luxury. Often, it is true, the merchants who traded in these *ghelman* educated them with great care just as they taught music, dancing, and poetry to the most beautiful girls who were destined for princely harems – so that intellectual accomplishments should be added to their physical attractions and thus enhance their price. (Surieu 1967, 170)

As in Greek society, rules for the types and numbers of gifts in courtships existed, especially when the affair took place in the royal court between the king and his favorite *gholams*. In his *Siyasat Nameh*, the eleventh-century vizier Nezam al-Molk advised the shah to reward his favorite *gholams* generously and to promote them to a new rank each year, depending on their service, devotion, and talent (Nizam al-Molk 1962, 132–134). Favorite *gholams* could therefore become

---

[9] See Zakani 1964, 207. English translation in Surieu 1967, 170.

wealthy and powerful men. "Many of them became army commanders, grand viziers or ministers, and there were some who rose as high as the throne itself, like the Emir Subuktagin, founder of the Ghaznavid dynasty." Most became royal bodyguards upon growing a beard and reaching adulthood (Surieu 1967, 170).

Countless Iranian kings and emirs were former pages and slaves. Not all the slave soldiers were of erotic interest to the ruler, and paths to advancement did not necessarily depend on the erotic component of the relationship. However, some slave soldiers were concubines and were rewarded for their companionship (see "Gholam" in Dehkhoda 1946–). Occasionally slaves fell out of favor and were summarily discarded or killed. Sultan Sanjar (r. 1097–1157) rewarded some boy concubines handsomely. But he was also known for his sadistic treatment of his former lovers (Shamisa 2002, 73–74).

The beloved could also be the *amrad* of a person more powerful than his lover. Many passionate and erotic love poems, in which the lover describes the beloved's secret and sporadic nocturnal visits, refer to such situations. It is easy to see how flirting with the slave of a jealous emir or sultan could have very serious repercussions. Kings routinely ordered the castration of courtiers caught in acts of illicit sex with the king's male slaves, whether consensual or forced.

Though the Prophet had condemned sexual mutilation, castrations continued to be performed in the Muslim world until at least the late nineteenth century. Eunuchs were a regular feature of harem life. Some were castrated in Mecca before sale, some were condemned convicts accused of sexual molestation, and some were men with natural deformities. After castration, they were considered neither male nor female, and as asexual beings they could be trusted inside the harem (Floor, "Barda," 771; Scholz 2001, 197–198).

Homosexuality and homoerotic expressions were embraced in numerous other public spaces beyond the royal court, from monasteries and seminaries to taverns, military camps, gymnasiums, bathhouses, and coffeehouses (Fig. 3.3). *Luti* (strongmen) were known for their homosexual practices ("Luti" in Dehkhoda 1946–). They congregated in social and athletic gangs to practice wrestling, and were employed to hang around the streets for the protection of local clerics and political figures. Some shunned marriage, believing that relations with women would diminish their physical prowess. *Lutis* were bound by a code of honor that called for courage, devotion, and mercy toward the weak, but they were also known for unsavory deeds, including rape, robbery, and murder (Floor 1987, 243–266; Martin 2005, 113–32; El-Rouayheb 2005, 16). In the twentieth century, as *lutis* gradually disappeared from urban Iranian

Figure 3.3 Traditional gymnasium (*zur khaneh*)

society, the connection between their name and their sexual activity was lost. In literary works and in cinema *lutis* were portrayed as honorable strongmen who took care of their community, especially their women folk. *Luti* reticence toward heterosexual relations was interpreted as chivalry, concern for family honor, or especially self-control.

Until the mid-seventeenth century, male houses of prostitution (*amrad khaneh*) were recognized, tax-paying establishments. Bathhouses and coffeehouses were also common locations for sexual encounters. The French traveler Sir John (Jean) Chardin (1643–1713) recalled large coffeehouses where young male prostitutes entertained customers. Male dancers, many of them Georgian *gholams* and servants, braided their hair like women, dressed in revealing clothes, and performed erotic dances. The most popular coffeehouses were the ones reputed to have the best-looking boys, whose services customers could purchase (Chardin 1811, IV:69). Intellectual conversations took place in Safavid coffeehouses as well as "homoerotic interaction between servers and clientele in the form of suggestive dancing and music making by young boys who would be available for sex with customers" (Matthee 2005, 173). During this eclectic and spirited age, opium houses served beverages laced with the drug, and clerics and Sufis openly debated politics and theology in coffeehouses. Women could walk in gardens and public spaces without a male chaperone, and all freely enjoyed music and dance (Babayan 1998; 2002).

By 1694, when religious orthodoxy was ascendant, and the *mojtaheds* (jurisconsults) became the only mediation between God and the believers, a decree prohibited many common practices such as music, dancing, and drinking. "Sodomy, prostitution, and gambling were banned. Coffee houses were closed down. Opium and 'colorful herbs' were declared illegal" (Babayan 2002, 485). Such activities were now deemed illegal and incurred fines and punishments, though they did not completely vanish (Matthee 2000).

Rituals of courtship and patronage: old practices and new sensibilities

Were homosexual relations in medieval and early modern Iranian society also bound by rituals of courtship, what Foucault termed the "ethics of love"? In Greco-Roman antiquity certain rituals emerged in the relations between *erastes* (adult male) and the *paidika* (adolescent boy); Foucault held that the first recorded ethics of love in the Western world developed around these relationships, rather than heterosexual relations. Kenneth J. Dover, one of Foucault's main sources, provides the best account of these relationships and their accompanying code of honor. The *erastes* would use a variety of gifts to court the *paidika*, also furnishing the youth with social contacts that could advance his career. He advised and trained him in the arts of manhood and ultimately introduced him to "philosophical truths." The *paidika* was expected to refuse, resist, flee, or escape the *erastes'* sexual advances. Eventually, he might agree to mutual masturbation and "thighing", but was not supposed to permit "penetration of any orifice in his body." If he agreed to engage in amorous relations, his consent was supposed to derive from a sense of admiration, gratitude, and affection for the *erastes*, as well as the duty and desire to please him, rather than out of any sexual feelings of his own (Dover [1978] 1989, 103). Athenian society publicly maintained the fiction that these youths were incapable of experiencing any sexual pleasure or sensation. A youth who admitted to taking pleasure was the object of great humiliation and dishonor. One rule stipulated that a *paidika* should never submit for money, which would reduce him to the level of a prostitute. Another indicated that he should not initiate a sexual liaison, which would have been regarded as shameful, and yet another specified that once he grew a beard, the relationship should end. The young man then took his place as a citizen in the city-state, entered into a respectable marriage, and in all likelihood cultivated his own string of *paidikas* (Dover [1978] 1989, 224).

Similar rituals were practiced in early modern Ottoman Turkey. The youth acquired refined intellectual and artistic qualities through interactions with men in prominent positions. The boy's "intercourse (perhaps in both senses of the term) with the artistic and intellectual crowd was key to his success, rather than a hindrance of any kind" (Andrews and Kalpakli 2005, 51). These relations emerged out of the wider patronage system, in which slaves, servants, and apprentices of shopkeepers and artisans could increase their limited incomes by receiving employment and subsidies from their masters in return for sexual favors (Andrews and Kalpakli 2005, 143).

Some of these practices continued until the twentieth century in Iran. The work of the renowned poet Iraj Mirza (1874–1926) is one of the best-surviving accounts of male courtship rituals in twentieth-century Iranian society. It exhibits remarkable similarities to the descriptions cited in Dover. A progressive aristocrat, a brilliant satirist, and an advocate of women's rights, Iraj Mirza was the last major Persian poet to write openly about pederasty. In his early poetry, the narrator speaks of his desire for adolescent boys and suggests the relative prevalence of such relations at the time.

In an amusing piece by Iraj Mirza called "Counsel and Advice," an aristocrat expresses his love for a youth and asks him to become his beloved. He warns the young man that his days of remaining a good-looking, eligible adolescent are almost over, since the boy would soon grow a beard and become an adult. No poet would then compare his beautiful hair to silk or his rosy red lips to sugar. The aristocrat advises the boy to stop frequenting the hotels and clubs of downtown Tehran in search of one-night stands, to learn from the story of the "Ant and the Grasshopper," and to start thinking about his future.[10] The youth should select an older, established man as a lover, who could provide him with the basic necessities of life, an excellent education, and the possibility of a good government job or other secure position. He should focus on his studies, but if he wanted to be truly educated and refined, he should also find a mentor. The aristocrat offers himself as such a mentor/lover, promising the boy everything he could possibly imagine, including a good home, a loving relationship, the best tutors, and a wonderful wardrobe that would make him "the most fashionable man in town." He also pledges to protect the boy's reputation and keep the affair secret. The poet wants to be everyone and everything to the boy, "like a father and a mother." He would stay up at night to make sure the boy completed his homework, take him on

---

[10] Iraj Mirza had translated this folk tale by Jean de la Fontaine into Persian. Thanks to John Perry for this information.

weekend rides and hunting expeditions, and play music for him in the house. The aristocrat also mentions the importance of learning to write poetry and good prose: "After a couple of years as a guest in my house you will be an accomplished young man. You will learn Arabic, foreign languages, history, jurisprudence." Upon completion of this education, the aristocrat promises to use his connections to find the young man a good job, first as a clerk or a secretary in a government bureau, then as a manager, and maybe later as a government minister (Iraj Mirza 1972, 39–47).

Here we find all the elements common to earlier Greek and Ottoman rituals of courtship: the use of customary gifts to court the boy, training in the arts of manhood, an introduction to literary conventions, and, most important, mentorship and social contacts that would advance the boy's career. It is also evident that among members of the Iranian upper classes, the older partner felt obligated to maintain the reputation of the adolescent *amrad* and keep the affair secret, so he could later take his place as a respected member of the elite Iranian society.[11]

But other poems of Iraj Mirza force us to confront what might be called, in the language of Kenneth Dover, "the fundamental contradiction" within the Iranian homosexual ethos. Persian poetry did not distinguish between a male or female beloved. The inclination to a romantic bisexuality was common, and, by early twenty-first-century standards, quite remarkable. But Persian poetry suggests that elites disregarded many social and ethical conventions where their relations with the lower orders were concerned. Pedophilia, for example, was visibly tolerated in elite society when the boy was a slave or a servant.

Classical poetry reflects this. Terms that refer to a lad in a homosexual relationship sometimes identify him as an adolescent, and at other times as a child. The term *amrad*, for example, refers to an adolescent boy who has grown a mustache but not yet a beard. Similarly, a *now khatt* is a youth who has just grown a mustache. However, a *tefl* is a child between birth and puberty, while a *kudak* refers to a child who has not yet reached puberty. There could be variations on such terms: *tefl-e amrad* or *kudak-e amrad* could refer to a nine or ten-year-old, indicating the young age of the boy, while *javan-e amrad* refers to an older teenager.[12]

---

[11] In response to changing sexual norms in Iran, Iraj Mirza later altered his position. In "'Aref Nameh," he disavowed male same-sex relations and praised the pleasures of normative heterosexuality (Iraj Mirza 1972, 120–163). On this point, see also Najmabadi 2005, 148–149.

[12] See the following terms in the lexicon of Ali Akbar Dehkhoda (1946–): "Rish," LX:269–272, "Tefl," LXXX–LXXXI:275–276, "Now Khatt," CXXVI–CXXIX:852, "Kudak," XCV–XCIX:416–417, "Amrad," VIII–XII:180–181, "Bacheh," XVII–XXI:670–671, "Gholam," LXXXVI:219–221, "Gholam va Bandeh az Nazar-e Tarikhi," LXXXVI:271–275.

What distinguishes modern homosexual relations from premodern status-defined ones is that the latter involved significant social inequality, usually age-based or class-based, between lover and beloved. In medieval Iranian society, the vast majority of boy concubines were slaves, who came from Africa, Central Asia, the Caucasus, and parts of Iran. Slave concubines included "Turks, Armenians, Romans, Indians, Ethiopians, Nubians" ("Gholam" in Dehkhoda 1946–). The use of Turks as sex slaves was so common that after the tenth century CE, the term Turk became synonymous with the beloved or *shahed* ("Gholam" in Dehkhoda 1946–).

From time to time, great poets such as Saʿdi or Rumi wrote about the sexual molestation of boys or the castration of former beloveds of angry kings and sultans. But even poets who are remembered for their tolerant poems, their criticism of religious bigotry, ethnic chauvinism, and mistreatment of women, treated stories of unsolicited sexual advances toward boys as entertaining anecdotes.[13] The modern reader cannot escape the fact that classical Persian poetry is brimming with accounts of non-consensual sex with junior male partners. The poets seem to have regarded these encounters as "pleasantries," even if they involved violent sexual molestation. Rumi joked about the repeated rape of a destitute, beardless youth who could not protect himself from his attackers even when he barricaded himself behind a wall of bricks (Rumi 1996, verse 3843). ʿObeyd Zakani mocked the power games in these relations. Ambitious boys worked their way to powerful positions by becoming sexual partners of members of the political or clerical elite (Zakani 1964, 207). Iraj Mirza captured the coercive or even violent side of such status-defined homosexuality, which speaks to elite men's dominance and power. In one poem he described a man courting a youth with tenderness and affection. In another he recounted the rape of a boy in the middle of the night. Covered in pornographic detail, the perpetrator gloated about denying the boy the compensation of a watch (Iraj Mirza 1972, 294). A classical poet such as Saʿdi could write about homosexual incidents in one poem and religious homilies in another (Southgate 1984, 415). One can be amused by the frank expressions of same-sex desire, but as in child marriage, one can also be taken aback by the carefree presentation of child molestation and sexual coercion.

Mystical love, or a Persian ethics of male love

The examples explored above involve relations between males of unequal status. But Persian Sufi poetry, which is consciously erotic as well as

---

[13] The poet Saʿdi is a good example. For his witticisms see Saʿdi 1996, 190–194.

mystical, also celebrated courtship rituals between people of more or less equal status. The strong relationship between master and disciple in the Sufi orders probably reinforced the unequal paradigm of sexual relationships within the monasteries. Annemarie Schimmel has explained the inner dynamics of some of these Sufi orders. The disciple (*morid*) worked with a master (*pir*) who advised him on the path of unity with God. Sufi writers often compared the mentor to a physician who tended to a sick person and gradually healed him through a strict diet. The apprentice was like a sick patient and was expected to have complete trust in his master. Rules of apprenticeship varied from order to order. In some orders three years of service were expected of the disciple, after which he was admitted into the circle of the Sufis. Poverty, deprivation of sleep and food, repentance, and hard work were parts of the apprenticeship. The apprentice was expected to perform humiliating physical tasks, from sweeping the floors to cleaning the latrines. Gradually, and as a result of such hardships, he grew more patient. He learned to be content with the simple pleasures of life. At this point, the apprentice received the dark blue garment of the Sufis (*kherqeh*), and sometimes an earring connoting his devotion to the *pir*. He then embarked on the more difficult last two stages of acquiring mystical knowledge and love (Schimmel 1975, 130–139).

In medieval Persianate societies,[14] becoming a Sufi meant pursuing a spiritual love that was also "produced, sustained, and consummated corporeally." One began the journey by becoming enamored with the master, who deliberately made himself attractive. This male–male corporeal love was mediated through the five senses of seeing, hearing, touching, smelling, and tasting of the body of the beloved, though not through sexual intercourse, according to the surviving literature. At the summit of the Sufi hierarchy, when the disciple became a master, he became simultaneously the lover and the beloved. In this way Sufi authority was transmitted through an "unbroken intergenerational chain" (Bashir forthcoming).

In the courtly *ghazal* poetry composed by many Sufi mystics, love was defined as an aristocratic diversion not suited to ordinary people. Love was also a prerequisite for the pursuit of manliness (*mardanegi*) "in its dual sense of aristocratic manly virtue and humanity" (Meisami 1987, 256, 255 n. 32). The bond between lover and beloved was also based on a form of chivalry (*javan mardi*). Love led one to higher ethical ideals, but love also constituted a contract, wherein the lover and the beloved had specific obligations and responsibilities toward one another and the love that bound them both (Meisami 1987, 258).

---

[14] Societies influenced by Persian language and culture, from the Balkans to India.

In Persianate mystical traditions, the fellowship of the Sufis comprised more than a powerful aid in the complex search for the divine.[15] Rumi compared earthly love to a wooden toy sword given children to practice the art of swordsmanship. Love had a certain "growing power: it illuminated the path toward the perfection of the soul. Love was higher than faith. God was a 'hidden treasure' that longed to be known and loved. In fact, as 'the beloved,' God needed a lover for his own perfection" (Schimmel 1975, 290–291). In the words of Rumi:

> Not a single lover would seek union
> If the Beloved was not seeking it.
>
> (*Masnavi* in Book 3, verse 4393 [Rumi 1996])

Intellectual, bookish knowledge was useless in the search for the divine, but earthly love could serve as a model for mystical love. Nezami (d. 1203), Sana'i, 'Attar, Rumi, and Jami recreated dramatic love stories that expressed the sense of longing and described the journey toward a higher ethical ideal as part of a passionate love for God. Most narratives concerned heterosexual love affairs,[16] but not all. The story of Sultan Mahmoud of Ghazni and his male slave Ayaz[17] became the quintessential homoerotic love affair in Persian and Turkish literature. "Mahmoud and Ayaz took their place right alongside such legendary heteroerotic lovers as the Arab Majnun and Layla and the Persian Khosraw and Shirin."[18]

One of the best-known examples of love and reciprocity in mystic circles appears in an account of the life of Rumi, the greatest Sufi poet in the Persian language, whose followers founded the Mevlevi order known for its ritual whirling. While living in Konya in 1244, Rumi forged an intense bond with Mawlana Shams Tabrizi, a mystic and accomplished teacher who claimed to have reached union with God. Theirs was a unique relationship since both were mature and renowned masters. Franklin Lewis writes that contemporaries defined their relationship as falling in love, which Franklin qualifies as "Platonic love of a disciple for his teacher." Rumi took Shams home, "where they lived happily for a year

---

[15] The best example of this appears in *Manteq al-Tayr* ('Attar 1963), the classic poem of Farid al-Din 'Attar.

[16] 'Attar's story of the *Sheik of San'an* is a good example of a fable in which earthly love (in this case heterosexual) moved one to a higher ethical domain and the comprehension of God ('Attar 1963, 67–88).

[17] Ayaz was known for his long, beautiful hair. During a drunken spell, the sultan, who feared losing self-control and sleeping with Ayaz, ordered him to cut his hair short. Once sober, the sultan regretted his foolish request. This incident became the subject of a famous verse by the poet laureate 'Onsori and others. See for example Jami 1958, 303–305.

[18] Rowson, forthcoming.

or two before the disciples of Rumi began to act on their jealousy" (Lewis 2001, 159). Various accounts have suggested that resentful disciples of Rumi stabbed Shams and threw his body into a nearby well.[19] After the disappearance of Shams, Rumi's mystical poetry continued and gave birth to some of the most beautiful poems in the Persian language. Rumi also used Shams's name as a pen name in much of his poetry, signaling his unity with his beloved. Rumi had other mystical love relationships and eventually composed the *Masnavi*, which has been called the "Persian Qur'an" (Schimmel 1975, 313–315).

Devotees of Sufi poetry have often denied its earthly and carnal dimensions. They have suggested that Sufi love poems were not literal expressions but symbolic representations of the concealed beauty of the divine. We may never know the true nature of the relationship between Shams and Rumi. We do know that many of their contemporaries considered the lack of a hierarchical relationship between the two most unusual. "They embraced each other and fell at each other's feet, 'so that one did not know who was lover and who was beloved.'" (Schimmel 1975, 313). Rumi celebrated moments when social formalities were abandoned in their lives: "How sweet it is when there are no formalities between lover and beloved. All these conventionalities are for strangers, [but for the lover and beloved], whatever is not love is forbidden to them" (cited in Lewis 2001, 181). But Shams lamented the lack of clear boundaries, "I need it to be apparent how our life together is going to be. Is it brotherhood and friendship or shaykh-hood and discipleship? I don't like this. Teacher to pupil? (Tabrizi 1990; cited in Lewis 2001, 163).

Many admirers of Sufi poetry have pointed to the mystics' break with orthodoxy and their exploration of a more intimate relationship with God. Others have celebrated the Sufi message of tolerance, especially their rejection of socially imposed boundaries between different religions, and their belief that Jews, Zoroastrians, Christians, and Muslims were all created by God (Nasr 1977, 123). Can the homoeroticism of some Persian mystical poetry be viewed as a definite cultural theme, not just a break with religious orthodoxy, but also a departure from the requirements of status-defined homosexuality in mainstream Iranian society (Fig. 3.4)? This is an intriguing question. In this rigidly hierarchical society, as much so as the Greco-Roman world that preceded it, one of the most important social barriers was between the "active" lover and "passive" beloved. Yet it appears that some mystic poets such as Rumi may have aspired to a new and more reciprocal ethic of love within their

---

[19] Lewis takes issue with this conventional reading of the disappearance of Shams (Lewis 2001, 187–193).

Figure 3.4 Courtly love, by Reza 'Abbasi, 1630

small communities. When Rumi and his contemporaries insisted that in the most exulted state of love the distinction between the lover and beloved disappeared – noting in the accounts of Rumi and Shams that no one knew "who was lover and who beloved" – they may have been moving beyond status-defined homosexuality, beyond a relationship that always involved an implied "active" lover and a "passive" beloved. In ultimate love, then, reciprocity and consent were essential.

Sufi women and female homoerotic traditions

Much like the Greco-Roman philosophers and the more orthodox Muslim jurists, mystics maintained a bifurcated concept of humanity that associated the body with degradation and lowly existence, while linking the mind and the heart to the beautiful, the universal, and the sublime. The mystics viewed the experience of longing for the beloved as an attribute of the heart, but they derided bodily experience that did not contribute to the mystical path. Because women were responsible for childbirth and the daily domestic routine, they were more associated with the body and its debasing functions. A man's labor to provide for his family and community also depleted resources that he might otherwise devote to the Sufi order. Thus, for some men, women and their attachments to the world constituted impediments in the path to union with God (Schimmel 1975, 428).

Nonetheless, some Sufi circles were more accepting of women than orthodox Muslim seminaries. Women attended Sufi lectures, and from the late eighth through the tenth century CE, there were many female Sufi mystics, poets, and calligraphers. The Prophet Muhammad had said, "Paradise lies at the feet of the mothers," and this was noted by many Sufis. Old women and poor widows with children were regarded as voices of conscience and sources of wisdom in Sufi literature (Schimmel 1975, 426–435). Since sexually active women were viewed with apprehension, and even seen as a source of evil, many Sufi women remained single. For them, the path to the Almighty was through absolute renunciation of earthly love. Pious Sufi women, such as Rabi'a al-'Adawiyya of Basra (717–801), were praised for their chastity and complete lack of interest in men. Others, such as Rabi'a Quzdari (d. 940) of Balkh, who fell in love with a slave, were killed.[20] There was often a complete double standard with regard to the concept of earthly love as a "bridge to the divine." Sufi men were encouraged to use homoerotic relations as a pathway to spiritual love. Sufi women were generally expected to traverse this long road without (heterosexual) mediation. Did this also preclude homoerotic unions between women?

In Iran, as in many other Muslim countries, certain Sufi shrines were exclusively for women (Smith 1928). Female visitors might make a vow in hope of resolving family problems or to express gratitude for a wish that had come true. Nancy Tapper has defined such visits to Turkish Sufi shrines as a "celebration of female sexuality and fertility and of the friendship, solidarity, and support among women" (1990, 249). The shrines were places where bonds of sisterhood could be tied. As with brotherhood

---

[20] On Rabi'a al-'Adawiyya, see Smith 1928; on Rabi'a Quzdari, see Rajabi 1995.

vows, sisterhood vows sometimes had homoerotic or homosexual dimensions (Schimmel 1975, 426–435; Smith 1928).

Documentary evidence of female homoerotic relations in Sufi shrines, convents, and other institutions is extremely scarce. Brief references to female same-sex relations in harems appear in several European travelers' accounts and Persian advice books. Jean Chardin noted the near openness of female homosexuality in Safavid harems. The women of the East, he wrote,

have ever been said to be given to the Lesbian vice. I have heard it said so often, and by so many people, that this is so, and that they have means of mutually contenting their passions, that I hold it for very certain. They are prevented, so far as may be, from these practices, for it is said that they diminish their charms and render them less receptive to the passions of men. Women who have been in the *seraglio* tell strange tales of the passionate love-making of the females therein, the jealousy between them, and the jealousy of one favorite to another, how furious it may be; and they tell also of their hatreds and their treasons and the evil turns they play. They accuse one another and divulge each other's shortcomings. (Chardin 1811, VI:24–25; English trans. in Surieu 1967, 135–136; slightly altered)

Sisterhood vows seem to have been common between elite urban women. The most authoritative Persian lexicon, the *Loghatnameh* (1946–), includes several references to female homosexuality and sisterhood vows. It suggests that the two were the same, a designation that was lost by the late twentieth century, when bonds of sisterhood or brotherhood were assumed to be asexual. Here are select entries from the *Loghatnameh*, with clear references to the sexual dimensions of such relations:

Khāhar khāndegi. Adopting someone as one's sister. Sisterhood vow; two women having sex (*mosaheqeh*). (Dehkhoda 1946–, 40–44, 828)

Tabaq zadan. Also *sahaq.* Taking sisterhood vows. A practice performed by women who desire other women (*zanan-e hakeh*). Rubbing and brushing against one another's special parts of the body, as in the following poem by Khaqani:

> Look at Baghdad and you see all classes of women performing sex
>   (*tabaq zan*) with one another.
> You will see silver mortars for sifting saffron,
> But you won't see any pestles ...
> When they place their plates (*tabaq*) on top of each other,
> You will hear wild screams all the way to the skies. (Khaqani)[21]

(Dehkhoda 1946–, 80, 155–156)

---

[21] See also the following references in Dehkhoda (1946–): "khāhar khāndegi," XL–XLIV:828; "khāhar khāndeh," XL–XLIV:828; "tabaq zadan," LXXX:155–156; "mosaheqeh," CXI:301; "charmineh," CXVIII:175; "machachang," CXI:487. See also Shahri 1990, VI:348–349.

The most detailed discussion of sisterhood vows appeared in the late seventeenth-century *Kolsum Naneh*, written by Molla Aqa Jamal Khānsari (b. 1605), in a chapter entitled "On Sisterhood *Sighehs*" (Khānsari 1999, 60). Here Khānsari, a male jurist from an established clerical family at the Safavid court, took up many folk traditions concerning Iranian women in a mocking tone. In his view women *mollahs*, who performed religious ceremonies for the female community, endorsed sisterhood vows and considered it a requirement for entry into heaven after death. One who abandoned her "sister" in life committed a sin and would die a "Jew or a Christian" (Khānsari 1999, 60).

Ali Javaherklam has written about the continuation of such practices in the twentieth century (Khānsari 1999, fn. 112). Through these scant sources we learn that bonds of sisterhood were common among married women, while single women were prohibited from entering into such relationships. Tradition dictated that one who sought another as "sister" approached a love broker to negotiate the matter. The broker took a tray of sweets to the prospective beloved. In the middle of the tray was a carefully placed dildo (*Arus chock* or *Arus hak*) or doll (*Arus kuchak*) made of wax or leather. If the beloved agreed to the proposal, she threw a sequined white scarf (akin to a wedding veil) over the tray. She then tipped the broker and sent the tray back. If she was not interested, she threw a black scarf on the tray before sending it back. Vows of sisterhood were performed on special days of the year at some of the many shrines around the country, accompanied by drums, the sharing of sweet juices, and other festive practices. Often, the ceremony was performed on March 20, the last day of the Persian calendar and on the eve of Nowruz (Persian New Year), a day when the world turned upside down. Sisterhood *sighehs* also took place on another joyous day of the Shi'i calendar, the 'Eid of Ghadir Khom, the day when according to Shi'i belief Muhammad designated Ali his successor.

Before exchanging vows of sisterhood, it was customary for the two women to socialize for several months. They might send gifts to one another, including spices and herbs, which symbolized their love and longing for each other. Sometimes they planned a short trip to see if they were mutually compatible. After six months or more of courting, they exchanged sisterhood vows, sporting a variety of scarves as symbols of their friendship. If their husbands resented these relationships, women might visit the shrines and secretly exchange vows anyway. According to Khānsari, on Friday evenings at the end of Ramadan, the fasting month, "sisters" spent the night together. A husband who did not permit his wife to be with her sister, or to visit the shrines, was often regarded as unjust. The community saw such behavior as grounds for a wife to initiate divorce proceedings and believed that such a man would be punished in the hereafter. Occasionally, a husband would divorce his wife because he resented her "sister." Many divorced women maintained these relationships, never remarried, and worked as seamstresses or hairdressers to support themselves (Khānsari 1999, 60–63, 89–91).[22]

The street and the court in the early modern era

Given his position as the court gynecologist and obstetrician, Dr. Polak was in a good position to observe such relations and his account confirms the continuation of sisterhood vows in the mid-nineteenth century. He observed that some marriages remained harmonious because the wife and husband maintained separate sexual interests:

Tribady – or *tabaq* – among women is widespread, though not to the same extent as pederasty [among men]. A certain friendship pact between women is performed within certain ceremonies in particular mosques on the last Wednesday before New Year's Day (*char shanbeh suri*). The rituals and the day point to its heathen origins. Once the pact is entered into, the women maintain an inviolable commitment. This act is called *khāhar khāndegi* (sister recognition). It is worth noting that, just as men who have relations with individuals of their own kind (*sui generis*) develop a repulsion toward women, so too do these women develop an opposite repulsion. Thus there is often an agreement or tolerance of one another. (Polak [1861] 1982, 43–44)

Qajar and early Pahlavi historian Shahri casually referred to various sexual venues used by harem women and suggested that they engaged in "*mosaheqeh* and homosexuality, as was the practice of their husbands," in addition to secret affairs with men (Shahri 1990, VI:61). Shahri devoted a chapter to the subject of sex between women in his classic study of Tehran. Though he did not speak of sisterhood vows *per se*, he divided the women in such relationships into two categories: (1) those who were deprived of male companionship, because they were not married or because their husbands ignored them in favor of prettier co-wives; and (2) those who were seduced or were innately predisposed to the practice. In this latter case, he writes, "it is part of her nature and she will not be satisfied even if she has a husband and child, in the same way that men who are inclined to homosexuality retain their relations [with other men] even if they have a wife or children. Woe to the man who ends up with a wife like this!" (Shahri 1990, VI:348–349).

---

[22] Although Khānsari poked fun at these practices and may indeed have embellished his accounts, briefer ones can be found elsewhere. For details, see the notes by editor Bahram Chubineh in Khānsari 1999, fns. 112–119. See also Babayan 1998.

In the era of Naser al-Din Shah and Mozaffar al-Din Shah, Iranian society remained accepting of many male and female homoerotic practices, among them the staging of dances by *mukhannathun* (effeminate men) in coffee shops (Aubin [1908]1983, 248–249). The state distinguished between permissible and illegal homosexual acts. Bringing male (or female) prostitutes to lower-middle-class homes was illegal, but purchasing or hiring a boy as a servant for the exclusive sexual pleasure of the master (in middle-class or elite homes) was permissible. Here a man could hire a boy as his long-term servant/concubine without any social recrimination. Handsome boys from poor families were hired at elite homes around the age of eight and were known as *gholam bacheh* (page boys). Polak made a number of observations about the practice:

> Though this vice, *livat* [*lavat*], *betsche bazi* [*bacheh bazi*], is strongly rebuked in the Qur'an and can even be punishable by death, it is nevertheless today generally widespread, among the lay people, especially ... officers, schoolteachers, and even clerics. It is so overt that no one makes an attempt to conceal it. In almost every house of standing there is such a boy, even many, who are there to serve this purpose. No one is reserved about introducing them publicly. Indeed, one takes pride in possessing a splendid specimen. One is especially jealous about them. They are carefully watched and protected from seduction. (Polak [1861] 1982, 41)

He goes on to say that men often fought bloody battles over these boys: "One uses all possible means of seduction: money, [professional] advancement, even violence, in order to take possession of a boy" (Polak [1861] 1982, 41). At the same time, the abduction and rape of boys remained serious crimes:

> Though pederasty is quietly tolerated, the punishment for the abduction of a boy is often significant. Often the abductor, because of legal action against him, has all of his genitals, including his penis, cut off, at which point the individual will seek to be part of the eunuch service. Several of those violently mutilated received positions as governors and ministers. (Polak [1861] 1982, 41)

By the 1880s the kidnapping and molestation of boys were still major offenses, but the punishment had been generally reduced to imprisonment and flogging. The police in Tehran were vigilant about missing children, and every attempt was made to find and reunite them with their families within a few hours (see for example Shaykh Rezaei and Azari [1885–1888] 1999, I:181, 266, 397). If a common soldier or peddler took an eight- to ten-year-old boy to a garden or a religious seminary with the intention of raping him, and was caught, he might be beaten by the citizenry and then turned over to the police (Shaykh Rezaei and Azari [1885–1888] 1999, I:17, 39, 50, 103; II:428). Taking a prostitute to one's house was also a criminal offense in middling residential neighborhoods. If a man paid a male or female prostitute for sex and took him or her to his home, and if this became public knowledge, the police would arrest and punish both the prostitute and the customer (Shaykh Rezaei and Azari 1999, II:511).

At the same time, consensual and semi-open pederastic relations between adult men and *amrads* (adolescent boys) were common in various sectors of society. Police officers remained derisive in their description of the *amrad*, but did not interfere unless the men disturbed the neighborhood, as in the following example:

Muhammad who is an *amrad* youth was a companion of Mirza Muhammad Yavar of the Royal Armory. [On Nowruz of 1887] Yavar bought him a new suit and asked for a receipt from the youth so he would not leave him. In the midst of these events, they broke up. The youth left him and moved in with Mirza Aqa the Photographer. Often the louts [*lutis*] and hoodlums gathered at the door of the photo shop to gaze at him. Yesterday the Lieutenant from the Armory went there on behalf of Yavar and demanded his eight *tumans*. They had an argument over the matter. The police brought [Muhammad] to the office to investigate the matter. (Shaykh Rezaei and Azari 1999, I:388)

Hence, the *amrad* Muhammad was not brought in because of his sexual orientation, which is discussed in a matter-of-fact although derogatory sense, but because he was expected to return Yavar's gift once they broke up and also because he got into a fight with the Lieutenant. Muhammad was also not identified as a prostitute (who was paid for his services) but as an *amrad* (who received gifts as compensation), showing that such distinctions continued to exist.

But the elite lived by different rules. In the court of Naser al-Din Shah, the distinction between pedophilic (attraction to children) and pederastic relations was not always maintained. Here, the keeping of favorite boy concubines – sometimes mere children – was an acceptable practice. The custom of bringing boy concubines on trips was also common among the king's retinue. Polak noted, "During camping in tents in the summer and expeditions, no one other than the king is allowed to bring women with him into the camps. Thus the retinue manages during this time with the allowed boys" (Polak [1861] 1982, 42).

In the harem of Naser al-Din Shah, young Malijak was the shah's favorite from the time he was a small child. Although the shah denied his attraction, rumors of their sexual relationship were widespread. 'Ayn al-Saltaneh called Malijak "the shah's concubine" and reported that the king loved him more than anyone else ('Ayn al-Saltaneh 1995, I:593). Many contemporaries found the king's infatuation with this sickly boy to be bizarre and disgraceful. But in his memoir, Malijak recalls proudly, "the king's love for me reached the point where it is impossible for me to write about it ... [He] held me in his arms and kissed me as if he were kissing one of his greatest beloveds" (Malijak 1997, I:76, 101). On another occasion, when he was asked about the shah's attraction to him, Malijak answered with another question, "Why do you think [Sultan] Mahmoud desired Ayaz?" thus comparing his relationship with the king to the epic love of Ayaz and Mahmoud (quoted in Azad 1985, 422). When Malijak was a small boy, the shah shielded him from other men. Seven or eight girls became his playmates and attended the bathhouse with him. In violation of Muslim tradition, the shah prevented Malijak's circumcision, a ritual marking a boy's passage to manhood (Malijak 1997, I:101). As he grew older, Malijak became a restless boy whose pranks in the harem were legendary. By this time, he also had several pages and slaves of his own (Navaei and Malekzadeh 2005, 23).

In 1873, when the shah was planning his trip to Europe, the most pressing issue facing him was whom he should bring from the harem. The shah settled on four companions: his favorite wife Anis al-Dowleh and Malijak, plus two attendants. Anis al-Dowleh objected that the presence of a boy concubine in Europe would embarrass them all. But the shah ignored her. In Istanbul, the city's dignitaries gave a twelve-year-old Circassian slave girl to the shah as a concubine. To avoid a public scandal in the West, she was dressed in a boy's outfit and taken along to Europe. By the time he reached Moscow, the shah decided to send Anis al-Dowleh and her female attendant back to Tehran. The presence of a fully veiled wife, who could not receive European dignitaries, had proved to be an embarrassment. He continued the trip with Malijak and the Circassian slave girl. The shah's entourage did not escape attention in Europe and became the subject of much gossip ('Ayn al-Saltaneh 1997, II:1105; Bakhtiari-Asl 1996, 63–70; Nategh 2006, 34).

Boy concubines were expected to be interested in girls, and Malijak had his own series of female beloveds. At one point, he fell in love with Taj al-Saltaneh, and hoped to marry her, but Taj's mother disapproved of the match. For a while, he courted her and wrote her love letters, even though Taj was engaged to another boy. When Malijak reached the age of fifteen, he married another daughter of the king, Akhtar al-Dowleh. The king approved the match and oversaw the details of the ostentatious ceremonies. Shortly before the wedding, Malijak was circumcised at the insistence of his new mother-in-law, but the marriage ceremony still broke with tradition. Instead of sending the groom to fetch the wife, the bride was taken to the house of the groom on her wedding night. In this sense, Malijak continued to be treated as if he were a woman (Malijak 1997, 109).

A form of serial love ('eshq-e mosalsal) was also commonly practiced in the court and among elite men and women. Their love interests could shift back and forth from girl to boy and back to girl. As in the Ottoman Empire, love objects were often in love with others as well (Andrews and Kalpakli 2005, 129). Soon after their marriage, Taj's husband Hassan fell in love with a female Russian dancer who was part of a traveling circus. Later, he became enamored of a male dancer, on whom he spent a fortune. Taj also seems to have had lovers of both sexes. She had a secret affair with a male friend of her husband and later developed an intimate relationship with a beautiful seamstress (Taj al-Saltana 1993, 82, 91).

Michel Foucault argues that the notion of the homosexual person is a modern construct and that before this, "the love for one's own sex and love for the other sex" were not "two exclusive choices, two radically different types of behavior." Even though Europeans spoke of sexual inclinations and predilections, men were not *identified* by their sexual activity until the eighteenth century. In Iran, too, one person might be described as inclined toward women, another as fond of both men and women, and a third as inclined toward adolescent boys. Contemporaries of Naser al-Din Shah casually pointed out that he was inclined toward women, even though he also kept boy concubines. They noted that Mozaffar al-Din Shah and Muhammad Ali Shah were predisposed toward boys, despite the fact that both men had wives, and Mozaffar al-Din Shah had a small harem. Hence, compared to the contemporary Western regime of sexuality, late nineteenth-century Iran was less judgmental about sexual orientations. But it was not entirely free of such judgments. Some boys and men were *identified* by their sexual activity. A young male concubine was routinely termed an *amrad*, a pejorative term, and an adult man who sought sexual submission (*ma'bun*) was considered to be perverted.

As we have seen in this chapter, Muslim-Iranian typologies regarding homosexuality predated the nation's encounter with the modern West. Iranian society, like much of the rest of the world, did not conform to our modern sensibilities concerning age, sex, class, and mutual consent in sexual relations. Distinctions between consensual adult sex and pedophilic or pederastic abuse or rape of a boy were less clear. In middle-class society, abduction and rape of boys were prosecuted, and bringing prostitutes of both sexes to one's house was forbidden, but in elite circles sex with domestic boy concubines or female prostitutes who passed as temporary wives was common. In status-defined homosexuality, if the man and the youth were of the same social class, the man kept the relationship discreet in an attempt to guard the youth's reputation. But if the man and the boy were not of the same social class, then the upper-class man made less effort to conceal the relationship.

Part 2

Toward a Westernized modernity

4   On the road to an ethos of monogamous, heterosexual marriage

At the turn of the twentieth century, Iran's population stood at around 10 million, with 200,000 in Tehran. Ninety-five percent of the population was illiterate. Average life expectancy remained under thirty due to high infant mortality, scarcity of health and hygiene facilities, and famine. Although little internal migration took place from rural to urban areas, several hundred thousand Iranians were living abroad in Russia and neighboring countries, often as migrant workers (Bharier 1971, 4–5, 26). In addition to these influences from abroad, through merchants and migrant workers, Western culture was spread through new educational institutions. These included missionary schools founded by American Presbyterians, secular Western ones formed by the Alliance Française and Alliance Israélite Universelle, Baha'i schools, other Iranian schools, and the first modern institution of higher learning, the Dar al-Fonun, which was formed in the mid-nineteenth century (Arasteh 1969, 164; Nikbakht 2002, 200; Ringer 2001; Shahvar 2008).

It was in this period that three broad and overlapping political discourses on gender and modernity emerged in elite urban circles. (1) A new nationalist discourse of "scientific domesticity" embraced modernity in the areas of health, hygiene, and education. It emphasized industrialization, education, and new health measures that improved standards of living, reduced child mortality, and gave women greater authority within the home, all with the aim of turning Iran into a modern country. Most proponents of this view did not want to radically alter existing gender or sexual patterns or question the *shariʿa* in terms of family and personal law. (2) A social democratic discourse supported all the above together with civil liberties and social reforms to ameliorate the lives of the urban and rural poor. Proponents of this view wanted to redraw the boundaries between the public and private arenas and alter many gender norms, even when these reforms came in conflict with the *shariʿa*. (3) A conservative religious discourse reacted to Western modernity with great hostility. It opposed reforms that threatened male prerogatives and saw most forms of modernity, from women's education to industrialization, urbanization, and democracy, as threats to the established order. However, these conservatives also used modern institutions such as newspapers and the Parliament to establish their own counter discourse, and in this way planted the roots of what become an Islamist discourse later in the century. Implicit in all of these discourses was the fact that redrawing the boundaries between the public and private arenas also disturbed the (male) homosocial environment and its semi-clandestine sexual norms.

Western encounters: shock, denial, and accommodations

Greater interaction with the West in the nineteenth century had resulted in a gradual adoption of some modern gender and sexual norms in Iran. Elite Iranian men were not accustomed to the public display of European women's faces and bodies in ballrooms and other arenas. Many were also taken aback by the institutionalized monogamy of the West and viewed European women as powerful matriarchs who had emasculated their men (Tavakoli-Targhi 1993; 2001a). During a trip to Europe in 1838, Mirza Fattah Khan Garmrudi wrote with astonishment about seeing "half-naked" women in ballrooms and made a series of outrageous claims about them. He was convinced that European women slept with numerous men each night and were prone to bestiality. Since Western women often carried puppies, Garmrudi concluded that the dogs were sex toys: "The husbands of such women are very happy and content with this arrangement and they have a right to be so. Women are so sexually aggressive in this country that no man, no matter what his potency and ability, can satisfy a woman" (Garmrudi 1969, 956).

Other humorous misunderstandings arose. In the early nineteenth century, Iranian visitors to the West debated whether the ballrooms, theaters, coffeehouses, and gardens, where unrelated men and women interacted in public, were houses of prostitution or the paradise on earth promised to the faithful in the Qur'an that was populated with beautiful female (*houris*) and male angels (*ghilman*). Some assumed that European men, who shaved their beards and wore tight-fitting clothes, were *amrads* (Garmrudi 1969, 951). Later, they realized that polite European society held same-sex relations in great disdain. Afsaneh Najmabadi has suggested that when elite Iranian men traveled to Europe and came across European memoirs that discussed male homosexuality in Iran, this troubling reflection of their own norms through Western eyes encouraged them to "dissimulate and disavow male–male sexuality in Qajar Iran" (Najmabadi 2005, 37). Of course, many public expressions of affection between Iranian men were asexual, but the key point is that Iranian intellectuals felt it necessary to distinguish between various expressions of affection. They began to "explain" to European visitors that what they had perceived as homosexuality in Iran – for example, men holding hands, kissing, and embracing in public – was simply homosocial behavior. Such dissimulation appeared in the work of Garmrudi, who wrote:

[James Baillie] Fraser has vulgarly denigrated Iran and has gone to extremes in this regard. Among his charges is that the men of Iran have excessive desire for beard-less teenagers and some men commit obscene acts with them. Yes, in the midst of all nations of the world, some fools, due to the predominance of lascivious spirit and satanic temptations, commit some inappropriate acts. It is far from just that the people of Farangistan [Europe], with all their imperfect attributes and obscene behaviors for which they are ... particularly famous – the establishment of homo-houses [amrad-khaneh] and whore-houses, where they go at all times and pay money and commit obscene acts – characterize the people of Iran with such qualities and write about them in their books! (Garmrudi 1969, 962; cited in Tavakoli-Targhi 2001a, 69)

The open display of heterosexual affection in European public spaces, and the Europeans' disdain for (public) homosexuality, seem to have influenced gender expectations among elite Iranians. Soon it became more fashionable in some Iranian circles for men to appear in public with women, or to ride a carriage or share a meal with them. Men also began to show public affection toward women, to serenade them in poems, and to write about such experiences in detail (Najmabadi 2005, 54).

New discourses on monogamy and compulsory heterosexuality

At the turn of the twentieth century, a host of Iranian diaspora news-papers, such as *Akhtar* (Istanbul), *Habl al-Matin* (Calcutta), *Soraya*, and *Parvaresh* (Egypt) began to advocate women's education and other gender reforms. In 1899, the Egyptian Qasem Amin's Arabic-language *Tahrir al-Mar'a* (Liberation of Women) caused a great sensation within the Muslim intellectual world, whether in Cairo, Beirut, Istanbul, Tabriz, or Tehran. Amin criticized veiling and seclusion, as well as polygamy and the male prerogative of repudiation. In 1900, a modified Persian translation appeared in Iran under the title *Tarbiyat-e Nesvan* (Education of Women), which helped unleash a new discourse on gender reforms.

Those who called for the reform of marriage laws in Iran belonged to two different camps. Some were adherents of the new Babi and Baha'i religions that had broken away from Shi'i Islam in the second half of the nineteenth century. Others were liberal Shi'i intellectuals who called for reforms within Islam. Babism discouraged polygamy as well as divorce by repudiation. One of its leaders, the brilliant religious thinker and poet

Tahereh Qorrat al-'Ayn, had left her husband to become an advocate of the new religion. She is remembered for her courageous public unveiling at a Babi convention in June 1848. There, she broke completely with Shi'ism and inaugurated Babism as a new religion. The Babis rejected many social taboos against women's participation in society. Conversations between unrelated men and women, which were unacceptable in the wider Muslim society, were permitted if the topic concerned "serious and significant" issues. Babis were encouraged to proselytize, and regularly entertained guests in their homes for this purpose. Women attended such gatherings, where the veil was not enforced (Amanat 1989; Bayat 1982).

An offshoot of the Babi movement was the Baha'i religion, led by Mirza Hussein Ali Nuri Bahaollah (1817–1892). He forbade slavery and made the education of girls and boys a requirement of the new religion in his *Most Holy Book* (1870). If Baha'i parents neglected their duties in this area, other Baha'i institutions were required to step in and take on the responsibility of educating the youth. Despite their progressive approach, neither the Babis nor Bahaollah banned polygamy outright, although they expressed a strong preference for monogamy. The tradition was simply too entrenched among the clerics and upper classes to whom the new religion appealed in the late nineteenth century. Bahaollah recommended monogamy, but allowed a limited polygamy of up to two wives. He himself had two wives and apparently lived an unhappy family life as a result. It was Bahaollah's son, Abdolbaha (1844–1921),who declared monogamy mandatory, reacting in part to his own childhood experiences (Cole 1998, 171–172).

The Babis and Baha'is were severely repressed, but in the second half of the nineteenth century, several secular Muslim intellectuals also campaigned for companionate monogamous marriage. Some lived in Transcaucasia and wrote books and articles that were eagerly read by reformers inside Iran. The two most radical thinkers of this period were the Azeri playwright and linguist Mirza Fath Ali Akhundzadeh (1812–1878) and the Iranian freethinker Mirza Aqa Khan Kermani (1854–1896), both of whom encouraged women's education and monogamous marriage.

Akhundzadeh was an outspoken critic of the African slave trade in the Middle East who penned a searing critique of castration of slave boys in Mecca, one of the first such criticisms by a prominent Muslim intellectual. Akhundzadeh expressed his views in a fictional epistolary form, in a series of letters between two characters, Prince Kamal al-Dowleh and Prince Jamal al-Dowleh. In one letter, Kamal al-Dowleh complains:

There are many humans in Africa who capture young boys, castrate them with great cruelty, then sell them like animals in Muslim lands. ... In a village near

Mecca, slaveowners have a hospital for such innocent children, complete with surgeons and barbers. First the barber cuts off one hundred percent of the boy's organ, then the surgeon struggles to save the boy. A third of the boys do not survive. The rest are sold at three to four times the price to make up for the loss. Who is the cause of such misery of the boys? Muslim pilgrims who purchase them during Hajj and other events. (Akhundzadeh 1985, 73–74)

Akhundzadeh also adopted a radical discourse on women's rights. His plays featured resourceful female characters who fought for their rights within the family. He also published a daring criticism of prevalent marriage practices in Muslim communities, going so far as to place the blame on the example of the Prophet himself. In analyzing several verses in the Qur'an, Akhundzadeh pointed out that in one account, the Prophet had gone to the house of his adopted son Zeyd Ibn Harith, caught a glimpse of his beautiful wife Zainab, and admired her. Zeyd decided to divorce his wife so the Prophet could marry her. Muhammad objected strenuously, whereupon the Angel Gabriel appeared to him and insisted that he should marry Zainab (Qur'an 33:37). In condemnation of this incident Akhundzadeh wrote:

How do we know if his wife Zainab was also willing to marry the Prophet? It may be that in divorce a woman's agreement is not needed. But the law states that a woman must consent to marriage. When did your God receive Zainab's consent, and through whom was this conveyed? Perhaps Zainab, who was young, did not want to marry an old man who already had twenty-two wives and slaves. In fact, it is said that initially Zainab did not consent to this marriage, but that she ultimately agreed when the angel Gabriel brought word from God. (Akhundzadeh 1985, 119–120)

Akhundzadeh continued this line of provocative argumentation. His characters explored several other well-known incidents involving the Prophet's conflicts with his wives, among them the famous story of his young wife 'Aisha's necklace. One night, when 'Aisha was nineteen, the caravan left her behind in the desert. The next morning, she arrived with a handsome man named Safvan Ibn Mu'attal at her side. She claimed that she had fallen asleep on her camel the night before and had lost her necklace, and that Safvan had helped find it and return her home. This story is important in the history of Shi'i Islam and is said to have played a role in the ensuing political conflict between Ali, the first Shi'i Imam and 'Aisha, Muhammad's favorite wife. Ali found 'Aisha's behavior scandalous and advised Muhammad to divorce her after this incident. Muhammad refused to do so, and the enmity between 'Aisha and Ali grew. After Muhammad's death, the power struggle between 'Aisha and Ali escalated, and peaked once the third caliph Uthman (r. 644–656) was killed and Ali became the fourth caliph (r. 656–661). They fought in the Battle of the Camel at Basra (656 CE), where Ali defeated ʿAisha's army at the cost of around 10,000 deaths on both sides.[1]

The necklace incident is notable because Muhammad eventually decided to forgive his wife, regarding the whole matter as nothing but an "invented slander." In the same chapter of the Qur'an where Muhammad called for the harsh punishment of adultery (100 lashes), he also established the rules against false accusation of adultery. Now there had to be four male witnesses to the actual transgression or the accuser would be punished: "Those that defame honorable women and cannot produce four witnesses shall be given eighty lashes" (Qur'an 24:1). This might have been aimed at those like Ali who had accused his wife of infidelity. In addition, the Qur'an states, "If a man accuses his wife but has no witness except himself, he shall swear four times by God that his charge is true, calling down upon himself the curse of God if he is lying. But if his wife swears four times by God that his charge is false and calls down His curse upon herself if it be true, she shall receive no punishment" (Qur'an 24:6).

Akhundzadeh could have used this story, as many have done, to draw attention to the relative leniency of the Prophet and the fact that the Qur'an gave women a powerful tool with which to defend themselves when accused of adultery. Instead, his character Kamal al-Dowleh followed the standard Shiʿi commentary by placing some of the blame on ʿAisha, a villain in Shiʿi historiography. He also criticized ʿAisha's father, Abu Bakr (first Muslim caliph, r. 632–634), for marrying his young daughter to an old man. The marital conflicts of the house of Muhammad stemmed from the institution of polygamy. The young wives of Muhammad were flirtatious, tempting Muhammad's closest followers in hopes of finding a younger husband once the Prophet passed away. Basing himself on the authority of the Ismaʿili leader Hassan Sabbah (d. 1124), Kamal al-Dowleh pointed out that this scheming resulted in the following Qur'anic verse, which banned Muhammad's wives from marrying after his death: "If you ask his wives for anything, speak to them from behind a curtain. This is more chaste for your hearts and their hearts. You must not speak ill of God's apostle, nor shall you ever wed his wives after him; this would be a great offense in the sight of God" (Qur'an 33:53). He also charged that it was these few verses from the Qur'an that had sentenced generations of Muslim women to seclusion and deprived them of a good life. Future Muslim reformers, he advised, should grant women and men equal rights and require monogamy (Akhundzadeh 1985, 117–139).

---

[1] For details of this story see Abbott [1942] 1985; Spellberg 1994; and Stowasser 1994, 94–95.

Another outspoken opponent of polygamy and advocate of companionate marriage was Mirza Aqa Khan Kermani, a convert to Azali Babism[2]
who later became an agnostic and freethinker. He moved to Istanbul,
where he collaborated with the exile Persian journals *Akhtar* (Istanbul)
and later *Qanun* (London). Kermani considered the clerical establishment
to be corrupt and ignorant. As one of the first nationalist Iranian intellectuals, he also adopted a contemptuous and derogatory tone toward Arabs
(and to a lesser extent, Jews), whom he saw as the source of all of Iran's
problems (Pirnazar 1995). Kermani called for a reform of Muslim law
and the abandonment of religious rituals of Arabian origin, including
the pilgrimage to Mecca and the Shi'i ritual of Muharram (Bayat 1982,
160–161). In his *Sad Khetabeh* (One Hundred Lectures), Kermani continued Akhundzadeh's fictional dialogue between Kamal al-Dowleh and
Jamal al-Dowleh in order to assail the evils of the veil, age differences in
marriage, and polygamy. Iranian intellectuals and elite society were gradually becoming aware of the link between sexual promiscuity and venereal
disease, and Kermani's characters tied such diseases to temporary marriage
and pederasty (Kermani 2006, 165).

Historian Willem Floor notes that by this period venereal disease had
become endemic in Iran, though, unlike in Europe, they had not yet
become socially stigmatized because the connection to sexual promiscuity
was still unknown to most people. Syphilis

was spread through the promiscuous behavior of the males either through frequenting male and/or female prostitutes and/or the contracting of temporary wives
in the major pilgrimage and trading towns. The prevalence of sodomy and pederasty (*bacheh bazi*) either in cabarets and coffeehouses or in peoples' homes through
the contracting of musicians and their dancing boys (*gedas*) also contributed to the
transmission of this disease. Many eighteen-year-old boys had syphilis because of
the widespread occurrence of pederasty. (Floor 2004, 34)

In advocating companionate marriage, the character Kamal al-Dowleh
also commented on the class and social dimensions of sexuality. He spoke
about destitute men and women who remained single because they could
not afford to marry. He described women's extramarital affairs during
visits to shrines (and other destinations) and the plights of young women
married to wealthy but considerably older men. The main culprit was
strictly arranged marriages. Unhappy marriages between couples who felt
no attraction for one another started on the nuptial bed, right after the
anxious defloration of the young wife by her husband (Kermani 2006,

---

[2] The Azali Babis were a minority of the Babis who followed Sobh-e Azal, after Bab's death.
The majority of Babis later gravitated toward Bahaollah, founder of the Baha'i religion.

174). Women in polygamous marriages cared little for their husbands' health, wealth, or general happiness. "They saw their husbands as not their own," Kamal al-Dowleh states, arguing that the women's lives were ruined because of unavoidable hatred and jealousy in such marriages (2006, 163).

The writings of Akhundzadeh and Kermani were revolutionary by the standards of the time and had an important impact on elite Iranian society in the decades that followed. Both writers were also opposed to same-sex relations. Akhundzadeh's character discussed Muslim poets who openly admired *amrads* and "refused to condemn this unethical conduct" (1985, 179). Kermani's character believed that because of the veil and the consequent lack of social interaction between men and women, pederasty was rampant. He maintained that if women unveiled, and if marriages became based on mutual attraction, relations between husband and wife would improve. This would also bring the practice of pederasty to an end:

In any nation where men are deprived of the great joy [of seeing women's faces], the practice of pederasty [*bacheh bazi*] and sex with slaves [*gholam baregi*] has developed of necessity, because handsome boys look like women and this is one of the mistakes of nature. In Iran, this travesty has attained the ultimate ... The reason for this practice is the veiling of women, which exists in Iran. As a result, men are deprived of that natural inclination that emerges after seeing women. Therefore they are drawn out of desperation to pederasty and love of boys. The poet Sa'di of Shiraz, the pervert Khaqani, and other poets of Iran in their great *divans* simply prove this point. (Kermani 2006, 173)

Here, various elements of the modern discourse on sex and marriage began to emerge: women's education, unveiling, and an end to polygamy became key demands of this generation of thinkers. Sexual slavery, pederasty, polygamy, and all forms of homosexuality were lumped together as perverted traditions that had to be eradicated. Calls for changes in sexual relations were at the root of the reform movement in Iran and emerged alongside other social, political, and economic demands at the turn of the twentieth century. It would take several more decades and a social revolution before these new values, whose consequences were not fully anticipated at the time, became more accepted norms among the dominant sectors of society.

Modernity and a new disciplinary regime for elite (female) bodies

In a well-known essay on Foucault, the feminist philosopher Sandra Bartky critically appropriated his notion of the modern disciplinary body and used it to reflect on the situation of women in the West. Whereas

Foucault had focused on male bodies – soldiers, students, workers, or prisoners – Bartky took up control over women's bodies, a topic the French philosopher did not cover. She argued that modern disciplinary practices affected women differently from men. Modernity produced a new notion of femininity, both in gesture and in appearance. Bartky divided such practices into three categories: (1) those that aimed to produce a body of "a certain size and configuration"; (2) those that demanded from this body a "specific repertoire of gestures, postures, and movements"; and (3) those that transformed the body into a new "ornamental surface" (Bartky 1988, 64). Long before Bartky wrote about the disciplinary practices of modernity and European women's bodies, astonished Iranian women were commenting on the awkward outfits of European women visitors to the harems. After meeting with Mary Sheil, a Qajar princess reported to her sister in Shiraz:

> I am writing because I thought you would like to hear an account of her looks and the stories she recounted. Her clothes were most interesting and appeared uncomfortable. Her dress had an open neckline, the bodice went down to an abnormally narrow waist, the skirt was in the shape of a bell, and the whole thing was trimmed in much lace. She was wearing a poke bonnet on her head, and her hands were covered with gloves. Later I discovered that they wear something underneath like a cage [corset] with bones in it to make their waists narrow. In reality they are prisoners in their costumes ... The women's court dress consists of a petticoat, bodice, and train four zars [*zar*: approximately a meter] long! Their headdress has to have exactly three feathers and a veil of white tulle. Their gloves, shoes, and fans have to be white, and they must carry bouquets of flowers. They talk of the freedom people have in Europe, yet it seems to me that they lack any because so many rules and regulations exist for eating, drinking, dressing, sleeping, and even just existing. (Cited in Mahdavi 2004, 70–71)

While many Iranian women joked and laughed about the confining Victorian outfits along the lines above, some elite Iranian men liked the modern bodies of European women, and encouraged the adoption of similar practices by their wives and concubines, though only in private and for the enjoyment of the man. A surviving essay by a member of the Qajar aristocracy, appropriately entitled *Ta'dib al-Nisvan* (Disciplining of Women) reveals how some members of the aristocracy used their knowledge of Western culture to construct a new and more confining discourse concerning proper behavior and dress of upper-class Iranian women. *Ta'dib al-Nisvan* was written in the early 1880s by an anonymous member of the Qajar family (Mathers 1927). Later it was translated and published in both English and French. Virtually nothing is known about the author, who kept his identity secret, probably fearing retaliation by the women whom he was addressing (Adamiyat and Nategh 1977, 20–21). He is referred to below as QA (Qajar aristocrat).

Ta'dib al-Nisvan (Javadi *et al.* 1992) followed the style of the medieval Mirror for Princes genre of literature. It differed from the classical advice books and the religious manuals of Shi'i theologians, which also contained detailed rules of conduct for women, in that QA based his demands on the modern Western etiquette of behavior and hygiene. *Ta'dib al-Nisvan* was divided into ten sections, with titles such as "A Wife's Proper Behavior," "Watching One's Language," "Holding Grudges," "Ways of Walking and Carrying Oneself," "Table Manners," "Hygiene and Proper Attire," "Bedtime Manners," and "The Morning After" (Fig. 4.1).

Throughout the text, QA adopted a defensive tone. He selectively appropriated some modern bodily practices for women that were ostensibly based on hygiene and science, and that appeared to be compatible with Shi'i Islam. Women were expected not only to have modern docile bodies, but also docile minds, which would assure their lifelong obedience to their husbands.

Rules for ornamentation appeared in sections 5 and 7 of the essay. QA gave detailed suggestions on makeup and attire, such as how a woman should use eyeliner and rouge on her face, henna on her hair, polish on her nails, and rosewater on her body, and whether she should wear her hair long or short. A proper woman wore the kind of clothes her husband liked and changed her outfit once a day. She never touched dirt, and she washed her hands with perfumed soaps instead of ordinary ill-smelling ones. She kept her hands in silk gloves, even if she was sitting by a heater (*korsi*), so that her hands would remain attractive and smooth at all times (Javadi *et al.* 1992, 54–55, 61–63).

He gave similar detailed instructions on rules for proper body movement, gesture and behavior (Javadi *et al.* 1992, sections 3, 4, 5). A proper woman would never raise her voice, disagree with her husband, flail her arms about in all directions, or move them excessively. In general, she never adopted a hostile and angry posture, but remained kind, gracious, and deferential toward her husband (Javadi *et al.* 1992, 45–48, 49–50, 51–54).

QA also presented detailed rules of conduct for proper behavior in bed. Husband and wife should sleep in separate beds unless they were having sex, since sleeping in the same bed "reduced affection." The woman should wear gowns made of soft cloth, and come to bed "fully perfumed and clean." During the day she was expected to be weak and submissive, but in bed she should use erotic and provocative language and carry on with "utter shamelessness." More important, she never said no to her husband's demands for sex, at any time or in any place. If she resisted, he might turn to a lower-class temporary wife, who would gratify him at all times, be that "in the toilet cubicle or under the stairway" (Javadi *et al.*

Figure 4.1 Page from the *Ta'dib al-Nisvan* manuscript

1992, 80–81). A well-behaved wife woke up early, cut short her prayers, and made herself attractive for her husband. She was expected to be discreet about the couple's amorous experiences the night before, not sharing them even with her female friends (Javadi *et al.* 1992, 73–83).

Another series of regulations dealt with a woman's language and thought processes. If her husband accused her of wrongdoing, "even if she did not commit the crime," the correct response was to "admit to her guilt and apologize to him." If her husband pushed her into a fire, "she should imagine that fire a garden of flowers," and willingly enter it. When she died, God would reward her for her total submission to her husband (Javadi *et al.* 1992, 38–39, 41–44). QA frequently brought in selective references from the Qur'an and other religious texts to prove his points. He based his arguments on a circular logic, where the existence of sexist laws proved women's natural deficiency, and hence justified discrimination against them (Javadi *et al.* 1992, 88).

A decade later, in 1895, Bibi Khanom Astarabadi (1858–1921), a performer in the Qajar court, wrote an angry response to *Ta'dib al-Nisvan* entitled *Ma'ayeb al-Rejal* (Vices of Men). Like many other women in the family of the *'ulama* and those connected with the court, Astarabadi was well versed in Persian literature and religious texts, although the spelling and grammatical errors in her essay reveal a lack of formal education. She was a popular performer in women's gatherings of Qajar high society. Bibi Khanom was married at age twenty-two or twenty-three to Musa Khan Vaziri, a migrant from the Caucasus who had joined the Persian Cossack Brigade, and they had seven children.

Ma'ayeb al-Rejal (Javadi *et al.* 1992) was a proto-feminist work. Astarabadi said she wrote it because her female friends were angry at the pedantic and misogynistic advice in *Ta'dib al-Nisvan* and wanted someone to respond to it. They encouraged the more educated Astarabadi to write the essay. What makes the work unusual is the remarkable openness of its language, and the ease with which the author speaks of women's personal lives and their most intimate concerns. Because *Ma'ayeb al-Rejal* was written for an audience restricted to women at court, it lacks the inhibitions that later appeared in published writings, including progressive social commentaries in newspapers during the Constitutional Revolution.

Astarabadi's response shows that socioeconomic changes and increased encounters with the West had altered women's expectations in marriage. On several occasions, Astarabadi argues that since Iranian women lacked many of the social, economic, and educational opportunities enjoyed by their European counterparts, Iranian men had no right to make such odious demands (Javadi *et al.* 1992, 124). The hypocritical QA never mentions the greater freedoms enjoyed by Western women, but has the audacity to ask Iranian women to mimic the demeanor of Western women. He advises women "to take delicate steps, to speak gently," to follow proper table manners, "to eat quietly with the tips of their fingers," to be clean, and to keep a clean house. Such words meant little to a poor Iranian woman: "Any idiot knows that cleanliness is better than dirt; there is no need for all this nonsense." Bad hygiene was the result of poverty, she writes. Furthermore, if ordinary women wore silk gloves and followed the etiquette appropriate to European restaurants and ballrooms, who would supervise the fields? Who would watch the children in a one-room dwelling? For "poor folks like us," she continues, men and women who sleep under the same cotton comforter for "thirty years" and could ill afford to change it, such calls for cleanliness were meaningless. The solution to the problems of the nation was not more flimsy "advice" but fundamental reforms in all aspects of society: governmental, religious, administrative and military affairs, and in the lives of ordinary citizens. Men had to educate themselves rather than give women ill-conceived advice (Javadi *et al.* 1992, 141–142).

Astarabadi expresses anger toward QA, and men like him, who deprived women of education and social contact, reducing their lives to housekeeping and child-rearing: "God has created men to be lovers of women, not their tormentors." Instead, men told women that God had created them for only two purposes: service to men and procreation. A woman could not leave the house without her husband's permission and was told "never ask for anything even if you die from hunger; ... in disputes and in arguments remain silent; never give any of your husband's belongings to another person without his permission; [but] if you have any wealth of your own do not deprive your husband of it" (Javadi *et al.* 1992, 102). For her part, Astarabadi advises women:

You should listen to such advice only if you have a believing and decent husband who is chaste; one who is kind and considerate to his wife; does not have intolerable demands of her; is not fault-seeking, abusive, or reckless – a man who is not obstinate, has no extra-marital affairs, and does not run away from home. [Listen to such advice] if he is a lover of women, not a lover of boys [*amrad baz*]. Do not listen to your husband if he is yet another shameless man who divorces his wife for no reason. If he does not have these good qualities, it is better that you free yourself. The sooner you rid yourself of him the better. Free yourself before you grow old and are burdened with sons and daughters. (Javadi *et al.* 1992, 102)

As the above shows, one of Astarabadi's major complaints involved men's extramarital affairs, both heterosexual and homosexual. She spoke frankly of sexual relations, extramarital affairs, and pederasty, subjects that concerned women and had been discussed by male intellectuals such as Akhundzadeh and Kermani. At one point, she recalls a humorous anecdote involving a friend's husband who had homosexual inclinations:

> There was a man who had a very beautiful wife but he was not interested in her. Every day he picked a fight with her over some minor issue, then left the *andaruni* angry and in his nightgown. One night he called his servant in the middle of the night and asked him to find an *amrad* for him. The poor servant went in search of an *amrad* but could not find anyone. So he went to the house of a prostitute who had a tall and handsome brother and asked for him. The sister said, "My brother is away on a trip, but I can come instead." The poor servant said, "My master is a lover of *amrads* (*amrad baz*) and he will not want you." She said, "I will dress like an *amrad* and pretend to be one. Hopefully he will not find out and will give you a reward." Out of desperation and greed, the servant agreed. At the sound of the door, the husband rushed out to the door barefoot and anxious. He passionately embraced the woman who looked like an *amrad*, as if she were a *ghilman* from heaven, and with much excitement and without undressing her, threw her on the bed facedown. (Javadi *et al.* 1992, 126–127)

Eventually the husband found out that he was having sex with a woman. He called the servant, who was watching from behind the door, and complained about the prostitute's lack of a penis. The servant offered his services for a three-way arrangement. In the moralistic ending of the story, the husband found this offer highly amusing. Laughing at this turn of events, he fell off the bed, accidentally cut his penis, and lost consciousness. The servant and the prostitute collected all the valuables in the house and ran away. Later, the wife found her husband lying unconscious and called the doctor. Soon the entire neighborhood learned about this humiliating incident, which forced the man to make a long trip abroad (Javadi *et al.* 1992, 127–128).

If this story suggests that a husband's extramarital affairs, including homosexual ones, were humiliating experiences for a wife, Astarabadi's own story indicates that the arrival of a co-wife, even a lower-class one, was devastating to the first wife. When first married, Astarabadi and her husband Musa Khan Vaziri had been much in love. At this time she had decided to forego her considerable *mahriyeh* of 400 *tumans*, a decision she later regretted. After nine years and several children, she found it physically impossible to respond to her husband's sexual demands. By this time Musa Khan was a colonel in the army and a respectable member of Qajar society. Like many other women of her class, who dreaded the presence of a second '*aqdi* wife of equal social status in the house, Astarabadi decided to hire a childless widow as a maid, intending that she would become the *sigheh* of her husband.

Unfortunately, Astarabadi had underestimated the maid's ambitions and her husband's desire. Before she had the opportunity to work out such an arrangement, her husband took the maid as his *sigheh* wife and called for divorce. Astarabadi found herself back in her uncle's house, where she stayed, heartbroken and worried about her children. She decided that her only option was reconciliation with her husband. At first he would not take her back, apparently because the new wife would not agree to it, but in time he relented. Astarabadi returned, but was now the humiliated co-wife in her own house, while the former maid enjoyed the position of "lady of the house." Eventually, the former maid tired of the bickering and hostility in the family and left, after which Astarabadi's life returned to a semblance of normalcy. Yet the deep emotional scars of this affair remained with her and became the motivation for writing *Ma'ayeb al-Rejal* (Javadi *et al.* 1992, 189–198).

QA had based his claims on two seemingly irrefutable authorities, religion and modern science. His limited knowledge of Western societies and his familiarity with authoritative religious texts that justified women's subordination led him to prescribe a number of disciplinary practices that urban middle-class Iranian women found impractical, illogical, and humiliating. Astarabadi's cogent arguments against QA, coupled with her own compelling life story, constituted a remarkably strong challenge to QA's misogynistic discourse. She rejected a selective reading of Western modernity that allowed more disciplinary practices to be imposed on women's bodies without also granting Western-style social and political rights. Occasionally she also reinterpreted religious sources to produce a more egalitarian interpretation of Shi'i doctrines. Although she had reconciled with her husband by the time she wrote *Ma'ayeb al-Rejal*, the marriage unraveled again soon after the essay began to circulate. Musa Khan Vaziri took a second temporary wife and fathered another child, at which point Astarabadi left him permanently. In 1906, she became a leading constitutionalist and founder of a new school for girls.

The critical modernity of the Constitutional Revolution

The Constitutional Revolution began with the political protests of dissident intellectuals, clerics and theology students, merchants, artisans and guilds, and urban women. The protesters focused on both democracy and national sovereignty. Women took part from the earliest stages of the movement. They facilitated the strikes, lent their moral and financial support to the constitutionalists, and occasionally even defended them physically against the forces of the shah (Malikzadeh 1992, II:355; Nahid 1981, 55–58). By August 1906, Mozaffar al-Din Shah had granted the protesters the right to form a Parliament, and to draft a modern constitution.

Figure 4.2 Woman on left tells woman on right to send her daughter to a
modern government-approved school for girls, 1913

The merchants and intellectuals who led the Constitutional Revolution
had asked the leading clerics to help build a mass movement that opposed
excessive political and economic concessions to Western powers, but the
more secular leadership did not allow the culturally conservative clerics to
dominate the movement. This helped the revolution to become an important turning point for gender relations. Urban middle- and upper-class
women of Tehran and other major cities joined it and supported the new
Parliament (Bamdad 1977; Bayat-Philipp 1978; Nategh 1979; Nahid
1981; and Afary 1989, 65–87). Without institutional support, they created
a network of women's associations, schools for girls, and hospitals
for women, and contributed to the intense political debates of the period
(Fig. 4.2). Some women challenged the conservative wing of the clerics in
the newspapers, often relying on new interpretations of religious texts in
order to press for their rights. Some adopted social democratic rhetoric,
which had become popular in the revolutionary period, and wrote about
social and economic issues of the poor. A few also criticized polygamy and
divorce by repudiation. With the support of male journalists and parliamentarians, women managed to place their rights to education and political participation on the national agenda.

Between 1906 and 1911, more than 200 periodicals began publication.
Many were politically progressive, and some were recognized for

their literary accomplishments (Browne 1914, 26). These new publications were filled with calls for an end to economic concessions to the European powers and with demands for more limits on the authority of the shah and the clerics. They also petitioned for the enactment of a host of civil liberties. Iran's first Parliament (1906–1908) took several historic actions. It restricted the authority of the shah and his ministers. Popular provincial councils known as *anjomans* were formed throughout the country, and provinces gained administrative and financial autonomy. These *anjomans* founded modern elementary schools, thus undermining the authority of the traditional religious schools (*maktab*). *Anjomans* in northern cities and large villages pushed for greater regional autonomy. In 1907, the new constitution granted formal equality before state law to male citizens, thereby undermining the authority of religious law, which kept non-Muslims (*dhimmis*) in a second-class status. In 1911, the franchise was expanded to include men of all social classes. Recognized religious minorities (Zoroastrians, Christians, and Jews) were each allocated one or two representatives in the Parliament, but the Babi and Baha'i minorities were denied representation. Women were denied the right to vote, as they were in contemporary Western societies, where democratic reforms often barred women from access to some of the new public spaces.

The Constitutional Revolution was influenced by three modernist ideologies: liberalism, social democracy, and the homegrown Babi movement. Liberalism had arrived through greater contact with Europe and through Presbyterian missionary schools. Social democracy spread from Russia to Iran through migrant Iranian oil workers and merchants in the Caucasus who had experienced the 1905 revolution. Armenian Iranians, who had close ties to their brethren in the Caucasus, also played a pivotal role in the course of the revolution (Berberian 2001; Afary 1996). Marxists of the Russian Social Democratic Workers Party had influenced the creation of the Iranian Organization of Social Democrats in Baku (then part of the Russian Empire), which campaigned for the rights of workers, peasants, and women. Branches of this organization emerged in many Iranian cities after the revolution. Social democrats also helped radicalize the newly formed popular *anjomans*. Many leading intellectuals of the Constitutional Revolution, including parliamentarians, journalists, and authors, privately held social democratic convictions and were therefore sympathetic to women's rights. A few spoke out against the veil and men's right to repudiation. Most focused on education and the need for women's schools and associations rather than on these more controversial issues.

The revolution witnessed a large grassroots movement by Muslim Iranian women to start girls' schools. American Presbyterian missionaries had opened the first such schools in Iranian Azerbaijan in 1838. Similar ones opened in Tehran, Mashhad, Hamadan, and Rasht and included a small number of Muslim students. American Presbyterian women instructed young elite Iranian girls on monogamy and what could be defined as non-erotic heterosexual marriage, focusing on hygiene, nurturing of the family, and loyalty to one's husband.[3] Zoroastrians, Baha'is, and Jews had established their own community schools for girls. The secular Alliance Israélite had opened the first modern school for Iranian Jews in Tehran in 1898 (Nikbakht 2002, 200). During the revolution, women appealed to the Parliament for help in forming schools and associations. But ranking clerics in the Parliament responded that women needed only a limited education to prepare them for their domestic chores (*Majles* 6, December 30, 1906, 3).

Some women joined the wave of revolutionary activism rather than wait for the male leadership to offer them institutional support. These upper- and middle-class women, often from progressive constitutionalist families, encouraged their relatives to spend their resources on the education of their daughters rather than on large dowries. In the first three years of the revolution, they created councils that established a variety of women's schools, health clinics, orphanages, and adult education centers in Tehran and other cities. These societies also became involved in social and political campaigns (Afary 1989). Still, only a small number of women attended the modern schools, and the traditional *maktab* schools remained predominant. By 1914, when Iran's population was about 10.9 million, there were only sixty-three modern girls' schools in Tehran with a total of around 2,500 students (*Shekufeh* 2[20], 1914, 3–4; Bharier 1968, 275).

Taj al-Saltaneh and her sister Eftekhar al-Saltaneh were active in the Anjoman for the Freedom of Women. By this time, disillusioned with her marriage and the Qajar aristocracy, Taj had gravitated toward social democracy and became interested in women's issues (Afary 1996, 196–297). Others belonged to the leading clerical families, or came from Babi or Baha'i families, where the education and socialization of women were religious tenets (Qavami 1973, 128–141). Sediqeh Dowlatabadi (1881–1961), the daughter of the most important Azali Babi theologian in Isfahan, opened the first girls' school in that city. In later years, she established the Women's Association of Isfahan and began publication of the weekly *Zaban-e Zanan* (Women's Voice) (Sheikh al-Islami 1972, 88–99; Qavami 1973, 140). American missionaries and Iranian students

---

[3] E-mail exchange with Thomas R. Ricks, September 4, 2007.

of the American School in Tehran were also active in the *anjomans*.[4] Other members of the women's *anjomans* crossed the barricades, defying fathers and brothers who opposed the revolution. Some who had little education and no family support also joined the movement, and many risked their lives and even got killed. When royalist forces besieged the city of Tabriz in 1908–1909, some women joined the resistance in male disguise, and several lost their lives in defense of the revolution (Qavami 1973; Afary 1996).

Not all constitutionalists belonged to the respectable classes. The courtesan Robabeh worked secretly to remove dangerous royalists in her bordello. When a certain Mirza Hussein, who had received military training in Russia, was suspected of aiding the royalists, Robabeh invited him to her house. According to one account, "when Mirza Hussein, received into her confidence, slept with his head pillowed in her lap, she, with her own pink hands, drove the thin point of the Caucasian knife through his eyeball far back into his brain" (James 1909, 43).

The revolution achieved a milestone by ending the institution of the harem. At the stroke of a pen, the new Parliament restricted the court's budget and brought the harem establishment to an end. It also extended assistance to the discarded harem wives and concubines by providing them with small stipends for a few years. The new king, Muhammad Ali Shah (r. 1907–1909), and his son Ahmad Shah (r. 1909–1925) each maintained one *'aqdi* during their respective reigns (Navaei 1995–1996, 55).[5] By the first decade of the twentieth century, some Qajar princesses, traveled abroad and lived more independent lives. Taj al-Saltaneh got a divorce and moved to a garden villa in a wealthy suburb of Tehran ('Ayn al-Saltaneh 1998a, III:2010, 2201). She followed her grandmother's penchant for male lovers and held many social events where music, alcohol, and sexual flirtations were common. Her married sister Eftekhar al-Saltaneh had an open affair with the celebrated poet of the Constitutional Revolution 'Aref Qazvini (Amanat 1993, 56–58). Thus, near the end of the Qajar era the extramarital affairs of elite women, which had previously taken place quietly inside the harem, became somewhat more conspicuous, and occasionally caused public distress.

The first Parliament also addressed the subject of domestic slavery. On one occasion, the social democratic deputy from Azerbaijan Hasan Ahsan al-Dowleh demanded a "notice to the state that slavery be abolished" (*Mozakerat-e Majles*, 5 Rabi' al-Avval 1326). On another occasion a petitioner from Kerman demanded an end to the internal slave trade in

[4] Among them was Mary Wood Park Jordan (wife of Samuel Jordan), who joined the *Anjoman-e Azadi-ye Zanan* (Anjoman for the Freedom of Women). See Armajani 1974, 33.
[5] Thanks to Manoutchehr Eskandari-Qajar for some of this information.

Baluchestan, where "children were separated from their parents and brought to Kerman and from there to Tehran where they were auctioned like animals." In response, some religious deputies maintained that "selling of Muslims was prohibited" by Islam and pressed for measures that outlawed the practice altogether (*Mozakerat-e Majles*, 5 Rabiʿ al-Thani 1326).

Two stories on slavery took center stage in this period. One was the tale of the Daughters of Quchan, a group of peasant girls in the province of Khorasan, who were sold to Sunni Turkoman brigands so that their parents could pay their back taxes to the local governor. The second was the tale of the women of the Bashganlu tribe, who were also kidnapped by Turkoman brigands. These two stories were combined and turned into one grand narrative. The repeated telling of these tales of destitute Shiʿi girls being sold to Central Asian Armenians by Sunni Turkoman slave traders helped forge a new sense of national identity. It became an emblem for all that was wrong with the nation (Najmabadi 1998b).

Constitutionalists insisted on adherence to international anti-slavery treaties, which the Iranian government had signed, and received the backing of several progressive clerics in the Parliament. Henceforth when *kanizes* ran away, and the police returned them to their owners, newspapers and women's *anjomans* protested, as in the following story recounted in the social democratic newspaper *Iran-e Now*:

'Ala' al-Saltaneh had a *kaniz*. He gave her to Hajji Mirza, the slave merchant, to sell for him. The poor *kaniz* ran away from the grip of the Hajji and saved herself. Unfortunately, the bazaar police commissioner caught the poor *kaniz* and returned her to the slave merchant, so he could give the proceeds to 'Ala' al-Saltaneh to add to his enormous fortune. Shame on the buyer! We ask the authorities to stop the actions of such ignorant Hajjis and 'Ala' al-Saltanehs. A long time ago, the Iranian government signed the treaty banning the slave trade and prohibited it. (*Iran-e Now* 45, 1909, 2)

Following the publication of this article, three women came to the offices of the paper and offered to buy the *kaniz*'s freedom. They learned that the *kaniz* had fled a second time but once again had been returned to the slave merchant and tortured. *Iran-e Now* published the names of the individuals involved, further humiliating them (*Iran-e Now* 46, 1909, 2). On another occasion, when a *kaniz* ran away and left her small child behind, *Iran-e Now* protested, "We are amazed that in the twentieth century and at a time when people in our nation are struggling for political freedom and sacrificing their lives, human beings are being sold as if they were animals" (*Iran-e Now* 98, 1909, 2–3). Thus, by shaming elite slaveholders, and appealing to anti-slavery treaties, constitutionalists pushed for the eradication of the last vestiges of urban slavery and succeeded in doing so.

Several southern border towns continued the slave trade for a few more decades, however.

Modern justice and the place of women and minorities

Constitutionalists strove to unravel a number of legal ambiguities and forms of social and political discrimination. They introduced the ideas that Iranian (male) citizens should be treated equally before the state law regardless of their social standing or religion, that mutilation and amputation were cruel and inhumane punishments, that slavery had to be fully abolished, and that laws should be uniformly enforced in different cities and towns. As constitutionalists began to place legal, social, and economic changes on their agenda, some of their early clerical supporters withdrew their support. The secular–religious coalition fragmented over issues such as freedom of speech, assembly, and publication; equality before the law for non-Muslims; land reform; and women's education.

Many Shi'i clerics now joined the royalist camp. Among them was Sheikh Fazlollah Nuri, Tehran's most eminent cleric, who opposed the new girls' schools and women's associations. He warned that new rights for women would lead to "prostitution" and intermarriage between Muslims and non-Muslims, thereby undermining what he saw as the very foundations of Islam (Zargarinezhad 1995, 161).

Alongside these two discourses in early twentieth-century Iran – the social democratic and religious ones – a nationalist discourse of scientific domesticity had also emerged. It advocated selective progress on gender issues to build a modern nation-state. Motherhood gained greater respect in this new nationalist discourse, which saw women as educators of the nation (Rostam-Kolayi 2002). The new women's journals of this period, *Danesh* (1910–1911) and *Shekufeh* (1913–1917), epitomized such cautions. *Shekufeh* objected to unveiling on the grounds that it would introduce untold social maladies in the institution of the family, as had happened in the West (2[23], 1914, 4). Both journals avoided the subjects of gender inequality, sexuality, and grand politics, and focused instead on hygiene, disease prevention, education, home economics, childcare, and proper etiquette.

These were by no means minor issues at the time. In elite Iranian society, fathers controlled many aspects of their young sons' and daughters' lives. Wives were viewed as merely vessels to bear children and, later, deputies to carry out the fathers' wishes. The new discourse on scientific domesticity empowered women by emphasizing the nurturing qualities of mothers and their role in the children's education. Hence both the "regulatory" discourse of scientific domesticity and the "emancipatory" discourse of the social democratic press contributed to women's growing ability to carve out a more productive role for themselves in society. Both strands worked to reduce the accepted authority of men, giving women greater private and public rights and opening the door for increased educational, political, and professional opportunities. At the same time, the discourse of scientific domesticity assured the public that women who enjoyed the advantages of modernity would not abandon chastity and modesty, and would stay within the acceptable confines of moral decency (Najmabadi 1998a, 98–103; 1993).

Love in marriage and the scandal of women's suffrage

There was a brief hiatus in the constitutional movement after the shah temporarily took over and closed down the Parliament in June 1908. After the summer of 1909, when constitutionalists once again regained control of Tehran and reopened the Parliament, elite urban women's activism increased. They organized open forums on a variety of social and political issues, and some deputies vocally supported them. In 1911, Vakil al-ra'aya of Hamadan, who had petitioned the first Parliament on behalf of the women's *anjomans*, asked the second Parliament to grant women's suffrage. Although unsuccessful, his call caused a sensation, sparking coverage in the London *Times* ("Women's Rights in Persia" 1911a and 1911b). Activist women also published reports in progressive newspapers. Astarabadi, the author of *Ma'ayeb al-Rejal*, who now headed the Maidens' School, invited women to attend regular weekend meetings at her house to discuss "the advantages of constitutionalism and the disadvantages of autocracy" (*Iran-e Now* 150, March 7, 1910, 1).

The nascent women's movement raised funds through women's conferences and plays. Proceeds helped to establish schools for orphaned girls, adult education programs, and women's hospitals. Intellectual women such as Taj al-Saltaneh addressed controversial issues such as polygamy and repudiation (Fig. 4.3). In the context of the revolution and its radical ferment, Taj candidly describes her forced marriage, her secret abortion, and her husband's bisexual inclinations, including a love affair with a twenty-year-old male dancer:

This beloved husband of mine was a devotee of the god of hedonism. He derived enormous pleasure from being with simple youths [*amrads*] ... My dear husband, so prone to losing his heart, was head-over-heels in love with this youth. Everything he owned, everything he could snatch away from people through force or oppression, went into satisfying the young boy's whims and caprices ... It lay within my power to expel the boy from my house, but it was not in my power to purge him from my husband's heart ... My husband loved him ardently, intensely. Had I cherished any real love in my heart for my husband, I would

Figure 4.3 Taj al-Saltaneh

most assuredly have suffered terribly; but I only harbored conjugal respect and affection for him, so I was not particularly concerned with what he did, and left him alone. (Taj al-Saltana 1993, 270–273)

The lack of courtship between girls and boys before marriage and the need for love within the institution of marriage were central themes in Taj's memoir. In her view, there was little shared affection between husbands and wives in elite circles. Couples married without mutual love and sought emotional fulfillment outside marriage. Men like her husband, who married for social position and wealth, turned to male and female lovers for companionship, and spent their time away from their wives and families, drinking and socializing. Their lonely wives threw extravagant parties, bought expensive furniture, clothing, and jewels, and hired many handmaids and servants. Here Taj made parallel arguments concerning men who turned to male and female lovers for companionship and women who hired handmaids and servants, and included references to her own inclination toward a young seamstress. Taj became one of the first Iranian women to call for romantic love within marriage. "If women were unveiled and, as in all civilized nations, men and women could see each other, want each other, and join in a permanent union of love, would this not be preferable to a life spent alongside mistresses and companions?" (Taj al-Saltana [1914] 1982, 101–102; see also Mahdavi 1987, 188–193). Elsewhere in her memoirs, the now social democratic Taj linked female prostitution to poverty. She argued that among the urban working population, the male head of household's meager income was never adequate to cover all the expenses of his household, which typically included several women – wife, mother, daughters, sisters, and often nieces. Some poor women turned to prostitution to support themselves and their families. If women were able to earn an honorable living, these families could live in dignity, she concluded (Taj al-Saltana [1914] 1982, 100).

Another champion of companionate marriage was the Baha'i poet 'Esmat Tehrani (d. 1911). Her essays appeared in *Iran-e Now* under the pen name Tayereh. Born to a Babi–Baha'i family in Tehran, she was married at the age of thirteen to a guard in the court of Naser al-Din Shah and had three daughters. Her husband, Mehr Ali Khan Zanjani, a fierce persecutor of the Babis and the Baha'is, brought his prisoners home to be tortured. In reaction to her husband's cruelty, and under the influence of an uncle who was a convert, Tayereh adopted the Baha'i faith herself. When Zanjani found out about her conversion, he became violent in an attempt to force her to recant. First, he nearly beat her to death, and then he almost buried her alive. Next, he placed her on the roof on a cold snowy night. Finally, he tried to suffocate her. Somehow, she survived these torments. When Zanjani died in the mid-1880s, Tayereh, who was thirty-one at the time, turned to activism. She used her inheritance for her Baha'i activities, wrote poetry, opened a school for girls, and devoted the remainder of her life to the cause of women's rights (Beyza'i [1966] 1996; Cole 1998, 180). In her articles for *Iran-e Now*, Tayereh drew on these life experiences, writing about the predicament of women and men in unhappy marriages, and about polygamy and repudiation. She tried to convince her readers that the key to the nation's progress was the advancement of its women, since educated women would raise better citizens and therefore build a stronger nation (*Iran-e Now* 65, November 13, 1909, 3; see also Afary 1996, chapter 7).

Molla Nasreddin and the campaign for normative heterosexuality

Girls' education, scientific domesticity, and companionate marriage were goals of the Iranian advocates of women's rights in this period. But an equally significant new discourse on gender and sexuality emerged from the Russian Caucasus and influenced the Iranian Revolution. During the period of the 1905 Russian Revolution Azeri intellectuals in the Caucasus, who saw themselves as part of an Iranian diaspora, articulated the most radical discourse on gender and sexual reforms. In 1906, *Molla Nasreddin* (1906–1931), a sophisticated Azeri-language satirical newspaper, began publication in Tbilisi (in present-day Georgia, but then under Russian rule). With its colorful cartoons, the paper immediately captured the imagination of large sections of the Muslim world. Its founder and editor, Jalil Mamed Qolizadeh (1862–1932), was a celebrated playwright. His wife, Hamideh Khanom, was an early Azeri feminist, and several talented poets and artists also worked with the paper.[6]

Molla Nasreddin advocated a progressive reading of Islamic texts and was the first newspaper in Iran and Central Eurasia to reinterpret Qur'anic verses in light of modern gender concerns. Its humorous stories and poems challenged the conservative social and political practices of the orthodox clerics and the prevalent Western colonial discourses. *Molla Nasreddin* (henceforth *MN*), which began with a circulation of 1,000, was soon smuggled across the border to Iran, where it reached a wide audience in the coffeehouses and *bazaars* of Tabriz, Tehran, and Rasht. It also gained an audience in many cities of the Russian Empire, India, the Ottoman Empire, and Egypt. With its lithographic illustrations, poetry, and satirical columns, *MN* embarked on a refashioning of gender and sexual mores for the Shi'i communities of Iran and the Caucasus (Figs. 4.4, 4.5).

Although most members of the editorial board were secular social democrats, Jalil Mamed Qolizadeh and his colleagues showed great respect for Qur'anic verses and sayings attributed to the Prophet Muhammad, though not necessarily for other Muslim religious sources, and in this way pioneered a critical modernist Shi'i discourse. The paper argued that the entrenched patriarchal traditions of Iran and the Caucasus violated the spirit of the Qur'an. For example, in their criticisms of face covering (*rubandeh*), a common tradition among Shi'i Azeri communities of the Caucasus and Iran, Qolizadeh turned to Qur'anic verses (33:59, 24:31) to argue that the Prophet had never required it. The original spirit of these verses had been lost or hidden to the believers, he wrote. The Prophet had merely required women to cover their private parts and not their faces. Qolizadeh goes on to blame male chauvinism for such misreading of the Qur'an:

---

[6] For more details, see Afary, *From Mullah to Goya*, forthcoming.

Figure 4.4 "New wife and old wife," 1907

Figure 4.5 Condemnation of child marriage: "Women and socks are the same. One size fits all," 1907

What kind of men are we? ... We imprison our women in the house but enjoy ourselves at parties, where we embrace the [male] musicians. We imprison our women in the house, but take as a temporary wife any woman whose [bare] ankle we fall for; we imprison our women in the house, but spend the daily bread for our sons and daughters on blond foreign prostitutes. (*MN* 20, May 19, 1907)

At a time when Iranians were engaged in a passionate debate about the new concept of freedom (*horriyat*), and the scope and limits of the term, *MN* satirizes the practice of repudiation, linking it to the concept of freedom:

No nation has the freedoms we have in marriage and divorce. For example, I marry a woman today. Tomorrow, if I want to, I can divorce her ... No one has the right to tell me why I divorce her or why I do not divorce her. This is freedom. I keep her or I divorce her, as I wish. However, among us, a man seldom tells his wife, "I want to divorce you." Usually he looks for an excuse, and harasses her so much that she puts on her veil, and leaves for her father's house. Then the man says, "Thank God!" He goes to a *molla* and divorces her ... The freedom that has been given to Muslim men has been given to no other nation. (*MN* 20, May 19, 1908)[7]

MN also initiated a new discourse on same-sex relations. In the Shi'i communities of Iran and the Caucasus, criticisms of homosexuality were common. After all, homosexual sex was a religious violation that required repentance. Contempt for the "passive" junior partner was also well known. Political accusations of homosexuality (the charge that an important person had been an *amrad* as a youth) were occasionally leveled. But *MN* introduced a different discourse on homosexuality, a secular and modernist critique that would shape Iranian debates on sexuality for the entire century. *MN* turned its attention to the subject of pedophilia in its generic meaning, that is, the practice of committing very young girls to arranged marriages and maintaining boy concubines in schools and seminaries.

Numerous cartoons and columns in the pages of *MN* satirized the customs of child marriage and pedophilia. The gifted poet of *MN*, Ali Akbar Saber, captured the trauma of a newly married girl who held onto her nanny and begged to be saved from her elderly husband (Saber 1992, 6). Other stories and cartoons suggested that young men were also victimized by strictly arranged marriages.

MN also broke new ground with its cartoons and satirical columns on dancing boys and boy concubines (Fig. 4.6). A fierce debate was going on between the proponents and opponents of modern schools. The opponents of modern education charged that girls would be molested there,

---

[7] *MN* simply ignored the fact that the Qur'an had authorized repudiation and polygamy.

Figure 4.6 "Dancing boys," 1906

and the proponents disagreed. *MN* turned this debate on its head, accusing the religious teachers of molesting young boys in the *maktabs* and seminaries and advised parents to enroll their sons in the modern schools, where teachers would presumably protect them from such harassment (*MN* 7, May 19, 1906; 28, July 18, 1910).

A second type of discourse on homosexuality concerned married women whose husbands kept *amrad* concubines. Through various satirical columns and cartoons, *MN* suggested that these men had a vested interest in maintaining the (male) homosocial public spaces where semi-covert pederasty was tolerated. The men opposed unveiling and, more important, the presence of women in public parks, schools, and coffeehouses, because such freedoms for women made it more difficult for men to maintain the separate realms of wife and *amrad* (*MN* 23, June 13, 1910). Thus, *MN* was suggesting that male opposition to unveiling was rooted in more than a desire to safeguard the honor of women. Veiling and gender segregation preserved male privileges in homosocial spaces that would have to be relinquished if women were to enter public spaces.

While the new discourse had positive aspects, since it addressed the rampant problem of pedophilia, it also had limitations, for *MN* created a

Figure 4.7 "Now they perform brotherhood vows! (Better say they get married)," 1910

discourse that castigated all forms of same-sex relations, as well as the rituals associated with it. Among others, it mocked the rites of exchanging brotherhood vows before a mollah and compared it to a wedding ceremony (Fig. 4.7). The paper also charged many conservatives with pedophilia, an accusation that may or may not have been true, but was extremely effective propaganda.

The articles and illustrations in *MN* were so provocative that the editor received death threats and went into hiding. In the Shi'i centers of Iran and Najaf, the *'ulama* banned *MN*, calling it blasphemous. On several occasions Muhammad Ali Shah and the conservative clerics tried to stop its distribution, but the Iranian Parliament intervened. The paper remained enormously popular with Iranians who viewed Mamed Qolizadeh and his Azeri colleagues as expatriates who were able to write on the Constitutional Revolution from the safety of exile.

MN also became a model for several Iranian newspapers of the era, although these papers had to operate under greater restraints. The most important was *Sur-e Israfil* (1907–1908) of Tehran. The celebrated poet Ali Akbar Dehkhoda, editor of *Sur-e Israfil*, followed the lead of *MN* in opposing veiling and exposing the hypocrisy of clerics who preached one set of beliefs and norms of behavior but practiced quite another (*Sur-e Israfil* 17 [November 20, 1907], 7).

Dehkhoda's columns centered on the harsh treatment of women by fathers and husbands, and denounced child marriages and polygamy. He criticized parliamentary deputies who refused to support the new educational and social institutions for women. He also accused *akhunds* (low-level clerics) of taking advantage of their religious positions to turn their offices into brothels. In one of his columns that is considered the first modern Persian short story, and is entitled "Qandarun," the villain is an *akhund* who marries for money, enters into several temporary marriages, and shamelessly spends the last penny of his wife's dowry (Dehkhoda 1908, 7).

However, neither Dehkhoda nor any other journalist in Iran went so far as Qolizadeh and *MN* in challenging prevalent sexual norms. Iranian revolutionary leaflets (*shabnameh*) commonly berated major political figures for their sexual transgressions. They focused on the extravagance of these affairs, such as the large number of male or female concubines a politician maintained. Revolutionary leaflets accused adult men of having homosexual sex with other adult men, "of thirty-year-olds propositioning fifty-year-olds and twenty-year-olds propositioning forty-year-olds, right in front of the shah," rather than adhering to the man–boy regulations of status-defined homosexuality (Sharif-Kashani 1983, I:xiv, 19, II:481). Some leaflets repeated the allegation that major political figures had been *amrads* in their youth (Sharif-Kashani 1983, II:487; III:752). Others turned to a religious condemnation of homosexuality (Sharif-Kashani 1983, II:501, III:789). For example, when the social democrat Hasan Taqizadeh defended the rights of religious minorities, he was accused of advocating a society that tolerated both republicanism and *lavati* (homosexual transgression) (Sharif-Kashani 1983, II:529, 755). These criticisms differed from those introduced by *MN*, which had predominantly focused on pedophilia. *MN* had castigated the older adult male partner and showed sympathy for the children and junior partners, hence turning traditional tropes of status-defined homosexuality upside down.

Sur-e Israfil generally avoided such matters. Dehkhoda's satirical columns made only a few brief references to same-sex relations. These are seldom condemnations; more often they describe a character or social event. In one story, Dehkhoda depicts a youth with a "pistachio mouth" and "almond eyes," whose beauty "rivaled the sun and in age was ten, perhaps twelve or thirteen, or maybe fifteen" (*Sur-e Israfil* 18, November 28, 1907, 7). In another satirical column, Dehkhoda narrates the life of a man, Azad Khan, who falls in love with a young waiter in a coffeehouse but cannot court him because this "requires money," and he is destitute (*Sur-e Israfil* 5, June 27, 1907, 8). Thus, in his two most prominent discussions of homosexual love, Dehkhoda reproduced standard tropes of same-sex love in Persian poetry. He dwelled on the exquisite beauty of a *shahed* or on the gift-giving rituals of courtship. Here we see some of the differences between Qolizadeh and Dehkhoda, the two most eloquent and influential secular writers of this period. While Iranian readers became familiar with the modern criticisms of homosexuality in the pages of *MN*, two more decades would pass before most Iranian intellectuals came to support discourses explicitly favoring normative heterosexuality and companionate marriage.

After 1912, when the revolution came to an abrupt halt as a result of Russian military intervention, orthodox clerics were able to revert to some earlier patterns of gender segregation. During World War I, houses continued to be divided into private and public sections, lower- and middle-class girls were still married at or before puberty, and women covered their faces with the *rubandeh* in public, though modern schools for girls continued to function. For a while the *chadors* actually became longer and thicker and the *rubandeh* wider and longer, coming all the way to the knees. "If a woman showed a corner of her eye, her husband or *vali* would be punished. Public meetings and conversations between men and women, even if they were married, were prohibited and led to police investigation" (Shahri 1990, VI:298–299). Change was more perceptible in elite circles, however. Slowly, companionate marriages were becoming more acceptable in these classes. Girls married somewhat older, and women traveled abroad. But there was little change among the *bazaari* and clerical families or the urban poor. Few girls in these strata attended modern schools, and many merchants continued to maintain polygamous households. According to Clara Colliver Rice, more than any other group the *bazaari* merchants kept the "custom of having more than one wife. The poor cannot afford it, and the upper classes have come so much in contact with Western ideas and ways that they realize its disadvantage" (Rice 1923, 47). The activists' struggle for greater gender reforms had to await the impact of another revolution that would occur not in Iran, but in Russia, Iran's neighbor to the north.

5   Redefining purity, unveiling bodies, and shifting desires

The rise of the Pahlavi dynasty in 1925 coincided with a new era of gender and sexual politics in Iran, a time when a new and more educated middle class emerged whose unveiled women appeared in public on their way to school, in women's organizations, and in jobs. This educated elite was fascinated with many aspects of modernity, from Bolshevism and Fascism to Freudian psychoanalysis, gramophones, and cinema. Reza Shah's reign (1925–1941) saw changes in gender norms in four specific areas: (1) increased reforms in health and hygiene that reduced the spread of venereal and other contagious diseases; (2) educational and legal reforms that mitigated social hierarchies; (3) reforms in dress codes and the ascendancy of modern mannerisms, and (4) reforms that contributed to normative heterosexuality and attempted to outlaw male homosexuality. Many of these reforms consequently clashed with existing practices, producing ambiguity and anxiety in the realm of sexuality. Often, Western cultural and social values were forcibly grafted onto indigenous practices, creating hybrid forms in which old and new cohabited uneasily.

Resistance stemmed partly from the fact that in Shi'i Islam, as in a number of other religions such as Zoroastrianism and Judaism, the body is a source of shame and ritual impurities. Accordingly, not only unveiling, but also modern clothing for men or women, participation in team sports, and greater socialization between the sexes violate notions of honor and centuries-old traditions of segregation. The new practices introduced under Reza Shah also exposed believers to ritual pollution and possible damnation in the afterlife, which contributed mightily to the antagonism of the old middle classes toward these gender reforms. But another source of unease remained unstated, and little discussed, even long afterwards. Unveiling disrupted male homosocial spaces, especially when gender reforms encouraged normative heterosexuality and pushed same-sex relations further to the margins of society.

142

European upheavals and the emergence
of Reza Shah Pahlavi

In 1921, the seemingly devout modernizing military leader Reza Khan took power in Tehran. By 1925 he had unified the country, established a new dynasty, and adopted the name Reza Shah Pahlavi. Many nationalists, socialists, and clerics backed the new monarch. Nationalists admired him for unifying the nation. Clerics hoped he would stop Mustafa Kemal Ataturk's secularizing reforms from spreading to Iran. Leftists hoped he would dismantle the archaic agrarian relations and usher in a new era of capitalist development that would eventually lead to socialism. But the shah disappointed and surprised both his admirers and his critics. He created a strong and unified central government, a modern army and bureaucracy, and crushed autonomous and separatist movements in the nation. He also established an authoritarian regime, blocked all independent political and social organizations, skillfully co-opted or silenced dissident voices in the Parliament, encouraged secularization and sharply reduced the powers of the clerical establishment.

Reza Shah introduced modern disciplinary practices regarding women's and men's bodies, a process that accelerated after urban men were required to wear Western suits and hats in 1928, and women were unveiled in 1936. Foucault's thesis that modern liberties have always been accompanied by new administrative and disciplinary mechanisms is borne out in Iran (Foucault [1975] 1977, 136; Afary and Anderson 2005, 80, 197).

In the 1920s, unveiling and gender reforms in Soviet Central Asia and the Caucasus were the talk of the town in Iran. The Soviets abolished *shari'a* law and granted women new rights. In 1922, they also decriminalized homosexuality (Healey 2001). The Soviet Union legalized secular marriage based on the mutual consent of the partners and upheld the right to unilateral divorce by either partner, as well as the right to abortion. New laws gave women the vote, erased the distinction between legitimate and illegitimate children, introduced equal pay for equal work, and set up co-educational schools. The Soviet Union banned polygamy and started a wide campaign for unveiling. Hundreds of unveiled Muslim women volunteered to be translators and assistants for *Zhenotdel*, the government organization for women. Soon, the number of divorces initiated by women increased. But male communist leaders in Central Asia had mixed reactions. While some supported these activities, others tried to sabotage the process, and still others tried to take sexual advantage of the newly unveiled women. The years 1927–1928 witnessed a mass retaliation against unveiled Central Asian women. The communist leadership, now under Stalin's control, accepted some of the demands of the conservative community and eventually closed down the *Zhenotdel* (Massell 1974; Stites 1978).

Despite these setbacks, gender reforms in the Caucasus and Central Asia continued to influence the intellectuals in Turkey and Iran. The secular, authoritarian rulers of these two countries gradually appropriated the issue of "women's emancipation," originally a signature issue of progressive democrats and socialists. The state became the enforcer of some patriarchal powers. In their efforts to transform Iran and Turkey into "Westernized" nations, Ataturk and Reza Shah used gender reforms as a vehicle for nation-building, modernization, and capitalist development, thereby also ideologically disarming Turkish and Iranian leftist forces.

The Russian Revolution also impacted Iran more directly. In the summer of 1920, the Red Army entered Iran in pursuit of White Russian forces. This allowed a revolutionary Soviet-backed movement, the Soviet Socialist Republic of Gilan, to emerge in the Caspian region. The short-lived republic frightened the landed elite and the conservative clerics, who feared that a successful communist movement in Iran would confiscate their property and destroy their way of life. A decade earlier, they had been scandalized by the milder reforms of the constitutionalists; now they faced avowed Iranian atheists and communists in the Gilan Republic. Many feared that the republic was the opening wedge of a Soviet Socialist Republic of Iran. Leaders of the Gilan Republic were not entirely secular, however. The inclusion of several progressive clerics in this Islamic–socialist alliance contributed to its local credibility and popularity. The more radical elements in the republic supported the confiscation of large landholdings and the vast *vaqf* religious endowments, and the replacement of some *shari'a* laws with modern secular ones. Most important for our discussion, the Gilan Republic also supported the unveiling of women, a highly controversial measure at the time (Fakhra'i 1977).

The threat of communism encouraged Britain to shore up its influence in Iran. In 1919, an Anglo-Persian treaty made Iran a quasi-protectorate of Britain. But the treaty was suspended in 1920 because of nationalist opposition in Iran. Faced with numerous autonomous movements in Iran, and the Soviet Union's renunciation of most of the Tsarist concessions in Iran, British officials in Iran were forced to change their policy and back a strong Iranian central government that could suppress the autonomous movements and prevent Iran from gravitating into the Soviet orbit.

While the new government had come to power with British support, it soon asserted its autonomy from Britain by signing the Russo-Iranian treaty of 1921. Reza Khan consolidated his authority by forming Iran's first modern army. In 1921–1922 government forces took back control of the Gilan province and in the next three years other autonomous regions were also pacified. In 1924 the Fifth Parliament ratified Reza Khan's modernization program, which included the adoption of the metric system and the Persian solar calendar (vs. the Islamic lunar calendar), the requirement of a family name and birth certificate for every citizen, the abolition of aristocratic titles, and compulsory military service. In 1925, a majority in the Parliament brought the Qajar dynasty to an end and supported Reza Khan as founder of the new Pahlavi dynasty.

Reforms of the Reza Shah era

Reza Shah was a complex figure, and it is not easy to sum up his role in modern Iranian history (Fig. 5.1). In a little more than a decade, the shah established a centralized state, unified the nation, and built a rudimentary economic structure.[1] As Ervand Abrahamian notes, the regime embarked upon "transforming the multiethnic empire into a unified state with one people, one nation, one language, one culture, and one political authority" (Abrahamian 1982, 142). In this process, the state also ended the remnants of domestic and foreign slave trade, and the segregation of women and ethnic and religious minorities. With the help of Western and Iranian reformers, the shah created a state bureaucracy and an army representative of the nation's diverse makeup (Cronin 1997). Less than 50 percent of the nation's citizens spoke Persian. Now an ambitious project of public education in Persian aimed to integrate women, ethnic minorities, Sunni Muslims, and non-Muslims into the state.

   Though he often used Western technicians and academics in rebuilding the country, the shah's insistence on Iran's political and economic independence strengthened his popular support. These educational and professional advances helped create a modern middle class and significantly increased the numbers of the intelligentsia, a group whose commitment to modernity and secular nationalism led it to back the state in carrying out its reforms, at least initially. Abrahamian notes:

The same intelligentsia grew to total nearly 7 percent of the country's labor force, and developed into a significant modern middle class whose members not only held common attitudes toward social, economic, and political modernization, but also shared similar educational, occupational, and economic backgrounds. The intelligentsia was thus transformed from a stratum into a social class with similar relationships to the mode of production, the means of administration, and the process of modernization. (Abrahamian 1982, 145–146)

---

[1] On Reza Shah's rule, see Banani 1961; Mirza Saleh 1993; Abrahamian 1982; Keddie 1981; Ramazani 1966; Alamouti 1990; Clawson 1993; Ehlers and Floor 1993. On abolition of slavery see Mirzai 2004, 212–214.

Figure 5.1 Reza Shah Pahlavi

However, the growth of this new middle class soon resulted in a wide national and cultural gap. As Nikki Keddie has argued, "Reza Shah's work for rapid modernization from above, along with his militantly secularist cultural and educational program, helped create the situation of 'two cultures' in Iran ... The upper and new middle classes became increasingly Westernized and scarcely understood the traditional or religious culture of most of their compatriots. On the other hand, the peasants and the urban *bazaar* classes continued to follow the ʿ*ulama*, however politically cowed most of the ʿ*ulama* were in the Reza Shah period." (1981, 111; see also Chehabi 2003, 205).

Most biographers of Reza Shah agree that he was at best indifferent toward religion and hostile toward the conservative clerics, to whom he gave only lip service. He made a point of sampling local beer at annual trade fairs, commenting on the quality of the brews. At the crown prince's wedding reception he made a toast with a glass of champagne, a dramatic gesture that announced his utter disdain for prohibition. But the shah also knew how to use the power of religion to enhance his authority. In 1924 Reza Khan was willing to support a republican form of government in Iran and assume the title of president. But the ranking clerics opposed this move, fearing the president would follow Ataturk and abolish the *shari'a*. As a result, Reza Khan agreed to establish a new dynasty (Qazi 1993, 394; Banani 1961, 42).

By 1927, Reza Shah's reforms were clearly moving in a direction that would challenge the clerics. Many of these reforms had long been on the agenda of constitutionalists and leftists. In keeping with the dominant version of Marxist theory at the time, most socialists and communists believed that the shah represented the new bourgeoisie and that he was dismantling Iran's archaic "feudal" economic and social relations, thus paving the way for a new capitalist mode of production. Capitalism would eventually lead to democratization, under which trade unions and socialist organizations could expand. Leftists and nationalists wanted a strong centralized government that could resist British intervention and prevent the fragmentation of the country. For all these reasons, many leftists and nationalist intellectuals of this era initially supported Reza Shah and helped him institute a top-down cultural revolution.

In the late 1930s, government institutions put this agenda forward through public lectures in modern schools, colleges, and lecture halls. This form of modern education was aimed at creating loyal citizens who would support the shah and his rule, and who could be peacefully integrated into the new society administered by the expanding state bureaucracy, rather than creating a generation of critical thinkers (Menashri 1992, 111; Akhavi 1980, 39–42). In 1939, two other government-run organizations became active alongside the new schools and the colleges, the Institute for the Development of Thought (Sazeman-e Parvaresh-e Afkar) and the Institute for Propaganda (Sazeman-e Tablighat). Their mission was to propagate modernity, nationalism, and loyalty to the shah through public lectures, radio programs, newspapers and magazines, textbooks, theatrical performances, and patriotic music.[2]

Health, hygiene, and rituals of purity

In the 1830s British and American missionary groups built Iran's first modern hospitals and Iranian advocates of modernity focused on combating

---

[2] For the organization's bylaws and various reports of activities, see Delfani 1996, 1–3.

Figure 5.2 Water distributor complains to women for contaminating the stream; Women respond that running water is ritually pure so long as it looks and smells clean, 1913

contagious diseases. The state moved cemeteries to outside cities, filled urban ditches, built public toilets, and required health passports at borders during epidemics. Residents of cities were encouraged to build on elevated sites, and Tehran began to build up.[3] However, these reforms were woefully inadequate and by 1924 there were no more than 900 physicians in the country, 1 for every 11,000 people. The problems went beyond the inadequate number of physicians and nurses. In the Constitutional era the state had enacted public health measures and planned for vaccinations against smallpox and diphtheria, but "upon hearing that smallpox vaccines contained serums from human sources, the clergy waged an effective propaganda against vaccination and rendered the government's efforts useless" (Banani 1961, 63). A League of Nations report demonstrated that sanitary reforms often conflicted with religious practices of the community: "The manner of killing animals in the slaughterhouses, the washing of the dead, and their burial, are all performed in the manner laid down by the religious laws. The belief that all running water which is open to the air is good and safe for drinking is taught by the religion" (cited in Banani 1961, 63) (Fig. 5.2).

[3] Mohamad Tavakoli-Targhi, "All that was Holy is Profane" lecture presented at Toronto University 2007 and Banani 1961.

Reza Shah's government gave the health campaign a higher priority and turned it into a state policy. By the late 1930s Tehran had a certified medical school and there was now 1 doctor for every 4,000 people. Pestilential swamps had been drained and municipal slaughterhouses had taken control of the slaughtering of animals. By 1941, in addition to the new Ministry of Health, the number of nurses and hospitals had increased. New organizations were formed, like the Red Lion and Sun charitable organization (Iran's equivalent of the Red Cross), and the Organization for the Care of Mothers and Children, while a number of orphanages were also instituted. Smallpox vaccination became compulsory, with certificates of vaccination required for all schoolchildren and job applicants. Schools, factories, and brothels were routinely inspected, and treatment of venereal disease became mandatory (Banani 1961, 65).

A new group of women's publications was important in disseminating and promoting the new rules of hygiene and other reforms that affected the health of women and children. High infant and maternal mortality rates were blamed on poor hygiene and ignorant midwives. This discourse benefited women, because it encouraged the training of professional nurses and midwives in modern colleges. The press paid close attention to the problem of venereal disease, as it affected both women and children, and not only men. Women's magazines carried articles about the effects of venereal diseases on infants, and women were advised to demand a clean bill of health from their fiancés before marriage. Nonetheless, health and sanitary standards remained low throughout the country, and infant mortality rates high. According to a 1949 study conducted by Overseas Consultants, after several decades of public education campaigns, and the creation of a new College of Midwifery, infant mortality rates remained substantially high (Kashani-Sabet 2006, 23).

One impediment came from the orthodox religious jurists, who continued to deny a relationship between certain religiously sanctioned practices and diseases, as the following three examples demonstrate.
1. Shi'i regulations for purification required immersion (*ghosl*) of the body or object in a pool of still water for complete ablution. When the government closed the public bathhouses, and installed more sanitary faucets and showers in houses and public baths, many clerics protested. It took years, and much persuasion by doctors, and eventually by some progressive clerics who prescribed appropriate regulations for *ghosl* using modern gadgets, before the public accepted faucets and showers as proper alternatives.
2. Islam forbade alcohol. Yet health officials and women's journals recommended alcohol for cleaning wounds and for sterilization. Clerics viewed both rubbing alcohol and vaccination as ritually impure

practices that contaminated the blood, and they instigated considerable resistance to both practices. In some remote regions of southern Iran, families refused to vaccinate their children or follow proper hygiene until after the 1979 Islamic Revolution, when local health clinics established by the theocratic state made these practices more acceptable.

3. Clerics denied any link between temporary marriage and the spread of venereal disease and generally opposed any measure that diminished men's sexual prerogatives. They asserted that temporary marriage reduced men's inclination to visit prostitutes and thus decreased the spread of disease. For its part, the state-orchestrated discourse on marital hygiene never resolved the hot-button problem of temporary marriage, focusing only on population control and reduction of prostitution. The Marriage Act of 1931, which recommended health certificates for men before marriage, still permitted an unlimited number of temporary wives, although such marriages now had to be registered (Schayegh 2004, 335–361; Kashani-Sabet 2006, 21).

The new health measures succeeded in replacing some of the old purification rituals and *shari'a* recommendations. Faced with stiff legal penalties, and with scorn and derision from doctors and scientists, the religious establishment relented on some issues. Clerics came to accept showers as a substitute for baths, medicinal use of alcohol, and vaccination.[4] With the gradual abandonment of some rituals of purification, Iranian society became more socially integrated. New public bathhouses, now equipped with showers in individual rooms, were opened to men (and separately to women) of all religions. Likewise, coffeehouses, restaurants, and other public dining areas began to serve women and religious minorities, although unveiled women and those traveling without family continued to be unwelcome in old-style coffeehouses.

In the *bazaars* and among the devout middle classes, many continued to observe the customary rituals of purification in modified form and with some subtle changes. In this way, modernity instituted a double life for pious Muslims. Outwardly, they behaved as modern citizens of the state, ignoring religious hierarchies and engaging not just in business and trade with women and non-Muslims, as they had always done, but also mingled socially, shaking hands and sharing tea or meals with them. Inwardly, many *bazaaris* harbored a constant sense of anxiety since they continued to believe that a pious Shi'i Muslim who ignored the proper rituals of purification after encounters with *najes* (polluted) individuals had "nullified" his prayers and supplications to God and the Imams.

---

[4] For an example of this recognition, see Khomeini [1943] 1984, 275.

Educational reforms

In the early 1920s, Iran had only ten public schools for girls, who comprised nearly 17 percent of all students. In Tehran, with a population of 250,000, private girls' schools, women's societies and journals were more acceptable than elsewhere. Here, in addition to American and European missionary schools, and those affiliated with religious minorities, there were fifty-eight modern private girls' schools, where about 3,200 Muslim girls studied, often for a couple of years. Many other cities lacked such schools, and education was limited to the traditional *maktabs*. Shiraz, for example, had no new schools, and a controversy broke out when a modernist intellectual (*farangi mo'ab*) tried to form one ("Rowzeh Khăni" 1920, 3).

By 1933, the situation had improved. Around 45,000 girls, nearly 23 percent of all students, were attending 870 girls' elementary and high schools, most of them public (Menashri 1992, 110; Sanasarian 1982, 62). The curriculum had also changed. The hours devoted to *shari'a* studies and Arabic (the language of the Qur'an) were drastically reduced, and those devoted to science, mathematics, and foreign languages were increased. Tehran University, Iran's first, was inaugurated in 1934; twelve women were admitted in 1936 though their male classmates initially refused to interact with them (Bamdad 1977, 98–99).

Non-governmental women's organizations and journals advocating scientific domesticity, unveiling, and other gender reforms were active in the 1920s. The best-known association of this type was the progressive Patriotic Women's League (1922–1932), which sponsored the second regional Conference of the Women of the East in Tehran in 1932. Participants came from a variety of religions and countries, called for the reform of marriage, divorce, and inheritance laws, equal wages for equal work, greater political rights for women, greater emphasis on women's education, and especially unveiling (Salami and Najmabadi 2005) (Fig. 5.3).

Soon after the conference, however, Reza Shah ordered the Patriotic Women's League disbanded and encouraged the formation of the government-controlled Ladies' Center (Kanun-e Banuan), with Reza Shah's daughter Princess Shams as its nominal head (Fig. 5.4). Many activists remained on the board, such as the long-time feminist Sediqeh Dowlatabadi who directed the day-to-day affairs of the center (Fig. 5.5). However, gender reforms were henceforth to come only from the top, decreed by the royal family. The activities of the center were initially restricted to unveiling, vocational training, home economics, education, charity, and the shaping of patriotic female citizens. Financially secure and respected by the authorities, the Ladies' Center became an important institution that attracted many members. Over time, the Center's discourse

Figure 5.3 Modified veil worn by elite women of Tehran, 1931

Figure 5.4 Members of Kanun-e Banuan after unveiling

Figure 5.5 Sediqeh Dowlatabadi, circa 1930

shifted from a focus on "patriotic motherhood" to that of "patriotic womanhood." Student members spent more time studying literature, math, science, and foreign languages than domestic topics like sewing and home economics (Paidar 1995, 105; Kashani-Sabet 2005, 38).

Legal reforms

A more secular Civil Code and Penal Code replaced the *shari'a* courts in all matters except the highly sensitive family law. The Ministry of Justice, which comprised judges with degrees from secular law schools, now handled most other legal cases. The clerics maintained control over marriage, divorce, and the appointment of trustees and guardians, although there were also minor changes in these areas. The new Civil Code benefited women in several ways. It raised the legal age of marriage for girls from nine to fifteen and for boys from fifteen to eighteen. On the one hand, the court could give special permission to a father or *vali* to offer a girl as young as thirteen or a boy as young as fifteen in marriage. On the other hand, an eighteen-year-old woman could now petition a marriage bureau if her *vali's* refusal to allow a match of her choosing was deemed unreasonable (Article 1043). Marriage contracts had to be registered in civil bureaus, which allowed urban women to stipulate contractually the right to divorce if the husband took a second wife. A woman who agreed to become the second wife of a man would be also notified before marriage if her future husband had another wife (Bagley 1971, 50). The law also required registration of temporary marriages, a provision that was ignored by most (Woodsmall 1936, 120). A husband who did not provide his wife with maintenance, and refused to divorce her, also became subject to arrest. These changes in family law strengthened the state, producing what historian Parvin Paidar has called "educated mothers and subservient wives" (1995, 112). The regime scrapped laws and customs that violated its new modernist concept of a housewife and mother, but reaffirmed women's sexual subordination. Husbands retained the right to repudiation, while a new Penal Code sanctified "honor killings." A man who killed his wife and her accomplice for committing adultery was exempt from punishment; a brother who killed his sister, or a father who killed his daughter, for the same crime received the minimum sentence of one to six months' imprisonment. Oddly enough, this conflation of crimes of honor and crimes of passion was rooted in French rather than Islamic law. The 1810 French Penal Code (which was abolished only in 1975) was the basis for the Iranian Penal Code of 1926 (Zerang 2002, I:365). Article 324 of the French Code, on crimes of passion, became the foundation for crimes of honor in the legal codes of numerous Muslim nations (Abu-Odeh 1996, 141–156). Women also continued to be denied the right to work or travel without permission from their husbands.

Although Reza Shah encouraged many gender reforms, he saw no need to ban polygamy outright or even end temporary marriage, even though these practices had declined in popularity among the urban middle and upper classes. German diplomat Wipert von Blücher, who lived in Tehran in the 1930s, reports that in that city, with a population of around 300,000, "approximately one thousand men had two wives, approximately one hundred had three, and very few had more. The highest number [concerned former Prime Minister Farmanfarma] with eighteen wives" (Blücher 1949, 184). More and more, women pilloried the tradition of polygamy, which was viewed as an outmoded cultural practice, and awareness among men of its emotional and psychological toll increased as well.

Historians have wondered why the shah stopped short at this point. Banning polygamy and temporary marriage would have involved a major confrontation with the clerical establishment, but it is unlikely that Reza Shah refused to do so solely for this reason. After all, he supported the even more controversial measure of banning the veil, a more direct affront to the clergy. Perhaps he hesitated because most Iranian men, including intellectuals, wished to have a modern-looking wife at home, but did not want to surrender the privileges of polygamy and easy divorce. A brief look into Reza Shah's own life might further explain this matter.

Reza Shah married four times, first with a temporary wife. Little is known about this marriage, which produced a daughter whom the shah supported. The second wife of the shah was an ʿaqdi one: Taj al-Moluk, the daughter of his superior officer in the Cossack Brigade. She became his official queen, and bore him four children, including Crown Prince Muhammad Reza Shah. After becoming army commander in Tehran and moving up the social hierarchy, Reza Khan married two additional women, both from the former Qajar dynasty: his third ʿaqdi was Turan Amir Solaymani. He divorced her after she gave birth to a son, finding her too haughty and upper class for his taste. He was devoted to his fourth ʿaqdi, ʿEsmat Dowlatshahi, and stayed with her until the end of his life. She bore him another five children. In her memoirs, Queen Taj al-Moluk recalls the trauma of having to endure this last, more favored, co-wife and writes that "like all other women, I hated my co-wife. But I had no choice and had to control myself and tolerate the situation" (Ayramlu 2001, 41). As Reza Shah's story suggests, polygamy remained socially advantageous to men. He discarded a lower-class temporary wife and married the daughter of his superior officer. Later, he took a third and a fourth wife from the aristocracy, bolstering his humble social background. Most men were likewise reluctant to give up such privileges which increased their power at home and in society.

The making of modern, docile bodies

Besides educational and legal reforms, Reza Shah's third major reform was aimed at creating modern Iranian citizens in both appearance and in conduct. In 1927, when Nowruz (Persian New Year) coincided with a religious holiday, Queen Taj al-Moluk and her female attendants visited a shrine in the religious city of Qom. The queen was wearing her *chador* somewhat loosely, given the festive time of year. Her casual observance of the veil caused some commotion in the shrine and brought a reprimand from one of the attendants. She telephoned her husband to complain about this treatment, and he immediately drove to Qom. Upon entering the courtyard of the shrine, the shah went on a rampage. First he beat several theology students with his stick. Then he ordered the arrest of the attendant who had insulted his wife, giving him a good thrashing before sending him to jail. Finally, the shah smacked the Chief of Police of Qom.

This story might explain why Reza Shah became the darling of many Iranian constitutionalists despite his humble background and lack of any formal education. For decades, constitutionalists had advocated women's greater social and political participation in society, including the need for unveiling. Now they found an unexpected ally in the new and secular monarch, who not only incorporated such views into state policy, but had the power to enforce them. The incident in Qom constituted the first major clash between the shah and the clerics over veiling. It was the prelude to some more serious confrontations in the following decade.

Two of the shah's most dramatic initiatives, a decree on a uniform dress code for men and a ban on veiling for women, were part of his project to modernize and Europeanize the nation. Until now, clothing and headgear had been clear markers of gender identity, religious affiliation, and social position. The new dress code enacted by the shah undermined social, religious, and tribal distinctions based on appearance and substantially reduced gender segregation. In this way, the unified dress code also built a more cohesive sense of national identity (Chehabi 1993; Sahim 2002).

In December 1928, the shah ordered all urban Iranian men, except for properly credentialed clerics and theology students, to discard their cloaks and more traditional headgear in favor of European-style clothing, including a hat that came to be known as the Pahlavi hat. The government also encouraged female students to unveil. By the late 1920s, greater interaction with the West had slightly altered women's clothing. Women wore lighter veils, many no longer wore a *rubandeh*, and a very small number of elite women in Tehran had abandoned the veil altogether. Ministers and deputies in the Pahlavi government were asked to attend social functions with their wives unveiled. Schools also promoted the new campaign. Following his visit to Turkey in 1934, Reza Shah embarked on a more radical, less gradualist program of unveiling. He certainly knew the risks of such an action: in 1928, the reformist King Amanollah of neighboring Afghanistan, and his wife, Queen Soraya, had visited Iran. Clerics, both in Iran and Afghanistan, fiercely objected to the presence of the unveiled queen. The next year, the Afghans overthrew Amanollah, turning their backs on his modernization agenda.

Despite this discouraging precedent, in January 1936, Reza Shah issued a formal decree ordering women to unveil. For the next five years, under the project known as Women's Awakening, a "veritable panopticon" was deployed to implement Reza Shah's new dress code with administrative and disciplinary mechanisms enforcing these measures. Local authorities arrested anyone on the streets who resisted the new orders. They prevented veiled women from entering public baths, theaters, stores, bus stations, and, eventually, even shrines. Respectable women had to unveil, but prostitutes, who had been unveiled or had worn casual veils, now had to veil. The state was transforming "the symbol of virtue into a symbol of vice" (Chehabi 1993, 218; see also Chehabi 2004).

Public reaction to compulsory unveiling was mixed. The veil was largely an urban phenomenon, as rural and tribal women had long worn more colorful and less restrictive clothing, something the authorities and the media now emphasized to encourage similar practices in the cities. Police records suggest that the media's celebration of national diversity in clothing gradually made it easier for some women to drop the veil (Ja'fari et al. 1992). The new decree became popular among men and women from the upper and new middle classes, composed of teachers, nurses, doctors, and civil servants. By the 1930s, many young educated men, who had been exposed to Western gender practices, simply refused to marry a woman sight unseen. Women in these communities eagerly purchased European-looking suits and hats for the special day when they came out unveiled (interview with Monir Pirnazar, May 13, 1995).

Other more devout sections of the population were reluctant and even hostile, since the veil had marked the physical boundary between acceptable and unacceptable gender roles, and its elimination by decree had resulted in a crisis of identity for both men and women. The strongest opposition to unveiling arose within the old urban middle classes, clerics, merchants, and artisans. In some homes, women decided to remain indoors for years, while some prominent clerics prevented their daughters from attending school (Ja'fari et al. 1992). Reza Baraheni recalls the crisis in his family when unveiling became law:

Since there were no showers in Iranian homes, women had to go to a public bath. The husband would put his wife in a large sack and carry her like a bale of cotton to the bath. I remember from my childhood, when my father would carry his mother in the sack, empty his load in the bath, and then come back for his wife. He once told me that Reza Shah's policeman had asked him what it was that he was carrying. He had improvised an answer: pistachio nuts. The policeman said, "Let me have some," and started tickling Granny. First she laughed, and then she wiggled her way out of the sack and took to her heels. My father was arrested. (Baraheni 1977, 52)

In addition to unveiling, the state expected urban women to conform to a Western aesthetics of the body. Unveiled women could have adopted the loose and colorful outfits of provincial women, such as those of Gilan, but instead they were told to follow a Western European dress code. Many poor women, who could not afford presentable modern clothing, resisted the new order for that reason. Newly unveiled women were also expected to walk, talk, and interact in a modern Western way and elite society enforced these new norms. Suddenly, both men and women began to pay closer attention to women's gestures, height, and bodily dimensions, and these began to affect a girl's chances of finding a proper suitor.

A common grievance of this period was that professional young men, who were emancipated from their patriarchal families, delayed marriage or never married. Another complaint was that young women were becoming too uninhibited, even loose in their morals. Jewish families were thought to be very strict with their daughters, while Armenians were regarded as more lenient. Urban, upper-middle-class Muslim girls were seen as somewhere in between. The conservative writer Prince 'Ayn al-Saltaneh Qajar had complained about the supposed promiscuity of fifteen and sixteen-year-old Muslim girls, even before they were unveiled by the state:

In previous times girls of such advanced age would be married. Now husbands are scarce, and there are too many unmarried available girls with fully developed bodies. The girls' schools have ruined them and perverted [their conduct]. Four times a day, the girls walk back and forth to school without any impediment. Since the girls are older, boys harass them. ('Ayn al-Saltaneh 2001, X:7207)[5]

Parents worried if their fifteen-year-old daughter was not yet engaged, but they no longer knew how to raise a daughter for a proper marriage. If they taught her dance and music, suitors might ask for a more traditional girl, but if they raised her in the old ways, suitors might ask for a more modern wife ('Ayn al-Saltaneh 2001, X:7704).

Unveiled women's entry into public spaces created a variety of other problems. Until this period, husbands, sons, and male servants did most of the shopping in urban, middle-class families. When women went to the baths, visited friends and relatives, or, in more recent decades, attended schools and went shopping, they tried not to attract much attention. Suddenly, after 1936, unveiled bodies became the center of attention. If an unveiled woman entered the *bazaar* to shop and a pious Muslim merchant looked at her, shook her hand, and talked to her, he had committed three major sins, each of which required immediate repentance, starting with ritual ablution. This problem was never completely resolved during the Pahlavi era. As late as the 1970s, many *bazaar* merchants refused to interact with female customers and demanded that a male family member accompany the women or come in their place.

Cinema as agent of modernity

The new middle class was eager to observe and emulate Western mannerisms, and cinema became the easiest way to learn to do so. Between 1925 and 1935, Tehran became a more modern urban center with new

---

[5] Girls went home for lunch break and returned in the early afternoon.

shops, cafés, movie theatres, broad paved roads, and modern state buildings. The number of movie theatres expanded, while several film studios and acting schools were established. Over 400 American, French, German, and Soviet movies were shown each year, with the US becoming the major exporter of films to Iran. In the 1930s, the nation with a population of 13–14 million had thirty-four movie theatres, with nine in Tehran and four in Tabriz. Hamid Naficy estimates that in 1931 alone, the residents of Tehran went to the movies more than a million times, while on average each person saw five films. State policies helped this trend. In England, Queen Elizabeth's ban on Catholic rites and passion plays in the late sixteenth century had channeled public interest into more secular theatrical productions. In Iran the ban on Muharram processions and passion plays increased the audience for movie theatres. The state encouraged men to bring female relatives to the cinema, and although clerics issued a variety of proclamations against women's attendance, these had little effect upon the new middle classes.[6]

Cinema also contributed to the project of normative heterosexuality in this class: first, it created a new public space where young men and women could spend a few private hours together. Cinemas in northern Tehran, where the new middle and upper classes congregated, became prime dating locations. As Naficy points out, "young girls and boys, who were not customarily allowed to walk the streets together or to meet openly in cafés and restaurants without chaperons, found the darkness and safety of the movie houses conducive to the charged moments of privacy, intimacy, and eroticism" (Naficy in press, chapter 5, 582). Cinema encouraged heterosexual love by showing movies that emphasized Western ways of courting, thereby helping to alter norms of courtship and marriage. Not only foreign films but also the first Persian-language sound movies by director Abdolhussein Sepanta focused on heterosexual love, among them the extremely popular *Lor Girl* (1933), followed by *Shirin and Farhad* (1934), *Black Eyes* (*Chashm-e Siyah*, 1936), and *Leyli and Majnun* (1937). The latter two films were based on poems by the twelfth-century Nezami Ganjavi, perhaps the greatest romantic epic poet in Persian literature.

In south and central Tehran, however, and more conservative southern cities, where audiences remained exclusively male, cinema had a different effect on sexuality; it created new safe havens for homosexual relations. According to one report:

---

[6] For information on cinema in this period I am grateful to Hamid Naficy who shared his forthcoming book on the history of Iranian cinema with me.

For the deprived and the vast majority of the youth, especially the *pesar baz* (those inclined to relations with boys), cinema was the best place where with 10 *shahi* they could buy a ticket and spend several hours in debauchery, touching, kissing of this and that person, killing time and enjoying themselves. (Shahri 1991, I:284)

The project of normalizing heterosexual eros

The Pahlavi era saw as great a shift in homosexual as in heterosexual mores. The state passed new laws against pederasty and male prostitution, and the resultant crackdown saw male prostitutes more frequently arrested than female ones. The 1933 Penal Code prescribed a prison term of three to ten years for the rape of boys and a term of one month to a year for encouraging a youth of either sex under the age of eighteen to pursue illegal sexual activities, including *lavat* (sodomy). According to Shahri, the state encouraged the *zan baz* (men who were inclined to heterosexuality), but chastised, arrested, and punished the opposite faction (men who were inclined to homosexuality). Thus the visibility of this second group gradually diminished, while those of the *zan baz* and female prostitutes increased (Shahri 1990, VI:339). Journalists who condemned homosexuality were also allowed ample opportunities to publish their views at a time when the press heavily censored other publications. All of these changes decreased the visibility of same-sex relations, pushing them further and further to the margins of society.

The male homosocial environment had persisted through the early 1930s, although in somewhat attenuated form in more traditional sectors of society. The mentorship rituals between a guild master and his apprentice boy concubine had continued without much change. Ja'far Shahri presents a revealing picture of male homoerotic relations at this time. Men of all social classes commonly employed a more lower-class boy in their workplace who performed a variety of menial and office tasks, such as bringing tea and running errands. The boy could be much more, however. He could be "the motivation for one's living," and a person "without whom no one really had any desire to go to work" (Shahri 1990, VI:318). The boy concubines had different titles in various professions:

In the royal court he would be known as the "*gholam bacheh*"; in the military, as the "orderly"; among the elite, as the "servant"; in the merchant community he was the "revenue collector"; the notary called his boy "the scribe"; the rich called him "servant"; ... the peddler, hawker, porter, walnut seller, whey seller, berry seller, syrup seller called him "son"; the hoodlum, thief, gambler, and others [of similar professions] called their boys their *mochul* [snack]. At any rate, whoever earned a living and made enough to feed two people kept a boy. Some men remained loyal to their boys and would not leave them until the lads grew beards and became men with wives and children of their own. (Shahri 1990, VI:319)

A poor handsome boy served other more commercial functions as well. Much like Western advertising models, boys attracted customers. The coffee seller, cigar seller, baker, or barber who kept an attractive boy in his store often made more money. Admirers visited the store on one pretext or another, just to catch a glimpse of the handsome boy behind the counter. Some waited outside the store until the evening when "they could walk the boy to his home" (Shahri 1968, 206).[7]

As in the nineteenth century, a poor boy's adult lover was bound by many courtship rules, the most important one being to help his future prospects. Often the master found a wife for his apprentice from his own family. In this way, the young accountant might become a merchant's brother-in-law, marrying his master's sister. After the merchant's death, if there were no sons interested in taking over the business, the accountant might inherit it and become responsible for the financial affairs of the merchant's widow and children (Shahri 1990, VI:320–321).

Other social rules of interaction applied in male homosocial spaces. No one was supposed to gaze at another man's boy, just as no one was supposed to look at another man's wife or fiancée. Such transgressions were punished harshly; they could lead to rape and even murder. Shahri pointed out that adult men of the same age could also be sexually involved. While a guild master might terminate his relationship with a boy when he grew a beard, "there were many active men (fa'el) who made love to people their own age, and many who remained passive (maf'ul) lovers of other men, though they themselves had a wife and several children" (Shahri 1968, 206). Here relations were more companionate though frequently one partner was much wealthier than the other. Adult male couples enjoyed each other's company in public without shame: "No one worried about the labels fa'el (active) or maf'ul (passive). Male couples formed the vast majority of every male gathering, and few men appeared without a companion ... Some men never married and stayed with the beloved of their youth until they became old. Throughout this entire time, they never uttered a word to hurt the feelings of their beloved and ultimately left their entire fortune to him" (Shahri 1990, VI:321, 324).

The unveiling of women and normalization of heterosexual eros created a host of new issues in urban communities. Most importantly, perhaps, unveiling challenged the authority of the male patriarch. Until this period, at least among the elite and the middle classes, the veil had reduced the chances for mutual attraction to play a role before marriage, which made it

---

[7] This quotation is from Shahri's fictionalized account of the period, but it is very similar to his historical account (1990), cited above. Thanks to Houchang Chehabi for providing this source.

easier for parents to arrange marriages. Now a young man could see the unveiled girl on her way to and from school and could more easily venture his opinion and reject a prospective bride whom his parents had carefully chosen. Many urban professional middle-class men did so as they were financially emancipated from their highly patriarchal fathers. In addition, unveiling and the concomitant ending of women's seclusion allowed young women to become objects of desire and thus to compete more easily for the attentions of men. Unmarried urban girls, who had been unable to compete openly with boy concubines for men's attention, could now do so.

Attempts to normalize heterosexual eros came from several other directions as well. As in other parts of the world, public baths had been locations for casual, homosexual sex. Beardless boys attended to adult male customers as they undressed, or scrubbed and massaged their bodies (Shahri 1990, I:483; El-Rouayheb 2005, 42–43). In the 1930s there was a rigorous campaign against public baths for reasons of hygiene. Clerical and *bazaari* families built private baths so that the women in their families would not have to go into the streets unveiled to reach public baths. The construction of private baths in homes reduced the popularity of public baths and drove many out of business. Once the government banned the use of communal pools in public baths for hygienic reasons, new and more modern public baths appeared that had a series of tiled, private rooms, each with a separate shower and dressing area. Customers of various religions and ethnicities could rent these baths for a few hours a day. Patrons could still bring a boy concubine or a male prostitute to the small room in the new baths, but this required advance planning and limited the choice of partners.

Intellectuals and the new (homo)sexual norms

Leading constitutionalists enthusiastically joined the campaign against homosexuality. Sex with adolescent boys became culturally less acceptable. However, the gradual acceptance of a more modern gay lifestyle was not yet occurring. In the early 1920s the influential journal *Kaveh* (1916–1921), published in exile in Berlin and edited by the famous constitutionalist Hasan Taqizadeh, had led the movement of opinion against homosexuality. By the 1920s Taqizadeh had become an utterly uncritical modernist. In an oft-cited statement, he called upon Iranians to "become European in appearance and in essence, in body and in spirit." Only this would enable the nation to catch up with the West (Taqizadeh 1920, 2). Members of the editorial board of *Kaveh* supported greater women's rights, including in marriage and divorce. Their notion of modernization now included the normalization of heterosexual eros and the abandonment of all homosexual practices and even inclinations. The paper claimed that Iranian men "curse their wives in private (*andaruni*) and love and adore men in public (*biruni*)." Only heterosexual love was legitimate, and a man who remained trapped in same-sex inclinations was therefore backward. Such a man "had difficulty accepting the civilization of the clean-shaven Europeans." Presumably he would confuse the beardless European men with *amrads*, and remain oblivious to the (heterosexual) mores of the West ("Nokat", *Kaveh*, 1920, 2). *Kaveh*'s articles were a continuation of the discourse initiated by Akhundzadeh and Kirmani in the nineteenth century and further developed by Jalil Mamed Qolizadeh in the pages of *Molla Nasreddin* in the early twentieth century.

Iraj Mirza now became an unexpected advocate of the new sexual mores. Known for his earlier homoerotic poems, he transformed himself into a strong critic of male homosexuality. He joined other leading political figures of this period in encouraging compulsory heterosexuality for men. In '*Aref Nameh*, a hilariously provocative narrative poem, he admitted that as a young man he had been fond of beardless boys, but when he became older, he shifted his desire to women. He now blamed the veil for the pervasive homosexuality of Iranian society. True patriotism required support for modernization, which in turn required switching one's sexual orientation from boys to women. True morality required both unveiling and compulsory heterosexuality (Iraj Mirza 1972, 128–139; Najmabadi 2005, 148–150).

Other intellectuals and educators pressed for the elimination of poems with homosexual themes from school textbooks. Here, the best-known advocate was the noted historian Ahmad Kasravi, who helped shape many cultural and educational policies of the 1930s and 1940s. Kasravi had been trained as a junior cleric in his youth, but under the influence of the Constitutional Revolution he changed into a harsh critic of the clerical establishment. Later in his career, Kasravi became a distinguished judge, a professor of history at Tehran University, a prolific journalist, the author of a classic study on the Constitutional Revolution (Kasravi 1984), and the founder of a new and secularizing political movement known as *Pak Dini* (Purity of Religion) which operated within the authoritarian Pahlavi order. *Pak Dini* developed a broad following. It embraced a "rational" modernity and denounced all viewpoints that its author viewed as irrational, among them Shi'ism (but not Islam as a whole), Baha'ism, Sufism, and Social Darwinism (Jazayery 1978; 1973, 193). Clerics were predictably outraged, among them the young Ayatollah Khomeini, who fiercely attacked Kasravi and his followers.

Kasravi also supported socially engaged forms of poetry that addressed concrete problems. He extolled the "wholesome" poetry of Parvin E'tesami, who wrote of women's hardships in a segregated world, and also admired the poetry of *Molla Nasreddin*, which had advocated monogamous hetero-sexuality (Kasravi [1944] 1977, 53).[8] The poems of the great Sufi masters, which dealt with homosocial love, wine, and drugs, did not fulfill these criteria. For Kasravi homosexuality was a measure of cultural backward-ness. The Sufi poets themselves lived a "parasitic life," Kasravi opined, and their writings encouraged fatalism and determinism (*jabriyat*). Poetry of this kind was dangerous and had to be eliminated. Kasravi and his supporters went so far as to institute a festival of book burning, held at the winter solstice. Books deemed immoral and harmful were thrown into a bonfire in an event that seemed to echo the Nazi and Soviet-style notions of eliminating "degenerate" literature (Kasravi [1944] 1977, 132–133).

Many high-school students and military officers supported Kasravi's position. In Tehran, a group of students proposed a society for "fighting against the harm done by the poets" (Jazayery 1981, 312). Most of the educated elite disagreed, however. In 1935, the Literary Society (Anjoman-e Adab) invited Kasravi to present his views. Although most members continued to differ with him, the Society ultimately agreed to set some limits on the publication of new poems. From then on, poets could publish in only six specified subject areas, and the *ghazal* form of poetry, dedicated to same-sex love, could "no longer be written" (Jazayery 1981, 313).

Kasravi subsequently published this lecture in his journal, *Peyman*. He condemned classical poets, such as Khayyam, Rumi, Sa'di, and Hafez, and called for their writings to be eliminated from high-school textbooks. After the publication of this article, however, Prime Minister Muhammad Ali Foroughi (in office 1933–1935) ordered Kasravi's journal itself censored, for Foroughi was partial to Sa'di. The Education Ministry had published a new edition of Sa'di's *Golestan* (Garden of Flowers), for which Foroughi had written an introduction specifically praising Sa'di's concept of love. Foroughi and Kasravi had a meeting, where Kasravi urged the prime minister to eliminate some of Sa'di's homosexual poems from school texts. With apparent reluctance, Foroughi ordered all the nation's high schools to skip the controversial chapter 5 of *Golestan*, entitled "Love and Youth," most of which dealt with homosexual love. Kasravi still objected, knowing that the students would be eager to read the skipped sections of their textbooks. Later, Kasravi asked Foroughi to ban the publication of homoerotic poems in daily newspapers. This time the prime minister ignored him, but the controversy continued. The next prime minister, Mahmoud Jam, who held office from 1935 until 1939,

---

[8] For a discussion of Kasravi's views on literature, see Katouzian 2002, 171–194.

acceded to Kasravi's demand (Kasravi [1944] 1977, 135). Kasravi's opposition to classical Persian poetry continued to isolate him within the intellectual and academic community. Denied the rank of professor, he resigned from Tehran University in the late 1930s.

New technologies of power, or women's emancipation?

Contemporary feminists have expressed ambivalence toward Reza Shah's reforms. Some have argued that his repression of the religious establishment, together with his support of unveiling and new health, educational, and employment opportunities for women, reduced women's oppression, especially because he undermined the position of the clerics. Others such as Parvin Paidar have held that his new Penal Code and Civil Code served more to codify existing patriarchal relations and to give new authority to *shari`a* laws (Yeganeh 1993, 5). What is clear, however, is that women's bodies became a site of politics. The state constrained women's activism and reacted to the fact that women married later and in general were becoming more independent from their fathers and husbands. The matter of unveiling, raised early in the century by secular democratic activists, was now being institutionalized by an authoritarian government. By the mid-1930s, previous efforts to introduce women's rights and other social reforms at the grassroots level had been co-opted by the state.

As in many other authoritarian states, there was no due process and no free press, and no one was immune under Reza Shah's regime of fear, including several ministers who were executed (Qazi 1993, 75–121). The shah left the more democratic and leftist advocates of women's rights with few options, at least as most of them saw things. Many in the educated elite and new middle classes aligned themselves with an authoritarian modernist government, hoping to achieve some of their social objectives. At the same time, a small elite committed to modernization monopolized the new wealth generated from oil and industrialization. Over time, advocates of women's rights came to be identified with the state, its authoritarian policies, and its elite cronies.

In Iran and other Middle Eastern societies, modern scientific advances served to refute religious and customary practices. Researchers and medical doctors explored the consequences of veiling on women's health and concluded that veiling contributed to osteomalacia (softening of the bone due to lack of exposure to the sun and vitamin D) and tuberculosis, which was exacerbated by "constant re-breathing in of germs behind the veil" (Woodsmall 1936, 290). Other studies linked high infant mortality rates to polygamy and suggested that as rates of polygamy declined, and a woman's sense of security in her marriage increased, rates of infant mortality also declined (Woodsmall 1936, 299).

A new medical discourse on health and hygiene replaced the older religious one on pollution and purification. "Unclean" Jews and Armenians were moving out of their ghettos. Women with partially exposed bodies were entering public spaces and rising to new positions of authority, while ranking clerics stayed home in protest. The clerics, who stood to lose the most in this immense power shift, reluctantly accepted most of the changes. Many abandoned the cloak, entered the state bureaucracy, the judicial system, or the new educational institutions. They also revised some rituals of pollution and purification that for decades had made the clerical establishment the butt of jokes by the Western educated, although some such practices remained intact.

Both veiled and unveiled women were now harassed on the streets. Veiled women were hounded by the police, who ripped *chadors* and large scarves off the heads of frightened women. But unveiled women were also pestered, since most men saw their bodies as an open invitation to sexual harassment. Every movement of the unveiled woman came under public scrutiny. The old discourse on women's modesty, proper ethical behavior, and moderation did not die out, but was recast. Women were urged to "wear simple dresses" and to "act modestly." Government directives asked women "not to compete with other women in dress and fashion," not to "imitate European fashion," and to beware of "financially ruining their families" through the purchase of Western-imported clothing and accessories (Sha'bani and Zargarinejad 1992, document 30).

Women were also asked to internalize the old ethical code of conduct that had previously been observed through the veil. As the conduct of the unveiled woman became the subject of great attention, a series of questions dogged her: Had she looked people in the eye? Did she smile too much? Was her dress modest enough? Did she carry herself respectfully while walking on the streets? These questions sought to measure a woman's propriety. Women as well as men enforced these new standards of behavior, especially older women upon younger ones. In Foucauldian terms, one could say that unveiling had constructed a new panopticon. Unveiled women could be more easily observed and therefore subjected to various forms of social control.

Reza Shah's authoritarian modernization of sexuality and gender relations took place without democratic debate or discussion. Unveiling was not accompanied by personal autonomy or economic security for women. A woman still needed her father's permission to marry, her husband's permission to work or travel, and had extremely limited rights to divorce and child custody. Her husband retained the right to take other permanent and temporary wives. A daughter's inheritance was still half that of a son's. There was no campaign to equalize inheritance laws or to revise divorce and custody laws. Male reformists who welcomed unveiling balked at ending these and other male prerogatives. Public debate on Reza Shah's reforms had to await his expulsion from the country by the Allied forces in 1941. When that discussion came, however, it did not take the form of a wholesale rejection of Reza Shah's gender reforms, let alone of modernity as a whole.

Female desire and normative heterosexuality in modern Persian literature

During this period, a radical transformation concerning sexuality took place in the literary circles as well. The most celebrated poet of this era was Parvin E'tesami (Fig. 5.6). In 1935, she published 150 poems in her first *divan* (collection of poems), to great acclaim. E'tesami was shy, saw few visitors, and remained reticent about meeting male admirers of

Figure 5.6 Parvin E'tesami

her work even after the 1936 unveiling. Farzaneh Milani writes that her poetry expresses "perhaps most eloquently the push and pull between self-assertion and self-denial, between self-revelation and self-concealment, that many women must have felt who wanted to unveil but could not do so easily or at once" (Milani 1992, 102). E'tesami's best-known poem, "The Iranian Woman," written on the occasion of the 1936 unveiling, captured the sense of joy some urban women felt at entering the public arenas, but also their ambivalence toward the new ethos of modernity, especially concerning their obligation to maintain the old standards of social propriety. The poem began by condemning women's oppression in the era before unveiling, but it ended with a warning to women to guard their chastity for fear of what might happen:

> Walk on the straight path, because on crooked lanes
> You find no provision or guidance, only remorse.
> Hearts and eyes do need a veil, the veil of chastity.
> A worn-out *chador* is not the basis of faith in Islam.

(E'tesami 1985, 107–109)

Female desire and normative heterosexuality became the subjects of popular novels and literary works by male authors. Flouting the custom of not calling a woman by her first name, authors such as Mohammad Hejazi and Sadeq Hedayat named their short stories or novels after their female protagonists, as in Hejazi's *Ziba* (Beautiful [1961]), *Parvaneh* (Butterfly [1953]), and *Arezu* (Dream [1965]), or Hedayat's *'Alaviyeh Khanom* (Madam Alaviyeh [1933] 1959). Most secular and leftist authors of this generation contributed to a new anticlerical literature. But some also explored the complicated relationship between sexuality and religion, and the ways in which premodern and early modern Iranian society had allowed more ambiguous sexualities.

Female prostitution became a favorite topic of a new generation of writers. Many novels, such as Morteza Moshfeq-Kazemi's *Monstrous Tehran* (*Tehran-e Makhowf*, 1941/1942), revolved around the sexual exploitation of women. These modernist morality tales portrayed women as helpless victims of unscrupulous fathers, mothers, and husbands. The novels also introduced and popularized a new genre of heterosexual erotica. Readers avidly followed the female protagonist's many escapades as they read about the allegedly scandalous nightlife of the wealthy elite ('Abedini 1990, 35).

Among the first generation of these writers, Muhammad Ali Jamalzadeh stands out for his critique of prostitution, which took aim at both the clerics and the more modern, educated elites. He portrayed poor women with great sympathy, showing that they longed for loving relationships. While he recognized the power of female sexual desire, he argued that it had to be scrupulously controlled to avoid societal chaos or breakdown (Jamalzadeh 1947).

Others, such as Sadeq Chubak, who were influenced by social realism, wrote more freely about both male and female sexual desire. In his view, a woman's passion was neither a vice, the result of simple ignorance, nor of Western influences, as many had assumed, but a natural feeling, one that appeared in everyday life, during prayer, various religious rituals, or travels to shrines (Ghanoonparvar 1993, 268–275).

Sadeq Hedayat, the most creative writer of this generation, dealt with the pain of sexual desire and the traumas associated with modern marriage. Hedayat was influenced by Indian mysticism, as well as by a host of Western writers and thinkers, among them Nietzsche, Freud, Dostoevsky, Poe, Woolf, Proust, and Kafka. His stories depicted the gradual normalization of monogamous marriage and normative hetero-sexuality among the elite and the new middle classes, and the alienation that permeated an atomized, urbanized society (Fig. 5.7).

In France, Hedayat became familiar with the Parisian gay culture and explored the homoerotic writings of Oscar Wilde, André Gide, Marcel

Figure 5.7 Sadeq Hedayat

Proust, and Jean Cocteau ("Gerayesh-e Jensi" 2005, 20). His body of work expressed the dilemma of European-educated Iranian leftist intellectuals who returned home, full of excitement and socialist ideas. His characters faced disillusionment upon reaching the conclusion that pervasive illiteracy, poverty, excessive religiosity, and superstition have contributed to an insurmountable gulf between the masses and themselves as Westernized intellectuals ('Abedini 1990, 59; Katouzian 1991).

Hedayat focused on the unresolved Oedipal complex, as seen in stories exploring abusive relationships between mothers and sons, or mothers and daughters. Repressed desire and other bottled-up emotions produced authoritarian personalities with sadomasochistic tendencies that culminated in murder and suicide. Hedayat was concerned with everyday power and resistance. Often in his writings, desires that could not be gratified were channeled into religious devotion, asceticism, and sadomasochistic behavior, including child abuse. While Iranian nationalist poets celebrated the role of the mother, Hedayat problematized motherhood in some highly unconventional ways (Hedayat 1979, 206). Employing Freud's archetype of the domineering mother, Hedayat created elite male characters that had been traumatized by maternal figures. Excessive attachment to the mother and fear of the father kept the boy in a perpetual state of regression.

Hedayat's intellectual debt to Freud can be seen in his surrealist masterpiece, *The Blind Owl* ([1936] 1957), a tale with strong homoerotic overtones that was published the same year Iranian women were unveiled. Literary critic Michael Hillmann later suggested that *The Blind Owl* was "far and away the most important piece of fiction in the Persian language" (Hillmann 1978). The story concerns a poor painter driven to madness as a result of repeated encounters in dreams and hallucinations with a repulsive old man and a beautiful woman with magnificent eyes. The tale is told in the first-person singular and set in no particular time or place. As if to underscore their universality, the characters have no names, and are identified only through their familial relations or occupations, such as the Man, his Wife, the Aunt, the Odds-and-Ends Seller, and the Butcher. In the second part of the tale, the reader learns that the woman in the story (who looks just like the man's mother) is the man's wife. But the man cannot make love to her because she repulses him, even though he loves her. The wife has multiple affairs with men who often resemble the narrator's stepfather. In the end, while making love to his wife for the first time, the man kills her in a moment of passion. He then mutilates her body, places it in a suitcase, and buries it.

A generation of literary scholars has explored Hedayat's affinities to Freud. Meghdadi and Hamalian (1978) have pointed out that three prototypes appear under various guises and different names in the novel: the narrator, a father figure, and a mother figure. The central character is desperately in love with his mother (wife) and terrified by his stepfather (wife's lovers), but he reaches no healthy resolution of this Oedipal conflict. In this revised Freudian scheme, fear of castration does not lead to the emergence of a strong male ego and "normal" heterosexual desire. Rather, the woman/mother/whore is castrated/mutilated, making it impossible for the man to achieve pleasure in a heterosexual relationship.

Hedayat took Freudian theory to its logical conclusion. The urbanized, sexually emancipated women of Hedayat's stories, often nicknamed "whores," were simply too demanding. They emasculated men and drove them to insanity. This pattern repeated itself throughout his fiction. In *The Doll Behind the Curtain*, an Iranian man who is studying abroad finds it impossible to communicate with women or to engage in a hetero- sexual relationship (Hedayat 1993, 245–257). He can neither become intimate with his Iranian fiancée nor communicate with the European women he meets at school. The rituals of heterosexual courtship are too daunting for him. Women want men to entertain them. They want men who can dance and can "carry on a conversation with women, pursue them, dress well, give compliments on a variety of dreadful subjects" (Hedayat 1993, 251). The central character eventually falls in love with a mannequin in a European storefront. He purchases the life-sized doll, brings her back to Iran, and informs his relatives that he will never get married. *The Doll Behind the Curtain* bore some similarity to the story of "Pygmalion" by the Roman poet Ovid (d. 17 CE), where an artist falls in love with a beautiful statue of a woman. In "Pygmalion" the artist becomes ecstatic when his statue comes to life, whereas in *The Doll Behind the Curtain* the seeming animation of the mannequin terrifies the man who subsequently shoots her. In Hedayat's stories only silent, passive, or dead urban women could be loved, it appeared.

Can we conclude that Hedayat's anxieties stem from his anger at the compulsory heterosexuality of the modern urban world?[9] In his brilliant descriptions of the coffeehouses, caravansaries, and passion plays of Iran, Hedayat focused on rituals, mores, and beliefs that gave meaning to the lives of the poorer classes. He also scorned socialists who hoped to revolutionize and modernize Iran by recruiting the downtrodden masses. His poor characters were not naïve and simple, but clever, cunning, and

---

[9] Repulsed by a bourgeois capitalist order that created lonely individuals and sanctioned only heterosexual desires, Hedayat sometimes cherished the aristocratic, homoerotic values of what he saw as an Aryan, pre-Islamic Iranian society. This led him to a gross form of anti-Semitism toward both Arabs and Jews (Pirnazar 1995).

duplicitous. While the urban intellectuals of Hedayat's stories are paralyzed with fear, the dispossessed social classes rely on religion, destiny (*qesmat*), and sexuality to make sense of their chaotic world and downtrodden lives. Hedayat's stories portrayed masterfully the harsh lives of ordinary citizens, especially poor women, who were burdened with temporary marriages, multiple children, poverty, filth, and the sheer exhaustion of daily life. Indeed, he found more life, and more will to live, in the dirty, crowded dwellings of the masses than in the posh but intensely lonely abodes of the urban intellectuals depicted in his stories. Perhaps, like Foucault, Hedayat was fascinated by the gender roles of a world where individuals were not burdened by modern choices.[10]

In *'Alaviyeh Khanom* (Madam Alaviyeh), the story of a group of *ta'ziyeh* (passion play) performers on a pilgrimage to the city of Mashhad, Hedayat portrayed the sexual mores of the older Iranian society, where temporary marriage was routine, and heterosexuality was not a norm (Hedayat [1933] 1959). In the world of the protagonist 'Alaviyeh, groups of unrelated people often room together each night, and no one seems to obey the modern rules of sexual propriety that were gaining ground among the urbanized new middle classes. 'Alaviyeh has three or four affairs and temporary marriages in just one year. Twelve-year-old 'Esmat has also been married three times. The sexual identities of several characters of the story remain undefined. 'Alaviyeh is secretly the driver's mistress. She is blamed for sleeping with another male passenger and is accused of having lesbian sex (*tabaq zani*) with 'Esmat. Her young handsome employee, Mochul, who recites the passion plays, is labeled a "beardless boy."[11] After a fight with 'Alaviyeh, Mochul leaves the group and finds a job as a masseur in a public bath, a popular occupation for men with homosexual inclinations.

This busy world of dirt, poverty, and multiple sexualities stood in sharp contrast to Hedayat's comfortable, urban, upper-class world. Much like Nietzsche, Hedayat believed that the latter condition bred weak, indecisive, and effeminate men. Many of the intellectual men in his stories found compulsory heterosexuality unbearable. Occasionally, they obtained solace in fleeting homoerotic exchanges – a touch, a kiss, an embrace. But as the title of Hedayat's short story "Dead End" (1993, 295–312) suggested, there was no way out for them. They married under family pressure or for economic reasons. They experienced the wedding night as an unbearable humiliation and developed an abiding hatred for their "emasculating"

---

[10] We explored this side of Foucault in Afary and Anderson 2005; see also Almond 2004.

[11] *Mochul* was another common name for boy servants who were also boy concubines (Shahri 1990, VI:319).

wives. And, as with Hedayat himself in real life, who killed himself in 1951, they sometimes chose suicide as a way out.

The immense popularity of Hedayat's fiction in the 1930s and 1940s suggests that modern gender norms had created many new anxieties in upper- and middle-class society. For advocates of women's rights, these changes were the first steps toward the positive accomplishments of greater modernization and Westernization. But many men and women found these changes to be disconcerting and unsettling. Although most Iranians supported scientific and industrial forms of modernization, there was greater wariness concerning the cultural innovations of modernity. Some preferred the old order, with its intimate social relations and more ambiguous sexual practices, to the new, urbanized, alienated, capitalist order with its regulated heteronormativity and its demanding urban women. In this way, the negative verdict on modernity entered the cultural realm, as well as the political arena.

6 Imperialist politics, romantic love, and the impasse over women's suffrage

In August 1941, Allied forces occupied Iran, with the Soviet Union stationing forces in the north, and Britain taking control of the south. In September, the powers accused Reza Shah of pro-German sympathies and forced him to abdicate in favor of his twenty-two-year-old son, Muhammad Reza Shah (r. 1941–1979). Paradoxically, despite war and foreign occupation a weaker monarchy brought a degree of democratization to the nation. Progressive nationalists, both inside and outside the Parliament, revived the legacy of the constitutional era by campaigning for political reforms. Numerous political organizations and trade unions also emerged, among them the Stalinist Tudeh (Masses) Party.

Oil had become an important part of Iran's economy by the 1920s, and by World War II it assumed a pivotal place in the nation's international trade. As the war drew to an end in late 1944, the Soviet Union, competing with the West for postwar global hegemony, demanded the right to extract oil in the northern Caspian region. The Tudeh Party backed the Soviets, arguing that the United States and the Soviet Union should be treated equally and that Soviet demands for oil concessions be honored as part of the fight against fascism. But nationalists, led by MP Dr. Muhammad Mosaddeq, maintained that neither the Westerners nor the Soviets be given such lucrative concessions in the future.

A second postwar controversy was over the Soviet Union's political and military support for autonomy movements in the northwestern provinces of Azerbaijan and Kurdistan in 1945–1946. Iran protested to the United Nations, and the ensuing conflict between the United States and the Soviet Union over this issue became a marker in the emerging Cold War. In December 1946, the Iranian military moved back into Azerbaijan and Kurdistan, as the leaders of the two autonomous regions fled into the Soviet Union.

With the expansion of print media, radio, television, and cinema in the 1940s the modernization of gender and sexual relations accelerated. Ahmad Kasravi's campaign against the homoeroticism of classical Persian literature resulted in a nationwide discussion on the subject of pederasty.

References to the love of boys came to be censored in textbooks and even in new editions of classical poetry. A militant Islamist assassinated Kasravi in 1946 but Kasravi's ideas continued to be implemented in the nation's educational system. Classical poems were now illustrated by miniature paintings celebrating heterosexual, rather than homosexual, love and students were led to believe that the love object was always a woman, even when the text directly contradicted that assumption.

Mosaddeq formed the National Front in 1949, a democratic political opposition group composed of nationalist, liberal, and social democratic tendencies, and nationalized Iran's oil, ending Britain's extended period of control through the Anglo-Iranian Oil Company. In his role as Iran's prime minister (1951–1953), Mosaddeq infuriated British Prime Minister Winston Churchill who secretly called for his ouster. The November 1952 election of Dwight D. Eisenhower as US president ended US restraint in this matter and encouraged those in the CIA who backed British plans. Britain warned of a looming communist danger in Iran and pushed for a coup. A period of relative political freedom, which had begun in 1941, came to an abrupt halt as the joint Anglo-American-sponsored coup of August 1953 overthrew Mosaddeq and returned Muhammad Reza Shah to more absolute power.

Although Britain and the United States played the main roles in the coup, we will see below that differences within Mosaddeq's own coalition over broader social and cultural issues, including women's suffrage, contributed to the weakening of his government from within. In the crucial years 1951–1952, women's suffrage became a divisive issue within the nationalist movement. As in many other countries, Iranian leftist political parties made an arbitrary distinction between the educational, economic, and political rights of women, which they encouraged, and sexual and marital rights, which they advised against. Yet it was not easy to distinguish these two sets of rights from one another, as the conservative clerics knew well. The battle over women's suffrage and the empowerment of women, which nationalists and leftists supported and clerics opposed, contributed to the breakup of the nationalist coalition in early 1953 and facilitated the overthrow of the government soon afterwards.

The growth of communist sentiment and gender reforms

The 1940s brought several old and new gender concerns to the fore, including demands for companionate marriage, more attention to the concerns of working women, women's suffrage, and elimination of homo-erotic poems and prose from educational materials. Between 1941 and

1953 over seventy political parties and a dozen women's organizations were formed (Amin 2008, 8). With its progressive social agenda, the Tudeh Party, the country's largest and best-organized political party, attracted young intellectuals from all of Iran's religious and ethnic groups. Its women's branch, established in 1943, called for greater educational and employment opportunities for women, better working conditions, vacation time, childcare centers, equal pay, and colleges for women. In 1944–1945, Tudeh Party deputies and women leaders of the party called unsuccessfully for women's suffrage, while the Soviet-backed Democratic Party of Azerbaijan gave women the right to vote in party elections, a first for Iranian women (Vatandoust 1985, 110–111; Abrahamian 1982, 336; Behfar 2000b; Cottam 1979; Atabaki 1993).[1] The Tudeh also recruited impoverished women who struggled for workers' rights and organized trade unions. Some like Raziyeh Ebrahimzadeh took up revolvers, fought against the state, and endured years of imprisonment and torture in Pahlavi prisons. In the process, they also broke through centuries of class and gender barriers, becoming the harbingers of a new generation of leftist women (Ebrahimzadeh 1994).

While many aspects of the Tudeh platform gained the party a wide following among the educated public, including women students, the party eventually lost some of its appeal because it violated nationalist sensibilities by supporting Soviet demands for oil concessions and the autonomy movements of Azerbaijan and Kurdistan. The Tudeh Party functioned openly until 1949, when it was framed for an assassination attempt on the shah. However, the party operated semi-legally through a variety of front groups until 1953. It also continued to compete for influence in leftist and nationalist sections of opinion with the National Front.

The relatively open political climate and new economic opportunities of the era allowed more women to study at institutions of higher education, teach in schools, and work in factories and offices. A few women entered hitherto male-dominated professions such as medicine, law, and the natural sciences. Others earned degrees in the humanities and the social sciences. The progressive satirical newspaper *Baba Shamal* encouraged gender reforms and campaigned against the return of the veil (Figs. 6.1 and 6.2). In addition to the Tudeh-sponsored Democratic Union of Women (Jam'iyat-e Democrat-e Zanan), there were other left-leaning organizations which campaigned for suffrage such as the Women's Party (Hezb-e Zanan) and later the newspaper *Progressive Women* (Fig. 6.3), which supported the social democratic ideals of Khalil Maleki, a leftist

---

[1] Although a women's political party was formed in the Kurdish Republic, they did not gain the right to vote (Mojab 2001).

ــ دیدی ؟ ! خوب شد چادر را سرم انداختم،وإلا حالا پیرمردکه مچ مایـر را
گرفته بود !

Figure 6.1 Woman to lover: "Good thing I wore my veil or he would
have caught us," 1948

intellectual and nationalist who sided with Mosaddeq after breaking with
the Tudeh.

In 1945–1946, the Women's Party changed its name to the Women's
Council (Showra-ye Zanan), and became an umbrella organization of
several women's organizations. Members of the Women's Party such
as Fatimah Sayyah and Hajar Tarbiyat built international ties with
women's rights organizations in Turkey, Europe, and the United States
in their attempts to gain suffrage and demand "complete equality between
the sexes" (cited in Amin 2008, 9; see also Matin-Daftari 2001; Sedghi
2007, 94).

The various women's organizations of this period were independent
of the government, but most, with the notable exception of the Women's
Party, functioned exclusively as auxiliary branches of leftist or nationalist
political parties. In this period, such institutional subservience was not
unique to Iran but characterized women's organizations in many parts of
the world. Although women's demands were a priority, they were often
"secondary and subordinate" to those emphasized by the predominantly
male political parties (Sanasarian 1982, 73). A second problem was that in
the area of gender politics, a strict demarcation existed between economic

حاجی جون بیا ! مام بتو بیست در صد تخفیف میدهیم !

Figure 6.2 Sign on the door: "Twenty percent discount to veiled women." Flirtatious veiled woman to *bazaar* merchant: "Hajji, I will also give you twenty percent discount," 1947

or political rights, on the one hand, and sexual or personal ones, on the other. Leftist and nationalist parties recognized demands that pertained to the former – concerning employment, pay equity, health, education, and the right to vote. Other demands that would have granted women greater individual rights or challenged the marriage and family structure were deemed unacceptable, with some of the left labeling them "bourgeois."

This distinction was arbitrary at a time when gender relations, and especially the institution of marriage, were undergoing a profound transformation among the new middle classes (Fig. 6.4). These cultural shifts

Figure 6.3 Cover page of *Progressive Women*, spring 1952

were not very evident in the political tracts, but captured in the literary works of the period, as discussed below.

Classical literature and the normalization of heterosexuality

After 1941, Kasravi's secular ideological movement, the *Pak Dini*, gained many new supporters. Advocates formed an organization and published the widely read daily newspaper *Parcham* (Flag) (Jazayery 1978). They adhered to some progressive principles, supported land reform and greater rights for women, including unveiling and divorce, but only a modest education for girls, one that focused on home economics (Kasravi 1974,

Figure 6.4 Modern bride and groom, Anvar (Pirnazar) Afary and Naim
Afary, 1950

1–20). Kasravi continued his opposition to all "irrational" religious and
ideological beliefs such as Shiʿism and Sufism, and devoted himself to
social reform. Members of Parliament and public intellectuals took issue
with his condemnation of homoeroticism in Sufi poetry and the *Pak Dini*
festivals of book burning. This unleashed a "Great Debate" that reverberated throughout the country:

From the classrooms to the halls of *Majlis*, from newspaper offices to literary circles,
students and teachers, politicians and journalists, were involved in a nationwide
argument. Emotions ran high on both sides, but more on the side of Kasravi's
opponents. A Tehran newspaper, *Azad*, called for a national trial (*Muhakimi-ye
Milli*) for Kasravi for his persistent attacks on the poets. (Jazayery 1981, 315)

Kasravi's critics argued that he ignored the symbolic and representational
nature of Persian poetry, and that "words such as 'love,' 'lover,' 'beloved,'
'wine,' 'wine seller,' 'drunk,' 'beggar,' 'sodomite' (*shahedbaz*), 'cupbearer,'
'tavern,' and many others, designate[d] not their apparent meaning, but

much more sublime spiritual concepts" (Jazayery 1981, 319). Kasravi disagreed: "It is often clear from the context that the poet intended the original meanings – the real meanings – and that symbolic interpretations are out of the question" (Jazayery 1981, 319). Others claimed that the poets talked about homosexuality but "had not actually been homosexuals." Kasravi responded as the judge that he was: "No man in his right mind would confess to a crime, or an immoral crime, of which he was not guilty" (Jazayery 1981, 320). *Pak Dini*'s platform enraged not only many progressive intellectuals, but also Kasravi's conservative opponents, who were furious over his condemnation of Shi'ism and advocacy of secularism. He was prosecuted on charges of blasphemy and the burning of the Qur'an, charges he vehemently denied. In response to numerous death threats, Kasravi requested and received police protection. In March 1946, in the midst of his trial in the Palace of Justice in Tehran, Mojtaba Mir-Lowhi (a.k.a. Navvab Safavi), an Iranian theology student in Najaf and founder of the terrorist Islamist Fedayeen of Islam (Devotees of Islam) assassinated him, claiming to be carrying out a *fatwa* from a ranking cleric (Pakdaman 2001, 1–36).

Kasravi had based his opposition to the homoeroticism of classical poetry on several assumptions. He expected the young generation to study Western sciences in order to rebuild the nation, and he regarded Sufi poetry as a dangerous diversion. As preposterous as it might sound, Kasravi argued that the revival of Persian poetry was a grand conspiracy concocted by British and German Orientalists to divert the nation's youth from the revolutionary legacy of the Constitutional Revolution, and to encourage them toward useless and immoral pursuits (Kasravi [1944] 1977, 18–19). As a lawyer and a judge who had presided over many cases of rape and molestation, he was also concerned with the moral and psychological harm inflicted on boys in pederastic relationships, and he advocated capital punishment for men who had sexually abused children (Jazayery 1973, 198 n. 1).

Most supporters of women's rights sympathized with Kasravi's project because he encouraged the cultivation of monogamous, heterosexual love in marriage (Kasravi [1944] 1977, 129). Kasravi believed that the great poets had been irresponsible lovers of boys. Sa'di, for example, had followed a boy, pleaded with him to accept his love, had "an affair with him," and then begged the boy to return when the boy temporarily left him. Yet the poet discarded the lad as soon as he "grew a beard," without any care or concern for his future. Kasravi saw this as cruel and "despicable" conduct. He compared this episode to that of a man who chased a girl, promised to marry her if she had sex with him, then discarded her, saying, "How could I marry such a girl? I need an honorable wife" (Kasravi [1944] 1977, 129). In this period, neither Kasravi nor feminists distinguished between rape or molestation of boys and consensual same-sex relations between adults. Kasravi reiterated the old claim that the *ma'bun* was a deformed and degenerate man, but added a modernist, scientific rationale for this judgment:

A man's, a proper man's, sexual attraction can only be for a woman. Those who are attracted to boys, and cannot control themselves, are improper men. They have some feminine elements within them. Such men are base and disreputable. For they are neither man nor woman and are deprived of the positive attributes of both sexes. (Kasravi [1944] 1977, 132)

One vocal feminist critic of Kasravi was his contemporary Dr. Fatimah Sayyah, a distinguished professor of comparative literature at Tehran University, and a leader of the Women's Party. She took issue with his wholesale attacks on Western novels as "ahistorical" and "amoral." But even she agreed that a state commissioner should censor improper and sexually provocative literature and ban its translation into Persian (Behfar 2000a, 63). It would take another sixty years for some Iranian advocates of women's rights to accept homosexual love as a legitimate form of eros that was not in competition with their own project of women's emancipation.[2]

The modern woman of the 1940s

Several Western-educated literary writers joined the campaign for women's rights in the 1940s. The new gender expectations of the postwar years appeared in the works of writers such as Ali Dashti (d. 1982), but were best captured in the fiction of Bozorg 'Alavi (d. 1997), a leading novelist and a founder of the Tudeh Party who was a close friend of Sadeq Hedayat. 'Alavi's stories, which frequently deal with upper-class women in modern relationships, explored the hypocrisy of male politicians and intellectuals who claimed to support democracy and justice, yet maintained authoritarian and patriarchal relations at home. The urban women of 'Alavi's stories were passionate and devoted to companionate marriage. Many belonged to elite cultured families that held salons in their homes, discussed the latest artistic and political developments, and listened to Western classical music. 'Alavi wrote about the generational conflicts of his time, depicting politically active and idealistic youth who clashed with influential but conservative fathers, brothers, and uncles locked in the past. Young people often lost these battles, but not without putting up a fierce resistance ('Abedini 1990, 138–144).

In one short story, "The Letters" ("Namehha"), Shirin, the daughter of a corrupt judge, rebels against her father's misdeeds. Through a series of

[2] For more on Sayyah see Sedghi 2007, 92–93.

anonymous letters, Shirin secretly confronts her father with the many instances of his disregard for or abuse of the law. In the end, her father's refusal to acknowledge his mistakes leads Shirin to leave home and join the leftist movement. The story captures the progressive political milieu of these young activists in the 1940s:

He was used to their nightly comings and goings. Girls who were the same age as his daughter; boys who were younger than her; mature workers; people whom [the judge] knew through their files. They came quite often to his house. They sat down, talked, wrote, brought typewriters, mimeographed papers. They listened to speeches on the radio, discussed politics and literature, and argued about the writings of Sadeq Hedayat. Sometimes one talked and the others listened ... Some came to receive a recommendation from him through Shirin ... They often played a record on the gramophone ... held intimate discussions, laughed, and danced. Some were college classmates of Shirin; others knew her from high school. He had read all their files. The local police chief had informed him about all of them. ('Alavi 1978a, 16)

'Alavi's most acclaimed work, the novel *Her Eyes* (*Cheshmhayash*), published in 1952, also takes place in the milieu of leftist politics (1978c). It narrates the life of Farangis, a young aristocratic woman who becomes involved with leftist Iranian student groups while studying art in Europe. Farangis studies at the best schools but eventually realizes that she lacks the talent to succeed as an artist. This recognition drives her to thoughts of suicide, but later leads her to join the student activists. Through them, she becomes acquainted with Master Makan, a famous dissident artist back home. She returns to Iran, falls in love with Makan, and uses the sanctuary of her influential father's house to support the leftist underground movement. She secretly types the fliers of the organization and uses her connections with high government officials to release a dissident who has been arrested. Ultimately, she sacrifices her future for the sake of her lover. When Makan is arrested, Farangis offers herself in marriage to the chief of police, an old suitor of hers, in return for the freedom of Makan, whom she never sees again.

Here 'Alavi portrays a new generation of elite Iranian women. While in Europe, Farangis dates both Iranian and European men, and back in Iran she is free to choose her marriage partner. Her love for Makan encourages her activism, but when Farangis sells herself in marriage in return for Makan's freedom, the ungrateful Makan never fully comprehends her sacrifice. The novel is thus about a young, upper-class woman who does not follow the customary path of marriage and family. Farangis has the impudence to pursue the arts as a profession, the overconfidence to follow her dream in Europe, the courage to become an activist, and the boldness to think that after a few months she could lead the resistance inside Iran:

The thought took root in me that individual people, no matter how weak and insignificant, at certain times – in extraordinary times – could become the force for colossal change. Even the destiny of a nation could be tied to the heroism of an ordinary person – not even necessarily heroism – but the courage of a small person who, like a tiny cog, takes her place in a big machine. I saw myself as such an instrument and expected great results from this devotion. I told myself: the movement against despotism is finally growing in Iran. The center of this movement … is in Europe, and I will be the link with the cells in Iran. The person who runs the movement is Makan. I will be a small cog that takes a little bit of space in a big machine. I will forward the orders to him. Soon, I will become the leader of the resistance and then even Makan has to be under my control! ('Alavi 1978c, 114)

Although 'Alavi portrays Farangis as an independent and courageous person, her story suggests that a woman's transition to a modern lifestyle might not lead to greater happiness and fulfillment. Despite all the money spent on her, Farangis never develops a profession or a sustained intellectual or artistic interest, either before or after her political involvements. Later on in life she becomes lonely and unhappy, and it is implied that this is because she never remarries and has no children to preoccupy her.

Thousands of young Iranian women who became politically conscious in the 1940s and early 1950s came from more modest families than the fictional Farangis. Many shared her exuberance and idealism, feeling that they stood on the threshold of history and could make momentous changes in their personal lives, their marriages, and life of the nation. 'Alavi's writings express sympathy for these women who made brave choices – who broke through centuries-old cultural taboos, refused to settle for arranged marriages, and attempted to find partners they loved, even if the marriages were not always successful. On the whole, 'Alavi's stories expressed optimism about the future of marriage in a thoroughly modern Iranian society. In such a free and democratic society, where young people could freely choose their marriage partners, there would be no extramarital affairs and no divorces. Such idealistic views about marriage were undermined in the decades that followed as modern marriages revealed their own deep problems.

'Alavi's short story, "A Fortunate Woman" ("Yek Zan-e Khosh-bakht"), presents the central character, Aqdas Khanom, as fortunate because she is a modern woman who meets her husband at work and dates him briefly before marriage. Other women ask her if he loves her. She does not know how to answer this question and murmurs, "Well, it was better than marrying a suitor whom you had never had a chance to speak to before." When rumors spread that Aqdas Khanom's new husband is having multiple affairs, her relatives blame her. Surely, it is her fault for not knowing how to handle such a fine husband! Soon, her unfaithful husband takes a mistress who gives birth to a child. Driven to desperation by the daily taunts of her acquaintances, Aqdas Khanom commits suicide. The news of her sad death travels fast, perplexing her friends and family: "How could a woman who was deemed so fortunate by all, a girl who had taken such a revolutionary step of selecting her own marriage partner, die so quickly and after only a year and a few months of married life?" (1978b, 104). On her deathbed, Aqdas Khanom criticizes the semi-modern marriages of Iranian society for not being modern enough, and condemns traditions that prevent prospective couples from greater socializing. Her message is that in a thoroughly modern world, such misfortunes and mismatches could be avoided:

A suitor is an ugly thing. Can you imagine? ... I am not even discussing the ceremonial entry of his relatives. The woman is brought in, like a naked slave to be examined ... A man you do not know comes to your home. A man who wants to kiss your lips, to touch your body, a man who immediately considers himself your superior and master ...
  I had hardly met him when the family surrounded me; every day and every night they made snide remarks ... I had no alternative [but to marry him], even though I knew I was throwing myself into a dungeon. (1978b, 109–110)

Romantic love also found its way in real life and even in royal marriages. Muhammad Reza Shah's arranged marriage in 1939 to Fawzia (sister of King Farouk of Egypt) had ended in divorce in 1948. The shah's second marriage in 1951 to Soraya Esfandiari of the Bakhtiari tribe was politically motivated but there was something unusual about it. The two fell in love from the moment they laid eyes on each other and were not shy about their mutual affection. Soraya, whose mother was German, had lived in Europe for many years and considered herself both a Muslim and a Christian. The young shah adored her because of her modern European background, which was something they shared, as both had studied at Swiss boarding schools. An attractive and confident young woman considered by some to be arrogant and condescending, she spoke four languages and had hoped to become a movie actress before her marriage. Soraya brought the latest European clothing styles to the palace. On the evening of her engagement party, she wore a décolleté chiffon dress with a white mink cape, breaking decisively with the image of the cloistered and veiled Iranian woman (Fig. 6.5). Many fashionable elite women followed her example and scrupulously complied with Western fashion dictates.

However, as in every fairy tale, there were complications. Soraya could not conceive, and the shah's mother and sisters, as well as the shah himself, were anxious for a male heir. Several solutions to this problem were proposed. The shah had a daughter named Shahnaz from his first marriage, and Soraya hoped that this daughter would be designated the

Figure 6.5 Engagement ceremony of Muhammad Reza Shah and Soraya
Esfandiari

first woman to lead the country. Another solution was to select one of the
stepbrothers of the shah (but their mothers were members of the Qajar
family, making them ineligible) or the shah's young nephew Patrick
(whose father had died in a plane crash and was perfectly eligible) as the
designated heir. None of these solutions was acceptable to the shah or his
advisors. The shah proposed that he take a second wife (in a temporary
marriage) and divorce her after she produced an heir. But Soraya was too
modern to share her husband with a second wife. Thus, the marriage
ended in divorce in 1958, despite the apparent continuing affection
between the two (Soraya 2003). When the shah announced the divorce
on the radio in a broken voice, it was a sad day. Their divorce mirrored the
problems in the lives of many educated citizens of the new middle class,
who also seemed unable to reconcile the requirements of an extended
patriarchal family with the possibility of happiness in their personal lives.

"Put the modern women back in their place"

Although secular, democratic groups expanded in this period, the abdication of Reza Shah strengthened the culturally conservative clerics, whose influence had diminished sharply under his rule. Most clerics and their supporters immediately called for the return of the *chador* (Figs. 6.6 and 6.7).[3] In 1944, Ayatollah Tabataba'i Qomi issued a *fatwa* calling for the lifting of government restrictions on veiling, and a significant number

زن و مرد ایرانی دیروز

Figure 6.6 The heavenly couple of yesterday, 1942

---

[3] For a discussion of the activities of the conservative associations of this period, see Tavakoli-Targhi 2001b.

Figure 6.7 The devilish couple of today, 1942

of women from the old middle classes reverted to the *chador*. Some were persuaded by the clerics on moral grounds; others faced a hostile environment at home or in their neighborhoods; still others did so out of religious beliefs or because they rejected Western notions of propriety and aesthetics of the body. However, even these women adopted a more casual *chador* that loosely covered the body. Many members of the new middle classes chose to remain unveiled. The *chador* once again became both a class and a cultural marker, defining a person's economic standing and attitude toward modernity.

The clerics' insistence on reveiling led to a new debate on homosexuality as well. Some opponents of veiling asked why the same limitations were not imposed on youth who were inclined to homosexuality since "the *amrads*' unveiled faces" caused as much consternation as those of women. One religious authority gave the following answer:

Yes, in the case of the *amrads* too *hijab* would have been proper. However, here we are faced with a natural, God-given barrier, which has somewhat neutralized the matter and reduced the *fitnah* [chaos caused by sexuality] to a considerable degree. That natural barrier is the lack of active passion on the part of the *amrads*. It is obvious that their nature does not include erotic feelings and passion for intercourse with men. Therefore, in their mingling with people of their own sex, mutual attraction and magnetism does not exist … Since *amrads* lack passion and most have strong wills and are resilient, they are less attracted by men. (Ja'fariyan 2001, I:653–654)

Hence the old argument that the boy in a same-sex relationship had no erotic feelings continued to be upheld in some quarters. It followed that women were capable of erotic feelings, and hence had to be veiled. The above argument also suggested that the *amrad* was still an acceptable object of desire (Fig. 6.8).

The number of urban, middle-class women who lived the more modern lifestyle was small, but their presence was widely felt in society, from the streets and the schools to movie theatres and political rallies. Inside the Fourteenth Parliament, conservative deputies complained about the academic education of girls in the public schools. MP Majd Ziya'i, from the northwestern province of Zanjan, argued:

classes for women should be tailored to their essential needs … Girls should have strong bodies to be able to bear children. All this reading makes their souls exhausted and their bodies frail. My own daughter, who is attending the second year of high school, works like crazy to memorize things. I asked her about her courses, and she showed me several books of history, geography, and grammar, readings that would be difficult for boys in the fourth year of high school … What use is all of this knowledge for girls, to know about the geography of the rivers of Africa? Why should her precious life be wasted [with such learning]? Then I learned that she had thirteen additional books on geography, health, zoology, geometry, algebra, chemistry, grammar, English, Persian, drawing, mathematics, and home economics. A fifteen-year-old girl has to memorize all this. The Minister of Culture, who is a specialist in education, must not allow such useless programs. For next year, let us give the girls a few books in sewing, foreign languages, cooking, housekeeping, religion, and ethics. (Majd Ziya'i 1945, 1785)

Thanks to a new generation of liberal and leftist instructors, including many women, educators ignored such complaints, and urban, middle-class girls continued to receive roughly the same rigorous education as

Figure 6.8 Leili and Majnun at the theatre of the Parliament. Cartoonists used homoerotic depictions when exposing intimate political alliances in the state, 1943

boys in high schools.[4] My mother Anvar (Pirnazar) Afary, who was a student at Nourbakhsh High School in Tehran, recalls that in her all-girls high school, students could choose between Home Economics or Sciences as their major (Fig. 6.9). She chose Sciences and was very proud of her selection. In 1948 a debate took place in her school about the advantages and disadvantages of the two fields, in which 400 students

[4] From 1941 to 1958 the number of female teachers increased from around 300 to 1,500 (Arasteh 1969, 93).

Figure 6.9 Students at Nourbakhsh High School, 1948. First row, second person from left is Anvar Pirnazar

participated. One of the students read a selection from a small book by Zahra Kia-Khanlari, their Persian Literature teacher, who was the wife of the highly respected educator Parviz Natel-Khanlari. In this passage, Zahra Khanlari had encouraged girls to study home economics. Everyone was surprised by this contradiction, since Khanlari had a Ph.D. in Literature. She went to the podium and explained that she had written this book when she was only thirteen and had changed her mind since then. Not only Khanlari, who was the granddaughter of Sheikh Fazlollah Nuri, the arch-conservative cleric during the Constitutional Revolution, but thousands of others had also changed their minds and had come to value women's academic education.

Ruhollah Khomeini: jihadism and compromises with modernity

Outside the Parliament, Ruhollah Khomeini was gradually bolstering his credentials as a conservative religious figure. His 1943 book, *Kashf al-Asrar* (The Unveiling of Secrets), attacked the reforms of the Reza Shah era, and denounced secularists such as Kasravi (Moin 1999, 61–62; Behdad 1997). *Kashf al-Asrar* was a blueprint for a future Islamist regime that could coexist with the monarchy. Khomeini proposed a return to archaic laws of retribution (flogging adulterers, cutting off the hands of thieves) and supported a militant interpretation of *jihad* to achieve this end. He accepted some slight modifications in Shi'i rituals of purification in conformity with modern concepts of health and hygiene. His proposals regarding the state were also semi-modern. Khomeini condemned Reza Shah's policies of economic development, industrialization, conscription, and propaganda as corrupt and Westernized, but he endorsed these same policies under his proposed Islamist state. In such a state a militant army would proselytize, and a bureau of Islamic propaganda would labor to win the hearts and minds of the people and to challenge Western cultural modernity (Khomeini [1943] 1984, 311–12).

On gender, Khomeini made few compromises with modernity. He opposed unveiling, mixed schools, women's employment outside the home, and socializing between unmarried men and women. The unveiling of women symbolized all the evils committed by Reza Shah. Khomeini warned, "The unveiling of women has caused the ruin of female honor, the destruction of the family, and untold corruption and prostitution" (Khomeini [1943] 1984, 270–271). Khomeini was not alone in his opposition to veiling. In 1948 a group of fifteen *mojtaheds* had signed a *fatwa* banning unveiled women from shopping in the *bazaar* and markets (Akhavi 1980, 63).

Some militant clerics backed the Fedayeen Islam, and were inspired by Egypt's Muslim Brotherhood (Kazemi 1999). In 1950, Navvab Safavi, leader of the Fedayeen Islam, published a manifesto that stated: "Flames of passion rise from the naked bodies of immoral women and burn humanity into ashes ... Cinemas, theatres, novels, and songs teach crime and arouse passion" and therefore must be banned (cited in Arjomand 1984, 209). Safavi's manifesto curiously advocates the formation of houses all over the country to facilitate temporary marriage. Other publications of the Fedayeen Islam contained virulent attacks on Baha'is and demands to reimpose the poll tax on Christians and Jews (Kazemi 1999, 473; Tavakoli-Targhi 2001b).

Debates on women's suffrage

In 1951 the issue of women's suffrage moved to center stage. In the summer of 1944, the Democratic Union of Women introduced a women's suffrage bill with the assistance of Tudeh deputies in the Fourteenth Parliament. Women leaders of the party such as Fatimah Sayyah and Maryam Firouz later pursued these demands in letters to the prime minister and insisted that women be treated equally with men and given equal representation in the legislative and judiciary. They also pushed for gender equality in academic institutions, including the distinguished Academy of Literature and Art (Farhangestan-e Adab va Honar) (Behfar 2000b, 59). In the spring of 1946, Minister Mozaffar Firuz called for reform of electoral laws that would grant women the franchise according to the "United Nations Charter" ('Azimi 1999, 22–26). These measures were vociferously opposed by the clerics who found women's suffrage and communism, alongside anti-Baha'ism, useful issues for energizing their base (Akhavi 1980, 63).

By 1951, when the subject of suffrage came up again, thousands of women in Tehran and other major cities, many of whom sympathized with the Tudeh and other leftist parties, participated in various demonstrations for the right to vote (Paidar 1995, 134). Once Mosaddeq took office as prime minister, a few concrete measures to extend the vote were adopted. In September 1951, women were granted the right to vote and hold office in trade unions. In November 1952, they acquired the same rights in district and village council elections (Matin-Daftari 2001).

Opposition to changing gender roles was not limited to conservative clerics like Khomeini. It also existed within the National Front, among clerics and non-clerics who were politically and economically progressive, but more conservative on gender issues. The debate on women's rights continued to affect Mosaddeq's somewhat fragile nationalist coalition throughout this period.

In August 1952, Ayatollah Abu al-Qasem Kashani, a leading member of the National Front, became speaker of the Parliament. He was a close supporter of the Fedayeen Islam and a rival of Mosaddeq for the leadership of the National Front. The controversial Kashani, who supported Mossadeq for a while, but then crucially changed side, and was important in breaking up Mosaddeq's coalition, espoused radical economic and political reforms, including land reform (Akhavi 1988, 92, 102–103). But he rejected social reforms concerning women and repeatedly supported patriarchal gender roles. He sent strict directives to the Ministry of Education demanding the removal of female teachers from boys' schools and of male teachers from girls' schools. Because gender segregation was somewhat relaxed in sports and music, Kashani demanded the closure of the handful of mixed public swimming pools and the elimination of Western music from the public schools (Kashani 1983, I:203). He also warned the Women's Council (Showra-ye Zanan) that their calls for suffrage were dividing the country as it faced imperialist threats: "All citizens, whether men or women, should refrain from presenting any demands that under the current sensitive situation would lead to conflict and unrest. Such actions will create problems for the government, for the Parliament, and for the nation, and will ultimately benefit the foreigners" (Kashani 1983, III:192).

Mosaddeq's government presented its draft electoral law to the Parliament in December 1952. Activists were disappointed to learn that women's suffrage was not included in the proposal, and the weeks that followed saw a vigorous debate on suffrage. On December 30, 1952, MP Mahmoud Nariman, a strong supporter of Mosaddeq, declared:

Article 8 of the Supplementary Constitutional Law states, "The people of the Iranian state are to enjoy equal rights before the law," and since Iranian women are citizens of this nation, they therefore must be included in this article and should have equal rights in the electoral law. [Furthermore,] article 2 of the Constitution states, "the National Consultative Assembly represents the whole of the people of Persia, who participate in the economic and political affairs of the country." Therefore, [according to this article as well,] women should be able to take part in the affairs of the nation through the election of deputies. (Ettela'at, 9 Day 1331/December 30, 1952, 4)

Foreshadowing the stance of the Islamic Republic, conservative deputies condemned public demonstrations in support of women's suffrage, tying them to Western imperialist designs on Iran: "This scene we witnessed on Thursday, before the Parliament, was a warning signal. If this kind of commotion, uproar, and turmoil continues, the situation might become much more ominous. I dare swear that only the British imperialists would benefit from such an uproar. Women's entry into the election process not only fails to reduce our burdens, but would also add to our problems, since the vast majority of the nation opposes it" (Ettela'at, 14 Day 1331/ January 4, 1953, 4).

Both opponents and supporters of women's suffrage continued to sign petitions and debate their respective positions in the press. Opponents raised a number of familiar objections. They argued that men and women were not equal: "It was as if we asked the bee to give us milk, and the cow to give us honey." Moreover, even in Europe few women had ever amounted to anything, whether as political leaders or as scientists: "A woman's brain is simply too delicate and too weak to swim in the ocean of thoughts and ideas" (Ettela'at, 8 Day 1331/December 29, 1952, 4).

Opponents of women's suffrage belonged to diverse social classes, although the majority belonged to the old middle classes, including clerics, merchants, and artisans. The head of the Bureau of Islamic Propaganda submitted a petition with 400 signatures to the leading newspaper, Ettela'at. It stated that, according to the Qur'an, "Men have authority over women" (Qur'an 4:34). It also claimed, "the Muslim nation of Iran opposes the participation of any woman in the elections. We thereby express our contempt for such a measure." A second petition, signed by merchants and artisans and addressed to Kashani, went beyond a simple condemnation of suffrage and called for "the expulsion of all female employees from government offices" (Ettela'at, 10 Day 1331/December 31, 1952, 1–4).

Some progressives opposed women's suffrage on the grounds that elite men would dictate women's votes, and further manipulate the elections. Dr. Ali Shaygan, a close associate of Mosaddeq, argued, "If a majority of the nation approves of women's participation in the elections, Dr. Mosaddeq would agree to it. But it is obvious that the vast majority of Iranian men and women oppose women's suffrage ... Dr. Mosaddeq has found it necessary to revise the election law as a result of the voting fraud we witnessed in the election to the Seventeenth Parliament ... Heaven knows what would happen if women were to participate in the [next] elections!" (*Ettela'at*, 10 Day 1331/December 31, 1952, 1–4).

Male and female supporters of women's suffrage put forth their own interpretations of religious texts to buttress their demand for greater women's rights. In an article entitled, "Do Not Deny Literate Women," Hussein Shajareh compared Iranian women to French women who had finally received the right to vote after World War II. Shajareh wrote that Islam had generally treated men and women the same way, "except for inheritance rights." Moreover, Islam had granted women certain rights that European societies had not. While French medieval law had denied married women the right to administer their own business affairs and placed a number of burdens on them, Islam had not limited women in these ways:

Why, therefore, should we prevent them from participation in politics today and deny their involvement in social issues by depriving them of the right to vote? ... Why should we privilege men? This is a form of discrimination and despotism. A democratic regime is based on the rule of the people. Half of the people are men and the other half are women. Why should we elevate the men so high, and pull the women down so low? At any rate, at the present time we must at least give literate women the same rights we have given to illiterate men. (*Ettela'at*, 10 Day 1331/ December 31, 1952, 4)

Supporters of suffrage also appealed to international law. They argued, "women had gained the right to vote even in the most backward countries, so why should the educated and intelligent women of Iran be denied this right?" They delivered petitions to *Ettela'at* in support of suffrage and questioned women's continued disenfranchisement "alongside the insane, the youth, and the criminals." The National Organization of Women (Sazeman-e Zanan-e Iran) sent a telegram asking the United Nations to intervene on behalf of Iranian women: "In the Name of the United Nations Charter and the International Declaration of Human Rights, ask Iran to give its women the right to elect and to be elected" (*Ettela'at*, 8 Day 1331/December 29, 1952, 4).

In January 1953, a few days after the December 31 petition by merchants and clerics in opposition to women's suffrage and employment, the city of Qom exploded in violence. The clerics, *bazaar* merchants, and theology students were responding to a rally in which supposed members of the Tudeh Party had chanted, "Death to Islam and the Qur'an." Nearly thirty years later, it was revealed that *agents provocateurs* under the direction of Khomeini had posed as members of the Tudeh Party and staged the event (Kazemi 1999: 472). In response to this "blasphemy," the rioters of Qom burned down the shops of suspected Tudeh sympathizers. A steady stream of letters from clerics encouraged similar protests elsewhere. Mosaddeq feared further religious unrest. Concerned primarily with maintaining their fractious coalition government, supporters of women's suffrage abandoned the campaign (Matin-Daftari 2001). The issue of suffrage had caused serious divisions inside the fragile nationalist coalition. In January 1953, the same month that religious protesters rioted against the Tudeh Party, Kashani publicly broke with Mosaddeq and shifted his alliance to the shah, giving up his anti-imperialist stance as well.[5]

Historians have marveled at the ease with which the Anglo-American coup of 1953 was carried out, suggesting that the nationalist coalition was

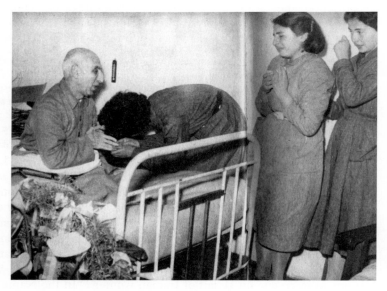

Figure 6.10 Muhammad Mosaddeq and high-school students, published on the anniversary of the August 1953 coup

---

[5] Kashani, Grand Ayatollah Boroujerdi, Navvab Safavi, and a number of other clerics openly backed the dismissal of Mosaddeq (Cottam 1979, 155–156; Gasiorowski 1987; Behdad 1997).

severely weakened before the coup. As in 1906–1911, Iran experienced the contradictions of a coalition between secular nationalists and politically progressive clerics. Mosaddeq had struggled to preserve the National Front at all costs, but the alliance fell apart because of its diverse ideological positions, not least on social and gender issues (Fig. 6.10). Recent writings on this period have documented American intrigues that fostered the breakdown of relations between Mosaddeq and the Tudeh Party just before the coup (Gasiorowski 1987; Kinzer 2003). While the United States and Britain played decisive roles in toppling Mosaddeq, the internal divisions in the nationalist coalition provided them with an opportunity to do so. Divergences within the National Front between the secular and religious factions over social and cultural issues, including women's rights, were crucial in the demise of the Mosaddeq government. A further complication was that not all advocates of women's rights were on the side of democracy. The shah's sister Ashraf and his wife Soraya had pushed for the ouster of Mosaddeq and backed the coup.

Close examination suggests that the political discourses and social affiliations of the major players in this period cannot be demarcated along strictly modernist versus anti-modernist lines. The same clerics who accused Mosaddeq of being too modern and too Westernized had no qualms about using modern technologies of power, including parliamentary politics, for their own purposes. Kashani supported the campaign to nationalize Iran's oil and sympathized with a number of leftist policies, including land reform. But he was against modernity when it challenged the patriarchal structure or redrew the boundaries between the public and private realms. Even Khomeini's far more conservative blueprint for an Islamist government embraced several modern institutions, including military conscription and a bureau of religious propaganda, provided they were under religious control. The reform bills of the Mosaddeq era, the new rights for women in trade unions and provincial councils, and the prospect of women's suffrage in national elections were all breaches of the conservative worldview of the clerics. In the end, the National Front cracked from within under the weight of these internal contradictions and disintegrated when Britain and the United States intervened.

7 Suffrage, marriage reforms, and the threat of female sexuality

Students and intellectuals largely supported the revolution of 1978–1979 which toppled the Pahlavi regime, hoping to see a more progressive social order in Iran. How and why they identified with Ayatollah Khomeini, ultimately making an Islamist theocracy possible, has continued to puzzle historians. Leftist intellectuals opposed Muhammad Reza Shah because he was backed by Western imperialist powers and because his reforms were "cosmetic" and "skin-deep." Although they supported in principle most of the gender reforms of the Pahlavi era, such as unveiling, employment, and greater social and political participation for women, they maintained that modern urban women indulged in a "vacuous modernity" of short skirts, makeup, and sexual frivolity, while the bulk of the population, especially peasant and working-class women, lacked basic requirements of life such as proper sanitation, clean water, decent schools, and adequate housing and food. While these critiques had validity, the leftists' comments also reflected their own deep sense of anxiety about the new gender relations introduced by greater interaction with Western modernity, especially the consumer society. The modernization projects of the authoritarian Pahlavi government might have had a limited scope in terms of the numbers of people who adopted a "modern" lifestyle, but Pahlavi modernization had a far greater symbolic impact, since its images permeated the new public spaces, including newspapers, television, cinema, billboards, the fashion industry, and popular magazines. Many urban homes had television by the late 1960s, and going to the movies was a popular form of entertainment. Pictures of women in revealing clothing and using provocative gestures filled the media. The advertising industry relentlessly propagated images of a more modern feminine body and a Western lifestyle. For their part, satirical magazines published cartoons featuring half-naked women. This served the dual purposes of lampooning the freedoms of modern women and advertising consumer products using attractive female bodies. In addition to being used as a marketing tool, women were also a prime target of the advertising industry. As the regime saw it, these changes in gender roles proved Iran's growing proximity to the West. Leftists saw this

198

as negative, however, and hostility to the new gender norms became the key factor cementing a political alliance that would have been unthinkable during the first half of the twentieth century, but nonetheless real now. This was a tenuous "Red–Black," anti-shah coalition of anti-imperialist leftists and conservative Islamists.

Ever since the Constitutional Revolution, advocates of modernity had pushed for greater women's rights through an implicit social contract. They had promised that if families encouraged educational and vocational opportunities for their daughters, these new rights would not interfere with society's expectations of women. It was unreservedly agreed that women would remain dutiful daughters, faithful wives, and self-sacrificing mothers, even as they assumed a more public role in society. Thus women's education would benefit the whole nation. But by the 1960s, a new generation of assertive women affiliated with the Parliament, the government bureaucracy, the legal system, and the universities began to undermine this implicit social contract by pushing for a series of new laws. Under the impact of second-wave feminism in the West, modern urban women demanded new legal, economic, and individual rights, including more rights in marriage. They also broke old sexual taboos, as seen in the feminist and sexually explicit poetry of Forough Farrokhzad. Her poems became the anthems of this new generation, shocking readers with their emotionally and sexually provocative messages. These events terminated the social contract over gender and galvanized a backlash against Western sexual mores, Western feminism, and the modern gay rights movement.

Foucault, Fromm, and modernity

Although the French post-structuralist philosopher Michel Foucault and the German critical theorist Erich Fromm belong to different branches of critical theory, both have theorized the impact of modernity on the family. Foucault concentrates on the eighteenth and nineteenth centuries, when Western societies developed new and increasingly detailed definitions of sexuality and began to control individual bodies in an attempt to reach maximum productivity and efficiency (Foucault [1976] 1980, 108). This process altered the role and function of the family. Foucault writes perceptively on how the new family, which was expected to respond to its members' diverse emotional and sexual needs, could not bear the boundaries imposed on it and gradually came under the scrutiny of medical doctors, especially psychiatrists. Henceforth, unhappy people were diagnosed with numerous mental "abnormalities," and the new field of psychology began to reshape them in order to fit them back into society, particularly into monogamous heterosexual marriages.

Foucault does not fully distinguish between the types of modernity that developed in France or the US and those that evolved in Germany in the 1930s. Research concerning commonalities among these forms of modernity, but also their differences, was a project of the Frankfurt School of critical theory, a group of exiles from Hitler's Germany who explored the roots of fascism. In their studies of the family, modernity, and authoritarianism, Erich Fromm and his colleagues Max Horkheimer and Theodor Adorno forged a synthesis of Marx, Freud, and Nietzsche, and concluded that the growth of individualism in modern Europe had resulted in a psychological trauma with significant political ramifications. As Fromm points out, modernity freed human beings from the hierarchical mold of medieval life, with its rigid class structure and well-known patterns of family obligations, and introduced the possibility of "freedom from" old social hierarchies. But the old social order had also provided a relative sense of security, because everyone's place in society had been predetermined. In the face of the economic instability and social atomization of the new liberal order, the modern notion of freedom became an unbearable burden for some, to whom freedom of choice meant insecurity and loss of identity (Fromm [1941] 1994, 35; 1955, 61). In Germany, this basic human desire for identity and rootedness led many to join the authoritarian Nazi movement. Some wished "to become one with the world by submission to a person, to a group, to an institution, to God," in order to transcend their loneliness and individual existence and to become "part of some body or something bigger than" themselves. Others expressed their desire for connectedness by moving in the opposite direction, toward domination of other people. An individual could "try to unite himself with the world by having power over it, by making others a part of himself and thus transcending his individual existence by domination" (Fromm 1955, 36). Through this symbiotic relation of submission and domination, a form of nonsexual sadomasochism, the individual gained a sense of attachment, direction, and power, though not necessarily a sense of integrity (Fromm 1955, 36; Chancer 2000).

These perspectives drawn from Foucault and Fromm can be applied to the Iranian situation in the 1970s as well.[1] Despite the many geographical, historical, and cultural differences between Iranian society and the modern Western ones studied by Foucault and by Fromm and the other members of the Frankfurt School, late twentieth-century Iran exhibited

[1] Fromm's works were well known to Persian readers in the 1970s, mainly his *Escape from Freedom* and *Art of Loving* and later *The Sane Society*. The average translator/reader found Fromm's prose much more accessible than that of other Frankfurt School theorists. Thanks to Ali Gheissari for his comments on this subject.

patterns similar to those in the West in the early twentieth century. The insights of the American feminist scholars Andrea Dworkin and Elinor Burkett, who studied right-wing women's groups in the United States, are also useful in illuminating Iran in the 1970s. These two feminist thinkers found patterns of uprootedness, loss of integrity, and symbiotic attachment to conservative movements on the part of women threatened by modern feminism, patterns that can also be seen in Iran (Dworkin 1983, 29; Burkett 1999).

Some followers of the Iranian Islamist movement of the 1960s and 1970s were ambitious men and women caught in a bind between premodern and modern social values. Many of them were the first members of their families to go to college. They gained a new sense of purpose and identity in the alien world of the secular university by embracing the Islamist movement's ethico-political structure. Many frequented the modern Islamist institutions where they found a new form of spirituality conducive to their academic achievements and more modern lives. In addition, large numbers of rural migrants had left the old hierarchical social order of the villages and moved into urban industrialized environments, where they experienced cultural alienation and psychological trauma. Cut off from their families and their ethnic and village networks, most of them barely eked out a living in cities whose mores they resented. In the West, as Foucault points out, the new middle classes turned to psychiatrists and psychologists, but in Iran, which had few such therapists, many members of old and new middle classes turned to religious institutions. In a modernizing authoritarian state, without any familiar safety net or cultural sense of affinity, the rural migrants found solace in the mosques and the new religious centers affiliated with the radical Islamists. Hardly any other public institutions had been established that could have provided them with a sense of community, and perhaps more importantly, basic forms of social assistance not offered by the state (Arjomand 1988, 97). Thus, at the Islamist centers, they might receive not only a comforting ideological message, but also more substantial things: food subsidies, better healthcare, and sometimes a small dowry for a daughter's wedding.

Economic development and suppression of dissent

After returning to power in 1953, Muhammad Reza Shah aligned Iran closely with the United States, which had succeeded Britain as the regime's main external support. With substantial revenues from both oil and US subsidies, a large-scale program of modernization was instituted. The Pahlavi regime trained a new generation of technocrats, encouraged industrialization and entrepreneurial activities, and created a new military. The shah spent the remainder of the 1950s eliminating his political opponents, particularly the Tudeh Party, the National Front, and other segments of the secular left, which he regarded as the most important threats to his regime. Mosaddeq was charged with high treason and tried by a military tribunal. He served three years in prison and was put under house arrest until his death in 1967. Labor unions came under the control of the state and business interests, with strikes declared illegal. Several hundred army officers sympathetic to the Tudeh Party were imprisoned or executed and the party itself banned. Liberal dissidents were silenced or co-opted by the regime. Martial law ended officially in 1957, but the newly formed SAVAK, a ruthless secret police force created with the aid of the CIA and Israel's Mossad, closely monitored and repressed the population, occasionally using torture. SAVAK agents were seemingly everywhere – in government offices, military barracks, private firms, university and school classrooms, and hospitals. Fear of arrest at the hands of SAVAK was pervasive, as the institution became a virtual panopticon in the Foucauldian sense.

Initially, the regime and the *ulama* seemed to get along well, in contrast to the Reza Shah era. To express his gratitude to those clerics who had backed him in 1953, the young Muhammad Reza Shah authorized a campaign against one of their *bêtes noires*, the Baha'is, and lifted some of the restrictions on Muharram festivities.[2] In these ways, the shah rewarded the clerics for their opposition to the left (Akhavi 1980, 77; Cottam 1988b, 113; Floor 1983, 80).

The White Revolution and women's suffrage

In the United States, a gradual shift in policy toward the Middle East was taking place. The 1960 election of John F. Kennedy signaled a further change in US policy in Iran. The Kennedy administration expressed some dissatisfaction with pro-US authoritarian rulers, including the shah, and encouraged greater political liberalization. To forestall communism, Kennedy's "New Frontier" proposed both a military buildup and internal democratization as key responses to the perceived threat of Soviet expansion. Between 1960 and 1963 the shah tried to present a more democratic face by establishing a state-sponsored two-party system, but he continued to manipulate elections to the Parliament, which caused

---

[2] Baha'is constituted Iran's largest non-Muslim minority. In 1979, the Baha'i community was estimated at 300,000, or less than 1 percent of the total population of some 40 million (Sanasarian 2000, 36–37).

repeated protests. In January 1963, in response to continued US pressure for reform, the shah launched his White Revolution, based on the following initiatives: land reform; sale of government lands to finance land reform; profit-sharing for workers in private-sector enterprises; nationalization of forests and pastures; a national literacy corps, which soon included women (Fig. 7.1); a health corps; a reconstruction and development corps; a series of urban and rural reconstruction projects aimed at building public baths, schools, and libraries, and installing water pumps; free and compulsory education for all children; and women's suffrage. Initially, women were granted only the right to elect and be

Figure 7.1 Women enlisted in literacy corps receive brief military training, 1968

elected to provincial councils. But after women civil servants staged peaceful protests to that end, the shah agreed to add full women's suffrage. The program of the White Revolution was put to a national referendum. The regime claimed that it passed by a landslide. While independent sources did not confirm this, it was clear that it had gained substantial support (Afkhami 2002, 124–136; Keddie 2003, 139–148).

The clerics strongly opposed these reforms, especially land reform and women's suffrage. Ruhollah Khomeini organized a gathering in Qom of senior clerics, who sent a telegram of protest to the shah:

> Women's entry into the Parliament breaks all rules of propriety and is against the *shari*ʿa. Moreover, it is against articles 2 and 27 of the Supplementary Constitutional Laws. The evils of women's entry into society and interaction between men and women are well known … Islam has made it clear what ought to be done with people who advocate the equality of rights for women in inheritance, in divorce, and such matters, which are essential doctrines of Islam. (*Asnad-e Enqelab-e Islami* 1995, 66–67)

All the high-ranking clerics stood opposed to the election of women to leadership positions (though not necessarily to their right to vote) on religious grounds. But they also asserted that such a move went against the constitution. In this way the ʿ*ulama* were able to enhance their nationalist credentials and present themselves as supporters of constitutionalism. As we have seen, women's suffrage had caused great controversy ever since it was first proposed during the Constitutional Revolution, and especially during the Mosaddeq era. In 1963, the National Front also came out against the White Revolution (including women's suffrage) because the reforms had not been the product of a democratic process.

The verdict on the White Revolution remains divided to this day. Supporters point to the fact that half of all village families became landowners, women were recognized as full citizens, and the literacy and health corps helped the village poor. Critics argue that land redistribution had few positive results and the White Revolution merely consolidated and centralized the shah's powers (Hooglund 1982). They note that peasants were not empowered. While the authority of big landlords was diminished, the reform had brought "peasants and nomads under direct government control" (Keddie 2003, 156). In many areas, the parcels of land were too small for farming, the new owners adopted inappropriate Western methods of farming, and the poorest peasants were left out of the program. The growth of mechanized agriculture and large agribusiness cooperatives pushed more villagers off the land and into the cities. Many sold their small parcels and moved to the city, in search of construction or factory work. For these and other reasons, a massive migration of villagers occurred. Between 1966 and 1978 at least 2 million villagers migrated to urban areas. The urban population of the nation increased from one-third of the total population in 1960 to one-half in 1978 (*Hesabha-ye Melli* 1981; Hooglund 1982, 147).

The new middle classes, though more prosperous, were also discontented. They did not gain the political reforms they had sought. The shah had intended to replace the authority of the old social classes (*bazaar* merchants, clerics, landowners, artisans) with that of a modern state and a Western-educated bureaucracy and business elite, but the prospect of independent centers of power frightened him. Thus, he refused to grant the new middle classes any meaningful voice in the decision-making process and prevented them from forming democratic political associations (Ashraf 1995, 19; Keddie 2003, 149–156).

The 1963 referendum, and the struggle against it, had another important effect, the realignment of the opposition. First, the struggle against the referendum brought the secular and religious opponents of the regime closer together. Second, it marked the end of the more secular National Front as the main opposition force and propelled to the center of opposition the more religious Iran Liberation Movement, led by Mehdi Bazargan and Ayatollah Mahmoud Taleqani (Chehabi 1990, 141–185; Floor 1983, 88). The most prominent leader of the religious opposition was Khomeini, who organized violent protests against the 1963 referendum. Later in 1964, Khomeini campaigned against the shah's granting of political immunity to American military personnel in Iran. While repeating past clerical diatribes against gender reforms and religious minorities, Khomeini added a new twist in his condemnations of the shah. He linked religious-based grievances to a type of anti-imperialist rhetoric that had up to then been more associated with the secular left. Khomeini was arrested and sent into exile first in Turkey and then in Najaf, Iraq.

By 1963, counting on US support and his new image as a reformist, the shah tightened the screws on the opposition. He outlawed the National Front and clamped down on the clerical opposition led by Khomeini. In the decade that followed, Iran experienced greater economic growth and relative political stability, thanks to increased oil revenues and the shah's friendly relations with the West. The government of Prime Minister Amir 'Abbas Hoveyda, whose father had been a Baha'i in his youth, oversaw the expansion of higher education. Many lower-middle-class students received financial aid to attend the new colleges and universities. These changes also benefited non-Muslims – Jews, Christians, Zoroastrians, and Baha'is – who entered educational, professional, and business careers in larger numbers than ever before. Iran's income substantially increased in the late 1960s and early 1970s when the shah negotiated a better deal with the international consortium and took some control over the production and sale of oil. Following the 1973 Arab–Israeli War, the shah led the efforts in OPEC to quadruple oil prices and further increased Iran's revenues. The additional income was used to accelerate the Five Year Plan and to purchase more sophisticated weaponry from abroad. Public discontent also increased, due to factors such as inflation, mass migration and urbanization, drastic food and housing shortages, and anger at conspicuous Western-style consumption on the part of the wealthy (Keddie 2003, 164–165). Public outrage at the regime also stemmed from cultural and social anxieties, especially regarding further changes in gender relations, which were fostered by the state-sponsored Women's Organization of Iran.

Urban gender reforms

Modernity, urbanization, and the new economy introduced many changes in women's lives. By 1966 nearly half of all boys and 35 percent of girls went to primary school (Bharier 1971, 38). In the 1960s and 1970s, improvements in health reduced infant mortality and helped create an increasingly youthful population. Although small, the proportion of women in the formal urban workforce increased gradually from 9 percent in 1956 to nearly 13 percent in 1976 (Nomani and Behdad 2006, 127; Kar 2000a, 141). Women remained a source of cheap labor in the older, labor-intensive industries and in the traditional, small-scale ones. The law required large modern firms to provide their employees with rudimentary day-care centers, social insurance, and healthcare facilities, though the smaller firms, where most women worked, were not required to offer such amenities (Ladjevardi 1985, 213–214). The law also required equal pay for equal work, regardless of gender, and a ban on child labor, but many factory managers ignored both of there policies (Sedghi 2007, 148). A majority of industrial workers in Tehran, many of them rural migrants, lived in more nuclear (and less extended) families, composed of husband, wife, and children. Often the elders and related kin arranged the marriage of the couple, with the young bride remaining least involved in these decisions (Vieille and Kotobi 1966). In some factories, however, demographic and economic changes were altering the institution of marriage. My father Naim Afary, manager of the Three Star Shoe Factory in Tehran, recalled that young women set aside their veil, and worked in uniforms and headscarves on the factory floor. Here, away from the authority of parents, men and women began to make their acquaintance, sometimes falling in love (Fig. 7.2). They depended less on their families for dowry and *mahriyeh*, as marriages became less strictly arranged (Interview, February 14, 2002).

Figure 7.2 Factory workers

By this time, a number of elite women already had important roles in national affairs. The shah's sister Ashraf Pahlavi headed several national and international organizations. In September 1963, six women entered the lower house of the Parliament, and two were appointed to the senate. Women could also enlist in the literacy corps, the army, the navy, and the air force (Sabahi 2002). Although their numbers were extremely small, images of women in uniform and at international festivals, sports events, and conferences filled popular magazines and helped to legitimize the shah's regime in the eyes of the Western world (Fig. 7.3).

Women's suffrage and greater involvement in the public sphere were decisive in ending the close alliance between the shah and the clerical establishment that had existed in the 1950s. The shah's statements on women's role in society confirmed that he was no feminist, but he did believe women's education and greater social participation would enhance the economy and contribute to the image of a modern nation that he wanted to project (Keddie 1981, 179).

Royal women provided a compromise figure between Western and Iranian models of femininity. The shah's personal life suggested some compromises between his role as a patriarch and as a modern brother and husband. Like Qajar princesses, royal Pahlavi princesses lived relatively

Figure 7.3 Soccer players

promiscuous lives by the standards of the times. This was known in
urban elite circles and tolerated by the shah. In 1959, with his youthful
and passionate marriage to Soraya behind him, the shah married Farah
Diba, whom the royal family chose while she was studying in France. After
a few brief meetings, the two were married in an ostentatious ceremony.
She soon provided him with a much-wanted heir, a boy they named Reza
(Fig. 7.4). Friendly, athletic, and immaculately dressed, Queen Farah,
who had studied architecture, helped to create a new image for Iranian
women. She became an international patron of the arts and supported
various philanthropic associations. She also held somewhat more liberal
political views than her husband and her powerful sister-in-law, Ashraf.
But given the twenty-year age difference between them and the shah's
numerous and barely concealed liaisons with other women, they did not
project the modernist ideal of companionate marriage very well. The
shah's affairs with glamorous women at home and abroad were kept off
the pages of the Iranian press, while Farah maintained the outward image
of a happy family. Women's journals were filled with the couple's pictures
on family vacations, and the queen never publicly expressed a whiff of
resentment, despite persistent rumors of discord ('Alam 2006).
    Women from the old middle classes of Tehran and northern cities
continued to wear a modified form of the *chador* or a large headscarf.

Figure 7.4 Muhammad Reza Shah, Queen Farah Diba, and their children

Without the face covering (*rubandeh*), the veil no longer provided anonymity, and the neighbors and community could monitor the comings
and goings of a veiled woman. As Michael Fischer (1978) has pointed
out, the veil now served as a "complex moral device" on at least several
levels. (1) The *chador* continued to give a highly religious woman the
freedom to use public spaces, including mosques, if she carried herself
according to the dictates of modesty, i.e. did not wear red nail polish,
laugh loudly, make eye contact with male pedestrians, or walk aimlessly.
(2) The *chador* was also a social and class marker, showing a woman's
community of origin and her degree of intimacy with the men around her.
Village women continued to walk about with head cloths but not veils;

Figure 7.5 Queen Farah and a group of northern women

working-class women tied their veils around their waists while working, in order to free their hands (Fig. 7.5); wealthy women of the old middle classes sported full veils, often black. Women loosened their veils around male relatives, but covered everything but an eye around strangers. (3) Many continued to use the veil for practical purposes: as protection from the elements, as a blanket when napping, as a towel after washing one's face, and as a cover for the breast during nursing. Modern women who usually went about unveiled sometimes resorted to the veil when they left home for a quick errand and did not feel like dressing up. (4) The veil also had religious and political significance. Women of all social classes and religious commitments wore their veils when entering shrines or going to Muharram religious gatherings.

By the 1970s, some college students had begun to wear a modified outfit, which soon became known simply as the *hijab*. Often, it expressed a woman's protest against both the regime and Westernized modernity. The young women's outfit consisted of a headscarf pulled over the forehead to cover all the hair, a loose tunic with long sleeves, and baggy pants (Fischer 1978, 207–208).[3] In contrast, women from the new middle and upper classes wore blue jeans or stylish miniskirts. Those who served in the health and literacy corps wore fitted uniforms ornamented with colorful scarves. High-school girls wore uniforms, though some who belonged to conservative families donned a *chador* to walk back and forth to school (Fischer 1978, 192).

The Women's Organization of Iran

In 1966, the shah approved the formation of the Women's Organization of Iran (WOI), chaired by his sister Princess Ashraf. While women's suffrage had a mainly symbolic value under the authoritarian regime, this was not the case with the changes in family law introduced by the WOI. These reforms gave urban, middle-class women greater control over their lives in matters such as marriage, divorce, and child custody, as well as diminishing the power of men. Under the leadership of the young, American-educated college teacher Mahnaz Afkhami, the WOI opened 400 branches, with a total membership of approximately 70,000. It set up centers for literacy and vocational training, healthcare, and legal counseling on marriage, divorce, and inheritance, as well as day-care facilities for urban lower-class women. At the initiative of WOI, the state provided three months' full maternity leave, which could be extended to seven months, and part-time employment for new mothers (Afkhami 2003, 266–267). The WOI also facilitated research on gender issues, such as critical studies of the sexist and derogatory portrayal of women in the media and in textbooks, which encouraged reforms in these areas. Others such as the American-educated Sattareh Farman Farmaian from the Qajar family established Family Planning Centers and trained a new generation of social workers (Farman Farmaian and Munker 1993). Many minority women affiliated with WOI also campaigned for the rights of women and children. Shamsi Hekmat, who served on the central committee of the WOI, successfully fought for women's inheritance rights in the Jewish community.

---

[3] The term *hijab* simply means "cover" in Arabic, from the root *hjb*, meaning "to cover, shelter or veil." Since the 1970s in Iran, however, *hijab* has also referred to this particular type of covering.

Mahnaz Afkhami recalls that WOI's programs evolved through communication and interaction with grassroots women who constituted the membership. Educated by the women it mobilized, from peasants and factory workers to urban professionals, WOI focused on economic self-sufficiency as the overriding purpose of its activities. Around the nucleus of vocational training and literacy classes, which provided job opportunities, a number of other needed services were developed. The opening of vocational classes quickly proved the necessity for instituting day-care centers. Childcare led to requests for better healthcare and birth control. Family planning led to the creation of village courts, where women received advice on divorce, child custody, and other legal matters. Afkhami suggests that members' concerns with social issues stood in inverse ratio to their class standing. Village and factory women were "extremely open and interested; they were brave, clearly saw their issues, spoke easily, were very eager to discuss their problems and even demanded from us what they expected" (Afkhami 2003, 67). Members of the upper classes were more vested in the patriarchal system and reluctant in their commitment to gender reforms. Professional women were somewhere in between. They were open to suggestions and did what was expected of them.

The organization was moderate in its expectations and sensitive toward social and cultural concerns. "Consciousness-raising" was the most important goal of the organization. But numerous other projects were also pursued. In a more urbane community, WOI would sponsor theatrical productions, while in a more devout area it might hold religious seminars. "In some classes all the women were veiled. In others they came unveiled. Elsewhere they would be half veiled and half unveiled. This flexibility made the organization very popular" (Afkhami 2003, 74). Gradually, unmarried young women also attended the meetings. Some clerics backed the organization. Future supporter of the 1979 revolution, Ayatollah Shariatmadari, for example, even allowed his two daughters to participate.

By 1973 it had become clear to the leadership that the old discourse to the effect that "women should be educated so they could be better mothers" was insufficient. Afkhami announced at a national meeting that women could not be expected to be fulltime mothers, wives, and modern workers, and that men and women should share the duties and responsibilities in the public and private spheres. "We are each and everyone of us a complete human being. We are not the other half of anyone or anything," she announced to a stunned group of delegates, whom, she recalled, received her statement with great applause (Afkhami 2003, 95–96).

Iran had become a world leader in the campaign for international women's rights. It was a relatively prosperous Third World country, a

Muslim nation with a government that supported women's organizations. It maintained good relations with the Eastern and Western blocs, as well as the non-aligned nations. Princess Ashraf led the UN Committee on Women at the International Women's Year Conference in Mexico in 1975 at which Afkhami also represented Iran. The Iranian delegation drafted a Plan of Action that was ratified by the conference. Arrangements were also made for a UN conference on women in Tehran in 1980, an event that eventually took place in Copenhagen because of the revolution (Afkhami 2003, 132).

The greater emphasis on women's education and the recruitment, from 1968 onward, of female high-school graduates into the literacy and health corps increased the number of female students at the elementary and high-school levels. Between 1970 and 1975, the number of girls attending school went up from 80,000 to 1.5 million, a significant gain, though still small given the total population of about 40 million. Half of all girls between six and ten were not attending school in 1974. The ratio of boys to girls was 3 to 1 in secondary schools (Menashri 1992, 183–184; Afkhami 1984, 335; Fischer 1978, 192). Shortly before the revolution, Fischer could write optimistically,

Today, there are few areas excluded to women; aside from an activist queen, there have been two women cabinet ministers [Farrokhrou Parsay, Minister of Education, and Mahnaz Afkhami, Minister of Women's Affairs], a number of senators and *Majles* representatives [fifteen women in the Twenty-Third Majles; three women in the Sixth Senate], mayors, city councilors, writers, architects, lawyers, doctors, senior civil servants, journalists, and university professors ... Iran still strains to catch up with Turkey, although it is decades ahead of Afghanistan and Saudi Arabia. (Fischer 1978, 191 fns. 3 and 5, 209, with bracketed insertions drawn from the footnotes) (Fig. 7.6)

Even *madrasahs* (religious seminaries) were changing. Qom had two *madrasahs* with separate classes for girls. The female teachers gave instruction in the classroom, and the males from behind a curtain. Women could become *mojtaheds* (jurisconsults), but their position was honorific since they could not issue *fatwas* for others (Fischer 1978, 210).

WOI's close identification with the Pahlavi family became more evident when the shah formed a new single party and asked all loyal citizens and associations, including WOI, to join it. Afkhami admits that in the highly traditionalist milieu of Iranian society it was easier to reform women's status by highlighting Pahlavi support for WOI. But in hindsight she laments the close identification of her organization with the royal court:

If Princess Ashraf or his majesty were interested in a project, or had certain views about it, many barriers before us were lifted, or perhaps we thought they were lifted. After a while we used the same strategy to prevent possible back-stabbing. I think this was a big mistake, which turned many groups, especially

Figure 7.6 Farrokhrou Parsay

intellectuals who opposed the shah, against our organization. ... In all the years I was head of the WOI neither [Princess Ashraf] nor the queen, nor the shah, nor the prime minister, nor anyone else, interfered in our affairs or gave us suggestions or advice, requested or ordered anything. We were the ones who used such "shorthand" methods to stop the opposition of the traditionalists and the bureaucrats as much as possible. Unfortunately more than twenty years after the Revolution I still have to answer for our own slogans, which had no relationship to the reality of our situation (Afkhami 2003, 217–218).

The WOI did play a role in the revolution though not the one its feminist leaders had expected. In 1978 many of its recruits joined the

Islamist demonstrations and lent their support to Ayatollah Khomeini. In one of the early demonstrations in the province of Kerman a group of veiled women joined the crowds against the Pahlavi regime. When Afkhami inquired about the political affiliations of the women, she was told by an executive secretary of WOI, "They are our own members. We kept saying, 'we should mobilize them', 'we should mobilize them'. We didn't say what we should mobilize them for. Now that they are mobilized, they say, 'death to the shah!' " (Afkhami 2003, 214).

Urban middle-class marriages

In the 1970s, urban marriages were becoming increasingly modern, and several months of courtship were now acceptable in the new middle classes, although both families had a voice in the process. Nobel Peace Prize Laureate Shirin Ebadi, who became a judge in 1975 at the age of twenty-eight, has recalled that she and her future husband Javad met through the recommendation of a mutual friend. After several informal meetings over coffee and ice cream, he proposed to her, but she suggested they see each other for another six months before making a decision. They met two or three times a week in Tehran's popular cafés and European-style restaurants, and eventually decided to marry. Javad then went through all the customary formalities of a betrothal. His family went to Shirin's house and asked for her hand, and they had a traditional wedding ceremony (Ebadi 2006, 27). Despite her otherwise extraordinary life, this account of her marriage was not so unusual for a person of her social position. Thousands of young urban women of her generation had similar opportunities. Most engagements led to marriage, but some were broken by the woman or the man. While a broken engagement would displease a young woman's family, there were no grave repercussions, and the girl usually found another suitor. Sexual mores were quietly changing among the new middle classes.

According to Tehran gynecologists, married women used birth control and continued to have abortions, now under the supervision of medical doctors. Some young urban women were engaging in premarital sex. When these relationships did not end in marriage, young women usually underwent hymen-repair operations, which remained "one of the most sought after procedures" (Bauer 1985, 122). Cyrus Pirnazar, a medical doctor and anesthesiologist, observed several such procedures in 1969–1971:

There were a lot of modern, urban girls between eighteen and twenty-four who were dating boys. Some tried to keep their virginity. Others went beyond casual contact and ventured into actual intercourse in certain times of the month to avoid pregnancy. When a serious suitor appeared on the horizon, the woman made an appointment with a gynecologist and arranged for a hymen-repair operation which cost 1,500 *tumans*. I understood that it was a prevalent practice among urban middle-class women. This relatively simple operation, which took 30–45 minutes, was sometimes performed in a hospital, where I gave them anesthesia. But it was often carried out in the privacy of a doctor's office, where the patient received local anesthesia. Women used their personal savings, asked the ex-boyfriend to help out, or if employed used their income. (Interview on January 7, 2007)

New marriage and divorce laws

The most important and controversial accomplishments of WOI were the 1967 Family Protection Law (and the 1975 amendment to it) and the Family Protection Courts, which dealt exclusively with family conflicts (Fig. 7.7). All marriage contracts now included certain rights to divorce for women (see text in Afkhami 2003, 253–264). These changes curtailed a man's uncontested authority to divorce his wife through repudiation at any time or for whatever reason. The Family Protection Law did not prevent a financially well-off man from taking a second wife, but it granted his first wife the right to sue for divorce in such a case. In 1976 regulations for taking a second wife, including temporary wives, became stricter. On January 7, 1975 the Minister of Justice Sadeq Ahmadi announced that while in the past multiple wives were permissible "Today, however, third and fourth wives are illegal, and the process of taking a second wife is

Figure 7.7 Family Protection Court, 1979. The speaker's face was blacked at the time of publication to protect anonymity

subject to several stiff conditions." A year later, on January 3, 1976, he issued a little-noticed and never-enforced circular to all offices of notary publics saying that a man who wished to take a *sigheh* wife was required "to make a declaration that at the time of taking the temporary wife he was not married to another woman" (*Echo of Iran: Iran Almanac* 1976, 351; see also Floor 2008). Thus as a matter of policy, though not reality, temporary marriage became illegal for already married men.

The WOI also succeeded in raising the legal age for marriage to eighteen for women and to twenty for men. In addition, a series of "internal memos" by the Ministry of Health, the Ministry of Justice, and the WOI tacitly legalized abortion (see text in Bagley 1971, 59–64; Afkhami 1984, 333; Afkhami 2003, 268–269). Still there were loopholes. Fathers could legally petition to marry off their daughters before eighteen (but not before fifteen). Also in poor urban and rural communities many continued to arrange a *sigheh* marriage for their daughters soon after menarche.

The greatest limitation of the Family Protection Law was the lack of financial support for divorced women. Neither the earlier Civil Code nor the Family Protection Law gave women any share in the property that the couple had acquired during their marriage. Still, as a result of these reforms, modern urban women seemed more confident about their place in the family and society. Many felt that life was getting better, this at a time when the standard of living was also improving. They dressed according to the dictates of fashion as much as their means allowed. They were also more assertive at home and in public. But the reforms had angered many urban men, both Muslim and non-Muslim, who complained that "uppity," educated women had stopped being loyal and subservient wives, also worrying that women were initiating more divorces. Many mothers-in-law agreed with this assessment. They might encourage more education and employment for their daughters but preferred more docile wives for their sons.

The Family Protection Law increased female-initiated divorces in urban communities (Ahmadi-Khorasani and Ardalan 2003, 284–285). As I recall from my own youth in Tehran, many such divorces were requested by young women who had chosen their husbands more or less freely, but became fed up with their husband's violence or extramarital affairs. Society was coming to the realization that a woman's freedom of choice in marriage did not necessarily produce permanent unions free of rancor. This led many to question the wisdom of modern marriages and to speak in favor of traditional marriages, which were widely seen as more stable. The perception that Iranian society was experiencing a higher rate of divorce was inaccurate, however. In fact the opposite was taking place. Although female-initiated divorces had increased, divorce rates overall had plummeted once men lost the right to repudiation and had to petition a court for divorce. As sociologist Akbar Aghajanian has shown, in 1966 the Iranian divorce rate (165 per 1,000 marriages) was higher than that of many Western European countries and several other Middle Eastern ones such as Iraq, Turkey, or Syria. After the introduction of the Family Protection Law, however, the Iranian divorce rate dropped by more than half to 81 per 1,000 marriages by 1978 (Aghajanian 1986, 750).

What really upset much of the public was the increase in the number of divorced women who were now living independently. Between 1966 and 1976 the share of female-headed households increased from 6.4 percent to 7.3 percent. In premodern Iranian society, young divorcees would become the second ʿaqdi or sigheh of a more well-to-do man, or would be absorbed into the large extended family networks. With the growth of monogamy and the nuclear family, and the emergence of greater educational and professional opportunities for women, more and more divorced women chose not to remarry and instead took a job and sometimes lived alone. This new phenomenon, combined with the high divorce rates in Europe and the United States, gave the impression to Iranian families that the same was happening in Iran (General Census 1966; Census of Population 1976; e-mail from Akbar Aghajanian July 2, 2008).

In 1975, the WOI was able to legalize an unprecedented right for Iranian women – a widow's right to custody (and sometimes legal guardianship) of her children. The courts gradually extended this right, sometimes granting divorced mothers custody of their children until the age of eighteen, as long as the mother did not remarry (Afkhami 1984, 333).

Among the other activities of the WOI was the campaign against honor killings. In the 1970s, WOI began the first movement against such killings in the region, with the publication of a book titled, *Wife Murder in the Name of Honor*. This publication brought great attention to the unjust law of French origin that had given a man the right to kill his wife (or sister or daughter) if he found her (or suspected her to be) in a compromising situation with an unrelated man. After much debate and struggle, the government finally agreed to amend the law (Afkhami 2003, 111).

Despite the WOI's many positive accomplishments, its secular orientation and close ties to the regime made it unpopular with the more religious sectors of society (Afkhami 2003). Conservative clerics portrayed feminism as a foreign, elitist concept aimed at the destruction of the Muslim family. Also, since all educational and social institutions were under the strict scrutiny of the secret police, and since Princess Ashraf remained the nominal head of the WOI, a wide gulf separated these pro-regime feminists from the popular opposition to the regime, including the leftist opposition, which attacked the regime's gender reforms as elitist and of relevance only to educated urban women.

Rural marriages and bikini-clad models

Despite such dramatic changes that affected women in urban middle-class communities, the institution of marriage remained much the same in many poor rural and urban communities. Paula Drew, a British cultural anthropologist, lived in Iran between 1964 and 1978, conducting her research in Tabriz and rural areas around Qom, and running a clinic for mothers and babies in an oasis community. Drew reported that rural marriages in her area were still entirely arranged by parents, even when based on mutual attraction. Though young people fell in love, such attachments were ignored or scorned by the family if social and financial considerations or kin approval were lacking. Girls were married at the onset of menarche and boys after puberty and after beginning to grow a mustache. The Compulsory Education Act of 1953 had required children of both sexes to stay in school until the age of fifteen, but parents were reluctant to send their post-pubescent daughters to school because of the increasing presence of male teachers, and because parents wished to marry their daughters earlier (Drew 1997).

Virginity remained a great concern within most urban and rural families, which meant that a divorced woman was still more marriageable than an unmarried one who was suspected of having an affair. However, some northern rural communities remained less strict and once a girl was engaged, the couple were allowed to spend time with one another (Bauer 1985, 121–122). As in many other parts of the world, after marriage men spoke of women as adversaries who had to be conquered and the young groom was ridiculed if he deferred to his wife. The groom's mother controlled the sleeping arrangements of the couple and knew their sexual habits. Drew points out that mothers-in-law rejected some modern conveniences that reduced their ability to spy on others:

There is a strong resistance among older women to the growing practice of installing hot water systems in the home. Although simplifying their dish-washing and laundry tasks, an automatic hot water system interferes with their ability to supervise the bathing practices of their husbands, offspring, and daughters-in-law, and thereby keeping tabs on their sexual behavior. Even in houses with a shower, the matriarch of the household often controls the means of igniting the hot water system. Similarly, she controls the supply of laundered undergarments and towels, keeping them tied up in bundles so that nobody can retrieve these essentials without her help. (Drew 1997)

Sex remained a common subject of conversation in village life. Sociologist Paul Vieille, who with a team of Iranian sociologists conducted research on peasants and industrial workers in and around Tehran from 1960 to 1968, points to its centrality: "The phallus dominates daily life, and it would not be exaggerating to speak of Iranian peasant society as a society centered on sexuality." People talked routinely about sexual matters: "Jokes, sexual boasting, questioning others' sexuality, fears for one's own sexuality, erotic stimulation" were among the topics discussed among men, among women, and even between men and women (Vieille 1978, 461–462).

Vieille's research found clear gender divisions. Only men had the right to express their desire. Women were seen as capable of erotic feelings, though their sexual activity was to serve their husbands' desire (Vieille 1978, 465). Although men expressed the wish to include women in their pleasure, they seemed to have little understanding or inclination to induce orgasm through foreplay. Moreover, there was little communication between husband and wife during or after sex. "The sexual act begins with intromission and ends with ejaculation, so that man and woman are physically united only in coitus ... sexuality thus appears to limit itself quite rigorously to coitus" (Vieille 1978, 462).[4]

Monogamy was still the norm in rural and migrant communities while temporary marriage remained less common. "Temporary marriage hardly flourishes, except around the great sanctuaries and places of pilgrimage, as brothels were formerly near the cathedrals of the West" (Vieille 1978, 466). Among more entrepreneurial and well-off artisans and village clerics *sigheh* provided men with cheap labor (often carpet weaving) as well as sexual gratification.

Villagers came in contact with modern sexual mores, however. American car ads, which displayed women in bikinis spread over massive Oldsmobile and Buicks, were common sights in Iran in the 1950s and 1960s. Semi-naked women could also be seen in ads for Western and Indian movies, for example in posters for James Bond movies. Home-grown tabloids such as *Ettelaʿat Haftegi* ran similarly revealing images. These pictures adorned coffee shops, garages, and even private sections of homes. Migrants often brought them back to the village as souvenirs.[5]

After 1967, state health programs included birth control. By 1973 fertility rates and infant mortality rates began to drop. Still despite the efforts of the WOI, modern means of birth control remained unpopular because of vast illiteracy and men's greater authority in sexual matters. In addition to *coitus interruptus*, anal penetration remained a common form of birth control, also used during menses (Drew 1997). A state report in 1973 concludes:

[4] Vieille also reminds us that there are no religious or cultural prohibitions to inducing female orgasm (Vieille 1978, 462).
[5] Thanks to Ali Gheissari for information on some of these practices. See also Drew 1997.

Another goal of family planning is to teach people that women also have a right to control their fertility. Both women and men should have a right to decide on the number of children they want. Elementary and secondary schools should teach youth that impregnating a women is not a sign of manliness ... Health and family planning ought to become a mass movement, beginning with villages and until a time when no unplanned and unwanted child is born. (Farrokhi 1973, 29)

Iran did eventually have such a mass movement for birth control but not in the Pahlavi era. Instead, by the mid-1970s the contradiction between the public display of bikini-clad Western models and actresses and village sexual practices pointed to the deep schism that had emerged in Iranian society. Beneath the seemingly placid surface of the shah's rapid modernization and secularization programs, a great well of sexual anxiety was developing. Villagers moved to the cities or sent their sons and daughters to urban areas to earn additional income, where they usually entered domestic service or became construction workers. The more the migrants were exposed to modern gender and sexual mores, the more they felt confused and perplexed about their village-based identity.

Sexism, erotica, and female desire

After the 1953 coup, Iranian literature experienced a crisis. A new literature expressed a sense of nihilism, and intellectual renunciation replaced the idealistic and committed literature of the 1940s. This was a melancholy generation "whose past was lost and whose future was stolen" ('Abedini 1990, 194). Many literary figures turned their backs on political and social commitment and aspired to the good life evoked by Hollywood movies. Some abandoned writing altogether. Others turned to translating Western works. Still others chose exile. Those who stayed in Iran often became more interested in religious themes in order to instigate a broad opposition to the shah. Each year, only about 660 books were published. In contrast, by 1973–1974 there were 432 movie theatres in the nation, with a potential daily seating capacity of nearly 300,000, 122 of them in Tehran (Naficy forthcoming).

By the 1960s, both the new and the old urban middle classes started to purchase television sets. Portable projectors showed documentary and feature films in many schools and small villages. The resultant exposure to the lifestyles of the rich and famous in the West had a profound impact on the public. At the time, the talk-show host and psychologist Naser al-Din Saheb al-Zamani complained that Western films

have helped create and intensify a sense of inferiority, dissatisfaction with and desire to escape from Iranian culture in order to blindly imitate Western cultural practices. Such sentiments have spread dramatically among our youth ... The easiest way to see this influence is through the spread of fashion, changes in taste, and people's modes of behavior. We have all seen how the imitation of a new style of dress worn by an actress, or the beautiful new hairdo of a popular star, travels with dramatic speed in our society. ([1964] 1999, 180–181)

Many popular journals and magazines followed the lead of the movie industry and turned to the subject of sex. Erotica and soft pornography became prominent and moved beyond the earlier focus on prostitution. By focusing on heterosexual love and sex, these media continued to encourage normative heterosexuality. In the guise of ethical advice to young people, authors such as R. E'temadi published serial novels about life in crime-ridden Tehran. These stories focused on young provincial students who came to the city to study but were sucked into the urban pathologies of addiction, alcoholism, sexual experimentation, and murder ('Abedini 1990, 200). This new and titillating literature, which was influenced by Indian, Turkish, and Japanese cinema, appeared everywhere, including respectable mainstream publications that supported modern reforms and even some women's journals.

Though most erotic texts were written by men and for men, a popular female cabaret singer made a unique contribution to this genre. Mahvash's *Secret of Sexual Fulfillment (Raz-e Kamyabi-ye Jensi)* was read by tens of thousands of people and went through more than ten editions (Mahvash 1957; Chehabi 2000, 160–162). The book, which was written in the guise of an autobiography and was rumored to have been composed with the help of journalist Ahmad Soroush, was part advice manual on marriage, part erotica, and part frank discussion of sexuality by a former prostitute (Mahvash 1957, 67).

The sections that read like advice manuals were not unlike the 1890s' *Ta'dib al-Nisvan* (Disciplining of Women) discussed in chapter 4. The author lectured women on cleanliness, charm and beauty, and fashionable clothes. She also told them to be flirtatious toward their husbands (and even toward other men) as a way of sustaining their husband's attention (Mahvash 1957, 21). In the erotic part she narrated tales of her supposed two marriages. The first was to a sadistic man who tormented her sexually, the second to an impotent man who enjoyed sharing his wife with others. Later, she worked as a prostitute in *Shahr-e Now*, the red-light district of Tehran, where she was discovered for her singing talents (54–67).

But *Secrets of Sexual Fulfillment* also made some keen observations about sexual practices in contemporary Iranian society. The author blamed parents for children's total ignorance of sexual functions, procreation, and sexual pleasure (Mahvash 1957, 8). It assured young people that masturbation in moderation was common and harmless (44–45). It urged parents to allow both boys and girls to date to ensure sexual compatibility before marriage. Men should be gentle on their wedding night, since a rough defloration could lead to a permanent loss of interest in sex on the part of the wife (51). A good husband kissed and caressed his wife's body, since "many secrets would be revealed through such caresses" (38). A loving husband made sure his wife reached orgasm, preferably simultaneously with him (40). Some women committed adultery because their husbands could not satisfy them sexually, either out of ignorance or because the men were much older and no longer interested in sex. Others sought solace in another man's arms because of their husband's infidelity (12).

Secrets devoted a section to homosexuality, which the book linked to lack of contact with members of the opposite sex. In this view, many engaged in homosexual relations when they shared a bed in "schools, prisons, hospitals, homes" in their youth (Mahvash 1957, 46). "Girls also engaged in sex with one another, and women drew close, and in a sad way gratified each other, as is commonly known in a lesbian relation (*tabaq-mizanand*)" (48). The author believed that these various forms of sexual deprivation resulted in prostitution and suggested that Iranian society accept healthy sexual interaction between men and women and legalize prostitution. Like France, Iran should grant legal recognition to sex workers, both to control the spread of venereal disease and to provide a more decent living for these women (49).

In polite society erotica appeared in other guises. *Towfiq* (1922–1970) was the country's most popular satirical magazine. Its illustrations lampooned Members of Parliament and government ministers, including Prime Minister Amir-ʿAbbas Hoveyda (though never the royal family), in bold and glossy sketches that usually managed to pass the censors. The journal opposed the Vietnam War and US foreign policy at a time when the shah had close ties with the United States. But *Towfiq*, which supported unveiling, also ridiculed modern urban women in semi-pornographic cartoons. In this respect, it was not so different from men's magazines in the West or Japan, with cartoons that displayed erotica and pornography.

Two kinds of women usually appeared in the paper's pages: (1) the tired and exhausted mother of the house, with numerous children, who constantly nagged her overworked husband about lack of money, and (2) the female sex object who was a student, a secretary, a nurse, a police officer, or a newly married woman. These young women were drawn with exaggerated features. They had protruding busts, small waists, voluptuous lips, and wore miniskirts. *Towfiq* seemed to express the sentiments of many Iranian men who saw their wives of many years as heavy financial burdens but saw other, younger women as potential sexual conquests.

Figure 7.8 Doctor to nurse: "The patient's heart races whenever you are in the room. You should leave to save his life!," *Towfiq* 1966

Nurses and secretaries were routinely portrayed as sexual objects (Fig. 7.8). Seemingly, their main purpose was to provide gratification for male employers and co-workers. In the pages of *Towfiq*, sex between a secretary and her boss or a nurse and a doctor in the hospital was commonplace (Fig. 7.9). In the cartoons men routinely pinched women on the streets of the big cities, and women were depicted as finding this a big compliment. *Towfiq*'s essays echoed the views of many conservatives, such as the historian Ja'far Shahri, who claimed years later that in the 1960s "the streets, towns, cities and villages were all filled with such prostitutes. The offices had become almost whorehouses to the point where only willing!! women were employed. Television and radio programs provided guides to such immoralities" (Shahri 1990, VI:297; exclamation points in the original). A 1959 cartoon in *Towfiq* suggested that unveiled women in Western dress had overstepped the boundaries of morality by appearing practically naked in public. The solution was to pass a law prohibiting such displays of "nudity" (Fig. 7.10). In another instance, *Towfiq* chose a simple construction worker ('*amaleh*), a transplanted rural peasant who had sexually harassed a young urban woman, as "Man of the Year" (Fig. 7.11). This type of satire, which targeted young modern women, for 1968 found a wide audience, which added to the paper's popularity.

Figure 7.9 Wife and secretary, *Towfiq* 1966

Also in its discussions of politics, *Towfiq* often attacked fashionable young women, accusing them of ignoring national concerns by purchasing Western consumer goods instead of products made at home. Men, and therefore the nation, were going bankrupt because women spent too much money on their makeup and clothing. A characteristic cartoon showed a man who had spent so much money on the appearance of his unveiled wife that *he* had to veil himself to escape his creditors. In these ways, *Towfiq* contributed to a new and contradictory discourse on gender and sexuality. (1) It presented female bodies as objects of desire; (2) it simultaneously degraded women and reduced them to sexual objects; and (3) it blamed modern urban women for male aggression in the public sphere, excessive consumerism, and even the nation's economic woes.

In the eyes of the old middle classes, women's emancipation and feminism became indistinguishable from the embrace of erotica by the media and Western consumerism. Often, the two were linked, as in many advertisements or in the "sex flick" genre of Iranian commercial cinema. Ads for cars, typewriters, and refrigerators routinely used sex.

Progressive intellectuals who continued to write about social and gender reforms were equally hesitant about women's rights. Because the authoritarian state had made gender reforms part of its social agenda,

Figure 7.10 The alleged undressing of women, from unveiling in 1936
to nudity in 1960, requiring "Anti-Pornography Laws," *Towfiq* 1960.
Published on the anniversary of Unveiling, known officially as
"Women's Day"

many writers trivialized and condemned such reforms in their protests
against the regime.

Even a best-selling novel about polygamy could not escape this duality.
Ali Muhammad Afghani's *Ahu Khanom's Husband* (*Showhar-e Ahu
Khanom*) was named the best book of the year in 1961 by the Society of
Iranian Books (Afghani 1962; 'Abedini 1990, 296). The novel, which
later became the basis of a popular film, focuses on a fifty-year-old baker
named Seyyed Miran who falls in love with Homa, a divorced beauty.
Seyyed Miran is already married to Ahu Khanom, the protagonist in the
story, and they have four children. Afghani produces a compassionate

Figure 7.11 "Man of the Year," *Towfiq* 1968

portrait of Ahu Khanom, a devoted working-class mother and wife, who endures a hellish life alongside her new co-wife. Homa, a modern and ambitious dancer with loose morals, is the novel's villain. After their marriage, Homa drives Seyyed Miran into bankruptcy with her extravagant expenditures on clothing and entertainment. In the novel's happy ending, Ahu Khanom reclaims her husband despite all the humiliation she has endured, while Homa leaves in search of another prosperous man to support her expensive tastes.

On one level, the novel is reformist in its criticism of polygamy and its sympathy for women who endured co-wives, but on another it is remarkably conservative. Homa is caricatured as an unveiled modern woman who believes in the equality of men and women, approves of the Pahlavi reforms, and manipulates her new husband into accepting a modern lifestyle. The novel expresses the bewildered sentiments of many educated Iranians in the 1960s, a generation that no longer approved of traditions like polygamy but disapproved of the regime and of the conduct of the modern urban woman.

The poetry of Forough Farrokhzad

At the turn of the twentieth century, three discourses on gender and modernity had emerged simultaneously in Iran: (1) a leftist social democratic one; (2) a nationalist discourse of "scientific domesticity"; and (3) an early Islamist religious discourse. In the 1960s, a variety of other discourses emerged under the influence of both consumerism and second-wave feminism in the West. In particular, a new generation of women writers began to focus more broadly on social, cultural, and political issues.[6] Among them, Forough Farrokhzad stands out for her poems and other literary accomplishments (Fig. 7.12). Her poetry is filled with references to daily objects in a woman's life, a clothesline, a shopping basket, a cup of milk, a pair of earrings, as well as preoccupations such as pregnancy, breastfeeding, a child's illness, or relationships with mothers or sisters.

Universally referred to by her first name, Forough was born to an urban middle-class family in Tehran. After finishing ninth grade, she married an older second cousin and gave birth to a son. Theirs was a marriage of love, of which her family completely disapproved. In 1955, she fell in love with another man, separated from her husband, and lost custody of her son, something that pained her for her entire life. Her first collection of poetry, *Asir* (Captive), appeared in 1952 when she was only eighteen. She went on to publish three other collections: *Divar* (The Wall, 1956); *'Osyan* (Rebellion, 1957); and *Tavallodi Digar* (Another Birth, 1959–1963). She also acted in and directed several films, winning the Oberhausen award in 1963 for *The House Is Black*, a documentary about the harsh living conditions at an Iranian leper colony. She died in a car accident in 1966 at the age of thirty-two (Farrokhzad 2002, IX–X).

An original woman who refused to be defined by others, Forough wrote poems that were frank, sexually explicit, and without stylistic ornamentation.

---

[6] This generation of women writers included Goli Taraghi, Mahshid Amir Shahi, Shahrnoush Parsipour, Mihan Bahmani, and Ghazaleh Alizadeh. For background see Talattof 1997. Among male poets, Ahmad Shamlu stands out as the only one who wrote about his wife, Aida, thus celebrating heterosexual love within marriage (Papan-Matin 2005). Thanks to Firoozeh Papan-Matin, Nasrin Rahimieh and Ahmad Karimi-Hakkak for their helpful suggestions on this section.

Figure 7.12 Forough Farrokhzad

Her poetry, which deals with the life of the modern urban woman, shocked readers who were unaccustomed to such open emotional disclosures by women. The critics attacked her mercilessly and accused her of living and writing about her "immoral life" (Milani 1982, 142).

This female-centered style of poetry, realized so evocatively in Forough's work, had actually been initiated by Jaleh Qaʿem-Maqami, who wrote during the Constitutional era but her writings did not appear in print until 1966 (Karachi 2004). In one poem about her marriage, Qaʿem-Maqami writes:

> What if I never married, mother?
> What if I didn't throw myself into this agony? ...
> A handful of bones, was I such a burden?
> Would father have been ruined if I didn't marry?

(Shakiba 1998, 152–153)

Simin Behbahani (1927–), a contemporary of Forough, had also moved beyond the traditions of classical Persian poetry, in which only men wrote lyrical poems about women or boys, and women remained silent (Milani 1994, 32):

> O, lost from my heart,
> Tell me the truth,
> Why have you come back tonight
> With the memories?
> If you've come back for the one
> Who stole your heart,
> I am not she: she's dead,
> I am her shadow.   (Behbahani, *Gozine-ye Asar*, Milani 1994, 33)

Nothing better expressed the alienation of the modern woman hemmed in by patriarchal structures.

Forough's poetry was far more sexually explicit than that of her female predecessors. It challenged the institution of marriage, even when not arranged:

> I sinned a sin that pleased me utterly,
> in arms that trembled with ecstasy.
> In that dark and silent meeting,
> O God, whatever happened to me?   (*Divar*, Farrokhzad 1982, 128)

The publication of this poem created a sensation at the Qom theological seminaries, where her work was immediately banned. It was simply assumed that the poem was autobiographical. Even more outrageous was that the narrator admitted to an affair while she was both married and had a child. In *Asir*, the narrator compares herself to a caged bird:

> I think of this knowing I shall never
> be able to escape this plight,
> For even if the keeper should let me go,
> I've lost all my strength for the flight.
> Every sunny morning a child
> behind the bars looks smilingly at me.
> When I start to sing my song of joy,
> his lips form kisses that he brings for me.   (*Asir*, Farrokhzad 1982, 123)

At times, Forough mocks vacuous upper-class marriages in which the woman basks in material comfort and calls herself happy:

> You can be like mechanical dolls,
> gazing at your world with glassy eyes.
> Your straw-stuffed form
> can sleep through the years in its velvet case,
> dressed up with sequined voile.

> To the pressure of any pressing hand,
> you can squeak inanely,
> "Oh, how happy I am!"   (*Born Again*, Farrokhzad 1982, 45)

Often, Forough denounces a woman's subservient position in marriage, as in the unequivocally feminist poem "Halqeh" (The Ring):

> Years went by and there came a night
> when a woman was brooding on that golden ring ...
> Bitterly the woman cried "Woe!
> Woe to this ring with its features
> that glitter yet and glow, whose meaning
> is slavery and near servitude."   (*Asir*, Farrokhzad 1982, 126)

After her untimely death, Forough was idolized by generations of women, who continued to mourn her loss. They held readings of her and memorized her work. Forough's poetry, bleak as it might seem, gave hope to a new generation of Iranian women, especially when she suggested that her example would be followed:

> In the garden I plant my hands.
> I know I shall grow, I know, I know.
> Swallows will lay their eggs
> in the nest of my ink-stained fingers.   (*Born Again*, Farrokhzad 1982, 91)

Forough seemed aware of the changes occurring in Iran, and of the sometimes-destructive radical movements in other countries of the Middle East. She left behind both hopes of a brighter future for intellectual women and troubling premonitions about a future she would never see:

> Instead of flowers our neighbors are planting
> machine guns and mortars in their garden grounds.
> Our neighbors are covering
> their tiled pools,
> and the tiled pools
> becoming ammunition caches
> without ever being asked
> And the kids on our street
> have loaded their briefcases
> with little bombs.
> The courtyard of our house feels sick.   (*Born Again*, Farrokhzad 1982, 110)

Modernity, industrialism, and freedom of choice

In 1961, Edward Galloway, a United Nations social scientist, was invited to Iran to conduct a study on juvenile delinquency in the cities. By then, 30 percent of Iranians were living in urban areas (*Hesabha-ye Melli* 1981).

Galloway used a body of fairly conservative, well-established, sociological concepts, which ever since the late nineteenth century have pointed to social disorganization and anomie as problems resulting from urbanization and, more generally, modernization. His UN study concluded that crime was on the rise in Iran's large cities. "It is reported that the number of young people who run away from their homes and come to the big cities is on the rise. It is also reported that in Tehran and other big cities rates of youth crime, prostitution, and especially homosexuality are on the increase" (Saheb al-Zamani [1964] 1999, 227). Evidently, Galloway regarded homosexuality as a social disease. He was probably unfamiliar with the culture's more accepting attitude toward semi-covert bisexuality. Urban honor killings had also increased when compared to the early twentieth century. Husbands, fathers, and brothers took advantage of article 179 of the Penal Code, which gave men light sentences of one to six months for murder of a related woman caught in a compromising position (Sedghi 2007, 142).

A series of warnings came in the wake of Galloway's report on the part of public figures such as Naser al-Din Saheb al-Zamani, who predicted that rapid urbanization would unravel society. Truancy rates, illicit drug use, alcoholism, and divorce rates had all shot up dramatically, leading to an "insurrectionary mood" in the country, he predicted (Saheb al-Zamani [1964] 1999, 253). In 1963, a follow-up report by a group of Iranian social scientists went further and demanded active state intervention to slow the modernization of the country. Its feverish pace had not only altered demographics, but also changed centuries-old social relations. Improved health had reduced infant mortality rates, and half of Iran's population of 21 million was now under the age of twenty. Men from rural communities were migrating to the cities, while women remained, resulting in a significant gender imbalance in both urban and rural areas. The report points out that in premodern societies parents

selected a spouse for the youth at puberty. The young person followed his father's profession through apprenticeship and pursued old ways of doing things. The notion of social, psychological, economic, or cultural dissonance is a new one ... With increased urbanization and industrialization, the social fabric of society changes. Soon, a person's individual personality becomes important. The large [extended] family is replaced with the small nuclear family, and the transition from childhood to adulthood, which previously took place naturally and without awareness, becomes more difficult and problematic. ("Seminar-e Masa'el-e Javanan" [1964] 1999, 279)

The report stated that the new generation was confused about how to reconcile older social expectations with newer Western-influenced ones. Young people declared themselves both liberal and socialist, conservative in religious matters and followers of mystical traditions of Islam, and did not know the difference among these stances. The new freedom of choice had led to extreme cultural dissonance:

In the modern world one has to constantly decide and choose. But we were not raised for such a world. The ability to choose, this type of independence of mind, has not yet taken shape among our youth. Today, by the age of twenty, a young person has to make more "ethical decisions" than his ancestors made during an entire lifetime ... New means of communicating ideas and news such as cinema, radio, television, newspapers, and magazines all accelerate this sense of confusion between old values and new temptations ... Today, the whole world lives in such a state of confusion ... This is why the dream of returning to the old social and cultural order, one based on a stable spirituality, has become a [international] demand. ("Seminar-e Masa'el-e Javanan" [1964] 1999, 280)

As Saheb al-Zamani and his colleagues were reporting on a worldwide hunger for spirituality, a new and more politicized interpretation of Shi'i Islam was gradually taking shape in Iran. The new discourse tapped into the public's deep spiritual longing, its disenchantment with the regime's modernization program, and its anxiety about the economic, social, and familial future.

8 The rise of leftist guerrilla organizations and Islamist movements

The dramatic changes discussed in the last chapter resulted in a backlash that led to an unusual alliance between leftists opposed to imperialism and consumerism, and conservative Islamists who were also hostile to Western culture. During the 1960s and 1970s some degree of convergence appeared in the writings of leading Islamist clerics Ayatollah Khomeini, Ayatollah Morteza Motahhari, and Ayatollah Mahmoud Taleqani, and the lay Islamist thinkers Jalal Al-e Ahmad and Ali Shariati, on the one hand, and secular leftist intellectuals on the other. Despite their numerous ideological differences, they shared, among other things, an overt enmity toward aspects of modern gender norms, particularly second-wave feminism. Such resentment was not limited to men, but could also be found among (1) a new generation of female college students who joined underground leftist organizations; (2) less educated Islamist women who entered the clandestine circles of Ayatollah Khomeini's supporters; and (3) women from old and new middle-class families who supported Ali Shariati and his modern oppositional religious center, the Husseiniyeh Ershad. In their personal lives, these women tried to combine new political objectives and the benefits of a modern lifestyle with older ethical and moral sensibilities.

In the course of the 1978–1979 revolution, many leftist and even women's publications encouraged their readers to accept Khomeini's leadership. This kind of support was facilitated by the fact that Khomeini's various pronouncements articulated a vision of a "third way" that would avoid the evils of (1) Western imperialism, which turned women into sexual commodities, and (2) Soviet communism, which destroyed family values. In Khomeini's ideal Islamic society, women would be educated and would participate in the political process. The state would assure that they became good mothers and wives, as well as productive members of the Shi'i Muslim community, while nearly everyone was to renounce Western-style feminism as part of the fight against imperialism. Young women and men from both the old and the new middle classes embraced this "third way" and joined the movement in large numbers, hoping to combine their commitment to education, employment, and political participation with the ethical values of Shi'i Islam.

Ritual pollution and sexual emancipation?

One way to understand how the gender discourse of modernity came into conflict with the gender hierarchies of Shi'i Islam during this period is to examine the religious advice books that counseled believers on the conduct of their daily lives. *Explanation of Problems (Towzih al-Masa'el)* had first appeared in the 1840s.[1] A cleric who hoped to become a prestigious *marja'-e taqlid* (source of emulation) was expected to publish such a work where he defined rituals of pollution and purification, and answered common questions regarding the daily observance of these rites. Similar works continued to appear during the Pahlavi era. Khomeini's *Explanation of Problems* (1947) is similar to those of other Shi'i jurists of the twentieth century in its detailed discussion of the rituals of cleansing and ablution. It will serve as my example in the following discussion.

These compendia defined religious propriety in two ways: Shi'i Muslims must follow the rules of the *shari'a* on imperative matters. On non-imperative matters, they are to follow the advice of a living *mojtahed*, who must be an adult Shi'i man with proper paternity (not born of a single mother) and religious training. The rules defining propriety in a typical *Explanation of Problems* are quite extensive, comprising more than 3,000 articles. Khomeini's manual included chapters on ritual cleansing (727 articles), daily prayer (822 articles), fasting (200 articles), tithing (284 articles), trade and business (200 articles), legal matters and power of attorney (110 articles), and marriage and sexuality (134 articles). The vast majority of the regulations are about ritual cleansing, since in Shi'i jurisprudence *taharat* (ritual purity) is of the highest significance. A Shi'i Muslim's daily prayer, fasting during Ramadan, and other religious obligations might be invalid in the eyes of God if the person were *najes*. Blood is one of a dozen items of *nejasat* (impurity), along with semen, sexual sweat, and urine. The touch of nonbelievers (including all non-Muslims) ceases to be impure once they convert to Islam. Khomeini, however, writes that even non-practicing Muslims are *najes*, and those who do not attend the mosque must be shunned. One must not join them for a meal, engage in business with them, live next to them, or marry a member of their family (article 897).

---

[1] For other examples see *Resaleh-ye* 1993.

Beginning with the Reza Shah era, the public abandoned some religious rites that were in direct conflict with modern sanitation, though these rites remained in most versions of *Explanation of Problems*. Many notions of *nejasat* lingered on, among them the idea that sex and menstruation made one impure. In Khomeini's manual a believer's daily practices – eating, drinking, sexual intercourse, and social contact with members of the opposite sex and non-Muslims – are all subject to detailed regulations. After each such contact, a believer must perform the proper rituals of *taharat*. This involves washing the face, hands, arms, and feet in a manner and style (with the appropriate quantity of water) that the manuals define. Full ablution, or *ghosl* (similar to Jewish *miqveh*), requires total immersion in water (articles 236–322). If people doubt whether they have performed the proper rituals correctly, that doubt will cancel their prayers and require them to repeat the rituals (articles 1168–1362). A woman's body is almost always associated with impurities because of sexual, menstrual, and other bodily secretions, including those of childbirth (articles 1634–1644). During menstruation, and after intercourse, touching sacred objects is prohibited; otherwise daily life continues (Fischer 1978, 205). Following sexual intercourse, a man must perform *ghosl* before praying or touching a copy of the Qur'an. These rules are internalized and become the guiding principles of daily conduct. As a result, casual social contact between unrelated men and women, or between Muslims and non-Muslims (or even non-practicing Muslims), creates severe psychological anxieties for a believer.

Khomeini updated his manual on several occasions.[2] Many Shi'is followed its regulations throughout the 1960s and 1970s with varying degrees of conformity mediated by the practical imperatives of daily life in a turbulent urban environment. Some sectors of society continue similar rites recommended by other ranking clerics today. We can understand the anxiety of a strict believer who enters modern society and interacts with others in the workplace, thereby violating hundreds of Shi'i rules and regulations on a daily basis. Esma'il Kho'i, a well-known writer, recalled that when he became a Marxist, his own grandmother viewed him as an unbeliever and therefore a *najes* person. Although she adored him and had helped raise him, Kho'i's grandmother washed the dishes he used at meals separately to avoid polluting herself and others in the household.[3] Prisons provide other examples. Islamist political prisoners in the shah's time kept

---

[2] No dates were given for these subsequent revisions, and the book has been reprinted with the original 1947 date.

[3] See Hossein Mohri's interview with Esma'il Kho'i, Radio Seda-ye Iran (Los Angeles), June 15, 2000. One can find similar stories in Orthodox Jewish communities who avoid more secular relatives.

their distance from leftists, refusing to join them for meals and shunning most other interaction. Non-Muslim Iranians have recounted numerous similar stories. They were usually not invited to share a meal. If they were, their dishes were washed separately.

In response to these political, social, and cultural taboos, two new, intertwined discourses of Shi'i Islam developed in the 1960s. One was that of the ranking clerics, such as Ayatollah Motahhari and Ayatollah Khomeini, who challenged many of the modernizing and secularizing trends of the Pahlavi era. They accepted some basic changes in hygiene and sanitation without modifying the prescribed rites of purification. The other was that of lay intellectuals with leftist leanings, who were not concerned with ritual purity but with the creation of a modern Islamic discourse. The latter included Jalal Al-e Ahmad and Ali Shariati, who prepared the ground for a new Islamist movement. They criticized such religious regulations as old-fashioned and even fanatical, and developed a new hermeneutics of Shi'ism based on Third Worldist revolutionary perspectives and European philosophy.

The ayatollahs and the lay thinkers denounced Iranian and Western women's transgressions of the boundaries of ethics and propriety, but neither group advocated a complete return to the nineteenth century. Both encouraged women's education and political participation, provided this helped to disseminate the new Islamist message. However, both continued to use the old language of defilement when speaking of modern sexual conduct. For the ayatollahs, the modern woman was a source of ritual pollution; for the radical lay thinkers, the apolitical Westernized woman was a duped agent of imperialist cultural hegemony as illustrated in the term *Westoxification*.

Religious institutions and the rise of Islamism

After the shah's government banned all independent political parties and trade unions in 1953, seminaries, mosques, and religious institutions with relative financial independence from the state gradually became centers of political dissent. This process accelerated after the shah's clash with the clerics in 1963. After 1965, modern *husseiniyeh*, or centers for the commemoration of Imam Hussein, mushroomed in urban centers. The benefactors of these centers, often *bazaar* merchants, also provided the poor and the needy with a variety of financial and health services, sometimes including a state-of-the-art hospital, which treated the poor without charge.[4] The regime exiled dissident religious figures to small

---

[4] These hospitals also treated more well-off patients, Muslims and non-Muslims, who were charged the regular fees.

provincial towns, but this policy only helped spread the Islamist message more widely. By 1974, there were 322 *husseiniyeh*-type religious centers in Tehran, 305 in the oil-rich southern province of Khuzestan, and 731 in the northwestern province of Azerbaijan. In Tehran alone, 12,300 other Shi'i religious societies existed. Some were named after the towns and provinces from which their members had immigrated to Tehran. Others were named after guilds and professional associations; these associations met people's needs for socialization and professional exchange (Arjomand 1988, 92–98). Loyal followers of the exiled Khomeini secretly controlled many of these associations ('Asgar-Owladi 1998, 8). Khomeini also sent letters to Iranian Muslim Student Associations in Iran, Europe, the United States, and Canada, encouraging them to join the revolt against the shah (Chelkowski and Dabashi 1999, 95).

Ayatollah Morteza Motahhari, a professor of theology at Tehran University, developed a politicized Shi'i discourse in a series of lectures between 1960 and 1963 (Motahhari [1974] 1988). Motahhari was one of Khomeini's closest allies inside Iran. In 1966–1967, as debates about the shah's Family Protection Law began, he published a series of essays in the journal *Zan-e Ruz* (Today's Woman) on issues such as divorce, alimony, inheritance rights, polygamy, and gender differences. The venue in which these essays appeared was significant, because *Zan-e Ruz* was not only the most popular women's journal but also tended to express the voice of the modern secular woman. Referring to ancient and modern Western sources, from Plato and Aristotle to Marx, Darwin, Will Durant, and Bertrand Russell, as well as the 1776 American Declaration of Independence and the 1789 French Declaration of the Rights of Man, Motahhari claimed that *shari'a* was equal, or superior, to Western law. In fact, all contemporary problems in family relations could be resolved if the gender regulations of the *shari'a* were applied in the true spirit of Islam. Hence, new laws to protect women's rights were unnecessary (Motahhari [1989] 1997). This did not mean that men and women were equal, however. Adopting a pseudo-scientific discourse, Motahhari argued that gender inequities were justified because men and women were "biologically different." Pregnancy and child-rearing functions sapped women's energy. Therefore, it was incumbent upon men to provide for them. Women did not benefit from economic equality, because it required them to shoulder two sets of responsibilities: their family chores, which were a woman's "natural and instinctual functions," and their modern job requirements (Motahhari [1974] 1988, 153–157).

Motahhari's "return to the *shari'a*" was in fact a hybrid discourse, for he borrowed Western ideas whenever they suited his purpose. For example, he lashed out against those who opposed women's right to an advanced education, because skilled female medical doctors and surgeons were necessary for the gender-segregated social order he envisioned. He also adopted the practices of Protestant charities in the West. He believed that creating Islamic charities and social services, as well as reenacting Islamic rituals, would bring about a more ethical Muslim community, create a healthier identity for women, and put an end to destructive Western influences (Motahhari [1974] 1988, 69).

In contrast to Motahhari, who challenged gender equality through theological discourses, the more blunt Khomeini, whose exile protected him from the wrath of the shah, openly declared the marriage reforms null and void. When the Family Protection Law gave women the right to demand divorce under certain conditions and to reject a husband's taking of a second wife, Khomeini issued a *fatwa* from exile, declaring that it was against Islam:

Women who are divorced [according to the rulings of Family Protection Law] should consider their divorces null and void. They are still considered married. If they remarry, they have committed adultery. Men who knowingly marry such women are also committing adultery and must be punished according to religious law. Their children will be considered illegitimate, without inheritance rights. (Khomeini 1947, article 2836; see also Yavari 1981, 98)

Like Motahhari, Khomeini appropriated some aspects of modernity that suited his purposes. In spring 1963, for example, he had distinguished between women's suffrage and the election of women to positions of authority: "It is permissible to give women the right to vote in the elections, but giving women the right to be elected will lead to prostitution" (Khomeini 1999, I:191). In 1978, as the revolutionary movement gained momentum, Khomeini encouraged an even greater degree of women's political participation. He repeatedly asked mothers to participate in the demonstrations against the shah and told them not to fear giving martyrs to the cause, just as the sister and wives of Imam Hussein had done during the Battle of Karbala in 680 CE (Khomeini 1999, III:472). In 1979 he advised them to participate and vote in the April referendum on establishing an Islamic Republic. Once that was achieved he also approved of the election of Islamist women to the Parliament, stating, "they have the right to vote, to elect, to be elected" (Khomeini 2005, 42).

The lay Islamist thinkers Al-e Ahmad and Shariati

Lay thinkers also articulated a more militant expression of Shi'i Islam. Initially, the two most important ones, Jalal Al-e Ahmad and Ali Shariati, gained much greater popular support among the educated youth than any of the clerics had achieved, including Motahhari or Khomeini. Al-e Ahmad came from a clerical family, but became a communist, also coming under the influence of the militant secularist Ahmad Kasravi. When the clerics, led by Ayatollah Khomeini, became leaders of the opposition in the 1960s, Al-e Ahmad renewed his interest in Islam, making a pilgrimage to Mecca in 1964 (Richard 2003, 189). Al-e Ahmad's discourse in the 1960s was a mélange of Islam and modernism. He not only criticized the West, but accused Baha'is, Jews, Christians, and Zoroastrians of being agents of Western imperialism (Al-e Ahmad [1963] 1994, 40, 67, 78). Al-e Ahmad, who was married to the distinguished woman writer and academic Simin Daneshvar, was far more progressive than the clerics on some gender issues, for he supported unveiling, the education and employment of women at all levels, and their right to divorce. As with other leftists, he attacked Western-style consumerism and the entertainment industry. But he also believed that legal and religious limitations on women's social advancement had pushed them into frivolity. Al-e Ahmad was particularly scornful of the display of eroticized female bodies in public spaces:

In fact, what have we done? We have only given women the right to show off [their bodies] in society ... only the right to show off, to call attention to their appearance. In other words, we have pushed women, who are the guardians of tradition, family, ancestry, our very blood, into adopting a loose manner of behavior. We have brought them to the streets ... So each day they adopt a new fashion and walk about aimlessly. No responsibility, no social obligation, no character. None! (Al-e Ahmad [1963] 1994, 102)

Al-e Ahmad also criticized "effeminate" and "disinfected" men, a reference to dandies or young, heterosexual urbanites who spent much time grooming themselves and were preoccupied with the modern gadgets and technologies of a consumer society (Al-e Ahmad [1963] 1994, 147).

Ali Shariati was the precocious son of a nationalist preacher and Islamic scholar (Fig. 8.1). He went to France on a government fellowship where he was influenced by the French scholar of Islam Louis Massignon. He read Marx, Heidegger, Sartre, Frantz Fanon and other thinkers while completing a doctorate in philology. Upon return to Iran in 1964, he first taught at Mashhad University. In 1969 he began lecturing at the modern religious center Husseiniyeh Ershad, where he echoed many of Al-e Ahmad's views. Thousands flocked eagerly to hear his sermons and adopted the way of life he preached. Young women attendees, who had earlier worn more modern Western dress, began to adopt the *hijab* he recommended. Shariati's hybrid discourse suggested a solution to the crisis of identity they faced. He encouraged women's social and political participation and rejected the stereotype of the traditional homemaker and housewife. He advised Iranian women to learn more about freedom fighters in the Algerian, Irish, and Palestinian movements and criticized

Figure 8.1 Ali Shariati

the Western media for promoting frivolous female characters as role models, among them the emaciated cover-girl Twiggy, the Princess of Monaco (Grace Kelly), the women in James Bond movies, and even Jacqueline Kennedy, who, according to Shariati, had "sold out her dignity" by marrying the Greek tycoon Aristotle Onassis. Why had the press not paid greater attention to scholars at "Cambridge, the Sorbonne, or Harvard," women who spent their lives in the archives studying historical, scientific, and religious texts, he asked (Shariati [1971–1976] 1990, 74). Thus, Shariati differed from the clerics because he supported greater social and educational accomplishments for women and did not call for a gender-segregated society. Japan, a country that, in his view, combined an enthusiasm for Western scientific and technological advances with a respect for conventional gender norms, was the best model for Iran.

Shariati's "modern woman" had to fit two important criteria. Her embrace of modernity was not to interfere with her responsibility as a wife or mother, nor with her commitment to authentic Islam. Shariati held up Fatimah, the youngest daughter of Muhammad, the wife of Ali and mother of Hussein, as the ultimate role model for Iranian women. He praised her total devotion to her father, her unconditional support of her husband, her never-ending love and care for her sons, and her sacrifices for Islam. Similarly, he considered the four greatest women of history to have been Mary (mother of Jesus), Asiyeh (wife of the pharaoh who raised Moses), Khadijeh (first wife of Muhammad), and Fatimah. The devotion of each of these defiant women to the men in their lives made them exemplary and defined them as worthy individuals (Shariati [1971–1976] 1990, 147).

His praise for such women led Shariati to condemn the Western cultural revolution, especially the sexual liberation of women. Such emancipation was immoral and unethical, nothing but an advocacy of prostitution. The disparaging language he used to define the sexually emancipated woman of the West drew heavily from the Shi'i discourse of impurity and pollution. Shariati painted the modern Western marriage in bleak, melancholy terms. Westerners spent their youth in dance halls, bars, restaurants, and similar places of entertainment. When they finally chose to marry and form families, they were considerably older and less passionate about love and romance. Marriage was simply a rational union between two tired and exhausted individuals whose youth and vitality was gone. There was no real attraction, no majestic love, only a "boring" union of two people, often in a simple ceremony in a city hall. He regaled his young listeners with a lurid and highly exaggerated portrait of Western sexual promiscuity: "The man has tasted hundreds of warm, young bodies. How could he find this more experienced woman, a woman whose mastery of sexual relations he abhors, exciting? How could he keep her as his wife? And the woman, she has [slept] with hundreds of male lovers. Surely now that she holds this tired, middle-aged man in her arms, she wants to scream out!" It seems that to Shariati Western marriages were unsuccessful because the sexually emancipated woman emasculated her husband. Her carnal knowledge – those "hundreds" of lovers – was both revolting and threatening (Shariati [1971–1976] 1990, 89–90).

Shariati denounced another evolving gender norm in the West, the recognition of an openly gay lifestyle: "Have you heard the arguments of British Members of Parliament in defense of the *lavat* bill [homosexual rights]? They say, 'This is an objective reality and it exists in our society, therefore we must recognize it'" (Shariati [1971–1976] 1990, 58). He accused the West of recognizing a vice that the Middle East had refused. However, he failed to mention that the centuries-old master/boy-concubine relations persisted in many traditionalist sectors of Iranian society, especially in *bazaars* and seminaries.

Homosexual practices among youth or married adult men continued to be ignored or made light of as well. According to Paul Vieille, who studied rural villages around Tehran in the 1960s, "eight out of ten boys was said to have had at least one homosexual experience of one form or another before marriage, whether with their peers or with much older men. The practice is thus transmitted from generation to generation, though it is in decline" (Vieille 1978, 165). Naim Afary recalls how factory managers in Tehran were faced with such issues in the late 1950s:

When we opened the Three Stars Shoe Factory on the south side of Tehran, we hired a large team of shoemakers from a nearby province for the sewing department. Each senior shoemaker worked with two or three young assistants, mostly teenage boys. Since the shoemakers were away from their homes, they asked to sleep in the factory at night, and we gave them permission to do so. One day there was a big fight in the sewing department. After some inquiries, we learned that two of the senior shoemakers had been quarreling over a boy. We called the boy to our office. He was about fourteen and was quite handsome, with blonde hair and blue eyes. He candidly revealed that the two older men were in love with him (*khater khāh*). We were disturbed by his account and wanted to fire the shoemakers. But the boy insisted that he was a willing participant in these relationships. So we let him off but told the men in the sewing department that they had to find other sleeping accommodations. The shoemakers were quite upset with the change and collectively decided to leave the factory. After this incident, we hired only women for the sewing department, and this is how women came to be employed in our factory. (Interview, February 15, 2002)

Same-sex relations among women also continued on the sidelines. Paula Drew reported on lesbian practices at a nurse's training hospital in Tabriz (Drew 1997). In the all-girls high schools, close intimate relations with lesbian dimensions were also common. Those who were attracted to their own sex were called *baruni*. They wrote letters to one another, exchanged gifts, and became inseparable. Some *barunis* continued to remain lovers in school even after they had become engaged (Mahvash 1957; interview with Ladan in Afary 1992, 87–88).

By the 1970s, a small gay male subculture was gradually taking root in elite circles of Tehran, mostly as a result of interaction with American and European advisors who lived in the country. "JP," an Iranian gay activist now living abroad, estimates that close to 10 percent of the 50,000 American advisors who lived in Iran were homosexuals. Their presence gradually helped build a new gay culture. Several hotels in Tehran were known for their gay bars, such as the Marmar Hotel, the Tehran Tower, the Intercontinental Hotel, the Hilton, and especially the Bel Air Hotel, with its famous Chelsea Pot Bar, owned by one of the shah's brothers. As in the West, some were performers or fashion designers such as Keyvan Khosravani, owner of the Boutique Number One in Tehran. Most of the Iranian clients of these bars belonged to elite and royalist sectors of society. This small gay community remained discreet on the job and in family encounters, but the more tolerant atmosphere of the late Pahlavi era for elite gay men meant far less fear of arrest. There was even some talk of starting a modern gay rights organization (interview, July 2004).

Shariati addressed an audience that was ambivalent about the changing gender roles of the period. Iranian Muslims and non-Muslims alike were angered by the open manifestation of female desire and the emergence of an openly gay lifestyle in Western culture. Yet elements of this new culture were also appearing in the Iranian mass media. The project of normalizing heterosexual desire had moved to a new stage. Popular female singers such as GouGoush were consummate performers who drew attention to their revealing clothes, dance routines, and alluring voices. In addition, there were brief tongue-in-cheek references to gay men and the gay culture on Iranian television and in films. One of the most popular talk-show hosts of the period was the poet and singer Fereydoun Farrokhzad, the poet Forough Farrokhzad's brother. Though a married man, Farrokhzad exhibited stereotypical homosexual mannerisms and tolerated various remarks about his sexuality ("Mosahebeh ba Babak" 2005, 8–9). There were also various references to homosexual characters in television programs such as the popular series *My Uncle Napoleon*. While condescending and disparaging, these references suggested at least a small degree of acceptance for a gay lifestyle. Shariati's attacks on Western marriage and open homosexuality spoke to the many anxieties resulting from the emergence of similar values in Iran (Shariati [1971–1976] 1990, 89–90).

Three responses to modernity among dissidents, 1963–1979

By the 1960s Iranian society faced a crisis of identity, as religious boundaries that marked social and gender hierarchies and rules of propriety began to fade, and the unequal status of women was called into question. Religious anxieties over female *fitnah* (disorder) and ritual pollution were combined with cultural anxieties over unleashed female desire and new gender norms. Leftist intellectuals called for a future socialist revolution, which was to emancipate working-class women and end the frivolity of the modern urban lifestyle and its decadent sexual norms. But Islamist associations offered immediate as well as long-term solutions. Joining these large associations not only assured access to good medical care and other forms of social welfare, but also obviated the need to make difficult personal life choices. Erich Fromm had argued that the cultural anxieties of modernity led some people to trade the burdens of modern freedom for the security of an authoritarian movement. The clerics and the Islamist lay intellectuals encouraged a religious form of authoritarianism, albeit with pragmatic features.

Dissident Iranian women affected by rapid social and cultural changes and wishing to take political action against the government chose several pathways. (1) Some joined the underground leftist guerrilla organizations, especially the Marxist-Leninist Fedayeen Khalq (People's Fedayeen), formed in 1971 with activists who had belonged to the Tudeh Party and the Marxist wing of the National Front. Others joined the Islamic leftist Mojahedeen Khalq (People's Mojahedeen), which in 1965 emerged from within the more religious wing of the Mosaddeq movement (Abrahamian 1982, 483–495; Chehabi 1990, 211). These groups were instrumental in organizing the revolution, even though both the Fedayeen and the Mojahedeen were to turn against the Islamic Republic. (2) Many house-wives, college students, and young professionals became followers of Shariati in the late 1960s and attended his public lectures. (3) Other highly religious women, many from rural or *bazaari* backgrounds, joined the clandestine Islamist circles that supported Ayatollah Khomeini after 1963. In the remainder of this chapter I will explore these three types of responses in the 1960s and 1970s through personal narratives that provide a glimpse into why these women felt alienated in the face of Iran's modernization, and how they coped with this in their personal lives.

"One of the men": activist women in leftist guerrilla organizations

Among the guerrilla organizations that emerged in the late 1960s, by far the most sizable were the Fedayeen Khalq and the Mojahedeen Khalq, as well as a segment of the Mojahedeen which broke off and formed the Marxist-Leninist Peykar in 1975. These groups recruited many educated women from among the middle-class university students. Their leaders were university students from urban centers, especially Tehran. The Fedayeen tended to come from the modern sectors of the middle class, while the Mojahedeen tended to draw their members more from the old middle-class sectors, where Shi'i rituals remained an integral part of daily life. Mojahedeen women wore the *hijab*, which in this period con-sisted of a long-sleeved shirt, long pants, and a scarf (Fig. 8.2). Members of the Fedayeen did not wear the *hijab* but dressed in jeans, short-sleeved T-shirts, and Maoist shirts. Women in both groups avoided any hint of an overtly feminine appearance, eschewing lipstick, perfume, and even simple jewelry (Abrahamian 1989, 224).

The Fedayeen Khalq supported women's rights at a formal level, including the equal right to education and employment. They also addressed the concerns of peasants and working-class women, such as equal pay, medical care and childcare. A few women gained leadership

Members of the Mojahedin at weapons training on a range several kilometers outside Tehran.

Figure 8.2 The Mojahedeen Khalq at weapons training

positions in the organization. These women became involved in major decisions of the party and in missions concerning the life and death of members. Those who were killed in action or under torture gained the status of *shahids* (martyrs), a designation traditionally denied to women in Shi'ism. The Fedayeen secretly published semi-hagiographic accounts of the lives of some of its *shahids* in order to inspire political recruits and underscore the "righteousness" of their cause (Fig. 8.3). Despite their small numbers, the Fedayeen challenged the regime in small-scale armed attacks. These activities greatly impressed disaffected youth, especially college students, who were in awe of the organization and its heroic members (interview with Manij Marashi, September 23, 2004).

The Fedayeen advocated a "two-stage revolution," which relegated the issue of women's emancipation to some distant future after the socialist revolution. The organization praised and even idolized women's contributions and sacrifices, but ignored their present concerns about autonomy and individual rights. Women in leadership positions concentrated on the organization's principal political concerns – the poverty of workers and peasants, the shah's despotism, or the impact of Western imperialism – seldom addressing women's rights as such. The Mojahedeen Khalq, where women held about 10 percent of the leadership positions, formally supported the equality of men and women as well, but demanded

Figure 8.3 Women martyrs of the Fedayeen Khalq

an almost cult-like obedience to its leader and his agenda (Abrahamian 1989).

As with many sectarian Maoist groups in the West, leftist Iranian organizations were homophobic and showed little tolerance for a gay lifestyle, even within dissident student organizations abroad. Ladan, a lesbian activist of the period, recalls that within the left:

One particular taboo concerned the issue of homosexuality. [Some] considered homosexuality as abnormal, implicitly advocating the execution of homosexuals. Others identified homosexuality as a social pathology, so they didn't prescribe execution, but suggested long-term rehabilitation. (Interview with Ladan in Afary 1992, 93)

Haideh Moghissi was a founder of the National Union of Women, the women's association affiliated with the Fedayeen Khalq. In her *Populism and Feminism in Iran* (1996), she tells the story of women in the leadership of that organization. The Fedayeen recognized two categories of women leaders. The first role model was Mihan Jazani, the wife of Bijan Jazani, the founder of the organization. Mihan, who had a degree in philosophy, assumed all of the responsibilities of wife and mother, while Bijan devoted himself to revolutionary activities. After her husband's arrest, Mihan was held up as a model for other women in the organization. Years later, Mihan would complain that despite her long service to the organization, her financial contributions, and her struggles for workers' and peasants' rights, she was never treated as an independent person with a mind of her own. She was viewed as the "mother" of the organization and was expected to perform a nurturing role toward the young members.

The second role model was Ashraf Dehqani, the only woman on the central committee of the party. She earned her position by virtue of the years of torture she had suffered in a SAVAK prison and her courage in escaping from that prison. Ashraf was hailed for not breaking down under torture, and for being brave "like a man" (Moghissi 1996, 117). Activist women were thus offered two choices: to become devoted mothers and companions to their male comrades and to the organization, or to renounce their sexuality and family ties and become "one of the men."

Populist, anti-imperialist perspectives dominated the Iranian Left, which focused more often on anti-imperialism than on the struggle for democracy. The Fedayeen regarded the shah as a simple instrument of Western imperialism. At the same time, the organization implicitly used hegemonic Shiʻi-Iranian concepts and traditions to discipline women's bodies and minds and to control female sexuality within the organization. This attitude toward sexuality characterized leftist guerrilla organizations around the world and was based on the perception that one had to abandon personal needs and maintain a strict discipline in order to become a successful revolutionary. Mohsen Nejat-Hosseini, former member of the Mojahedeen Khalq, recalls that their underground group held routine sessions of "criticism and self-criticism." Here members confessed to personal weaknesses such as "wasting time, wanting an unnecessary food item, desiring a fragrant cup of tea or a luxury item, wanting to own something, sexual urges" and so forth. The most difficult challenge facing these young men was suppressing their sexual desires, a subject that was often discussed in group meetings. For some, the only solution was to leave the group and get married; others fought hard against these feelings. "I once witnessed a comrade beating his head against the wall to fight his sexual urges and blaming himself every time such 'satanic' thoughts came to his mind." Later, as more women entered the Mojahedeen, marriages between members became more common (Nejat-Hosseini 2000, 57). In this sense, the close affinity that developed between the Iranian Left and the Islamists during the 1978–1979 revolution was not merely strategic, based on a mutual anti-Western, anti-imperialist outlook. The two groups also shared some similar beliefs concerning Western culture and especially its new gender and sexual norms (Moghissi 1996, 3).

The Shi'i-Iranian veneration of pain, suffering, and martyrdom gained new meaning for these young, often secular, revolutionaries. But they were also influenced by the Latin American revolutions, the ideologies of Soviet communism, and the Chinese cultural revolution, especially the latter's view of asceticism as bringing one closer to the suffering masses, the men and women whose difficult lives were to be both emulated and exalted. Despite their avowedly secular orientation, leftist organizations were steeped in an Iranian-Shi'i culture that replicated many of society's gender expectations. The activists' glorification of "masculine" and "Shi'i" values such as self-discipline, self-sacrifice, bravery, strength under torture, and especially the renunciation of earthly pleasures, was an important dimension of the political culture of the Iranian Left. Under the influence of Maoism, they went far beyond the asceticism of Islamic mysticism. In leftist circles, wearing colorful clothes, drinking alcohol, using perfume or cologne, indulging in intense sexual passions or romantic love, and sometimes even marrying or having children were renounced by party members. Such renunciations indicated their commitment to revolutionary goals. Hence many intimate relations among comrades were kept secret. Party members feared that passionate love would undermine their revolutionary resolve in battle and under torture, or simply interfere with the superhuman qualities demanded of a revolutionary. Therefore, the leaders rebuked both men and women for expressing personal emotions and affection (Mansour Bonakdarian, personal communication, April 23, 2003).

Such an ascetic lifestyle made gender relations within the organization easier to manage (Moghissi 1996, 128). At least within the Fedayeen some leading male cadres quietly used their power and prestige to take sexual advantage of lower-ranking women in the group. But women who showed the slightest deviation from the organization's rigid code of conduct or in any way enhanced their sexual appeal were suspected of being vain and lacking serious revolutionary commitment and therefore held in low regard (Moghissi 1996, 132). Many women who were members of the organizations helped create this hostile atmosphere.

Traditionally, many societies, both East and West, have equated a denial of worldly pleasures (food, drink, stylish clothing, and sex) with moral integrity and especially self-control. Contempt for the body has almost always included contempt for women, whose reproductive functions (menstruation, pregnancy, childbirth, and nursing) have been assumed to chain them down to earthly, mundane duties and prevent them from adhering to lofty, spiritual principles (Bordo 1988). Only women who renounced their sexuality could hope to reach a higher state of consciousness. In this sense, the Iranian Left, with its renunciation of bodily pleasures, was yet another manifestation of this bifurcated view of the self and the world, where sexually active women were regarded with contempt. Issues such as a woman's right to select her clothes or to control her body were almost incomprehensible to the major leftist organizations of this period. They saw all issues through the prism of anti-imperialism, reducing all gender issues to economic causes. They endlessly quoted old communist sources for solutions to the problems of modern Iranian women. Even activists who had lived abroad and had been more exposed to modern, Western feminist ideas, including socialist feminism, held this attitude.

As Maziar Behrooz has argued in his study of the Iranian Left, the Fedayeen's ambivalent stance toward women's rights during the revolution was the trigger for the group's breakup and the unraveling of the secular Iranian Left as a whole (Behrooz 2000, 108; Shahidian 1994). Many on the left became so enamored of Ayatollah Khomeini's implacable anti-imperialist, anti-shah stance that they followed him uncritically. Most of those who remained skeptical of Khomeini still believed that unity against the shah had to be maintained at all costs. They assumed that the Islamists could be easily marginalized after the revolution, since they were "backward" or lacked organization and would therefore be unable to hold onto power.

These attitudes changed little, even after the revolution. In early 1979 well-known members of the Fedayeen such as 'Atefeh Gorgin (wife of the martyred Khosrow Golsorkhi), Mihan Jazani (wife of the martyred Bijan Jazani), and Haideh Moghissi became the leaders of the leftist National Union of Women (NUW), the largest secular women's organization of the period.[5] By this time, the NUW had turned against Khomeini and become aware of the looming theocracy. The NUW formed several

---

[5] Later all regretted not having spoken out more forcefully against reversals in women's rights.

committees that worked among teachers, nurses, and civil servants. It also opened a clinic in south Tehran that offered literacy and sewing classes, and occasional art exhibits. A research committee located problematic statements by Khomeini and other conservative religious leaders, which they reproduced in a pamphlet in order to warn the public about the impending Islamization of society. Yet the group continued to publish statements on women's issues by Lenin, Engels, August Bebel, Clara Zetkin, and even Stalin that offered class-reductionist old left arguments in the face of the impending theocracy (Matin-Daftari 1999).

Until 1981, leftist women poured their heart and soul into various social programs for the urban and rural poor. Nasrin Basiri, one of the founding members of the NUW, recalls the dedication of the group and the energy and love that the activists channeled into their volunteer work:

Twenty to thirty people worked in this office, and our meal was normally fresh hot bread and cheese, ... [and] hot tea with sugar cubes to quench our thirst. Rent was paid out of membership dues. Women who were employed, such as civil servants, who had more funds, paid more. The unemployed donated their labor ... My husband and I used our rather large car for the organization's transportation ... With others, we visited women in villages around Tehran. An artist in our midst produced flyers for our regular meetings or a calendar. A teacher worked with a group of students. With a few other women lawyers and others I researched the Qur'an and the publications of the grand ayatollahs. [To alert the public] we even compiled a book called *Women Under the Islamic Republic*, which was later published abroad. (Basiri 1999, 148)

The NUW's dedication was not unique. Other leftist groups carried out similar work around the country involving literacy campaigns, vocational training, and ideological recruitment. However, the NUW still continued to reject the label of feminism. Its stated purpose was to recruit working-class women to the Marxist cause. In fact, most NUW activists knew little about either feminism or workers since there were hardly any workers in the organization.

Basiri recounts how she recruited Hajar, the "first and last" worker to attend the NUW meetings she helped organize. Hajar was a poor relative of the better-off Basiri, and the two were related through an uncle's *sigheh* marriage. Hajar worked in the Starlight stocking factory. She was delighted by the invitation to attend the NUW meetings, in part because it meant that one of her upper-class relatives had finally acknowledged her existence. One night she came to a meeting with a friend. Basiri recalls:

The women and girls in the meeting all looked and dressed alike. They had extremely short hair or else tied their hair back with an elastic band. They turned out in long pants and shirts and had no makeup. We sat there on the floor, dusty, colorless, and completely engrossed in our debates. Hajar and her friend came late … Since it was the first time they had attended a women's meeting, they assumed it would be something like a party or a wedding. The two women had put on their best clothes. They wore pleated skirts. One had a white lace shirt with pearl buttons under her veil. The other one was sporting an embroidered shirt. Both displayed several rows of gold bracelets and were heavily made up by standards of the time. The one in the white shirt also had long, white, manicured nails. They came into the room and, with their high-heeled shoes, awkwardly sat next to us on the floor. They dropped their black veils on their shoulders and looked at us, smiling but somewhat perplexed by our appearance. (Basiri 1999, 151)

This anecdote captures some of the ways in which the urbanized, middle-class, leftist women continued to misunderstand working-class culture even after the revolution. Most assumed that the poor were concerned only with labor issues and daily survival. They never imagined them as women who cared about the aesthetics of their bodies. But most leftist women were equally ignorant about the history of women's rights in Iran and the legacy of international feminism. Hajar, a single mother, continued to come to the meetings and distribute the NUW's paper on her factory floor until she was fired by her boss (Basiri 1999, 151).

An artist's compromise with modernity

Zahra Rahnavard was one of Shariati's thousands of supporters in the 1970s. Her life story shows the ambiguous sentiments of women from the old middle classes who found themselves caught in a bind between their religious practices and modernity. Rahnavard has earned an MA in the arts and a Ph.D. in politics, and has written on art, literature, poetry, religion, and politics. Her writings have been translated into Turkish, Arabic, Urdu, and English. These have included essays with titles such as "The Uprising of Moses," "The Colonial Motives for the Unveiling of Women," "The Beauty of the Veil, and the Veil of Beauty," "The Philosophy of Islamic Art," "Islam, Modernism, Postmodernism, and the Arts," and "Women, Islam, and Feminism in Imam Khomeini's Thought." Rahnavard has also held several exhibits of her artwork. Her large sculpture *Mother* was situated prominently in the middle of a busy Tehran square after the revolution. She is married to Mir Hussein Musavi, a protégé of Khomeini, who was a prime minister of the Islamic Republic from 1981 to 1989. In 1999, during the era of reformist President Muhammad Khatami (1997–2005), she became president of the influential al-Zahra Women's University in Tehran (Fig. 8.4).

Rahnavard was born into a religious family with Sufi inclinations and has defined her life as a constant struggle between "modern and traditional" values (interview in Giviyan 1994a, 5; subsequently cited only by

Figure 8.4 Zahra Rahnavard

page number). Both her powerful grandmother, who headed the clan after her grandfather's death, and her mother were intensely religious.[6] Rahnavard's grandmother was a constant presence in their lives, scrupulously observing the rituals of *taharat*. She insisted that the grandchildren follow her example, taking them to visit the shrines of Shiʻi saints whenever she could: "Through religious narratives, she repeated the lessons of ritual purity and cleanliness over and over" (6). Rahnavard's mother stressed that all actions on earth, even simple ones like banging against the door or tripping, were preordained by God (6). Rahnavard's father was a military instructor at the War Academy who was torn by conflicts between his religious beliefs and his commitment to the military and the state. His resentment of the American military advisors eventually led to his forced retirement at the age of forty (5).

A bright student who ranked first in her classes, Rahnavard was introduced to the underground stream of Marxist literature in high school in the 1960s: "Except for Marx's *Capital*, I have read nearly all the other

---

[6] On the maternal side, Rahnavard's family claimed to be related to Navvab Safavi, the influential leader of the Fedayeen Islam.

works by Marx and Engels," she recounts (7). She also became interested in the arts, but had trouble reconciling her new political and philosophical interests with her religious commitments and her somewhat traditionalist artistic inclinations. The democratic principles of a modern society, the plurality of organizations, of newspapers, and of institutions seemed appropriate goals to her, but Rahnavard could not accept the alternative value system that modernity brought about: "Like two edges of a pair of scissors, Marxism and Modernism had declared a war against traditions and Islam" (8). What she particularly abhorred in modernism was the rejection of religious rituals in favor of sexual and moral freedoms:

The modernization that the shah and his American masters had planned for Iran involved opposition to religion, the elimination of beautiful Islamic and national symbols, and an emphasis on appearance and frivolity, Westernization, and sexual and ethical freedoms. Alongside such cultural goals, the political autocracy, dependent capitalism, the lack of political parties and newspapers, and the chaos in the government continued. Despite the efforts of many authentic [Muslim] families, this modernization was infecting families and corrupting the younger generation. (8)

By her own account, Rahnavard found little support for her views among her progressive high-school teachers and college professors, which made her feel more isolated (8). At the Teachers Training College of Tehran, one of her teachers went so far as to accuse those who went on the annual pilgrimage to Mecca and circled the shrine of Ka'beh of idol worship (10). Many left-wing and liberal activists of the 1940s had become teachers and professors by the 1960s and 1970s. They continued to express a fervent belief in social and scientific progress and an equally passionate opposition to Western imperialist powers, especially the United States. Rahnavard was attracted to her teachers' ideologies and began to explore the class contradictions of Iranian society. But she could not accept the secular perspectives of her professors or many of her college class-mates. She was convinced that for all their opposition to the regime, they had been "brainwashed" by the government and the West. As an ele-mentary school teacher, she was appalled by the poverty of her young students, whose parents were unemployed and sometimes addicted to drugs. When Rahnavard began to politicize her young students in opposition to the government, she was fired and accused of mental instability (10).

Unemployed, and unwilling to marry immediately, Rahnavard decided to pursue graduate studies in Islamic Arts. Tehran University in the late 1960s was a hotbed of left-wing ideologies and influenced by a range of philosophical and political perspectives, ranging from existentialism to various forms of Marxism, especially pro-Soviet communism and

Maoism. The overthrow of Mosaddeq in 1953, the Vietnam War, and the 1967 Arab–Israeli War, as well as the close ties between the state of Israel and the shah, all helped produce a new generation of intellectuals intensely critical of the West. This generation of leftists attacked not only Western political and economic domination, but also expressed strong hostility to Western cultural values. Empress Farah Pahlavi, however, supported the art department, which received substantial funding from the government for projects aimed at modernizing Iranian art. According to Rahnavard, "It was one of the shah's greatest investments. [He hoped] to train a new generation [of artists] who could revamp the art and culture of this nation and defile it with cultural imperialism" (10–11). During these years, Rahnavard studied art history, exhibited her works, became involved in the student movement, and joined clandestine leftist groups. However, she defines this period as one of the "bleakest" and loneliest of her life, calling it her "period of annihilation." She complains that once the religious scaffolding of her thinking cracked, she was no longer capable of making any sense of her world. Good and bad, sin and virtue, all became one big muddle:

I was like a miserable speck of dust floating between the sky and the earth … Nothing seemed to be in its proper place. An unrelenting earthquake, spewing tormenting verses everywhere … If someone, in describing an event, said that such and such an incident was good, I would be baffled by their ability to judge. Good and bad were ambiguous terms to me. I would ask, "By what measure is it good or bad," and my friends would laugh at me … I only had one clear classification in my mind. On the basis of my old memories and teachings in the family, I divided all events and things into two types: worldly and divine. Foods, objects, colors, accidents, people, shapes, even times of the day, clothing, directions, were either of a material, worldly nature or of a divine one. (11)

Unable to develop a secular ethic that was more in harmony with the expectations of a modern world, she withdrew from others and her sense of isolation intensified. Eventually, she turned to religious studies. By the late 1960s, Rahnavard had found a group of like-minded friends, both inside and outside the university, and became an Islamist political activist. This was the circle of Ali Shariati, who helped to galvanize her generation of students. In 1969, she married Mir Hussein Musavi, who shared her religious devotion and criticism of Western cultural values (11; Giviyan 1994b, 5). They married in a simple ceremony. She wore no wedding gown, and held no customary feast: "We were not happy. How could one be happy when the fully armed government tortured the youth?" It was "just the union of two people who were moving in the same [political] direction," a struggle to the point of "martyrdom" (11, Giviyan 1994b, 5). In this later description of her marriage, it is noteworthy that she played down any emotional feelings and glossed over the fact that this was not an arranged marriage, but a companionate one that the partners had entered freely.

In the early 1970s, Rahnavard began to teach art to women at Shariati's Husseiniyeh Ershad. By 1974, she had organized an Islamic art exhibition there, was running a study group in which students read Shi'i religious texts, and had published two pamphlets, "The Migration of Joseph" and "The Uprising of Moses." During these years, when Rahnavard maintained an active political life, her mother helped raise her two small children. When the government cracked down on Husseiniyeh Ershad, Rahnavard, who had achieved some fame as one of the first Islamist women writers to challenge the Pahlavi regime, fled abroad with her children (Rahnavard 1987, 31). In 1976, she joined the left-wing Confederation of Iranian Students in the United States, siding with the Islamist wing when it splintered the following year. She returned to Iran shortly before the revolution and, through her husband's connections, was able to join the circle of the supporters of Ayatollah Khomeini.[7]

Fromm argues that what he calls moral aloneness and lack of relatedness to values, symbols, and patterns are as "intolerable as physical aloneness" for human beings (Fromm [1941] 1994, 17). As a result, individuals turn to anything that spiritually connects them to the world. "Religion and nationalism, as well as any custom and any belief, however absurd and degrading, if it only connected the individual with others, are refuges from what man most dreads: isolation" (Fromm [1941] 1994, 18). Many Iranian students willingly followed Shariati and later placed their fate, and that of their nation, in Khomeini's hands. Rahnavard belonged to a generation of Iranian women that went to college and lived a life that seemed to offer many new choices, more than those available to their mothers and grandmothers. By becoming a political activist in the Islamist movement, she found a compromise solution. She returned to many of her familial ethical principles without abandoning her desire for new ones, such as an advanced education, professional and economic progress for women, and companionate marriage, albeit within the bounds of Islam.

An Islamist woman's escape from tradition

Some of the followers of the Islamist movement in the 1960s and 1970s were ambitious women from lower-middle-class families with little formal education. They seemed to gain a new sense of purpose and

---

[7] For her activities after the revolution see chapter 10.

identity as a result of joining the Islamist movement and adopting its ethico-political structure. Most came from highly patriarchal families, with little or no chance for advanced education and employment. Some managed to carve out a different identity for themselves by joining the secret religious cells. Their allegiance to a highly authoritarian and patri-archal movement that advocated women's subordination to men none-theless allowed them to gain a measure of personal power, to exercise leadership over others, and to live more gratifying personal lives. This often came at great cost to others, however, especially after the revolution.

Marziyeh Dabbagh, a key supporter of Khomeini, was one such person. By 1979, she had spent more than fifteen years in Khomeini's circle. In the fall of 1978, Dabbagh was one of Khomeini's bodyguards in Paris. After the revolution, she served as a military commander in the Iran–Iraq War. In the late 1980s, she went to Moscow as part of a delegation to negotiate with Mikhail Gorbachev. In the 1980s and 1990s, Dabbagh headed the Islamist Women's Society, which was affiliated with the government (interview with Giviyan 1992, 22; subsequently cited only by page num-ber). Dabbagh was elected to the Islamic Republic's Parliament for four terms (Fig. 8.5).

Dabbagh grew up in the early 1940s in an old, lower-middle-class family in the western city of Hamadan. Her father was a small bookseller who also taught religious ethics. Unlike Rahnavard, who married a com-rade while she was in graduate school studying the arts, Dabbagh went through an arranged marriage at the age of thirteen. The couple soon moved to Tehran, where her social isolation increased. This experience was a turning point for Dabbagh. As Erika Friedl has shown in her studies of pre-revolutionary southwest Iran, provincial and rural women who moved from small towns and villages to large cities were often more isolated than before. Having left behind their relatives and close family network, they missed the social events of their home communities, whether at public bathhouses, weddings, celebrations at the birth of a child, or funerals. Once they moved to the city, they also observed the strict veil of the old middle classes (Friedl 1991). In her interviews, Dabbagh remembers those difficult years in the late 1950s, after she had moved to Tehran, and shares the great sense of injustice she felt:

Why shouldn't girls study? Why shouldn't they choose their own husbands? There were many other questions, for none of which I had an answer. I had to find answers to my questions, to understand who brought about this cruelty, injustice, and discrimination against women, to learn how the distinction between me, as a "woman," and the other sex, "man," came about. I had many discussions with my husband. He said, "I don't know the answers; you should talk to someone who knows. It is best that you study jurisprudence because all comes from the

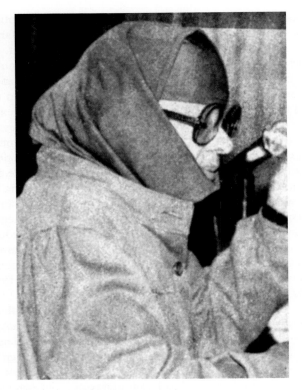

Figure 8.5 Marziyeh Dabbagh

Qur'an, the Hadith (Tradition), and the rules of Islam." (Giviyan 1992, 22–23; subsequently cited only by page number)

Dabbagh wanted to know why she had been deprived of such opportunities, while many other women she met in Tehran were not. She was questioning the theological justifications for gender subordination in her own life. Her husband's permission provided her with a way out. She could now leave the house for weekly lessons with a religious instructor, Hajji Ali Khăansari.

In 1963, when Khomeini was placed under house arrest by the state, Dabbagh joined a circle of his followers. Eventually she entered a study group in Tehran that was sponsored by a protégé of Khomeini, Ayatollah Muhammad Reza Sa'idi.[8] Dabbagh and sixteen other Islamist women

---

[8] Sa'idi was later arrested and tortured to death by the SAVAK (Akhavi 1980, 161).

met at the back of a nearby mosque for private lessons. There was now a new guiding principle in her life. She recounts that she no longer experienced her periodic "satanic temptations" to carry out sinful desires such as "buying a dress, going on a trip, or having a dinner party" (24).

By 1967, Dabbagh had proved herself the most dedicated member of the women's group and was being groomed for the next stage in the movement, becoming an underground revolutionary. Her new assignment was to travel to small and large cities and lecture to women, gaining new adherents for Khomeini. But in order to avoid the SAVAK and find a way into military circles, where she was supposed to concentrate on finding new recruits for the Islamist cause, Dabbagh needed to change her appearance. She had to look like a modern woman, and wanted to drive a car. But how could she drive a car when Khomeini had explicitly condemned women's driving? The solution was simple. In the Shiʿi tradition, each believer must follow a living *marjaʿ-e taqlid* and receive guidance from him on all difficult matters of life. But one can choose to change the *marjaʿ* one follows and select another. Khomeini, through one of his disciples, advised her "to find another *marjaʿ* [one who did not object to women's driving, and to ask for his permission] to learn [driving]; there would be no problem" (24). In other words, he taught her how to circumvent the technicality of ignoring his own rulings on this matter. But how was Dabbagh to learn to drive from a strange, unrelated man? Shiʿism solves such problems by sanctioning temporary marriage. Dabbagh would arrange a nonsexual *sigheh* between the driver and one of her daughters; thus, the driver became *mahram* (related), and she could take lessons from him. Finally, she had to change her appearance. She adopted multiple identities for different lectures, pretending sometimes to be the wife of a nonexistent engineer (25). In this way, she was able to enter the military circles and work among a group of officers' wives. She wore modest modern clothes, drove a car, traveled, socialized, and spent much time away from her family, all without feeling guilty, since Khomeini himself had sanctioned her activities.

Dabbagh's transformation shows that Islamist women could cross many forbidden boundaries for the good of the cause. At the very time that Khomeini was criticizing the advocates of women's rights for wearing Western clothes, driving cars, and mingling with men unrelated to them by birth or marriage, and blaming the government for encouraging such "immoral" acts, his disciple was engaging in all such activities and more, with his blessing.

In 1972, the SAVAK arrested Dabbagh, who was in her thirties, and severely tortured her. After a second detention, when her health began to fail, they released her. The SAVAK leadership had decided that it was politically imprudent to have a mother of eight (seven girls and a boy by this time) martyred in the shah's prisons. Soon, Dabbagh left Iran for Europe and other parts of the Middle East. She traveled to England and France, where she participated in hunger strikes on behalf of Iranian political prisoners. In Saudi Arabia, she distributed clandestine fliers among the pilgrims to Mecca. In the 1970s the secret cells loyal to Khomeini had sent 700 recruits to Syria and southern Lebanon, where they were trained in guerrilla tactics by the Islamist Amal organization. The cells used Khomeini's ties to Colonel Muammar Qaddafi in Libya and Yasser Arafat of the Palestine Liberation Organization to accomplish this. In Syria, Dabbagh helped set up a military camp that trained anti-shah combatants. With the help of the dissident Shi'i cleric Imam Musa Sadr, the Palestinian commando Abu-Jihad, and the Iranian activist Mustafa Chamran, Dabbagh trained Iranian Islamists in paramilitary tactics. She recounts that "after completion of guerrilla and destruction tactics," they were secretly sent back to Iran via the Persian Gulf, and often armed with explosives (28).

During these years, her parents and her married oldest daughter raised Dabbagh's other children. Dabbagh's husband, who supported her political activities, played a nominal role in the life of the children. He held a job in the southern city of Ahvaz, away from the family, visiting every two or three months. Thus, in effect, neither the mother nor the father of Dabbagh's children was living with them during the seven years before the revolution (28). In 1978, when Khomeini was expelled from Iraq and went to France, Dabbagh joined him and became his close advisor, bodyguard, and housekeeper.[9]

Fromm writes of the desire for total submission as an underlying principle of the fascist ideology and its adherents. The same applies to other authoritarian ideologies such as Stalinism and Maoism. Hitler's followers were told over and over that "the individual is nothing and does not count. The individual should accept this personal insignificance, dissolve himself in a higher power, and then feel proud in participating in the strength and glory of this higher power." Their idealism could lead them to willingly become a "dust particle" in this higher order (Fromm [1941] 1994, 231). Years later, after Khomeini's death, Dabbagh expressed this same desire for total submission in strikingly morbid terms. "I always wished for someone to cut me up and make a carpet of my pieces for [Khomeini's] feet. My feelings about him were the same until his death and will always remain the same. I wish we died and he lived and led society" (Giviyan 1992, 74).

---

[9] For her activities after the revolution see chapter 10.

As we have seen in this chapter, by the late 1970s, the conflicting early twentieth-century discourses on gender and modernity had gradually converged and overlapped on many points. Several ideological changes and accommodations with modernity in the anti-royalist coalition made this change possible.

First, for nearly a century, Iranian intellectuals had looked to the West as a possible model for gender reforms in Iran. They had supported calls for women's education and employment, and assumed that these changes produced better mothers and wives and strengthened the family and nation. But by the 1970s they no longer accepted the Western sexual revolution that was gradually spreading to Iran. Soon, there was an ideological split between those who advocated women's emancipation and those who supported a radical socialist and/or Islamic revolution.

Second, the antagonism toward the new gender constructs of the 1960s and 1970s also appeared among women. Even those who had benefited from the regime's gender reforms felt ambivalent about the rapid pace of change and the new dictates of modernity. Many found the aesthetics of a Western feminine body both morally repugnant and impossible to achieve. Western feminists too had written that the bodily norms set by the fashion industry and Hollywood created impossible ideals for women, but this point did not penetrate into the Iranian debate at this time. Also, the near-total identification of Iranian feminism with the Pahlavi regime over the past half-century had created a cultural rupture in Iranian society. As a result, the Islamist movement found it easy to gain the support of large contingents of women, including some branches of the government-backed Women's Organization of Iran.[10]

Third, Khomeini, unlike his ideological predecessor Sheikh Fazlollah Nuri in the Constitutional Revolution, did not completely turn his back on modernity. In the 1940s he appropriated some modern norms of hygiene and the requirements of a modern state. Later, he accepted select gender reforms, such as women's suffrage, education, and active political participation. As the story of Dabbagh shows, even before the revolution, the pragmatic Khomeini was willing to bend rules and allow his disciples to adopt a modern lifestyle in order to promote the cause. He also freely borrowed from Shariati and Third Worldism, frequently using terms such as "colonialism," "imperialism," "exploitation," and "social revolution," thereby creating a new anti-imperialist Islamist discourse.

Fourth, the writings of Shariati, which amalgamated Marxism and Islamism, and the lectures of Khomeini, which advocated a politicized,

---

[10] Personal conversations with Mahnaz Afkhami, November 17, 2004, and Mansour Bonakdarian, January 15, 2005.

"anti-imperialist" concept of Islam, were not so far from expressing the beliefs of many on the left who saw imperialism as the primary enemy and feminism as a Western import and therefore "decadent." Some sectors of the left briefly defended women's rights after the Islamist seizure of power, but others shared the Islamist view that those who demonstrated against Khomeini's rollback of women's rights were either naïve or outright tools of the imperialist powers, which wished to divide the revolutionaries in order to intervene in Iran, as they had in 1953. Thus, these three oppositional currents – secular leftists, supporters of Shariati, and followers of Khomeini – agreed that the preservation of the nation's independence and cultural identity depended on maintaining many existing gender norms, even though they differed in their articulations of what constituted this ostensibly authentic cultural realm.

Through a masterful synthesis of Shi'i religious traditions and leftist anti-imperialist discourses, Khomeini tapped into this discontent with modernity and its technologies of the body and succeeded in setting the ideological, organizational, and political agenda for the revolution. The initial result was a retrogressive religious dictatorship. It began by attacking the personal rights of modern urban women and went on to destroy all democratic and secular opposition, whether on the left or among rival, less authoritarian currents of political Islam. The regime became a rallying point for a militant Islamism throughout the Muslim world, in Algeria, Palestine, Egypt, Lebanon, Pakistan, Afghanistan, and even Saudi Arabia, transcending at times the sectarian divisions between Shi'is and Sunnis.

Part 3

Forging an Islamist modernity and beyond

9 The Islamic Revolution, its sexual economy, and the Left

The 1979 Islamic Revolution was not a wholesale return to the past; rather, the new state reinvented and expanded certain retrogressive gender and cultural practices and presented them as what Foucault has called a "regime of truth" through modern technologies of power. As part of its commitment to modernity, the Islamist state continued the literacy and health campaigns of the Pahlavi era. It also created, alongside the army and the police force, a parallel series of paramilitary forces. Once the regime attained some degree of authority, it established a new juridical discourse on sexuality, with the underlying theme of granting more power over women's sexuality and reproductive functions to the state and to men, while also reversing modern trends in love and marriage. The state encouraged polygamy (multiple 'aqdi) and temporary marriage, as well as the return of easy divorce for men. While these measures weakened conjugal bonds of affection, they also served to compensate men who had acquiesced to the strictures of the new theocratic state. In the name of morality and the preservation of women's honor, men of all social classes gained easier, cheaper access to sex, both inside and outside of formal marriage. The state reduced the age of marriage, and encouraged motherhood and large families, while limiting or closing other life choices for urban professional women. Small openings that had emerged for a modern gay lifestyle in elite urban circles vanished and were replaced with a partial return to practices of covert bisexuality in male and female homosocial spaces.

The long Iran–Iraq War helped the regime to consolidate its new policies including those on sexuality. In September 1980 Saddam Hussein attacked Iran, hoping for a quick victory. This caused a patriotic fervor across the whole country, as hundreds of thousands of Iranians mobilized in defense of the nation. Backed by the Western powers, Iraq initially made territorial gains, but was pushed back by the combined force of the Iranian Army and the parallel military organizations, the Islamic Revolutionary Guard Corps (Pasdarans) and the Basij (People's Militia). The latter sent over 100,000 recruits to the war front, including students, workers, and government employees, and thousands of impoverished youth, often mere boys recruited for "martyrdom operations," with the promise of paradise after death. They were dispatched on mine-clearing operations with staggering losses. In 1982 Saddam Hussein withdrew his troops from the disputed territories and attempted to negotiate a truce, but Ayatollah Khomeini chose to carry on with the war, which was helping him to cement his authority and to strengthen the foundations of the Islamic government. The war dragged on until 1988, when Iran was finally pressured into accepting a UN-negotiated ceasefire. Both nations suffered catastrophic damage. There is much debate about the number of dead and wounded. It is estimated that the war left at least 300,000 dead (200,000 Iranians and 100,000 Iraqis) and 600,000 wounded, and caused severe damage to urban centers and oil refineries ("Iran–Iraq War," 2004; Hiro 1990).

At home, the war allowed Khomeini and his allies to speed up the implementation of their harsh Islamist program and eliminate their moderate Islamic, nationalist, and leftist allies. By 1986, the Pasdaran had grown to 350,000 members grouped in battalion-size units, including a small navy and air force. The Basij, whose members were boys younger than eighteen, men older than forty-five, and those who had recently completed military service, had enrolled some 3 million armed volunteers at 11,000 centers, including many women's units. The Pasdaran received professional military training and operated on a fulltime basis, while the Basij consisted of those on active duty and others kept on reserve. Together, the Pasdaran and the Basij were considered the "eyes and ears" of the Islamic Republic. They served under the direct authority of Ayatollah Khomeini and his trusted followers, and were not subject to any elected bodies such as the presidency or the Parliament (Hiro 1990; *Iran: A Country Study* 2004, 11; "Pasdaran" 2007). While they undertook many such activities before the war, after it ended the Basij and the Pasdaran gave even greater attention to the surveillance and repression of the domestic population. Equipped with the latest weapons and subject to sophisticated riot-control training, they worked with the secret police and were instrumental in eliminating dissident groups. They spied on the general population. One of their most visible activities involved prowling around schools and factories to enforce the *hijab* regulations, often arresting youth for improper clothing and conduct. This could occur for as minor an infraction as a young man caught wearing a short-sleeved shirt. They also stopped cars to check for alcohol or use of makeup by women; they burst into weddings and arrested guests for improper dress, alcohol violations, or Western music. After the war they also broke into homes to destroy banned satellite TV receptors. These activities were coordinated by vigilantes who called themselves Hezbollah (Party of God). Hezbollah intimidated intellectuals by firebombing bookstores, disrupting social and political gatherings, and killing dissidents ("Niruyeh Moghavemat" 2006; "Pasdaran" 2007).

As the new revolutionary regime was placing greater limits on the rights of modern urban citizens, especially women, it simultaneously encouraged the more cloistered women of the old middle classes to become politically active in support of the Islamist cause. This is why Iranian women reacted to the policies of the Islamic Republic in such varied ways. Modern urban women condemned the severe restrictions of the new regime, which deprived them of numerous rights, but many from the old middle classes welcomed the new regime and actually gained greater rights. The latter group credited Ayatollah Khomeini, the revolution, and the war with emancipating them from rigid and patriarchal households and allowing them to become active participants in society. This was true even when this activism began by denouncing more secular supporters of women's rights. These disparate histories form the subject of this chapter and the next.

The Islamist panopticon

In 1978 Foucault hoped that the Iranian Revolution would become a countermodern revolution that would unleash a radical form of political spirituality for Iran and the broader Muslim world. But it would be a mistake to call the Islamist social order countermodern. Both the Pahlavi regime and the Islamist regime employed various techniques of modernity, particularly ones that operated directly on the body. Foucault's technologies of power can help us to analyze the modern disciplinary practices of the Pahlavi era and its harsh secret police, the SAVAK. But they can also help to delineate the modalities of power under the Islamic Republic.

Soon after the revolution, citizens found themselves under the constant gaze of an Islamist state that observed and regulated public (and in some cases private) bodily functions (Fig. 9.1). The Khomeini regime included all of the elements of a modern panopticon. Practices that were more or less voluntary during the Pahlavi era (and often before), such as fasting during the month of Ramadan, participating in the Friday prayer, or ritual mourning during the month of Muharram, were now strongly encouraged by the state. Ablution, daily prayer, fasting, and avoidance of contact with ritually "impure" people were no longer merely personal matters of faith for Shi'i Muslims, but legal requirements that the state sometimes enforced. Implementation was relatively simple. A hierarchical method of observation was established with the clerics at the top. Modern Islamist interpretations of old Shi'i regulations produced normative judgments, a set of rules that required continued observance. In Foucauldian

Figure 9.1 Revolutionary poster

terms, the religious judges compared, differentiated, hierarchized, homo-
genized, and excluded: in short, the new order began to "normalize" the
population. The concept of *taharat* now had an added meaning: the physical elimination and "cleansing of forces that posed a danger to the sacrosanct regime" (Chafiq 2006, 88). Sunni Muslims, non-Muslims, ethnic
minorities with potentially autonomous aspirations (Kurds, Turkomans,
Baluchis), secular Shiʻi Muslims, members of the left-wing opposition,
advocates of women's rights, and Shiʻi theologians with more tolerant

readings of Islamic law were all subjected to close surveillance. When they refused to go along, dissidents were routinely beaten, jailed, tortured, or executed. Officials of the former regime, leaders of the Baha'i community, and gay men were also executed, sometimes without trial. The so-called "hanging judge," Sadeq Khalkhali, had his men prowl the streets in search of political and religious suspects.

Khomeini's Islamist state gathered information relentlessly, first through the Office for the Promotion of Virtue and Prevention of Vice, and later through the revamped secret police, the Pasdaran, and the Basij. In addition, many ordinary citizens internalized the ethos of the new regime and eagerly imposed these rules on others, something the state counted on to achieve its goals. Many public spaces were resegregated along gender lines soon after the revolution. Only a week after Khomeini assumed power on February 11, 1979, *Le Monde* reported that Tehran University was "one of the rare places, perhaps the only one, where women come alongside men and hold discussions with them as equals" (Balta 1979). In June, beaches at the Caspian Sea resorts were segregated by sex. In the spring of 1980, unveiled women were knifed in the northwestern town of Urumiyeh and turned away by *bazaar* merchants in the southern port of Bushire (Tabari and Yeganeh 1982, 235). In many of these cases, the new rules were not yet directly enforced by the vigilantes and the clerical establishment, which in any case did not have full legal authority until spring 1981. Many citizens accepted the regime's ideology, based on the imagined community of early Islam, as a utopian ideal that would cleanse Iran of a century of Western spiritual pollution. They assumed that the gender hierarchies of the new regime constituted an important step in that direction.

After the revolution, the government of the Islamic Republic revamped a number of the Pahlavi institutions. Mosques, theological seminaries, and religious courts became the new centers of power. The state closed mixed secular schools, and segregated institutions of learning by sex. Religious bodies of knowledge (the Qur'an, the *shari'a*, the writings of Khomeini) came to dominate other forms of knowledge (humanities, social sciences, modern law, and even math and science). As a result, students could no longer enter the university without passing an extra exam in religious subjects. The courts of the Pahlavi era were shut down, secular judges were replaced by clerics, and female judges were altogether removed from the bench. The state tried to reverse a process of secularization that had begun with the Constitutional Revolution. The regime played down national non-Muslim rituals, such as the Nowruz New Year festivities, placing greater emphasis on Shi'i rituals and holidays. The new government tried to eliminate certain technologies of the body such as sports, particularly for women. Modern contact sports such as volleyball came to be considered transgressive, because bodies were exposed, though curiously no limits were placed on traditional wrestling matches, where contestants are partially naked. Some sports competed with religious events for public attention; for example, soccer matches often conflicted with daily prayers. As a result, televised soccer matches were stopped during calls for prayer and resumed when prayer was over until 2002.[1]

In the course of the revolution the *chador* and the *hijab* had become symbols of resistance against the Pahlavi regime. They represented the unity of women across social and class boundaries, as well as resistance to Western norms. Many leftist women donned the *hijab* out of respect for the more religious and traditional sectors in the revolutionary movement. By July 1981, however, the *hijab* and the *chador* had come to represent the political and ideological hegemony of the Islamist state. Women who worked for the state were often required to wear the all-enveloping black *chador*, the state's preferred dress code. All others had to observe a more modified form of *hijab*. The *hijab* of the Islamic Republic was starker than that of leftist Muslim groups such as the Mojahedeen Khalq. The regime's prescribed minimum attire consisted of a long and very loose cloak or overcoat, known as a *manto* [manteau], loose pants, and a large scarf covering the hair and neck, in black, brown, navy, or gray shades. The face could be exposed. Female vigilantes, known as Sisters of Zainab, monitored other women, who could be dragged to the offices of the Center for the Promotion of Virtue and Prevention of Vice and beaten, even for minor violations of the *hijab* requirements. At times, the struggles over the *hijab* or sports became life-and-death battles, because the Islamist state defined itself through bodily rituals that prevented "impurities" and maintained gender hierarchies. For women, showing strands of hair from under the scarf, wearing makeup, or maintaining other forms of a modern aesthetic of the body became modes of resistance.

The regime established its control not only through brute force but also through a coherent cultural discourse that demonized feminist accomplishments and linked women's rights both to notions of ritual impurity and to Western imperialist designs on the nation. It emphasized women as mothers, making the anniversary of the birthday of Fatimah (the mother of Hussein) into a Mother's Day holiday. But as against earlier notions of motherhood, a major part of a mother's virtue was redefined as the giving

---

[1] Thanks to Morteza Dehghani for information on this issue.

of martyrs to the Islamist cause. This received special emphasis after the outbreak of the war in 1980.

The degradation of the modern urban woman

By late February of 1979, the real power lay in the hands of the Revolutionary Council, a small, secretive group of clerics close to Ayatollah Khomeini. On the surface, the government of Prime Minister Mehdi Bazargan (1979) seemed relatively pluralistic, with no clerics and four members of the National Front as cabinet ministers. Feminists were comforted by the fact that Bazargan's wife did not observe the *hijab*. Khomeini's council frequently countermanded his minister's orders, however, and also changed its policies by fiat. Bazargan began to issue verbal attacks on "Marxists," whom he threatened to crush if they attempted to destabilize the country. The new regime also started to round up former officials of the shah's regime, some of whom were executed after summary trials. In addition, the new government maintained rigid control over the broadcast media. Public whippings were instituted as the penalty for alcohol consumption.

One potential source of opposition, the Tudeh Party, announced its unconditional support for Khomeini. The party's leading theoretician, Ehsan Tabari, likened the struggle between the shah and Khomeini to that between the Sunni Caliph Yazid and the revered Shi'i Imam and martyr, Imam Hussein (d. 680), and encouraged all its supporters to fully back Khomeini (Hashemizadeh 2007, 14). Since the Tudeh's loyalty to Moscow was legendary, this meant that the Soviet Union had made accommodations to the new regime. However, the two rival groups to the left of the Tudeh that enjoyed strong student support, the Fedayeen Khalq and the Mojahedeen Khalq, began to adopt increasingly critical stances.

On March 1, the Association of Iranian Writers warned that the "democratic character of the revolution must be preserved." Censorship had returned, along with renewed limits on freedom of expression. Vigilantes were intimidating newspapers and harassing public demonstrations and lectures. According to the Association, the vigilantes "cleansed" library books, and they also "brought to an end the rights of women, who had played an important role in the revolution" (Kanun-e Nevisandegan-e Iran 1979). A series of specific measures aimed particularly at modern urban women were promulgated during the first weeks of the revolution. On February 26, Khomeini issued a letter abrogating the Family Protection Law, which had been a milestone for women's rights. On March 3, the new regime prohibited women from serving as judges. The

Figure 9.2 Poster for International Women's Day gathering at Tehran University, March 1979

next day, Khomeini announced that initiating divorce would be an exclusively male prerogative. On March 6, the Ministry of Defense announced that women could no longer serve in the army. On March 9, women were banned from participation in sports, including the Olympic team. Thus, only a few weeks after Khomeini's return to Tehran, the state's intention of reversing decades of gender reforms was unmistakable.

A dramatic moment of resistance occurred on March 8, 1979, International Women's Day – the date of a historic demonstration by Iranian women (Fig. 9.2). This event drew global attention and the support of leading European and American feminists, including Simone de Beauvoir and Kate Millett (Millett 1982, 152). Progressive and leftist intellectuals around the world had generally supported the overthrow of the shah, though there was some uncertainty about the role of religion in a state that was to be led by a cleric. At the International Women's Day demonstration, the authoritarian character of Iran's new regime became apparent to many of its supporters, at home and abroad, who came to fear the new direction of the revolution and its implications for the fate of Iranian women.

On March 7, at a speech to thousands of supporters in Qom, Khomeini declared that, while he would not prohibit women's employment, he would require government employees to wear the *hijab* at work, "In Islamic ministries women should not arrive nude [unveiled] … It is permissible for them to go to work, but they must wear a *hijab* according the *shari'a*" (Khomeini 2005, 72). Several events commemorating International Women's Day had already been planned for the next day at Tehran University. In response to Khomeini's edict, thousands of angry urban women and their male supporters poured onto the streets near the university, where they held large demonstrations against the ruling. The demonstrations continued for five days. At their height, tens of thousands of women and men participated in Tehran. Some leftist men formed a cordon around the women, fighting off armed attackers from the Hezbollah. The demonstrators chanted "No to the *Chador*," "Down with the Dictatorship," and even the occasional "Down with Khomeini." One widely quoted banner read, "We Made the Revolution for Freedom, But Got Unfreedom," while others proclaimed, "At the Dawn of Freedom, There Is No Freedom." Hezbollah chanted in response, "You will cover yourselves or be beaten," but their actions were mainly nonverbal: stones, knives, and even bullets aimed at protesting women. As demonstrations continued, the government announced that Khomeini's directive had been "misunderstood." The new dress code was merely a recommendation, not a requirement, and the Family Protection Law would be restored. Both of these concessions were temporary. On Saturday, March 10, 15,000 women held a sit-in protest at the Ministry of Justice. The statement the women read out emphasized the important role women had played in the revolutionary movement and reminded the authorities that Khomeini had promised women all their social and political rights before assuming power. By March 12, the women's demonstrations had spread to numerous cities around the country. After a long public debate at Tehran University, during which the Fedayeen declined to help protect the marchers any longer, and other leftist groups urged the women to call off the march, thousands poured out into the streets again. But March 12 was the last large feminist demonstration. Another gathering at the national television station to protest biased coverage was far smaller. After that, the women's movement called off its public demonstrations, largely because of pressures from leftist groups such as the Fedayeen, the most influential group on the campus of Tehran University. The Fedayeen argued that the paramount issue now was the need to avoid strife in the revolutionary camp, which could pave the way for US intervention (Gueyras 1979).

In response to the women's demonstrations, the Islamists organized a counter-demonstration that involved more women than the earlier feminist protest. On March 16, some 100,000 demonstrators, many of them women clad in black *chadors*, rallied in Tehran to defend Khomeini and denounce the women's demonstrations of the previous week. While the crowd was larger, the Islamist women's demonstration enjoyed the full support of the regime, including free transportation, and freedom from harassment on the streets. Thus, from the first months of the revolution, the regime encouraged the political activism of women from more religious sectors of society, using them to clamp down on supporters of women's rights and on modern urban women more generally.

In their recollections of these events, several Iranian feminists have suggested that supporters of democracy lost an important opportunity to resist the Islamization program of the new government in March 1979, when the women's demonstrations were called off. Secularization from above, and denial of autonomy under the Pahlavi regime, had enfeebled the new middle classes and reduced many to a situation of apathy and hopelessness. Echoing regime charges, major leftist organizations like the Fedayeen and the Mojahedeen labeled the women's rights activists as "*agents provocateurs*" whose purpose was to derail the revolution (Moghissi 1996, 143).[2]

As the government of the Islamic Republic escalated its attacks on women's rights, democratic forces, such as the satirical journal *Ahangar* in Tehran, warned of the impending gender segregation and the imposition of draconian Islamic laws of retribution (Figs. 9.3, 9.4, 9.5). Members of the leftist National Union of Women (NUW) and other women's groups continued to call upon the Fedayeen and other secular leftist groups to help them organize around gender-specific issues, such as the campaign against the reimposition of compulsory veiling, the Islamization of family law, and sex segregation. But their requests for logistical support (renting a hall, announcing a demonstration) were repeatedly turned down. Many members of the Fedayeen maintained,

[2] Some of the text in the above paragraphs appeared earlier in chapter 4 of Afary and Anderson 2005.

عدل و نصفت

Figure 9.3 Justice under the Islamic Republic, 1979

"the *hijab* was not the issue of women workers, but that of petty-bourgeois and bourgeois women" (Basiri 1999, 151), while the Mojahedeen had enforced a mild form of *hijab* on their women members long before the revolution.

For a while, even with these difficulties, activist women made considerable inroads in small villages around Tehran with their literacy campaigns and discussions of social and economic issues. Yet leftist parties often used the women's organizations solely as a front to recruit members to the parent organization. As Ali Keshtgar, member of the Central Committee of the Fedayeen, recalled years later:

The women's question was about the toiling women and women of the working class. [Our] objective was to penetrate the NUW, using a handful of Marxist-Leninist

Figure 9.4 Map of Iran: anticipating full gender segregation of the nation, 1979

— مناسب‌تر نبوداگه این پتیاره،بجای اونه، یه کتاب توضیح المسائلی ، چیزی دستش میگرفت؟. . .

Figure 9.5 Punishment under the Islamic Republic: woman holding a book on human rights, 1979

women who would push for a Marxist-Leninist line, [then] capture the leadership organs in support of the interests of the toiling masses and ... shut out the intellectual women who were considered ... suspicious, petty-bourgeois, and counter-revolutionary. (cited in Moghissi 1996, 154)

In the above discourse use of the military terms such as "penetrate," "capture," and "shut out" pointed to the enormous hostility of the leftist leadership toward independent women's rights organizations. Many activists in the NUW eventually left the organization over these manipulative and authoritarian policies, as well as fear of arrest and persecution by the Islamist state which intensified daily. In their writings the women lament the fact that the NUW remained a mostly sectarian leftist organization and did not become more inclusive, cutting across ideological divides and focusing on the combating of male chauvinism and its social ramifications in all sectors of Iranian society (Azadeh 1999, 131–132).

Drastic reversals in women's rights

The speed with which the government of the Islamic Republic was institutionalized in 1979 stunned most of the non-Islamist, educated urban activists who had participated in the revolution. They had thought that overthrowing the regime would bring about a more democratic society that would improve the rights of women in family and marriage. Many women, who had worn the veil as a symbol of protest during the revolution, had not realized that a key part of the Islamist agenda was to reverse women's rights. Now they were on the verge of losing most of the rights they had taken for granted.

The 1979 constitution established the legal principles of the new Islamist state, which involved rule by an appointed cleric known as the Supreme Leader (*Rahbar*). The judicial system was entirely overhauled, and many reforms of the Constitutional and Pahlavi eras were jettisoned. The Islamic Civil Code included many elements of the *shariʿa* law of retribution. Women and men, Muslims and non-Muslims, no longer enjoyed equality under law. The testimony of two women now equaled that of a man. Evidence obtained from a Muslim man was worth twice that from a Muslim woman or a non-Muslim man. Life became particularly harsh for modern urban women. Lashing, amputation, and stoning were employed in administering justice, with the last punishment often reserved for women convicted of adultery (Afshari 2001, 55–69).

Khomeini declared the Family Protection Law "un-Islamic" and soon some provisions of the law were voided. The Islamist government was committed to reversing modern trends toward monogamous companionate marriage. Additionally, the Islamist state was determined to undermine modern urban women's individuality and autonomy, as it defined a woman's rights and obligations in relation to her male relatives. A "harmonious marriage" was based on male domination in the family and authoritarian relations, whether between husbands and wives or fathers and children. Within the family, women's main functions were defined as "childbearing, child-rearing, and housework," while gender socialization emphasized "feminine and masculine roles" (Kian-Thiébaut 2005, 46).

The universities were shut down from spring 1980 to fall 1983 as part of a "cultural revolution" aimed at expelling undesirable students and faculty members and revising the curriculum. The state did not oppose girls' education *per se*, instead working to indoctrinate women through a comprehensive Islamization of the school curricula. A series of segregation policies also limited urban women's career choices and access to advanced education. The traumas of this period are well described in Azar Nafisi's moving memoir, *Reading Lolita in Tehran* (2003).

As government day-care centers were closed down, many educated women were forced out of full-time office jobs and into low-paying and part-time employment (Nomani and Behdad 2006, 127). By 1983, women faced innumerable restrictions and violations of their rights, based upon the return to Islamic *shari'a* law, which defined a woman's legal rights as half of a man's.

New laws and regulations encouraged child marriage and polygamy, and prevented women from leaving abusive marriages, going far beyond the limitations of the Pahlavi era:

(1) The reinstitution of male guardianship regarding major decisions in a woman's life, such as a father's permission for marriage or a husband's permission for education, employment, change in domicile, or travel.

(2) The lowering of the legal age of marriage to puberty, which again was defined as nine for girls and fifteen for boys. Fathers and *valis* (guardians) could also arrange the marriage of a pre-pubescent girl or boy (in practice the age of women at first marriage remained constant).[3]

(3) The adoption of a pronatalist policy; a ban on abortion, as well as limitations on the use of contraceptives.

---

[3] As Nomani and Behdad have shown, the age of marriage remained constant from 1976 to 1986 (17.9 for rural women and 19.0 for urban women), while child marriage continued to decrease (2006, Table 4.1).

(4) New laws reinstated a husband's unilateral right to divorce. The couple would have to petition a court, which would encourage reconciliation, but if the husband refused, judges would issue a divorce certificate. Meanwhile, a husband could annul his divorce during the three-month 'idda period without his wife's consent.

(5) The return of polygamy and a man's right to take up to three additional 'aqdis without permission of his first wife. The first wife lost the right to sue for divorce in such cases.

(6) Policies encouraging temporary marriage, an institution that had largely fallen out of favor in the Pahlavi era, except around shrines and in poor urban sectors.

(7) Limitations on the custody rights of mothers; reversal of provisions favoring mothers' guardianship over their children after the father's death.

(8) Lighter sentences for husbands, brothers, and fathers accused of "honor killings."

Other laws curtailed women's access to public spaces and employment, further defining them as second-class citizens:

(1) Compulsory *hijab* for women in public. Even slight violations of the *hijab* dress code brought severe punishment. Violators, once rounded up, could be sentenced to as many as seventy-four lashes or imprisonment for up to a year.

(2) A ban on all co-ed. classes; resegregation of educational institutions, including cafeterias and many other public spaces.

(3) Partial segregation of parks, restaurants, movie theatres, beaches, buses, and all other public spaces. In public buses, women sat at the back, and men at the front.

(4) Restrictions on female state employees, resulting in the resignation or dismissal of 40,000 teachers between 1980 and 1985.

(5) Closing of state-sponsored day-care centers to discourage women's employment.

(6) Removal of women judges from the courts.

(7) Prohibition against women's singing and dancing in public.

(8) Ban on women's participation in public athletic events.

(9) Injunctions on public wearing of makeup and anything that enhanced a woman's physical appearance such as bright nail polish or form-fitting clothes.

(10) Regulations against public expressions of affection between men and women, sometimes leading to the arrest of engaged or married couples.

Figure 9.6 "Torture" by Shaqayeq

(11) Execution and stoning of women charged with *zina* (adultery).
(12) Arrest and execution of young activist women (and men), including members of the Mojahedeen and Fedayeen, on charges of opposition to the state (Fig. 9.6).[4]

Hezbollah goons sometimes stabbed and threw acid on young female activists on the streets before arresting them. Tens of thousands of dissidents, among them high-school and college students, journalists, doctors, teachers, workers, and housewives, young and old, were incarcerated and in some cases executed. Chahla Chafiq speaks of the emergence of a "sacred sado-fascism" inside the prisons, where men and women languished for months in solitary confinement and were tortured and raped. The perpetrators exemplified the definition of sadism as the desire for absolute control over another (Chafiq 2006, 100–101). Once the war ended in 1988, the remaining political prisoners were given a chance to join the Islamist *tavvabs* (repenters). In the early years of the revolution the *tavvabs* had joined the

---

[4] See Tabari 1984. Summaries of these changes also appeared in Tohidi 1991 and Tabari and Yeganeh 1982. I have also relied on Mir-Hosseini 1999; Kar 1999a; 1999b; 2000a; 2000b; Afshari 2001; Nomani and Behdad 2006, 76, and various newspapers in compiling this summary. I am indebted to Shahla Ezazi and Saeid Madani-Ghahfarokhi for their careful reading of this chapter and clarification of many issues. See also Ezazi 1998; Madani-Ghahfarokhi 2005.

guards and become enforcers of prison rules. In 1988, those who refused this offer, more than several thousand, were executed (Abrahamian 1999, 215).

In the early 1980s, some female prisoners were married as *sigheh* wives to their prison guards. Families often became aware of the death of their loved ones when the prison guards came to their homes and offered them an *ajr* (which a husband typically pays his *sigheh* wife) for their deceased daughters (Chafiq 2006, 123). These retrogressive laws and practices reverberated throughout society and reduced women to second-class citizens.

Marriage and the sexual economy of Iranian Islamism

Soon the state and ordinary men gained immense authority over women's sexual and reproductive capacities. Fathers, grandfathers, and paternal uncles (as male guardians) were given extensive guardianship powers over female relatives. Once again, a father or *vali* could choose to marry off a pre-pubescent girl to a much older man of his choice (Article 1041 of the Civil Code). While the *ʿulama* had historically differed on whether a woman needed her *vali*'s permission for first marriage, the state now established the more restrictive version of *shariʿa* on this question (article 1044 of the Civil Code). With so many limits on interactions between single men and women, semi-arranged marriages became increasingly necessary. Accordingly, extended family gatherings again became a crucial arena for finding spouses (Wright 2001, 176).

Once a woman was married, the state made it nearly impossible for her to avoid her husband's sexual demands. In the 1980s sexual and psychological exploitation in marriage became a husband's prerogative (Kar 2003; Aghajanian 1986, 751). Polygamy and temporary marriage gave married men easy access to other sexual partners. Moreover, this increased their power at home, even if they did not exercise these rights. The absence of community property in marriage continued to disempower married, divorced, and widowed women. This sexual economy was not a minor side effect of the Islamist ideology. Rather, it formed an important, though often unspoken, reason for male support or acquiescence in the face of Islamization.

The revolution and the war changed relations at home. Confident and highly educated urban women were shocked by the discrepancy in rights between men and women. In the final days of 1980, Shirin Ebadi was stripped of her position as judge. Soon she became a clerk in the same court over which she had once presided. While she was powerless in her job, she refused to accept subservience in her marriage. Ebadi asked her husband, Javad Tavassolian, to go to a notary with her and grant her the right to divorce and custody of any future children they might have. He agreed, much to the astonishment of the notary, and in this way they saved their marriage (Ebadi 2006, 53–54). But such legal rights depended entirely upon the husband's attitude.

After the revolution, leaders of various dissident and leftist parties encouraged their members to marry one another, hoping that marriage would avert government suspicion. Such "arranged political marriages" and even many love marriages proved fragile. In addition to the constant threat of arrest and possible execution, the young couple often realized that, aside from the political goals of the organization, they had little in common and scarcely knew each other (Farahani 2007).[5] Moreover, young leftist women rejected the types of manipulation implemented by wives of earlier times, who controlled men by feigning submission while entangling them in a web of overbearing familial relations. They had learned to verbalize their views, to argue passionately for social and political rights, and to demand equal treatment with men in political activity. Now they expected the same in marriage. But leftist men often had social and familial expectations not much different than those of their fathers, plus the Islamist state had further empowered them. Unlike Javad Tavassolian, many refused to give up these rights.

The life story of Vajiheh Reza'i, a member of the Fedayeen organization, was not so uncommon in the 1980s. She had married Massoud Reza'i for love and against the advice of her family in 1970. After a few years they moved to the United States, where she worked and he attended college, as both became leaders of the Confederation of Iranian Students. They returned to Tehran during the revolution. Vajiheh, who was now the mother of two children, quietly continued her political activities, while Massoud moved into the world of business. She was arrested in 1981 and spent a year in the dreaded Evin prison. Vajiheh was related to a grand ayatollah, however, and was released before the authorities realized that she was a key political activist. Constantly frightened about another arrest, Vajiheh was also concerned about her marriage and the future of her children. Massoud had become a successful company director and had started an open affair with his secretary. When Vajiheh asked him to end the affair, he beat her viciously, making it clear that she simply had to endure the situation. This went on for some months. On a vacation trip to the Caspian Sea, for example, Massoud brought along his mistress and rented two adjacent villas, taking his meals with his secretary. Desperate about her situation, Vajiheh offered Massoud three possible ways out: mend their relations and return to a monogamous marriage; divorce her;

---

[5] Thanks to Fataneh Farahani for sharing her dissertation, part of which deals with this subject.

or keep the appearance of a married life and turn theirs into an open marriage, where she could also quietly see others. He refused all three of these solutions: he would not divorce her; he would continue seeing his mistress or any other woman; and he would not permit her to see anyone else. Eventually, Vajiheh received a divorce by giving up her *mahriyeh* and the custody of her children. She fled on foot to Turkey to avoid another arrest at the hands of the Islamic Republic (Vahdati 2005; interview with Reza'i, September 16, 2007). Thousands of married women like Vajiheh came to the realization that their husbands had changed, as the men freely took advantage of the new laws. Many left the country in the 1980s, creating colonies of single Iranian women in major cities around the world, such as Istanbul, Berlin, Vienna, Paris, Los Angeles, and London. They became social workers, beauticians, small business owners, or went back to school. Often they channeled their anger into feminist activism.

Mehrangiz Kar, a human rights lawyer who spent two decades defending women in the Iranian courts, has documented various types of sexual violence aimed at married women. Of course, such sexual violence was common enough even before the revolution, especially in the provinces, where underage girls were illegally married. But the practice had spread further under the Islamic Republic. Medical doctors continued to report stories such as the following:

When I was an intern, I worked in the emergency section of the hospital. We had a phenomenon we called "the arrival of the bride" ... It meant a newly wed girl was brought to the hospital because of severe tearing and bleeding [of her hymen and vagina on her wedding night], and the doctors rushed to save her. (Cited in Kar 2000b, 476)

Men's unilateral right to repudiation (while curtailing women's right to divorce) disproportionately increased male authority in marriage (article 1133 of the Islamic Civil Code). In the first decade of the revolution, divorce rates shot up 200 percent in Tehran, leading to complaints in the Islamic Parliament (Maqsudi 2005, 14). Divorced women had limited child-custody rights, for boys up to the age of two and girls up to the age of seven. Also, the *'idda* waiting period was reinstated. Thus a husband who chose to take his wife back within three months of a unilateral divorce could simply do so, without considering her wishes, and the state enforced these practices. The courts expected women to tolerate most forms of sexual, physical, and mental abuse in marriage, and to continue living in the houses their husbands provided. Only male impotence, severe drug addiction, or intolerable violence (and here the bar was set quite high) could be admitted as grounds for female-initiated divorce. To avoid paying maintenance, men often abused their wives to make them leave their homes; then they petitioned the courts and claimed that their wives were disobedient (*adam-e tamkin*) (Kar 2000b, 140). Even in such cases, the courts often advised women to go back home and try to patch things up with their husbands (Kar 2000b, 159–161).

The law was explicit about men's sexual prerogatives. Article 1108 of Iran's Islamic Civil Code states: "If a woman refuses to have sex with her husband without a valid religious justification, she has no right to maintenance" (Kar 2000b, 144). The courts were largely indifferent to charges of sexual violence in marriage. Although Shi'i law recommends abstaining from intercourse during menstruation, some clerics rejected even this right for women. Kar concludes:

In Iran, legal and traditional concepts are such that a woman is denied any right in her marriage bed. Disobedience (*adam-e tamkin*) in its specific [sexual] meaning gives the man the right to have intercourse with his wife without any concern for her physical or psychological readiness. Sometimes the judicial authorities ignore a man's sexual perversion in his treatment of his wife and do not even consider such conduct bad behavior. (Kar 2000b, 143)

In the 1990s, when censorship was relaxed a bit, violence against women became a recurring topic in the women's press. The public learned that the authorities routinely ignored the pleas of abused and mutilated women. Many suffered inhuman abuses, among them being burned with cigarettes, set on fire, or disfigured by acid. Another common story of abuse concerned children left in the custody of their father's family after divorce, whose mother had neither custody rights nor even weekly visitation rights (Kar 2000b, 288–289).

Temporary marriage

During and after the war, the state pressured young war widows to remarry. Ranking clerics, and later President Hashemi Rafsanjani (1989–1997), advocated temporary marriage as a solution to the economic burdens of the war and the moral dilemma of having many young widows around. There were about 56,000 war widows, and many were asked to engage in temporary marriage with ideologically committed Islamists or disabled veterans. The state also used the issue of the war widows to promote polygamy for all women. At the time, even some Islamist women took issue with this rationale. Azam Taleqani argued:

There are 500,000 fewer women than men in our country … Yet we are told that we must accept that our husbands have the right to remarry. I even went to some of our religious leaders and asked them whether they were backing the family or planning to destroy it? Since it is obvious that the moment a second wife steps in, effectively the first wife is discarded and her life is ruined ... But they are forcing women in this country to accept polygamy. (Cited in Omid 1994, 201)

Despite the state's call for single men to marry war widows, old cultural norms that expected virginity at first marriage had not died out, preventing some widows from finding suitable husbands (Zahedi 2006, 275). In addition, widows who entered polygamous marriages seemed to be more prone to divorce (Aghajanian 1986, 751). By 2005, only 4,868 war widows had successfully remarried, and the rest who continued to receive their pension had either divorced after a second marriage or chosen to remain single ("Khanevadeh-ye Shohada" 2005, 57).

The state promoted temporary marriage as a solution to other social ills as well. A media campaign involving radio, television, newspapers, mosques, books and pamphlets, and, later, the Internet, promoted *sigheh* as a morally sanctioned substitute for Western dating. Many such websites are still operating, as of this writing. They encourage men and women to avail themselves of this "sacrament" and suggest *sigheh* as an ethically suitable alternative to masturbation and prostitution.[6] Posters in offices claim, "*Sigheh* is the sweetest pleasure given to Muslim women," and "the best medicine for passion."[7] Such statements are usually attributed to the Prophet and the first and sixth Shi'i Imams. Pamphlets and books also encourage young people to enter a temporary marriage, before contracting an *'aqdi* one, thereby avoiding the possibility of early divorce ("Ezdevaj-e Movaqqat" 1991).

In the 1990s, high-school principals encouraged their students to enter a *sigheh* "trial marriage" instead of dating, although most adamantly refused to do so. President Rafsanjani proposed the practice as a way of circumventing the state's strict rules against intermingling of the sexes (Tait 2007). In addition, prostitutes were asked to have short-term *sigheh* marriages with the Pasdarans, the Basijis, and other veterans under the auspices of the state in a "House of Honor" (Khaneh-ye 'Effat), a euphemism for legalized prostitution. However, the proposal had to be shelved after severe public criticism. The practice was more common among Islamist men and women who joined various regime-sponsored revolutionary organizations and worked side by side (Haeri 1989, 96–100). Hence some Islamist enforcers of morality, who wore heavy black *chadors* and covered much of their faces, lived freer sexual lives in some respects

---

[6] For more information see http://movaghat.blogsky.com/.
[7] Thanks to Houchang Chehabi and Mojhgan Fatoorehchi for sharing these posters with me.

than the young, secular women they arrested on flimsy charges of sipping coffee with male colleagues in cafés and subjected to lashing.

As we shall see in the next two chapters, the state lifted some of its most draconian measures in the 1990s. Meanwhile sexual mores began evolving rapidly and some urbanites increasingly lost their inhibitions about premarital sex. Iranian society had become less religious as a reaction to the theocratic state and also from exposure to Western sexual mores through the Internet, satellite TV, and interaction with the Iranian diaspora. In this environment, inhibitions about temporary marriage decreased and some decided to use the institution to their advantage in order to circumvent the state. In the old days, traveling men contracted *sigheh* marriages when they went to another city for a few weeks or months; now some young couples who were not ready for an *'aqdi* marriage used the practice to avoid the hassle of the morality police. Secular urban girls contracted *sigheh* marriages with their boyfriends to go on vacations and spend extended periods away from home. Young, educated men who could not afford to marry entered into *sigheh* marriages with their girlfriends, promising to have an *'aqdi* marriage when they were financially stable. Twenty-year-old Mahriar, a college student, reported that every holiday he and his friends contracted temporary marriages with their girlfriends and went to a Caspian Sea resort, where they rented a villa with no worries about the morality police (Shakerifar 2006).

As women became more selective in choosing husbands or realized that they could not have the man they wanted, many turned to *sigheh* out of loneliness and financial desperation. An increase in widowhood from war, high divorce rates, and female unemployment augmented the pool of women available for temporary marriage. By 1983, divorce rates gradually moved back up to 88 per 1,000 marriages. In addition, remarriage rates for divorced women remained half those of divorced men. Most divorced men married younger, never-married women, unless the men had fathered multiple children. As Aghajanian has pointed out:

Since it is undignified for a never-married Iranian man to marry a divorcee, her best prospects are widowed men or those interested in a second wife. The widowed men are usually older than the divorcee and have a number of children. It is only in very rare circumstances that a divorcee enters a remarriage and becomes a man's second ['*aqdi*] wife. Under these conditions, many divorcees choose to remain unmarried (Aghajanian 1986, 753).

Or else they quietly became the mistress or *sigheh* of a married man, once again a practice that was more common within the *bazaar* and clerical classes. Hence, some urban middle-class women who despised the custom reluctantly became *sigheh* concubines to wealthy married men, often those affiliated with the theocratic state, who bought them expensive villas and condominiums and annual memberships in posh health clubs. Most men and women kept such relationships semi-secret, because the stigma attached to the practice persisted. Love brokers also reappeared on the scene. Some were clerics who set up Internet sites for their business. They encouraged impoverished women and offered them weekend holidays at resorts with prosperous married men. As in premodern times, men also approached angry, desperate married women, sometimes with the help of love brokers. The broker and her connections produced fictitious certificates of *sigheh* marriage for these weekend getaways, and the men's influence and political connections allowed the couple protection from police harassment.[8]

The return of homosocial spaces

By the late Pahlavi era, Iranian society had substantially moved away from status-defined homosexuality (and the cultural practice of bisexuality) to normative heterosexuality and a celebration of companionate marriage among the new urban middle classes. In small, elite circles, there was also a gradual acceptance of the modern gay lifestyle by the 1970s. After 1979, the Islamist state made homosexuality a capital offense, and in the early years of the revolution, several people who were open about their homosexual orientation were executed.[9] However, while claiming an openly gay or lesbian identity became impossible, the new sex-segregated society became more accepting of covert bisexuality.

NK, a thirty-three-year-old female medical doctor who attended a sex-segregated public high school in Tehran in the mid-1980s, recalled an atmosphere where same-sex attraction was relatively common. At sporting events, the best player or the captain of the volleyball or basketball team was usually the focus of attraction. The students did not necessarily categorize such relations as unusual, but rather as an experience in the life of a young woman who would eventually marry. In a world where parents constantly told daughters to guard their virginity, the girls also felt relatively safe in same-sex relations:

My parents never talked to me about sex. I knew that sex violated the taboo of virginity (*bekarat*). But none of us knew much about virginity and there were a lot

[8] Interview with Vajiheh Reza'i, April 16, 2006.
[9] The International Lesbian and Gay Association (ILGA) estimated that from 1979 to 1997 at least 800 Iranians were executed on charges of sodomy. Most were said to be pedophiles and murderers despite the dubious veracity of such accusations. Others were political dissidents falsely labeled homosexuals. The number of people executed for engaging in consensual adult homosexual acts remains unclear ("Iran Asked to End" 1997).

of myths about it. Some thought it was a box-shaped membrane. Others believed it had seven layers. Only girls who had had sex with men could explain it to us, but they chose not to do so. In junior high school it was relatively common for girls to have sexual intimacy with one another. But unlike in the United States where people are labeled lesbians for such acts, no one pointed a finger at others or called them names. Sex with another girl was also considered safer than sex with boys for two reasons: (1) If adults found out about it their reaction was potentially less aggressive. (2) There was no perceived risk of losing one's virginity. With a woman you felt no matter what you did, you could not lose your virginity.[10]

During the war, similar relations reemerged on the frontlines. The war, which celebrated the heroism and camaraderie of men in the battlefield, revived many male homosocial and homoerotic expressions among the recruits. As Minoo Moallem points out, this homosocial world was celebrated in the war propaganda of the era:

Men, both old and young, go about their daily lives – playing, exercising, reading, talking, strategizing, hugging, sleeping, bathing – on a battlefield that is both a real and an imaginary landscape. The war zone is a place between death and life, a land without women, enabling the expression of homoerotic desire. In this homosocial world, men live in proximity to each other and take care of each other. Women do not exist; this is a city of men of different generations living in harmonious contiguity. Contingent upon but parallel to the "real" world, the battlefield is a space where men are left alone. (Moallem 2005, 115)

This male homosocial space received praise in mystical homoerotic poems about the war. It emerged as well in wartime references to the tragic martyrdom of Hussein, in terms that connoted passionate love ('eshq or mohabbat) and the camaraderie of lovers (yars):

The poetry of the battlefield describes a longing for the scent and the sight of the lover and promises the union of the martyr with the lover at the end of the path where the lover awaits. The motif of romanticized and eroticized longing in the poetic space of the battlefield continues in the union with Hussein … Ironically, tragedy is transformed into the homoerotic union of men, and the homoerotic union of men into tragedy. (Moallem 2005, 116)

After the war, Basij veterans continued to remember the war and its sacrifices in similar ecstatic and romantic terms. The Basij websites and print media, which remain active at the time of this writing, are filled with such letters and essays. They describe the war as an "epic event where brave young men created passionate scenes of love and devotion." They also define a Basij veteran as one who "takes responsibility," "shows passion," becomes "drunk" with ecstasy, and ultimately "unites" with his "beloved" as a result of such sacrifices. The essays repeatedly designate

[10] Interview with NK, November 13, 2006.

the Basij fighter (Basiji) as one who "prays to love." The "Basiji is a man in love" and the gathering of the Basiji is "a school of love" where one learns "the alphabet of love," "the scripting of martyrdom," and "unity with immortality" (www.basijinews.com, retrieved January 17, 2006). Are these poems simply reproducing familiar tropes of Persian mystical poetry, celebrating spiritual devotion in passionate homoerotic language? Or are they telling us something more about homoerotic and homosexual relationships in the war zone? Only future research can shed light on these questions.

Outside the battlefield, the segregated institutions and public spaces of the Islamic Republic allowed for the revival and continuation of not just homosocial expression of love but covert homosexuality. Since kissing, hugging, and holding hands are acceptable between men and between women, covert homosexual conduct and bisexuality were not so conspicuous. According to an Iranian gay activist, before the revolution, homosexuals could meet only in elite hotels and bars. Now, finding a willing partner in a park was easy for a man who had a car and an apartment. Some even called Iran a "homosexual paradise" (interview with JP, July 30, 2004).

Many Westerners remained confused about the place of homosexuality in Iranian society and assumed these changes meant greater tolerance for a gay lifestyle. In the mid-1990s, police ignored men who picked up other men in the parks and public arenas for sex, but there was no formal legal or social tolerance for an openly gay lifestyle in Iran. In 1996, the Swedish government denied the petition of a gay Iranian for asylum on the grounds that homosexuality was an acceptable cultural practice. The Swedish government based its claim on a secret report of its embassy in Tehran. The report claims:

The situation for homosexuals is that the risk for legal proceedings or harassment is utterly minimal as long as a homosexual relationship is handled in a discreet manner ... The police and justice administration do not take active measures to investigate into the existence of homosexuality, nor do they actively hunt homosexuals. All in all, the situation in practice in Iran is drastically different from the impression conveyed by the *sharīʿa*-inspired Penal Code ... the situation in Iran is relatively tolerant, since homosexuality is by no means unusual in Iran. Certain "health clubs" in Tehran are e.g. known to be frequented by homosexuals. Furthermore, it is by no means unusual to meet openly homosexual persons under otherwise heterosexual, private circumstances like social events. Judging by appearances, diplomats with a homosexual orientation posted in Iran have not had any problems to get in touch with "partners" in Iran. If anything, the situation is rather that homosexuals can conceal their orientation more easily in Iran than e.g. in Sweden, as physical contact between men – embracing, cheek-kissing, handholding – is culturally accepted behavior. [So, to be punished,] a homosexual couple must behave with great indiscretion, almost provocatively, in a public place. ("Activist Stunned by Swedish" 1996)[11]

Thus, in matters of sexuality (both heterosexual and homosexual), the Islamist state rejected many modern gender constructs but endured and often encouraged other, premodern ones. Polygamy, temporary marriage, and covert homosexuality – that is, hierarchical social relations where one partner is subservient to the other – were allowed and, in the first two cases, promoted, while more egalitarian heterosexual or homosexual relations (feminist and gay/lesbian rights) were pushed back. The Iranian gay activist Saviz Shafaie summarizes how these policies affected personal relations:

There is conditional permission for erotic games or even rape as an exercise of male power. Pretend it is a joke, or a put-down, and you can get by. But call it true love or honest and real sexual desire, and you are in trouble. If you cross beyond traditional sex regulations and fail to prove that your ultimate desire is dominating a woman, you would be considered a subject. If you act upon your passionate lust and disclaim it, you are safer than claiming an honest love ... Such sex is not based on mutual agreement, mutual freedom of choice, mutual political power, or mutual feeling and desire. When only one person controls an encounter by forcing another to submit, it sounds more like sexual exploitation and rape rather than a healthy sexual attraction. (Cited in Nichols 1997)

Shafaie's statement calls to mind Suzanne Pharr's essay, "Homophobia as a Weapon of Sexism." Pharr argues that opposition to gay rights stems from misogyny, and that openly gay men are threatening because their relationships challenge patterns of domination/submission in traditional heterosexual relations, and, we might add, status-defined homosexuality (Pharr 2001, 148). Shafaie confirms this analysis, based on the situation in Iran's Islamic Republic:

When women are labeled and treated as inferior to men, any woman or any person assumed to have woman-like qualities is devalued. The assumption that homosexuals are feminine and less than manly justifies a domineering man's aggression against them. Sexual liberation would not be possible in Iran without challenging "masculine" values and traditions that work against equality between sexual partners. (Cited in Nichols 1997)[12]

---

[11] In the 1980s there were persistent rumors that European governments often sent their gay diplomats to Iran since life for wives of married diplomats was difficult and many married men turned down such assignments. This document has since been removed from the website.

[12] Shafaie (1950–2000) went to Shiraz University and later received a graduate degree in Sociology from Syracuse University. He campaigned for peace and justice as an Iranian gay activist. His mother Mahin was his staunch supporter and often appeared on the same platform with him in defense of gay rights in Iran. Thanks to Mahin Shafaie and Arsham Parsi for background information on Shafaie.

By implementing these policies, the state aimed to discourage modern trends toward companionate marriage and a modern gay/lesbian lifestyle. However, many citizens resisted these trends, while others began to use them to their own advantage. Modernity had left a lasting impact on Iranian society that could not easily be reversed, especially in a globalized age.

10   Islamist women and the emergence of Islamic feminism

Islamist policies toward women did not take root through force alone. Many women from the more religious sectors of society embraced the new conservative ideology and worked to enforce its repressive policies. The regime recruited others through subsidies to families of veterans and martyrs from the revolution and the war. Still others were "lateral actors" who paid lip service to the Islamist order in order to achieve their own goals.

By joining Islamist organizations, young men and women broke with the established conventions of Iranian society, turning their energy away from their families to support the state's social and political causes. For some women, political Islam was more than a tool of resistance against Western modernity; it was also a way to cultivate a Shiʻi-Muslim style of modernity and freedom from the yoke of parents. By taking jobs in revolutionary institutions, women gained financial and personal autonomy. Many also joined the war effort. As in other wars in other places, Iranian women claimed that if they were equal to men in facing death, they should be equal to them in life and receive the same benefits.

In the second decade of the revolution, some former Islamist activists cautiously reevaluated their political orientations. They realized that "Islamic" policies had not succeeded in developing the economy in such a way as to seriously transform the nation's industries, making Iran more competitive in a globalized world. In fact, the growth of the state-sponsored foundations, the war, and the embargo by the US and other Western powers had actually set back industrial development in many respects, especially when Iranians compared their situation to that of countries like China or South Korea. Many also realized that the idealized notions of an Islamic way of life had helped create a political order that legally undermined women in marriage, family, and the workplace.

The result was that some former Islamists became advocates of women's rights. Commonly known as Islamic feminists, their number is not insignificant. Islamic feminists rely mainly on the writings of two groups: a new generation of religious reformers who have reinterpreted scripture to present more woman-friendly interpretation of marriage and divorce laws, and feminist lawyers who have called for the revision of family laws in light of international human rights norms.

In addition, the long-term effects of some Islamist policies have been contrary to their original intentions. This has led to a determination on the part of many children of the revolution to gain more individual rights in the public and private spheres. A growing coalition of Islamic feminists and more secular advocates of women's rights resulted, creating a vocal force in society. This chapter concerns there developments until the election of reformer President Khatami in 1997.

Necropolitics and the Islamist call to activism[1]

In 1978–1980 modern secular women felt betrayed by their more religious sisters who sided with Khomeini; they could not comprehend the latter's enthusiasm for an Islamic revolution. A closer look at Khomeini's writings sheds some light on this paradox. During the revolution, Khomeini encouraged women to join the anti-shah demonstrations. After the overthrow of the regime, he enjoined them to vote for the Islamic Republic (Khomeini 2005, 42; subsequently cited only by page number), he approved female employment with proper *hijab* (43), and he urged his female supporters to "enter politics" (43) and "to build this nation and educate" its people (44–45). Later, he asked women to enlist in the Literacy Mobilization Organization (Nehzat-e Savad Amuzi or LMO), established in 1980, and in a variety of reconstruction and military projects (52). He applauded women's efforts to form Islamist societies (53–54) and lent his support to the new al-Zahra Theological Seminary for women in Qom (56). Before the revolution, certain professions, such as acting and hairdressing, were castigated as symbols of Western decadence. These now became acceptable professions so long as the women observed proper *hijab* (70). Watching television programs, including some non-Islamic ones, was also an acceptable form of entertainment (75), and women studying or teaching in the university were now said to be commendable (75). Khomeini's supporters even portrayed him as a caring husband who shared the housework when there were too many guests (Akhtari *et al.* 1999b).

In the Islamic Republic the veil gained new shades of meaning. It was no longer only a sign of decency and propriety but also a symbol of *jihad*. Soon large war posters all over the country showed veiled women carrying guns or holding small boys destined for *jihad* (Shirazi 2001, 100). Khomeini urged women and children to "defend their Islamic and

---

[1] Achille Mbembe uses the term "necropolitics" in his discussion of militarized "death-worlds" and the promise of death as a political tool (2003). See also Postel (2006).

national honor" (159). He proclaimed that there were no religious prohibitions against women serving in the army or the Pasdaran (165), and encouraged women to complete "the military, partisan, and guerrilla training appropriate for a resurgent Muslim nation" (165). On the front and in the service of martyrdom, gender segregation was cleverly circumvented, leading Khomeini to praise "women [who] would accompany men, the Pasdaran, the Gendarmes, the Armed Services, the whole military, shoulder to shoulder" (381). These statements were accompanied by economic policies that benefited the less-privileged segments of rural and urban communities, including more access to basic food, healthcare, and education than in the Pahlavi era.

By 1981, allocations for education and health had increased (Hoodfar 1998, 5). Some of the initiatives of the Islamist state facilitated marriage for low-income couples. Banks provided low-interest loans. The Imam's Aid Committee offered *jahiziyeh* to prospective brides. Other institutions such as the Martyr's Foundation (Bonyad-e Shahid) and the Marriage Bureau (Edareh-ye Ezdevaj) helped arrange marriages (Paidar 1995, 279–280). Young couples were encouraged to have simple weddings, and members of local mosques offered to pay the groom's wedding expenses and the bride's *jahiziyeh*. Though the state had required a father's permission in the marriage of his daughter, some of these policies had the opposite effect. An impoverished father could seldom challenge his daughter's choice of marriage after she became an activist in an Islamist organization, found a partner approved by the religious leadership, and also received a small *jahiziyeh* and/or low-interest loan to start married life.

Thus Khomeini's messages during the revolution and the war were very different from his own writings decades earlier, let alone those of a conventional *mojtahed*. Although he reminded women of their responsibilities as wives and mothers, he mostly asked them to become active citizens in the new Islamist order, to contribute to the war effort, and to live in ways that were less conventional. It was a message that many young women from the more religious sectors were eager to hear. In return, Khomeini asked for women's complete devotion to four principles: (1) the observance of the *hijab* and other Shi'i rules of sex segregation; (2) hostility toward more modern women (feminists and leftists), and working toward their elimination; (3) compliance with the new state policies on marriage and divorce; and (4) loyalty to the Islamic Republic and its doctrines of *jihad* and martyrdom (Khomeini 2005, 69–76; 90–93; 171–184; 188–234).

The first three principles were not obstacles for women from more religious sectors. Because of their highly conservative fathers and husbands, most had continued to wear the veil, especially after marriage. Indeed the morality police were almost absent in the southern more conservative parts of Tehran and other big cities since these communities had always monitored their women (Amir-Ebrahimi 2006, 4). Women from middle-class *bazaari* and the rural poor had seldom participated in the modern forms of entertainment of the Pahlavi era. They rarely went to movies – certainly not unchaperoned – did not swim at public pools or beaches, did not bicycle on the streets or drive, did not dance or go to Western-style cafés, and had not usually attended the university. Many had not benefited economically from the Pahlavi industrialization projects. Moreover, they resented the more modern urban women who had availed themselves of such pleasures and opportunities. Most *bazaari* families arranged their daughter's marriage before she finished high school. Since the legal age of marriage under the Pahlavi regime was eighteen, parents arranged a *sigheh* marriage for their daughters, later having a *nekah* wedding when she reached legal age (Haeri 1989, 87). Polygamy, especially in the form of temporary marriage, was also more acceptable in this sector of society. Divorce was less prevalent, since marriage remained an arrangement between two families rather than two individuals, and consanguineous marriages were still popular (Aghajanian and Moghadas 1998, 63). Hence, women from the religious sectors had little to fear from the Islamist state and every reason to embrace its new dictates, which forced modern urban women to become more like them.

In addition, supporters of Khomeini quickly sensed the broader implications of his rhetoric in terms of releasing them from their domineering fathers and husbands. A young Islamist woman could now stand up to her family and demand to go to the university, to become active in an Islamist organization, to join the literacy, health, or reconstruction programs, to enlist in the women's auxiliary branch of the Basij, also known as the Basiji Sisters, to support the war effort, or even to choose her husband through such contacts rather than submit to an arranged marriage (Fig. 10.1). Shirin Ebadi recalls a *bazaari* family with three daughters who were her neighbors. Before the revolution, the eldest daughter married a deeply pious *bazaari* who immediately asked her to wear the veil and refused to let her visit her own parents unaccompanied by him. The second sister begged to go to the university, but also ended up in an early arranged marriage. Her husband was less conservative but still refused her a college education. The third sister had the good fortune to come of age after the revolution. She went to medical school and married a classmate of her choice (Ebadi 2006, 107).

But how did the government convince women to accept the principle of joining the Islamist *jihad* and offering up their children as martyrs? Fromm had held, in the manner of Freud, that both necrophilia (love of death) and biophilia (love of life) are common human traits, though social

Figure 10.1 Basiji Sisters, 1994

conditions could intensify one or the other tendency (Fromm 1973, 408).
Khomeini encouraged necrophilia in the early stages of the uprising
against the shah and pushed women and children to march at the head
of the demonstrations against the shah and to shed their blood and that of
their children: "Our brave women embrace their children and face the
machine-guns and tanks of the executioners of this regime … Sisters and
Brothers be resolute, do not show weakness and lack of courage. You are
following the path of the Almighty and his prophets. Your blood is poured

on the same road as that of the [martyred] prophets, Imams, and their followers. You join them. This is not an occasion to mourn but to rejoice (Khomeini 1999, III:510–512). Throughout the revolution and the war, he repeatedly invoked the examples of Fatimah, the Prophet's daughter and the mother of Hussein, who had raised devoted sons for Islam, and of Fatimah's daughter, Zainab, who bravely embraced the death of her brother Hussein in the desert of Karbala (14). The greatest contribution of women was to give martyrs to the war, though Khomeini reminded them that, as women, they were not themselves required to volunteer for death (172).

Here again there were concrete benefits in life for those who embraced this ethos. Soon after the war began, the state established combat-training areas known as Zahra Camps for thousands of women who were sent to the front, many of whom were related to the men already fighting there. Others joined the Basiji Sisters, received military training, organized rallies that boosted the morale of the troops, and engaged in more conventional support work, such as cooking for the soldiers, mending their clothes, and preparing their medicine. The Basiji Sisters also helped families of the dead soldiers and prisoners of war by offering classes for them. The organization continued to grow after the war. By 1994, several years after the war, the Basiji Sisters had 147 battalions where women received introductory, intermediate, and advanced military training from an all-woman officer corps. The organization incorporated emergency units that suppressed local insurrections and provided relief during natural disasters such as floods and earthquakes. Nearly 100 youth centers and 3,200 student military stations provided ideological, military, and educational instruction. The student unit was sometimes deployed for health campaigns such as mass vaccinations in rural communities, thereby garnering greater community support. Physical education and sports were a vital part of the training. Basiji Sisters competed in a variety of intramural teams such as basketball, volleyball, riflery, swimming, and karate. They attended summer camps at Caspian Sea resorts and went on sightseeing trips to Mashhad, Qom, and even Syria (Giviyan 1994d, 23–26).

Other women enlisted in the Literary Mobilization Organization (LMO) or became nurses' aides. In the cities, many joined the Zainab Sisters' morality brigade, which enforced *hijab* rules, rounding up more modern women on charges of *bad hijabi* (improper *hijabs*) and fining or flogging them. As Sima Nahan recalls, the Zainab Sisters became more aggressive whenever there was a "particularly bloody confrontation at the fronts, [perhaps] to confirm the righteousness of a ubiquitous slogan, a 'message' from the Unknown Soldier/Martyr: 'Sister, your *hijab* is more devastating to the enemy than the shedding of my blood'" (Nahan 2006).

The state provided salaries for many recruits. Other Islamist activists worked voluntarily but received benefits such as subsidized housing or extra rations (Poya 1999, 77–137; Reeves 1989). There were also many intangible benefits. Activists reported that they gained a new sense of purpose in life, felt superior to others for joining revolutionary or war-related activities, and were treated with fear and respect in their communities. Female veterans pursued new political and educational goals and some refused to go back to a conventional lifestyle after the war. Many viewed the war years as the best years of their lives.

Seventeen-year-old Mina became a nurse's aide and worked near the front in the southern province of Khuzestan. She spent several grueling years tending to casualties and witnessing painful amputations at military hospitals. Her fourteen-year-old sister Mitra changed her name to Zainab and became a member of the Zainab Sisters. Later a dissident leftist group strangled Mitra with her *chador*, leaving the body in a mosque. Despite these wrenching experiences and the death of her sister, Mina says:

> For those of us who were there, leaving the region and separating ourselves from the front and the war scene was difficult. I myself, when I returned home, anytime I received news of military activity in the [province of] Khuzestan, I packed my suitcase and could no longer stay. We took wing with the sound of the bugle. For us, being away from the region was hard. We could not adjust ourselves to the culture and traditions of families. Our best years were the years we spent in the region next to our warrior brothers. (Anisi 1999, 29)

Unable to live a conventional family life, Mina and tens of thousands of women like her channeled their energy into university studies and often received advanced degrees after the war. By 1999, this woman from a highly conservative religious family had received a graduate degree from the al-Zahra Theological Seminary in Qom and was applying for admission to a Ph.D. program in the same field (Anisi 1999, 24–29).

War widows and the empowerment of Islamist women

In his classic essay entitled "The Obsolescence of the Freudian Concept of Man," Herbert Marcuse shows that in modern Western democracies (and perhaps more so in Stalinist and fascist regimes) the emergence of a strong state undermines the authority of the father over the son and daughter. Already weakened by the onslaught of a modern economy, the father grants his children more independence in matters such as finding a job and selecting a spouse. But Marcuse did not believe that this independence led to the development of a critical autonomous subject. Instead, under the barrage of the mass media, came the birth of "the masses," people who unquestioningly followed the authority of the new leadership, who replaced the father (Marcuse [1963] 1989, 235). Farhad Khosrokhavar makes a similar argument about Iran when he points out that the revolution "dethroned the father" and turned Khomeini into a charismatic father figure for urban and rural Islamist youth (Khosrokhavar 1995, 309; subsequently cited only by page number). Those who identified with Khomeini (as well as leftists who identified with their own party leaders) broke with the established norms of Iranian society, which placed the good of the family ahead of everything.

College students were exempted from the draft, and many upper- and middle-class parents sent their sons abroad to avoid it. A smaller number of pious young men from the old middle classes volunteered for the front, as did some secular leftists (from various religions and ethnicities), the latter out of patriotic convictions. But the vast majority of the boys sent to the front came from poor families, both rural and urban. Many young Islamists from the latter groups, whom Khosrokhavar calls "martyropaths," placed the new regime ahead of the family, and were encouraged to do so by the massive media campaign of the revolutionary period. While ordinary patriotism was surely a major motivation, Khosrokhavar argues that for many such young men caught up in the war, nothing was as important as the revolutionary ideal of martyrdom. They gladly sacrificed themselves and their families at "the altar of their necrophile passion":

The Islamic state in the person of Khomeini takes the place of the dethroned father, adopts an affectionate tone, separates the Good and the Evil (enemies are the Evil, defenders of the Islamic order are the Good), and confers a sense of engagement upon the youth of the martial organizations (the Pasdaran, the Basij, the Construction Jihad, the Martyr's Foundation, etc). The youth use the state to cut ties with tradition. (320)

Khosrokhavar also writes of "martyropath women" and "martyropath families," in which mothers encouraged youngsters to go to war. The state compensated these families and communities by showcasing them in the media and providing generous restitution in case of death or disability on the battlefield (321). As noted earlier, the bond between mother and son is a close one in Iranian society, often much closer than that between husband and wife. Recognizing the mothers' ultimate sacrifice, the state honored them above fathers in war posters and placards. Hence the Basiji son and his mother gained ascendancy over the father in regime propaganda (346). If the son lived, he received many veterans' benefits from the state, and he and his mother exercised new authority over the household. If he died, his mother was compensated as a war widow. In either case, the mother's identity altered and she exhibited a new sense of entitlement from society. Khosrokhavar suggests that many "martyropath families" lived in rural regions, such as some of the villages around Isfahan that had experienced dramatic industrialization during the Pahlavi era. It was also in such villages that the Basij made off with children from their own communities, taking them to the front in order to claim that their village had given more volunteers and martyrs to the revolutionary cause than others (342).

Martyropath individuals and families were not in the majority, however, and the state often had to convince poor urban and rural families that fighting and dying for the Islamist cause was indeed a glorious undertaking. Sociologist Ashraf Zahedi shows in her study of war widows (2006) how the state persuaded some women that giving *shahids* (martyrs) deserved "celebration" and not mourning. First, regime propaganda drew on the sacrosanct place of martyrdom in the Shi'i culture and argued that war veterans, as well as Islamists killed in clashes with leftist and secularist groups, joined the pantheon of the Imams in paradise (Fig. 10.2). Second, wives, and even mothers, were assured that by giving a *shahid*, they themselves gained greater recognition in the eyes of the Almighty. Third, the whole country was turned into a memorial for the dead, where *shahids* were honored and immortalized. Streets, hospitals, parks, mosques, schools, and universities were named after them. Every block had its memorial shrines, known as *hejlehs*. These were figurative wedding chambers that celebrated the martyred and unmarried men's marriage in heaven. Worship and adulation of *shahids* was encouraged in rural and urban communities alike. These pervasive symbols comforted grieving widows and mothers of the fallen soldiers and assured them that their sacrifices were not in vain. Fourth, while an ordinary widow received no state assistance, the state fully compensated war widows and their families. Here there was no difference between families of Shi'i or Sunni Muslims or non-Muslim *shahids*. Agencies like the Martyr's Foundation, the Foundation of the Dispossessed (Bonyad-e Mostaz'afan), and the Marriage Bureau set up generous indemnification programs for the veterans and for the families of the *shahids*. Ashraf Zahedi points out:

The Iranian programs include pensions, health care, education, counseling, vacation, pilgrimage (specific to different religions), subsidized food and household appliances, free and subsidized housing, low-interest mortgages, interest-free loans for establishing a business, low travel fare and burial benefits. Benefits were not index-linked to inflation, and in the 1990s their value gradually decreased, but initially they provided many new opportunities for poor families. (Zahedi 2006, 274)

Parents of *shahids* received a monthly allowance plus benefits. War widows received a monthly allowance until they remarried, and preferential

Figure 10.2 Poster at a cemetery in praise of martyrdom, 1998

legal, educational, and employment training. War widows also acquired
custody of their children (*Jayegah* 1995, 89–90). If they remarried and
were divorced, the subsidies might be reinstated. Sisters and brothers
were not entitled to an allowance but could benefit from preferential
policies on university admission and employment as well as interest-free
loans. Children of martyrs obtained the most advantages.[2] Often they

[2] Zahedi 2006; e-mail communication with Ashraf Zahedi, January 31, 2007.

attended special secondary schools with high-quality teachers and small classes. They also benefited from a quota on university admission. Later additions to the program provided monthly stipends for unmarried daughters, dependent sisters, and granddaughters of some state employees who had died or were disabled in the service of the state. Such subsidies continued until the age of twenty-five if the women pursued graduate degrees (*Jayegah* 1995, 171–175). These incentives encouraged young women to delay marriage and go to university with their family's blessing.

How could the state afford to be so generous? The fabulously rich foundations, which were at the disposal of the Supreme Leader and his cronies, were not formally part of the government, did not pay taxes, and were never audited. As Nomani and Behdad point out, the Foundation of the Dispossessed alone owned 400 companies producing "many essential goods, from glass containers, tires, and motor oil to soft drinks, synthetic fibers, sugar, textiles, and dairy products." This Foundation, which took over the Pahlavi estate in 1979, also owned nearly half of Iran's hotels and was the largest real estate and construction company in the nation, with assets of about 12 billion dollars (Nomani and Behdad 2006, 45). In 2000, the Foundation for the Dispossessed supported 404,000 disabled civilian war veterans and provided regular stipends for another 121,000. In the same year, the Martyr's Foundation supported 448,000 individuals through its various programs (Messkoub 2006, 249–250; Sciolino 2005, 326–327).

The state found jobs for war widows and other Islamist women relatively easily. By 1986, due to factors like the emigration of the economic elite, state harassment of the more modern sectors, closing of government daycare centers, and limits on women's employment, female urban employment had dropped to 1956 levels, or 9.2 percent of the workforce, although women continued to be fully employed in agricultural and nomadic economies. A majority of those who lost their jobs were low-level and upper-level employees of private companies. In the same period "the number of upper-level female employees of the state increased from 174,000 to 308,000 … [For] every woman who lost her job as an upper-level private sector employee, 44.7 gained an upper-level job as state employees" (Nomani and Behdad 2006, 137–138). This suggests that it was not women's employment *per se* that the government despised, but employing those who had not joined the Islamist organizations out of conviction or family commitments. Widows, sisters, and daughters of the *shahids* thus gained unprecedented political clout along with economic independence.

The Martyr's Foundation gives the figure of 205,000 as the official death toll of those "martyred" in the war. The public and some scholars believe the figure should be much higher (Nomani and Behdad 2006, 68 fn. 4; Zahedi 2006, 272). Since most came from large, rural families, it is safe to assume the *shahids* left behind a significant number of female and male relatives eligible for benefits from the Martyr's Foundation. Historically, Iranian women have experienced a sharp diminution of economic and social authority after their husband's death. Inheritance laws give a widow a very small proportion of her husband's wealth (one-quarter of moveable assets if they have no children and one-eighth if they do). The rest goes to the children, the parents, and the siblings of the deceased. In most cases her son becomes the main provider for the widow (Touba 1987, 112). The war subsidies changed this situation for the widows, mothers, sisters, and daughters of *shahids* and for families of veterans. It was now a great honor, indeed the highest honor, to have given a *shahid* to the war (Ono 1998, 146). The state's compensation also changed the public perception of widowhood. Many widows and relatives of *shahids* used their new status to move up in the political hierarchy and become influential members of the community. In exchange, the state expected them to remain pious or, more accurately, to perform piety by scrupulously observing the *hijab* and codes of gender segregation (Zahedi 2006, 279–283). These measures encouraged poor rural and urban families, which were often much larger than urban middle-class families, to accept the death of a son in return for the benefits they received from the state. A mother who lost a boy in the war guaranteed the social and economic welfare of the rest of her family. The death of a soldier provided an unexpected economic windfall for the entire family. The relatives of the *shahids* went to school, and many received an advanced education. Some had additional earnings from employment, thereby increasing their prestige at home and among their kin. Many government institutions had a hiring quota for veterans and families of the fallen (*Jayegah* 1995, 190–225).

However, financial considerations were not the only reason the public bore the cost of the great sacrifice of the war. Regardless of social class, many women and men believed in the ideal of martyrdom and longed for an opportunity to join the pantheon of martyrs in the afterlife. By giving a son who joined the martyred Imams, the mother was also promised a place in heaven next to Fatimah and Zainab. And, of course, ordinary patriotism was also crucial. Saddam Hussein had launched an unprovoked attack, he had used poison gas (prohibited since World War I on the battlefield), he had the unofficial support of the US, and his regime broadcast vile racist propaganda against Iranians. All these played no small part in maintaining support for the war, despite the sacrifice of so many of the nation's youth.

The politics of education, urbanization, and employment

While the state continued to restrict modern urban women, it encouraged a series of policies that benefited the poor, also helping to create loyal citizens for the state. As Golnar Mehran of al-Zahra Women's University in Tehran notes, "Education in the Islamic Republic is used as a tool of politicization, Islamization, and socialization in training the New Muslim Woman to serve and struggle for the Islamic government" (Mehran 1991). The Pahlavi regime had established the first literacy corps in 1963 and later expanded it to include women teachers. In the first eight years of its activities, more than 82,000 teachers gave a basic education to half a million rural students, and oversaw the construction of thousands of roads, schools, mosques, bathhouses, and mortuaries ("Karnameh-ye" 1971). In five years (1966–1971) total literacy rates increased from 29 percent to nearly 37 percent. Literacy rates for women increased from nearly 18 percent to 25.5 percent (*Salnameh-ye* 1973–1974). Leftist student activists followed through with their literacy campaign in 1979–1981, and the Islamist LMO successfully continued it with a much larger budget after the Left was crushed. By 2001 literacy rates for girls over six years of age had reached 75.6 percent (UNICEF 2005). LMO provided educational opportunities for nontraditional students, with classes in schools, homes, factories, mosques, military barracks, and rural tents. After the war, new sex-segregated schools and health clinics were built in small towns and villages, where many young women were recruited as elementary school teachers and nurses for girls. Wealthy individuals who had supported the Islamic Revolution contributed to the project. Married women could now study at the LMO schools, which taught subjects such as immunization, dental hygiene, child-rearing, and, later, family planning. Girls proved to be better students than boys, in part because so few avenues for advancement and recreational activities were open to them.[3] Many highly religious families, reassured by the state's segregation policies, began to send their daughters to college (Howard 2002, 84–85; Dungus 2000; Kian-Thiébaut 2005, 47; Mehran 1991).

Here again the state had followed a two-pronged policy, expanding educational opportunities for the rural poor, while restricting them for modern urban women. The universities were closed between 1980 and 1983, in a period known as the Cultural Revolution. They reopened with a substantially revamped curriculum. Textbooks were changed to reflect the new sex-segregated values. Women were denied admission

---

[3] In provinces where Arabic, Turkish, or Kurdish were the dominant local languages, literacy rates were lower than in Persian-speaking ones (Zangeneh 2003; Howard 2002, 87–94).

in many fields, including most fields in Engineering, Agriculture, Aviation, Political Science, Law, Management, and even Veterinary Medicine (Kamguyan 2001, 78–79). By this period the authorities had dismissed many women faculty members who refused to wear the *hijab* and abide by the new regulations.

Another important change involved university admissions. After the revolution, the national entrance exam (*concours*) was revised to include a new quota system. A third of university places now went to rural students, and another third was set aside as the "revolutionary quota." The latter category included people from revolutionary organizations, war veterans, and relatives of *shahids*. Meanwhile new ideological requirements, and a religious test, reduced the number of secular students and minorities, while Baha'is were barred from admission altogether. By 2001, almost three-fourths of those admitted to the universities had received some form of Islamist affirmative action (Fig. 10.3). The state created other opportunities for rural women and men to gain an advanced education.

Figure 10.3 College student, Tehran University, 2005

The new Azad Islamic University, with a *concours* of its own, soon became the largest university in the country with numerous branches in small cities and provinces (Sakurai 2004, 397). In the early 1990s, due to efforts by several influential Islamist women such as Zahra Rahnavard, the new Supreme Leader Ayatollah Ali Khamenei lifted the ban on women's study in some fields. By the early twenty-first century, most state universities admitted women in all fields, though some restrictions continued at Azad University.

Classes at the universities were not completely segregated by sex. Boys sat on one side of the classroom and girls on the other, and the faculties included both men and women. Social facilities like cafeterias remained segregated, however. State and private funds supported all-girls colleges such as the al-Zahra Women's University in Tehran, the Fatimiyeh Medical School in Qom, and several theological seminaries; these segregated facilities benefited female students whose parents would otherwise have prevented them from enrolling. Later, as women became a majority of college students, funding for some women's colleges was slashed and quotas established in others (Ebadi 2002, 47–49).

The state's land-distribution program was modest but, combined with the land that was confiscated by the villagers themselves, had a substantial impact. After the revolution, about 6 percent of the nation's arable land was redistributed among peasants, who began immediately to cultivate it to establish ownership. Soon, smaller farms replaced some of the large-scale private farms of the Pahlavi era. This land takeover and state policies supporting the rural economy improved the standard of living of many villages (Nomani and Behdad 2006, 36; Ajami 2005).

There were also changes in lifestyle and worldview. To reduce migration to the cities, the state began to modernize rural areas, contributing to small-scale projects initiated by the Construction Jihad. For some of these projects, such as the national immunization campaign against infectious diseases, the state used Basiji members. As a result, at the turn of the twenty-first century a majority of villages had clean drinking water, electricity, paved roads, modern stoves and refrigerators, and access to modern means of communication (television, radio, satellite dishes), schools, and health clinics. Reduced infant mortality rates and smaller, healthier families were among the results of these changes (Kian-Thiébault 2005, 47; Ehsani 2006, 89; "Niruyeh Moghavemat" 2006).

Anthropologist Mary Hegland, who conducted her fieldwork in the village of Aliabad (near Shiraz), reported many improvements in the area. Before the revolution, Aliabad had been owned by an absentee landlord and had no clean water or electricity. During the revolution, peasants confiscated the land. In 2001, the newly elected village council divided the property among several thousand villagers. By this time, many residents of Aliabad had moved out of agriculture altogether and taken jobs in nearby chemical factories, or in companies around Shiraz. Villagers sold a significant portion of their newly acquired land to city dwellers and used the proceeds to buy cars, establish new businesses, or build modern homes.

Ironically, this real estate boom in village property in proximity to large cities, which was propelled by rising world oil prices, was also related to the state's segregationist policies. It had become fashionable for upper-middle-class families to build walled villas and gardens in the villages around big cities for weekend getaways. Here they could enjoy the cleaner air and break the *hijab* regulations and prohibitions against singing, dancing, and drinking alcohol. This new urban influx into rural areas contributed to the village economy in many ways. Hegland writes:

Shiraz had stretched out almost to the edge of Aliabad land. Villagers had left their old mud-brick homes consisting of rooms built around a central courtyard, with people originally living in upper-story rooms and animals housed in the lower-story rooms, within the old, high village walls. Most villagers now live in fired-brick, urban-style homes complete with ... amenities such as shower rooms, modern kitchens with fridge and hot and cold water, washing machines, air conditioners, telephones, and vacuum cleaners. (Hegland 2005)

Not all villages were urbanized to this extent. Those that were far away from big cities continued to practice agriculture and animal husbandry, but the trend toward rapid modernization and urbanization was visible everywhere.

These shifts improved educational standards for young girls and changed parents' attitudes toward daughters. Azadeh Kian-Thiébaut shows that 86.5 percent of her respondents now believed that men and women should have equal access to education (2005, 55). Hegland reports, "parents are concerned about girls having sufficient time for their homework. Girls do better at school than boys do, and continue their education at higher rates than do boys. Teenage girls may speak up freely, offer advice and guidance to adults, openly express their ideas, argue with adults, and go away to university in smaller regional cities, Shiraz, or even Tehran. Now female high-school graduates have as a main goal preparing for the *concours*" (Hegland 2005; see also Hegland 2009). Similarly, anthropologist Erika Friedl reports that in a southwest village she studied many rural girls are eager for advanced education, which they view as the sole path to economic independence. Parents often provide boys with capital and social networks to start a business, but the only way to economic independence for most girls is a college degree (Friedl 2003; e-mail from Erika Friedl, December 6, 2005).

These improvements in education, standard of living, and relations at home have not been accompanied by a substantial economic expansion and more jobs, rather they have been fueled by state subsidies. Indeed, the state has continued to discourage private employment for most women. According to the 1996 census, 13.4 percent of women over the age of fifteen were employed in the formal sector. The vast majority worked in carpet weaving, dairy farming, agricultural labor, teaching, clerical, and health-related professions (Nomani and Behdad 2006, 143). Double-digit inflation rates meant that most families could no longer live on one person's income. War, inflation, and the mass emigration of the educated elite and several million members of the modern middle and upper classes had opened some new employment opportunities and thousands of women took jobs in the private and public sectors (Alaedini and Razavi 2005, 71). As elsewhere in the world, women preferred state employment because of its secure pay and more flexible hours. But here there were other concerns: fathers and husbands encouraged their daughters and wives to work in state institutions because gender segregation was stricter there than in private firms. Also, the private sector found maintaining sex-segregated workplaces prohibitive and many simply refused to hire women (Nomani and Behdad 2006, 185).

Experts believed that the actual employment rates for women were higher than government figures suggested. Forty percent of the nation's farmers were women, yet they viewed their labor as an extension of housekeeping. Economists observed that "the structure of female employment is increasingly shifting toward private sector positions in professional services for more educated women aged 20–50 years in the urban area." In contrast, in the pre-revolutionary period, female employment was mostly for young uneducated women in rural areas (Bahramitash and Salehi-Esfahani 2007). Still, many urban women who contributed to the informal economy considered themselves full-time housewives. In a survey of 350 working-age women in the more affluent northern area of Tehran in 2001, about 94 percent were earning an income, but only 53 percent described themselves as employed (Moghadam 2009).

Lack of formal employment did not necessarily mean women stayed at home. Tens of thousands of women were volunteers in the family-planning institutions and NGOs. Unemployed middle- and upper-class women often pursued educational and cultural interests outside the home. Many attended English-language, cooking, and exercise classes, and transported their children to a variety of after-school activities. Even in the village of Aliabad, mothers took children to English classes in Shiraz (Hegland 2009). Through such activities, women developed greater self-respect and a new sense of identity. They no longer saw themselves as mere extensions of the men in their families.

Although deputies in the Parliament, and others working in high posts, were strictly vetted for their ideological commitment to the new Islamist order, some women pushed to reinstate small benefits for war widows and working-class women. Secular lawyers such as Mehrangiz Kar had advised women to arrange prenuptial agreements. Many Islamist women working within the state also encouraged such preventive measures. In 1984 prenuptial agreements were reintroduced, giving the wife the right to ask for divorce if her husband took a second 'aqdi. The new agreements guarantee a woman's right to continue her education, choose her place of residence, or work after marriage. Small barriers were also placed on men's unilateral right to divorce, including on their practice of extracting "mutual consent" from their wives for a quick divorce through a notary public. All couples had to petition the courts to receive a certificate of non-reconciliation. The courts determined a woman's right to compensation and the childcare arrangements, according to shari'a law ("Qanun-e Eslah" 1992). Even these small measures seem to have reduced the frequency of men's resort to unilateral divorce. Overall divorce rates declined to 63 per 1,000 marriages in 1993 (Aghajanian and Moghadas 1998, 59).

The deputies in the First through the Fifth Islamic Majles (1979–2000) achieved the following reforms: they curtailed a husband's right to prevent his wife's employment and reinstated some pre-revolutionary benefits, such as parts of the Family Protection Law, pregnancy leave, time off for nursing mothers, medical checkups during pregnancy, and regulations facilitating part-time employment for office workers, nurses, military personnel, and (later) factory workers. They also granted workingwomen the option of early retirement. While women benefited from such policies, the net result was stagnant employment rates, since the Islamist government expected private businesses to provide these benefits without state support. As a result, many industries used these policies as a reason to deny women employment altogether (Ebadi 2002, 62; Kar 2000a, 141–142; Salehi-Isfahani 2000; Shaditalab 2002a; Akhtari et al. 1999b, 154–159).

Women who entered the formal labor market soon noticed that they were denied promotion and raises on a variety of dubious religious and biologistic pretexts. After a few years on the job, women complained about the preferential treatment of men, networks from which they were excluded because of their sex, lack of childcare, and uncooperative husbands at home. They resented the appallingly high unemployment rates, the state's constant pressure on women to mind their "family responsibilities" and to accept either low-paying, part-time jobs or leave the labor force. It was now clear that the war and the state's need for women's labor had contributed to a new consciousness among the more religious and rural sectors of society. The social changes outlined above had reduced the huge cultural gap of the Pahlavi era between the new and old middle classes and between urban and rural societies, in the areas of women's employment, education, and consciousness (Poya 1999, 89–98).

Islamist women leaders: the uses of power

Between 1992 and 2000, the conservative Islamist magazine *Payam-e Zan* (Women's Message) published nearly 100 interviews with prominent Islamist women, giving us a glimpse into the lives and thinking of women who attained leadership positions in the government of the Islamic Republic (Fig. 10.4).[4] Many of those interviewed were parliamentary deputies, heads of government agencies, artists, doctors, journalists, and professionals who worked closely with the government. Others were female veterans, wives of influential members of government, religious writers, relatives of martyrs and veterans, village activists, teachers, and workers, all of whose ideological credentials were approved by the most conservative wing of the government.

All the women interviewed by *Payam-e Zan* come across as busy. Many hold full-time jobs, are responsible for a variety of volunteer organizations, and often attend graduate school. The reader wonders who is taking care of the husbands and children of these women while they repeat the mantra of the Islamic Republic that a woman should never neglect her husband and family.[5] In fact, not one of them appeared to be a conventional mother and housewife.

Fereshteh Erabi, editor of the conservative women's journal *Neda*, was a member of the Central Council of the Women's Association of the Islamic Republic. Initially, she served as *Neda*'s public relations officer, but by the mid-1990s she had become editor of it and several other publications. Erabi was married and had three school-age children (Giviyan 1993a, 14–18). Simin Ahmadi, a mother of three, graduated with a degree in sociology. She worked at Radio Voice of the Islamic Republic, where she ran its family programs. Ahmadi planned to continue her education and receive an advanced degree in sociology (Giviyan 1993b, 16). Tayebeh Sultani headed the House of Zahra Propaganda Association, which offered a variety of classes in the arts and on Islam

---

[4] The journal was published in Qom under the auspices of the Bureau of Islamic Publicity (BIP), with which many leaders of the Islamic Republic were affiliated. For a more detailed discussion of this journal see Afary 2001.

[5] Thanks to Elham Malekzadeh for information on this subject (e-mail on February 7, 2007).

Figure 10.4 Cover of *Payam-e Zan* (Women's Message)

for women. Tayebeh, who was partially disabled, had two children. She was preparing for the *concours* examinations (Kaviyanpour 1993, 20–33). Despite their hectic lives, all three repeatedly stated that women must not spend much of their time away from home and abandon their children to the care of others.

Married women responded to fairly detailed questions about their daily lives and how they juggled their responsibilities to husband and children with their political commitments and organizational obligations. Widows, especially of *shahids* (killed in the war or assassinated by clandestine opposition groups inside Iran), were asked about their earlier married lives. Interviewers also inquired in detail about their difficulties in raising their children alone. When respondents were single or divorced, however, interviewers neglected the standard questions about husbands, children, and household duties. Thus, we never learned how these prominent women negotiated their daily lives. With whom did they live? Why were they divorced? And why did they never remarry? Such personal questions were completely avoided in these cases.

Both Zahra Rahnavard and Marziyeh Dabbagh (see chapter 8) gave lengthy interviews to the journal as important leaders of the Islamist government. Dabbagh had the more illustrious career after the revolution. She took over the Queen Mother's automobile, thus symbolically anointing herself Mother of the Revolution. Dabbagh helped to found the women's auxiliary branch of the Basij Mobilization Organization (Basiji Sisters). She also headed the conservative Women's Society of the Islamic Republic (WSIR), an organization that the more educated Zahra Rahnavard and others from the younger generation of Islamist women had initiated (Giviyan 1993c; 1994d). Immediately after the revolution, Dabbagh became involved in the repression of the Left. She joined the Pasdaran paramilitary group and worked to destroy all rival organizations, such as the Kurdish Komaleh and Democrat parties, and the secret cells of the leftist Fedayeen and the leftist-Islamist Mojahedeen. She was proud to have persuaded scores of Islamist women to spy on and betray family members who had joined rival political organizations, such as the Mojahedeen and the Fedayeen, as seen in the following chilling account of political repression:

I was able to gather these women from various communities and set up classes for religious discussions for them in the mosques ... In this way, we turned them into loyal informants and agents ... I asked them to immediately report to us when men in their family held meetings or invited [strangers] to the home ... I remember one night six underground homes [of presumably the Fedayeen or Mojahedeen dissidents] were revealed to us by the mothers and sisters of the [activists] themselves. Our troops circled the houses and destroyed them. It was a very successful experience that was later repeated in other provinces. (Giviyan 1993d, 13)

But she was not only involved in repression, for she also helped construct a new Islamist politics of gender. Dabbagh served as a parliamentary deputy for four out of five terms between 1979 and 2000. She and a few other deputies were instrumental in proposing several laws related to women, among them the granting of child-custody rights to widows of *shahids*, and more generally part-time female employment, early retirement, and several changes in marriage and divorce laws. After 1984, as in the Pahlavi era, a woman could initiate divorce if she and her husband had signed a prenuptial agreement to that effect, though even then her right to divorce was not automatic. Under severe circumstances, such as a husband's prolonged imprisonment, addiction, impotence, infertility, or taking of a second wife, the first wife could now sue for divorce (Paidar 1995, 284). A second set of laws increased a woman's *mahriyeh*. According to Shi'i law a wife is not required to breastfeed her children, nor do house-work. The new law calculated the value of these services for the duration of the marriage, instituting a form of "wages for housework." Another reform of the Majles was to index *mahriyeh* to inflation rates. Previously, if a woman's *mahriyeh* was 50,000 *tumans* in 1960 and she was divorced in 2000, she still received the same *mahriyeh*, which was a pittance by that time. The new law adjusted her *mahriyeh* for inflation. A third set of reforms granted the mother custody when the child's physical and mental health was in grave danger. In addition, the state reinstated Family Courts, albeit with much less authority than in the Pahlavi era (Akhtari *et al.* 1999b, 154–159; Dabbagh 1995). At the same time, Dabbagh and her female colleagues in the Parliament were totally committed to the segregationist rules of the Islamist state. The Fifth Majles, for example, tried unsuccess-fully to increase gender segregation in clinics and hospitals, prohibiting male doctors and nurses from tending to female patients under any circumstances (Zamani 2000, 6–10). The deputies might have thought this measure would ultimately help to increase the number of female nurses and doctors in the country, but in promoting this policy Dabbagh and her colleagues showed a complete disregard for the immediate fate of women at risk of dying because of the scarcity of women doctors.

After Khomeini's death in 1989, Dabbagh's main concern became continuing his legacy and legitimizing the Islamic Republic to the out-side world. In 1995, in response to a human rights report on Iran that emphasized the status of Iranian women as second-class citizens, Dabbagh claimed that as a military officer and active participant in the revolution she had "never felt that women were behind men in achieving social positions" (Dabbagh 1995, 26). Two years earlier, however, she had complained in an interview aimed at her domestic audience about the lack of respect toward her and other women in the Parliament. Here she expressed her frustration that, for many deputies, women's issues were limited to "cooking, washing clothes, and sweeping" (Giviyan 1993d, 10).

As mentioned above, Zahra Rahnavard was younger and more edu-cated than Dabbagh at the time of the revolution. She and other younger Islamist women had hoped that their early devotion to the revolution would assure them leadership roles in the post-revolutionary society, and it did. Soon after the revolution, Rahnavard became a founder of the Women's Society of the Islamic Republic (WSIR), along with Aʿzam Taleqani, a daughter of the left-of-center Ayatollah Mahmoud Taleqani. Rahnavard also became an editor of *Rah-e Zainab* (Path of Zainab), which under a different name had been one of the country's leading women's magazines before the revolution. But when the WSIR criticized the regime's policy of forced Islamization, including the mandatory wearing of the *hijab*, the government quietly clamped down on Rahnavard and other Islamist advocates of women's rights. Supporters of the Islamic Republican Party (IRP) attacked chapters of the WSIR in Tehran and several other cities in May 1981 (Paidar 1995, 240–241; Giviyan 1994b, 4). More orthodox members of the IRP, such as Dabbagh, now received greater authority in women's affairs.

Rahnavard's husband, Mir Hussein Masavi, presided over Iran's government as prime minister in the 1980s. Thanks to this association, Rahnavard survived these attacks. She used her considerable oratorical skills, her talents as a writer, and her influential position to propagate Islamist values in Iran and abroad. She founded the International Association of Muslim Women, and in 1987 became director of the Cultural and Social Association of Women, a branch of the Ministry of Science that advised President Ali Khamenei (later Supreme Leader) on women's issues. One of her best-known publications was a travelogue written during a 1986 state visit to India that she made without her husband. Her polemics against Hinduism, Western feminism, and more liberal interpretations of Islam show an intolerance of competing ideologies and religious perspectives (Rahnavard 1987). Rahnavard expresses concern over the plight of India's Muslims in the face of the Hindu revivalists. She also denounces the condition of Indian women, making references to "dowry burnings," where wives with an insufficient dowry "accidentally" caught fire in their kitchens and died. These positions could have made her a strong feminist. However, Rahnavard seems oblivious to the parallels between the abuses that women and Muslims faced in India and those that women and religious minorities endured in Iran. Her compassion for Hindu women was channeled into the injunction that "all Indian women should collectively convert to Islam" to save themselves from the sexism of the Hindu culture (Rahnavard 1987, 118).

After her husband stepped down as prime minister in 1989, Rahnavard remained active in politics. Faced with persistent discrimination against women, she gradually changed her position. In 1990, Rahnavard joined the High Council of the Cultural Revolution, where she lifted some of the restrictions on women's employment. She published several more books and held exhibits of her artwork. Rahnavard admitted that her husband helped with the housework and that he was basically in charge of their daughters' affairs, leaving her free to pursue her intellectual and social interests. Their three daughters all received advanced educations (Giviyan 1994a; 1994b; 1994c; Omid 1994, 194).

Since 1997, Rahnavard has adopted a more progressive stance on women's issues, although she continues to insist that while the West commodifies women, "true Islam" does not. In 1997, when the reformist President Muhammad Khatami was elected by a majority vote, Rahnavard joined his camp and was appointed president of al-Zahra Women's University in Tehran. In a 1999 interview with the feminist journal *Zanan*, she complained that Iranian women were treated as the "second sex," presumably a reference to Simone de Beauvoir's book with the same title. She unsuccessfully supported new laws to punish the sexual abuse, rape, and murder of women by male relatives. She also spoke out against wifebeating and demanded that women be given custody of their children after divorce (*Zanan* 7[55] [Farvardin], 9). Her recent interviews and activities suggest that she has moved closer to the feminist camp, which might explain why President Ahmadinejad removed her as president of al-Zahra University in 2006.

The differences between Rahnavard and Dabbagh give us a more intimate view of the power relations inside Islamist organizations, especially concerning women. Rahnavard and Dabbagh became leaders of the Islamic Republic and upholders of its conservative morality by denouncing the rights that secular, urban, middle-class and upper-class women had gained during the Pahlavi era. Both of them helped to repress and silence a generation of secular and leftwing women's activists who had also participated in the revolution and who opposed the setbacks in women's rights that followed. By becoming leaders of the Islamist movement, Rahnavard and Dabbagh gained a high degree of political and even personal freedom in their own lives.

Dabbagh was able to break through numerous obstacles that bound women in traditional marriages in Iran and many other parts of the world. Her absolute submission to Khomeini allowed her to exercise her own absolute power over others. She owed her status as a political leader entirely to the Islamist ideology of Khomeini (rather than to her education or class background) and was committed to preserving it at all costs. Nonetheless, Dabbagh saw herself as a defender of women's greater role in society. She opposed gender segregation in the military during the war and insisted that both women and men should be able to contribute to the war effort. She supported unsuccessful bills in the Parliament that would have limited a husband's uncontested right to divorce and custody of the children, and she was angry at men who prevented their wives, including highly educated ones, from holding socially responsible jobs. Dabbagh even referred to many examples of sexism in the Parliament, such as the time when, despite her considerable expertise in military matters, she was excluded from the defense committee because she was a woman, while men who had no military experience were selected.

Dabbagh wanted women out of the home and involved in society and politics so they could contribute to her version of a militant Islamist society. In her view, women were to be liberated from conventional household duties in order to become soldiers and *shahids* for the Islamist cause. Those who dared to argue against this position and demanded choice, including the right to live under a more secular state, had no place in the Islamist social order. Nevertheless, we should recognize the emblematic impact of Dabbagh and other conservative women in high positions of power; for they indirectly created a niche for women in socio-political venues, thus opening the doors for others.

Rethinking Shi'i doctrines, reconstructing notions of femininity

As censorship relaxed somewhat in the early 1990s, a host of new women's publications reemerged. Some, such as *Payam-e Zan* (Women's Message), *Neda* (Voice), and *Payam-e Hajar* (Hajar's Message), remained committed to the state, though they claimed more rights for Islamist women within the state. Others had a more ambivalent position. Popular journals such as *Zan-e Ruz* (Today's Woman), *Khanevadeh* (Family), *Rah-e Zendegi* (Way of Life), *Zan-e Sharqi* (Eastern Woman), and *Khaneh va Khanevadeh* (Home and Family) published articles on pressing social and legal issues, among others divorce, child custody, drug and alcohol addiction, and prostitution. At the same time, they occasionally denounced feminism as a harmful Western import. A third group of journals such as *Zanan* (Women), *Hoquq-e Zanan* (Women's Rights), *Jens-e Dovvom* (The Second Sex), and the Internet site *Bad Jens* (Bad Gender or Evil), defined itself as *feminist*, using the English term.

Zanan, which began publication in 1991 under the editorship of the award-winning feminist Shahla Sherkat, was sold at many newsstands across the nation until it was shut down by the state in 2008. For nearly two decades, *Zanan* was the most prominent women's publication in Iran and remained at the forefront of a growing movement by women writers, academics, artists, and other professional women to reclaim some of the rights and organizations they lost in the 1979 revolution and to demand new ones (Fig. 10.5). The journal was a curious publication by Western standards. It included articles that might appear in any popular women's

Figure 10.5 Editorial board meeting of *Zanan*; sitting under the poster is editor Shahla Sherkat

magazine on topics such as food, diet, health, exercise, fashion, family psychology, science, and medicine. But *Zanan* was also a sophisticated literary and cultural magazine with an explicitly feminist agenda, as seen in its regular features on divorce, sexual violence, and child custody. It published serious reviews of films, novels, poetry, poems, musical perform-ances, and short stories by Iranian women. Secular feminist lawyers and sociologists worked with *Zanan*. The journal ran translations of essays by non-Iranian authors such as Mary Wollstonecraft, Virginia Woolf, Charlotte Perkins Gilman, Evelyn Reed, Nadine Gordimer, and Alison Jaggar, and published Iranian writers such as Shirin Ebadi, Mehrangiz Kar, Shahla Ezazi, and other Iranian writers living in the diaspora (Fig. 10.6). The pages of *Zanan* defined and explicitly defended feminist perspectives and politics. The journal featured original sociological studies on working-women, domestic violence, and prostitution, and its staff was working to establish the country's first shelter for battered women. Mehrangiz Kar, an attorney who wrote a column for *Zanan* on political and constitutional reforms in the 1990s, also gave concrete advice on prenuptial agreements that could grant women some rights at the time of divorce. Nobel Laureate Shirin Ebadi, who defended political dissidents and liberal editors in

Figure 10.6 Cover of *Zanan*, Nowruz 1999, celebrating the accomplishments of a new generation

court, was a regular contributor on the rights of women and children (Ebadi 2006) (Fig. 10.7).

In addition, *Zanan* took up the task of developing a new feminist interpretation of Shiʻi Islamic doctrines. Religious thinkers who wrote for *Zanan* deconstructed scripture to present a more liberal reading of the *shariʻa*. Women attended religious seminaries in large numbers and became well versed in arcane legalisms. Some reinterpreted religious texts in order to give them a more woman-friendly reading or to reveal ambiguity in the more sexist statements. In this way they de-legitimized the authenticity of some of the most blatantly sexist statements and provided alternative readings of orthodoxies (Mir-Hosseini 1999). In deconstructing

Figure 10.7 Shirin Ebadi, Nobel Prize winner 2003

the texts and reexamining the narratives that form Islamic jurisprudence, these writers emphasized Qur'anic verses and narratives that suggested a more egalitarian treatment of women and reinterpreted those that seemed to call for restrictions on women.

In the 1980s the state successfully used similar reinterpretations to recruit women for the war effort. But the conservative authorities refused to use the same flexibility of interpretation with regard to men's easy access to women's bodies and laws regarding marriage, divorce, polygamy, and temporary marriage. A woman's bodily and traditional social functions were routinely invoked to justify her unequal political status (Shakeri and Labriz 1992, 26–32; Yadgar-Azadi 1992a, 20–26; 1992b, 17–25; see also Tohidi 1996).

Sometimes even clerics joined this debate in *Zanan*. Ayatollah Mousavi Bojnurdi, for example, defended the rights of women to open bank accounts for their children. He held that while men were often the breadwinners of the family, "the real head of the family is the woman." Hence, her authority on financial matters had to be expanded (Bojnurdi 2002, 11). These arguments, and those in a similar vein, may seem rather limited from a secular feminist perspective, but they have had an impact on some sectors of the public and the clerical establishment. All such writings implicitly question the legitimacy of the regime, which, after all, refers to the same sources. Advocates of women's rights have entered the theological debate and proved their understanding of arcane issues in the course of demonstrating ambiguities and multiple meanings in Qur'anic verses and other texts. These facts are in some ways more significant than the substance of their arguments; they create the possibility that feminist theologians and legal experts will be taken seriously, even by conservative clerics. Moreover, they have opened a major ideological debate at a time of popular dissatisfaction with the heavy-handed patriarchy of the Islamist regime.

Another group of religious thinkers, such as Mojtahed Shabastari and the lay theologian Abdolkarim Soroush, apply modern science (including Darwin's theory of evolution) and a hermeneutical reading to Islamic jurisprudence as they explore new ways of thinking about religion in the modern world. Shabastari writes:

> We cannot speak of eternal human systems, whether in politics, economics, or in the family ... Historical evolution means that such changes have taken place without a previous plan ... Those who accept the historical evolution of human beings believe that the differences between men and women, both physical and psychological, took shape in the course of this historical evolution. They believe ... it is possible to speak of other forms of family, other forms of division of labor or legal systems, and gradually reduce the existing inequalities in favor of justice and equality.

After presenting this radical interpretation, which challenges the foundations of the dominant forms of Shi'i jurisprudence while relying implicitly on Darwin's theory of evolution and postmodern thought, Shabastari backtracks in the end, especially on gender. He concludes that such a rethinking "of course must not go so far as to endanger the principal order of the family" (Shabastari 1999, 20).

Abdolkarim Soroush, a lay thinker who has become the most influential advocate of religious reform, places great emphasis on the hermeneutical distinction between the text and the process of its interpretation. Islam may be perfect, unchangeable, absolute, and offer the highest wisdom, but the human individual's comprehension of Islam is incomplete, imperfect, everchanging, and therefore relative. Soroush argues that therefore our comprehension of religion is scientifically, socially, and culturally constructed and hence open to interpretation. He has moved beyond earlier liberal Muslim thinkers, who searched for verses and quotations in the shari'a that were compatible with modernity. Soroush takes a more contextualist view. He argues that God manifests himself in each historical period according to the understanding of people of that era. Therefore, the search for reconciliation between Islam and democracy is not simply a matter of finding appropriate phrases in the Qur'an that are compatible with modern concepts of science, democracy, and human rights. Drawing on the works of Immanuel Kant, G. W. F. Hegel, Karl Popper, and Erich

Fromm, as well as several twentieth-century Christian theologians, Soroush calls for a radical reexamination of all tenets of Islam, while maintaining its original spirit, which calls for human decency and concern for fellow human beings.

At the same time, Soroush clings to an unchanging set of ethical concepts and takes an essentialist stance on both gender and sexuality: "An important issue in relations between men and women is that women remain women, and men remain men ... We should not devise rules that remove women from the cycle of femininity and men from the cycle of masculinity" (Soroush 1999, 32). By thus conflating sex and gender, Soroush condemns women to subordinate positions. In the late 1990s, he disappointed his many female admirers by briefly taking a second wife, a twenty-five-year-old graduate student, while remaining married to his first wife. Soroush's second marriage was much more than a private affair. It suggested a persistent attitude among intellectual men, especially religious ones, who have too often opposed limitations on women's rights to education, employment, citizenship, and choice of attire, while refusing to address male sexual prerogatives in Iranian society.

Seminarian Majid Mohammadi wrote in the 1990s that gender and sexuality remain unresolved issues for the new religious thinkers. Many reformists were leftist Islamists in the 1980s. In the 1990s the same men came to advocate a variety of social and economic rights, but "gender concerns remained a red line or taboo." He added that the new religious thinkers "have accepted political, cultural, and economic freedoms. However, they have not accepted social freedoms, such as open contact between people of the opposite sex in public places, or freedom of attire [for women]." These thinkers have paid detailed attention to Western ideologies, from humanism and socialism to fascism, existentialism, and liberalism, but not to feminism – "not to the movement to redress women's rights." In Mohammadi's view, religious thinkers need to address neglected topics such as the rights of women, religious minorities, the disabled, prisoners, the unemployed, the elderly, and people of all sexual orientations. They have to move away from a religious interpretation of rights and adopt a human rights discourse on rights (Mohammadi 1999).

Mohammadi has since joined the camp of the secular dissidents, but many others have continued the task of constructing a more liberal Muslim discourse. They search Iranian and Islamic history for the roots of this new discourse in a more tolerant version of Islam and try to build bridges to modern Western discourses of feminism and human rights. Armed with these interpretations, a new generation of intellectuals has used Islamic principles to carry out a number of gender reforms, projects that could not be implemented during the shah's regime because the public saw such measures as opposed to Islam. Thus, far from an obstacle to modernity, the new and more tolerant version of Islam that was advocated by this new generation of dissident religious thinkers has been closing the social and cultural gaps that separate Iranian and Western cultures.

By the mid-1990s the nation's population had grown to 60 million people, half of them born after 1979. A new generation had come of age that resented the ascetic culture of the Islamic Republic, the strict enforcement of *hijab* regulations, and the celebration of *jihad* and martyrdom. The government had also shifted gears. The mass executions of the 1980s were abandoned. Now instead of the open arrest and execution of dissident intellectuals, the state might secure a death warrant from a friendly cleric, and use it to execute a dissident, a poet, or a translator. Individuals continued to be arrested on false charges of espionage and forced to confess on radio and television. Several died in staged car accidents or robberies, or were gunned down in back alleys (Ebadi 2006, 131–142). This did not dampen the rising dissent, but rather provoked more of it.

Paradoxically, some of the Islamic Republic's accomplishments in literacy, health, and family planning had helped give rise to this new generation of dissidents. The government faced a more urbanized, mobile, and politically aware population. The pre-revolutionary belief that secular public spaces were amoral and unethical environments for women had faded. Many religious families had felt comfortable with segregation requirements and sent their daughters to the university. This increased level of participation by women altered many old gender expectations and culminated in new demands for civil liberties and a more open relationship to the Western world. Muslim intellectuals who had previously supported the revolution gradually formed the nucleus of what became known as the reform movement. The dream of an Islamic utopia was shelved and replaced with a more sober understanding of reality. Many still held on to the legacy of Khomeini and the revolution, but wanted a kinder, gentler, and more diverse Islamic Republic.

11   Birth control, female sexual awakening, and the gay lifestyle

In *The History of Sexuality* Michel Foucault argues that beneath a variety of sexual prohibitions of seventeenth-century European societies a "veritable discursive explosion" around sexuality could be discerned ([1976] 1980, 17). At the end of the eighteenth century, sexual regulations had become ingrained in legislative discourse, and state intervention addressed numerous issues concerning sexual conduct, among them the legal age of marriage, the birth rate, fertility, and the frequency of sexual relations. Through its economic, legal, medical, and health policies, the modern state influenced the sexual conduct of its population in new ways, resulting in dramatic demographic changes. By the nineteenth century, a broader discourse on sexuality was taking shape beneath the blanket of Victorian morality. It was nothing less than "an apparatus for producing an ever greater quantity of discourse about sex, capable of functioning and taking effect in its very economy" (Foucault [1976] 1980, 23). Foucault's interpretation of course contradicted the common assumption of an absence of discussion of sexuality in the nineteenth century and a presumed "Victorian morality," followed by greater sexual freedom in the twentieth century.

Considered alongside trends concerning gender and sexuality in post-revolutionary Iran, Foucault's portrait of sexuality in the Victorian era offers valuable insights. Foucault can shed light on the repercussions of the new sexual austerities that were imposed after the revolution. In the 1980s the Islamist government instituted a dramatic reversal in human rights, especially regarding women's rights. The state revived premodern social conventions (repudiation, veiling, flogging) but enforced them through modern means and institutions, which meant a wider application. In its system of distributive justice, Muslims and non-Muslims, men and women received different treatment before the law. Defunct and suppressive Shi'i rituals of purity and penance were brought back, while polygamy and sex with underage girls were newly sanctioned. Openly gay men were severely punished, even executed.

However, the popular notion that Islamism has enforced a harsh form of sexual repression on the Iranian people does not convey the complexity of what has taken place. There have been significant improvements in women's education and health along with a remarkable drop in birth rates. How can such important reforms, which have many positive implications for women, coexist with harshly misogynistic laws and policies? Part of the answer is that before the revolution Iranian women had already made significant advances in these areas. But the other part is that the policies of the Islamist government cannot easily be categorized as "puritanical" or "moralistic." Rather, using Foucault's framework, we can argue that various factions within the state actively deployed a new "sexual economy" for the population. Sometimes, the Islamist state privileged patriarchal interpretations of gender norms over more modern ones. At times, it adopted modern projects alongside a discourse that presented them as practices indigenous to traditional Islam. In all cases, the state used modern institutions to disseminate these various discourses.

Studies of birth control and family planning in the United States provide us with yet another vantage point from which to examine the unintended results of family planning in Iran. As a result of industrialization, urbanization, and the adoption of contraceptive technologies, American society by the mid-twentieth century had experienced a profound change in its sexual mores (Burgess and Wallin 1954). As people began to live longer and fertility rates dropped, marriage became more than an institution for procreation. Women's demands for emotional and sexual intimacy increased. The emphasis on romantic, (hetero)sexual love led to new forms of normative heterosexuality. Good sex in marriage became important, and romantic love seemed necessary to a good marriage. After Margaret Sanger and the Planned Parenthood Federation initiated the birth-control movement in the United States, many sectors of society gradually set aside their opposition and embraced such ideas. Most Protestant churches and Jewish organizations (and many individual Catholics) approved of contraception, hoping thereby to strengthen the bonds of marriage (Gordon 1990; Neuhaus 2000; D'Emilio and Freedman 1997). Attitudes toward premarital sex also changed, with sex outside marriage becoming more acceptable. Widespread use of contraceptives helped make marriage a more companionate union. While this type of marriage involved a division of labor between breadwinner and homemaker, it was in some respects a more egalitarian and less patriarchal relationship than before (Amato et al. 2007). In addition, by separating sexual activity from procreation, "birth control proponents opened the door for non-reproductive relationships ranging from childless marriages to casual encounters to non-heterosexual relationships" (Ball 2005, 23).

As women became more sexually assertive, they also became less tolerant of men's extramarital affairs, both heterosexual and homosexual.

By the 1960s and 1970s, the United States had moved further toward what could be called "individualistic marriages." In this third phase in the evolution of Western marriage, romantic love retained its importance, but the partners had also to fulfill each others' psychological, and often occupational, needs (Amato *et al.* 2007, 16). Occupational compatibility became a central aspect of psychological and emotional compatibility in an advanced capitalist order in which a majority of women not only had to but wanted to work. According to a forthcoming book by Stephanie Coontz, the increase in women's economic independence in the 1970s and 1980s initially led to a rise in divorce rates, not because women's work and education created more bad marriages, but because they encouraged women to raise their expectations of fairness in marriage and gave them more resources to leave bad marriages. But as men and women adjusted to women's new bargaining power in and out of marriage, husbands and wives began to communicate better, spend more quality time together, and develop deeper emotional ties, leading to more satisfying marriages and sex lives for both partners. This helps explain why divorce rates in the United States have declined significantly for college-educated couples since the late 1980s, much more significantly than for less-educated or lower-income couples. The right to divorce also led to lower rates of female suicide and domestic violence and contributed to more compatible unions among those who remained married.[1]

Better heterosexual sex altered perceptions about other types of relationships. Many came to believe that women had a right to enjoy sex, whether inside or outside marriage, whether in heterosexual or homosexual relationships, and neither should be covert any longer. Soon a more vocal gay movement followed, one that fought against the hetero-normative social and legal institutions of American society and gained new rights for gays and lesbians. Although it suffered some setbacks during the early years of the AIDS epidemic in the 1980s, by the early twenty-first century it was achieving numerous political victories.

In Iran too, as the birth rate dropped, life expectancy increased, and changing gender norms saturated society through the international media; women's expectations of marriage shifted as well. Iranians had practiced arranged marriages for centuries, with less normative weight given to romantic love. During the Pahlavi era, companionate marriages gradually gained ground among the elite and the new urban middle

---

[1] I am grateful to Coontz, author of *Marriage and History*, for her helpful e-mail exchange of April 3, 2007; see also Cowen 2007.

classes. Nonetheless, parents still played a key role in introducing pro-spective couples, approving marriages, and negotiating dowry and *mah-riyeh*. In the 1980s leftist and Islamist party leaders adopted parental roles and were expected to give their consent before a couple could marry.

By the first decade of the twenty-first century, in urban and even rural communities, strictly arranged marriages and endogamous marriages (within kinship groups) became less common. Although daughters still needed their fathers' legal permission to marry in the Islamic Republic, at other levels the enforcement of Islamist strictures had slackened. Marriage was seen less and less as merely an institution for procreation, and women had come to expect intimacy and spontaneity along with a greater degree of emotional and sexual closeness. Moreover, the mean age of marriage for girls had gone up, and dating had become a more accept-able part of life. In a comparative study of Iran, Iraq, and Saudi Arabia, Mansoor Moaddel reported a significant shift in attitudes toward mar-riage in urban Iranian society between 2000 and 2005. In a 2000 survey, 41 percent of respondents considered parental approval essential for marriage, but by 2005 this had decreased to 24 percent. Moreover, by 2005, nearly 70 percent of respondents favored personal choice in spouse selection, and of these, 50 percent declared love to be more important than parental approval, though most still sought their parents' approval for love marriages (Moaddel 2008, 9).

In urban and northern rural communities, young men and women formed friendships on the streets, at the universities, and in the workplace, often with the intention of getting married. This occurred, even though the Islamist state had established many prohibitions against the mingling of unmarried men and women. After about a year of such semi-secret dating, a young man might go to the father's house and ask for his daughter's hand. Parents still helped their sons and daughters with the cost of a new home and regarded this as their responsibility. In part, this was because renting an ordinary two-bedroom apartment in Tehran, for example, required an exorbitant down payment, plus a monthly rent of $600 in 2007.[2] The idea of unmarried cohabitation had also gained limited social acceptance in the capital city, in spite of its nominal illegal-ity, while Valentine's Day had become a big day of celebration, much to the consternation of the government.

In addition to covert homosexuality in many social sectors, especially sex-segregated high schools, within Tehran's educated and cosmopolitan population a small, clandestine, gay subculture had also emerged, along

[2] Special thanks to Mahsa Shekarloo, Farah Ghadernia, Hassan Mortazari, and Samira N. for the helpful information they provided for this section.

with cyberspace publications in Persian that advocated a modern gay and lesbian lifestyle. Iran's gay and lesbian community desired legal recognition of homosexuality by the public and the state, as well as more egalitarianism within relationships.

Meanwhile surging rates of unemployment and rising expectations concerning marriage had led to dramatic increases in the number of runaways, prostitutes, drug addicts, and suicides among young Iranian women. Many women complained of domestic violence and their husbands' extramarital affairs and wanted a way out. These upheavals unleashed new anxieties about the changing sexual mores of the country. This chapter explores the link between politics and the shifting gender roles in this third generation since the Iranian revolution.

Women, the politics of reform, and the discourse of human rights

In the mid-1990s, the battles for a more tolerant society were fought in numerous and sometimes unlikely sites. Iranian journalists, lawyers, clerics, doctors and nurses, fashion designers, actors and film directors, college students, literary writers, and homemakers became activists in the reform movement. Reformists came from many different social and religious orientations, including both secular and moderate Muslims. Some were leftist Islamists who had participated in the revolution, fought in the war, or had relatives who were martyred. Many had contributed to literacy and health campaigns. Such early supporters of the theocratic state, including women who had suffered the loss of loved ones in the war, were by now increasingly dissatisfied with corrupt policies of the state and felt abandoned by it. Most reformist intellectuals went through a dramatic ideological transformation that was influenced further by the collapse of the Eastern European and Soviet systems. Veteran Islamists and more secular dissidents gradually reached a fragile truce in order to unite provisionally in a common cause. These organizations were reinforced by the increasing numbers of youth raised on satellite television and the Internet who resented the excesses of the theocratic state and its morality police. Reformists argued that opposition to the shah and Western domination had been only one dimension of the revolutionary agenda. Issues of more importance were the creation of a viable democracy and a new interpretation of Islam compatible with the requirements of modern life.

The May 1997 election of Muhammad Khatami as president strengthened the voices of women's rights advocates, who supported his run for office (Fig. 11.1). Khatami was one of four candidates who had been vetted by the Council of Guardians and allowed to run for office shortly before the

Figure 11.1 President Muhammad Khatami, 1997

elections, in order to give a greater semblance of democracy to the process. Although Khatami was not expected to win, much of the public embraced his platform, which was dedicated to curbing censorship, fighting fanaticism, and increasing tolerance on social and cultural issues. Of 33 million eligible voters, 29 million (88 percent) voted, an unprecedented turnout for an Iranian election. Twenty million votes (70 percent) went to Khatami, who did equally well in cities and in villages. Word-of-mouth indicated that Khatami would adopt a more liberal stance on gender relations, which brought women and young people out to vote for him in overwhelming numbers. He was reelected in June of 2001 with close to 76 percent of the vote, despite his limited success in carrying out his program in the face of resistance on the part of entrenched hard-liners.

In 1999, more than 7,000 women ran as candidates in the first nation-wide local elections under the Islamic Republic, In twenty cities these women candidates placed first in contests for council leadership positions, and in fifty-eight cities they took second place. A total of 784 women (about 11 percent of the national total), many in remote locations, were elected. In the 2003 elections, this number increased to about 1,400 in the councils.[3] The February 2000 elections brought a new generation of deputies to the Sixth Islamic Parliament (2000–2004), giving reformists a clear majority. Many deputies assumed they could simply reinstate greater social freedoms, changing the Islamist regime through legal, parliamentary means. Between 2000 and 2004, the reformists who dominated the presidency, the Parliament and the provincial and city councils, attempted to liberalize the system. One important organ that heavily campaigned for women's rights was the Center for women's Participation (Markaz-e Mosharekat-e Zanan), which was affiliated with the Office of the President. The Center was established under President Hashemi Rafsanjani, but played a more active role in the Khatami era. Under Khatami, its new director Zahra Shojai held cabinet rank as advisor to the president. Khatami appointed another woman, Masumeh Ebtekar, Vice President for environmental and women's issues. Women deputies also organized a caucus and introduced a series of laws pertaining to the rights of women and girls, managing to pass a few of them. The Parliament raised the legal age of marriage for girls from nine to fifteen, but the all-powerful Council of Guardians disagreed, and it was eventually set at thirteen. Women gained some rights to initiate divorce and Parliament exempted women's *mahriyeh* from taxes. Single women received permission to study abroad on government fellowships. Reformists also managed to reduce the severity of the *hijab* for children and high-school students by allowing more colorful uniforms and scarves (Ebrahimi 2001; Mohri 2003; Tariqi 2004; Madani-Ghahfarokhi 2005; Koolaee 2006).

President Khatami supported these efforts, including ones that would have equalized women's inheritance rights and given them greater divorce rights. But the right to inheritance and several other bills were either rejected or severely revised by the Supreme Leader, the Council of Guardians, and the Expediency Council. The latter is a tribunal that arbitrates between the Parliament and the Council of Guardians, usually siding with the Council of Guardians. More ambitious projects, such as calls for the adoption of the UN Convention on Elimination of All Forms of Discrimination Against Women (CEDAW), which the

---

[3] Information from Mehrangiz Kar and e-mail from Azadeh Kian-Thiébaut of August 23, 2007.

Khatami government had helped introduce, were ratified – with some reservations – by a parliamentary majority.

Fierce opposition to the CEDAW developed in Qom, where Islamist men and women held demonstrations against the new law. Conservative clerics declared that joining CEDAW would amount to "a declaration of war against Islam." Another accusation was that the CEDAW represented a perverted "Western sexual ethos and prostitution" that would result in the creation of mixed bathhouses. Eventually, the Council of Guardians rejected the proposed law on the grounds that it conflicted with several principles of the constitution and Islam, including inheritance and divorce laws, the *hijab*, and polygamy ("Iranian Leader" 2000).

Despite strong public support and enthusiasm, the Khatami era, which benefited from a period of high oil prices in the international market, did not succeed in overhauling the Islamist state, though it did provide greater opportunities for cultural expression and political criticism (Nomani and Behdad 2006, 211). Moreover, the reformers faced repression at every step, since the police and the legal system remained under the control of the Supreme Leader, as did military and foreign affairs. One result was that between 1997 and 2004, more than a hundred newspapers were closed down, and the state targeted political dissidents, journalists, and even some reform politicians. Many were arrested, murdered, or forced into exile, including a generation of student activists who held dramatic prodemocracy demonstrations in Iranian universities in 1999.

When many reformists were disqualified by the Council of Guardians, disillusioned voters stayed away from the polls and conservatives were elected to the Seventh Islamic Parliament (2004–2008). The new MPs halted the debate on the CEDAW and many other progressive gender reforms (Nazila Fathi 2004). Among them were large numbers of Basij and Pasdaran, whose ascendancy to the top decision-making institutions marked a new stage in Iranian politics. Women deputies affiliated with the Basij and with close ties to the rural sectors promoted a few progressive measures, such as reinstituting abortion to save the life of the mother and the appointment of women judges in an advisory capacity. However, for the most part they supported the new conservative agenda (Koolaee 2006).

The reformists were further weakened when US President George W. Bush included Iran in his "Axis of Evil" in a 2002 speech, and suggested that the United States might invade Iran. The powerlessness of the reformists in the face of these foreign and domestic challenges led to widespread public disillusionment. Following a decade of reformist control in the provincial councils, the Parliament, and the presidency, the 2005 presidential elections brought to power Mahmoud Ahmadinejad, a conservative populist and former member of the Pasdaran. The presidency, the Parliament, and the provincial and city councils were now in the hands of a new generation of populist conservatives, many of them veterans of the Iran–Iraq War.

The decision of nearly 20 million disillusioned pro-reformist voters to boycott the elections, voting fraud engineered by the office of the Supreme Leader, and the zeal with which the Basij got out the vote certainly helped bring Ahmadinejad to power (Hourcade 2006, 10–11). Various reports estimate that by 2005 there were at least 8 million "card-carrying" Basijis: 3 million active members (trained at military camps and used in domestic repression) and 5 million inactive members (individuals who received handouts and could be mobilized at election times).[4] Those who voted for Ahmadinejad did so out of Basiji loyalty and support for his economic agenda. They were moved by his piety, his promises of social justice, and his opposition to the pro-market economic liberalization proposals of his rival, Hashemi-Rafsanjani, plans which would have ended many government subsidies.

Ahmadinejad's election also expressed a backlash against the sexual revolution taking place in Iran. I was in Tehran just before the election and was amazed by the range of negative comments on the streets and in social gatherings about women's supposedly scandalous behavior. Many men, including young working-class men bitterly opposed to the government, nonetheless expressed outrage over young women's presumed sexual promiscuity and at the sight of girls and boys walking in the streets with clasped hands. In such conversations, public criticisms of the economy were almost always tied into stories of young women selling their bodies to Arab Sheikhs (and not Iranian clients) in the Persian Gulf to raise money for their dowries and support their families. As journalist Christopher de Bellaigue reported at the time, many of Ahmadinejad's supporters were deeply concerned with the "dramatic rise in prostitution, marital infidelities, and drug addiction," which they blamed on reformist social and cultural policies (Bellaigue 2005, 20). They remembered that, as mayor of Tehran, Ahmadinejad had arranged low-interest loans for newly married couples, thus encouraging the institution of marriage. As a presidential candidate, he promised not only to reduce the staggering unemployment rate but also to provide more generous financial support for young couples (Fathi 2005).

Supporters of Ahmadinejad tapped into these feelings by distributing a documentary film by director Massoud Dehnamaki (a former Basiji) entitled *Prostitution and Poverty* (2002). The film was aimed at poor urban and rural supporters of the state. It featured a series of interviews

---

[4] According to Basij Commander Mohammad Hejazi the number was closer to 11 million in 2005 ("Niruyeh Moghavemat" 2006). Political scientist Farideh Farhi suggested a figure closer to 8 million (Farhi, e-mail, February 9, 2007).

with poor urban women who had entered the sex trade in the Persian Gulf, often for a limited period. Some saved up to help desperate family members or to raise a respectable *jahiziyeh* to get married. These clever manipulations of social and cultural grievances, which played on Iranian prejudices against Arabs, contributed to the defeat of the reform movement.

The culture wars continue

Despite these political setbacks, feminist discourses continued to permeate higher education, the arts, and other cultural arenas. In 2005, women, who did exceedingly well in the *concours* entrance exams, made up 65 percent of first-year students at state colleges and universities in Iran. The field of women's studies found its way into the universities and into women's periodical literature. By 2005, there were also more than 100 publishing houses that catered to women (Dokouhaki 2005, 20). In a steady stream of new books and articles, feminist writers questioned and criticized major male political figures of the twentieth century for their limited perspectives on gender. A heated debate arose over the Western concepts of cultural relativism and universalism, accompanied by attempts to combine and reconcile the best arguments from both perspectives. Some Iranian feminists tacitly called for the recognition of gay and lesbian lifestyles on the grounds that gender and sexuality are socially constructed (Sherkat 1998, 2–4).

At the turn of the twenty-first century, and with the emergence of a "third generation" of dissident youth, Iranian feminism had also redefined itself. The first generation resisted the shah and started the revolution. The second one endured the harsh early days of the Islamic Republic and the war. This third generation grew up in the reform era and was not only more confident, but seemed determined to confront the state. For this generation, fashion was a feminist tool. In contrast to the revolutionary generation comprised of leftist radicals, or Islamists who abhorred bourgeois decadence, young urban women engaged in a constant struggle with the morality police by wearing makeup, painting their toe nails red, and streaking their bangs in vibrant colors. Before the eyes of the clerics and the morality police, they announced their claim to the streets and other public spaces by wearing form-fitting slacks and short, elegant *manteaux*. While these garments met the minimum standards laid down by the morality police, they were as far as possible from the normative drab black veils.

This third generation also reclaimed Muharram for itself, even as it participated in state-sponsored religious festivals. Their Muharram did not just stress atonement, repentance, or rituals revolving around the war. This Muharram also challenged the austere sexual conventions of the Islamic Republic, as young women donned fashionable black clothing, lots of makeup, and matching black nail polish and lipstick. Girls and boys flocked to "Hussein Parties" in public squares and listened to rhythmic renditions of Muharram music. Women held candlelit vigils while quietly distributing slips of paper with their phone numbers to men in the crowd who caught their fancy (Nasser 2006; Moaveni 2005, 56–59).

Competitive sports provided another venue for women's rights advocates. By 2004, the number of women athletes was estimated at more than 1.2 million. They received training from 32,000 women coaches in 10,000 public and private sports centers (Dokouhaki 2005, 20). Women often cross-dressed in order to attend sporting events with male friends, despite the continuing ban on women's attendance at soccer stadiums. Occasionally, the democratic opposition was able to express itself in sports stadiums. In September 2001, fans at two stadiums publicly expressed their contempt for the terrorist attacks at the World Trade Center in the United States by observing a spontaneous moment of silence in memory of the victims and chanting "America, Condolences" (e-mail from M. Amir Ebrahimi, August 31, 2007).

The Internet offered another sphere for new developments in gender relations. Persian bloggers numbered in the hundreds of thousands, making Persian one of the most popular languages in cyberspace. The Internet became a medium for dating and matchmaking. Local sources reported that an unmarried woman teacher from the restrictive city of Qom might set up a date with a man from the province of Qazvin and arrange to meet at one of the more elegant cafés of Tehran. The Internet also served as a forum for jumpstarting a new feminist movement. When a March 8 International Women's Day celebration and subsequent peaceful demonstrations became the target of club-wielding police and militia, feminists changed tactics. In Spring 2005, in an unprecedented move, a number of feminist groups formed a broad coalition to protest women's inequality in the constitution and held a rally with over 6,000 people. A year later, despite escalating state persecution, noted feminists Shirin Ebadi, Noushin Ahmadi-Khorasani, Parvin Ardalan (winner of the 2007 Olof Palme Award) along with others signed a petition calling for the repeal of discriminatory marriage and divorce laws. Soon, thousands of young women in their teens and early twenties had joined the grassroots One Million Signatures Campaign, also known as Campaign for Equality, which spread rapidly throughout the nation through the Internet; its influence was apparent in both big cities and small towns. As of this writing, activists quietly continue to go door to door to explain the

Figure 11.2 Parvin Ardalan

deficiencies of the laws to ordinary women, collect signatures, and plan
to submit them to the upcoming Eighth Parliament in 2008 (Ahmadi-
Khorasani 2007a; Casey 2007) (Figs. 11.2, 11.3).

Iranian cinema, which has gained increasing levels of world recogni-
tion, has also helped to redefine gender roles (Fig. 11.4). Female film-
makers Tahmineh Milani (*Hidden Half*, 2001; *Unwanted Woman*, 2005),
Rakhshan Bani E'temad (*Under the Skin of the City*, 2001; *Gilaneh*, 2005),
Samira Makhmalbaf (*The Apple*, 1998), and their male colleagues, such as
Bahram Beyza'i (*Bashu: The Little Stranger*, 1988), Dariyush Mehrjui
(*Leila*, 1997), Mohsen Makhmalbaf (*Nights of Zayandehrood*, 1991;
Gabbeh, 1995), Ja'far Panahi (*The Circle*, 2000), Majid Majidi (*The Color
of Paradise*, 1999), and Kambuzia Partovi (*Café Transit*, 2005) subjected
Iranian and Islamic patriarchal cultures to critical treatment. Their films

Figure 11.3 Women's rights demonstration, Tehran, 2006. Simin Behbahani (left), Noushin Ahmadi-Khorasani (right)

explore various themes concerning marriage, among them women's desire to be loved and respected in relationships, polygamy, repudiation, and physical and emotional violence against women and children (Naficy 2001; Tapper 2002).

In contrast to the romantic films of the 1970s, wherein a loving marriage ultimately solved all problems, the new Iranian cinema offered critical perspectives on marriage, often singling out incompetent, abusive, and uncaring male heads of household. Nationalists of the 1930s had called upon mothers to raise patriotic children, and Islamists in the 1970s and 1980s asked them to give martyrs. In the 1990s, women turned their backs on these political appropriations of motherhood. The new Iranian cinema suggested that women should protect children (boys and girls) from abusive fathers, the ravages of war, the market, and the state (*Bashu, Sara, The Color of Paradise, The Circle, Gileva*). These films called attention to women's nurturing role and the social consequences of its absence, and criticized the patriarchal prerogative of institutional marriages that empowered the paternal mother-in-law, and the division of labor in more traditional marriages. But they also called attention to the fragility of more individualistic, romantic marriages.

Feminist intellectuals reexamined the traditional images of peasant and working-class women in popular media, including novels, short stories,

Figure 11.4 Film poster

and documentaries. In the leftist literature of the 1970s, the female
peasant was an asexual being whose concerns were confined to work,
poverty, health, infant mortality, and the struggle against the bourgeoisie.
By the 1990s, this cardboard image of the heroic, peasant or working-class
woman was being rewritten. The new literature explored sexual desire
and sexual violence across social classes, the infidelities of married men,
violence in the home, illegal abortions, and the dogmatism of the old leftist
organizations. These observable shifts in gender representation stemmed
from the public's new attitudes toward marriage, family planning, religion, and social hierarchies.

Urban youth and premarital sex

In Tehran and a few other major cities, the difference between indoor and outdoor social lives among middle- and upper-class urbanites could not have been more extreme. In public, young women observed the *hijab* requirements, followed the rules of modesty, and averted their glances. Behind closed doors, however, they lived unrestrained sexual lives that stunned even visiting cousins from Los Angeles. Since outdoor forms of recreation were extremely limited, most socializing happened in private residences. Parents were often complicit in these trysts. A young man's parents might be in the house when their son invited his girlfriend over. Many middle- and upper-class parents with secular dispositions tolerated this kind of behavior because at home they could shelter their children from the morality police, who could jail and torture transgressors very easily. Outside the home, young people attended parties at friends' houses where casual sex and drug use were common practice. Some of these young women and men belonged to the more modern sectors of society dating from the pre-revolutionary period. They had culturally sophisticated parents who became economically disadvantaged as a result of the revolution. Others belonged to the tradition-bound *bazaari* and clerical classes, whose fortunes have grown markedly since the revolution. They moved into posh condominiums and houses equipped with the latest American gadgets and electronic devices, with ready access to global television and other media networks.

Pardis Mahdavi's fieldwork on these urban populations across several Iranian cities reported that many unmarried youth – in her snowball sample of about eighty young people between the ages of eighteen and twenty-five – had experienced premarital or extramarital sex. Dating often began in cyberspace and quickly led to sex. However, very few of those who engaged in risky sexual behaviors (whether heterosexual or homosexual) used condoms or even oral contraceptives. The women were too shy to purchase prophylactics from the local pharmacy, and the men were simply too careless. Most believed they were not at risk of contracting HIV/AIDS (Mahdavi 2007b).

One of my friends in Tehran, a history instructor at a local college, believes that the growing numbers of unhappy marriages and divorces have contributed to a sexual revolution, one in which many of her students have participated:

The rise in divorce rates stems from a variety of reasons: economic and cultural factors, women's greater awareness of their rights, their education, and their employment, which has reduced their dependence on men. For these reasons, many women no longer see marriage as a means to reach their hopes and ideals in life. They no longer regard sex as an obligation in marriage, but a form of pleasure for themselves. Hence they no longer find it necessary to preserve their virginity. Those who must be virgins to get married undergo hymenoplasty. There are many doctors who perform this expensive operation.[5]

Hymenoplasty today is somewhat more sophisticated than the hymen-repair procedure Dr. Polak described in 1865. The modern operation includes the use of gelatin capsules containing red dye that will rupture during nuptial intercourse, simulating the physical markers of virginal sexual experience. Hymenoplasty and various forms of vaginal reconstruction seem to be popular operations throughout the Middle East and even among expatriates in the United States and Europe, since they are advertised widely on the Internet.[6] Simpler methods of simulating virginity are also available. Some women regulate their menses by taking pills to coordinate their period with their wedding night. Iranian men are well aware of these changes and tricks, often joking that there are no real virgins left in Tehran and the other big cities. Feminists are divided on the merits of hymenoplasty. Some believe it reinforces existing power relations and affirms the patriarchal order, but Fataneh Farahani suggests that the increasing numbers of women who choose such operations might eventually diminish the significance of virginity:

The very rising of the hymenoplasty operation, and other tactics, in all probability, renders it impossible to distinguish between "the real virgin" and the "remade virgin." In these circumstances, the growing number of "false virgins," therefore, cast a shadow of distrust on all the women who appear to be "real" virgins. (Farahani 2007, 91)

Today more than ever it seems young women are "performing virginity." They engage in non-vaginal heterosexual intercourse or same-sex relationships. If they are not virgins on their wedding nights, women can simulate virginity. Most fake inexperience in sexual matters, proving that virginity has become a "social and cultural construct, rather than a biological truth" of ideal womanhood (Farahani 2007, 90).

The politics of birth control

While young unmarried urbanites engage in risky sex, the married population has relatively easy access to birth control. Soon after taking power

---

[5] Interview with an anonymous informant, February 8, 2007.
[6] See for example www.labiadoctor.com/hymenoplasty.html. For more information on this relatively comman procedure see: http://en.wikipedia.org/wiki/Hymenorrhaphy.

in 1979 the state instituted its own religious sex education, which served a different function. Rather than censoring all discussion of sex, the state initially took a more traditionalist stance, banning only progressive discussions of sex influenced by Western discourses. Shiʿi ʿulama pride themselves on adhering to the notion that "there is no shame in [discussing] religious matters" (la haya fi din). The religious manuals of the clerics, with their detailed instructions on proper sexual conduct and on the rituals and purification required after sex, became mandatory reading in school. During religious instruction in public schools, teachers spent a great deal of time describing proper procedures for ablution of the genitals and restoration of taharat. Instructors provided students with information about the anatomical and biological differences between men and women (menstruation, ejaculation, childbirth, etc.) from a religious perspective. Similar information was disseminated in neighborhood mosques and prayer sessions. Discussions of issues such as masturbation (viewed as reprehensible), vaginal discharge, and nocturnal discharge focused on avoiding ritual pollution before prayer (Drew 1997). In these manuals, shahvat (sexual desire) and interest in jemaʿ (intercourse) were seen as much stronger in women than in men. But women's haya (modesty) and men's gheyrat (honor) controlled excessive female desire (Mir-Hosseini 2004, 206). A high-school teacher from Qom recalls that children constantly asked for definitions and explanations of words like sodomy, bestiality, and a variety of other forms of sexual conduct they encountered in these religious manuals of sexual etiquette, demands that placed their parents and teachers in an awkward position.

Initially, the new regime adopted natalist policies. Couples with seven or more children received a plot of land on which to build a home. The state limited access to birth control and banned abortions. Families who sent their sons to the war were compensated with food coupons, monetary rewards, and expanded educational opportunities. Overall, fertility rates increased from 6.3 in 1976 to 7.0 in 1986, as Iran's population expanded dramatically from 34 million to 49 million (Dungus 2000; Aghajanian 1995).

When the war ended in 1988, the government faced a population explosion and a disastrous economy. Supported in this by Ayatollah Khomeini, the state began to encourage family planning. Modern approaches to reproductive health were integrated into religious teachings and implemented as part of state health policy. Birth control was reauthorized in 1989. The state also requested assistance from the UN Fund for Population Activities. The architects of the new birth-control program were Hussein Malekafzali and his colleagues Habibollah Zanjani and Muhammad Alizadeh. Each had held positions in the Ministry of Health since the

Pahlavi era. Their goals were to encourage birth spacing of three to four years, discourage early and late pregnancy, and limit family size at first to three and later to two children (Aghajanian 1995). The team reintroduced some of the birth-control policies of the pre-revolutionary National Organization of Women that had been shelved, and added many new features. This time, they had more success then under the shah.[7]

By the end of the twentieth century, Iran had become a model for other developing nations in the area of population control. Before the revolution, the annual rate of population growth had dropped from 3.1 percent in 1966 to 2.7 percent in 1976. This trend had reversed itself after the revolution, so that by 1986, the annual rate of population growth was 3.9. In the next decade (1986–1996), the annual rate dropped once again, this time more dramatically, to 2.0 percent. Total fertility rates also dropped to 2.0, below replacement levels, making Iranian rates comparable to those of South Korea, Thailand, and Malaysia. Between 1986 and 1996 there was a 50 percent drop in the number of women who married before the age of twenty, even though the state encouraged early marriage. The average age of women at first marriage increased from 19.7 in 1976 to about 22 in 1996, with the gap between rural and urban women at first marriage decreasing (Nomani and Behdad 2006, Table 4.1; Zangeneh 2005; Howard 2002, 107–111; Aghajanian and Mehryar 2005). By 2004, these numbers had further improved so that 74 percent of women of childbearing age were using various methods of family planning (UNICEF 2007). While many engaged couples delayed marriage due to financial problems, the success in population control was attributed to several other factors:

- As studies of fertility in other developing countries have shown, a rise in female literacy rates leads to a decrease in fertility rates, even when no other substantial changes are introduced (Jain 1981). Iran experienced a dramatic rise in literacy rates between 1985 and 2005, especially among rural women, which was the key factor contributing to a decrease in fertility rates overall.
- All forms of contraceptives (birth-control pills, condoms and other prophylactics, the IUD) became free and/or widely available for married couples. A condom factory, the only one of its kind in the region, was established. Hospitals and trained physicians in mobile units performed

---

[7] I interviewed Muhammad Alizadeh while I was in Tehran in April 2005, and he generously provided me with many details of their program. Ali Reza Marandi, a pediatrician and two-time Minister of Health (1985–1989 and 1993–1997), headed the project. He received the UN Population Award in 1999 and the World Health Organization Award in 2000 for the success of his organization in reducing the birth rate.

vasectomies and tubal ligations free of charge, and provided injectable contraceptives in both rural and urban areas.

- Thousands of midwives were educated about contraceptive technologies. The state also recruited female volunteers as intermediaries between the clinics and young couples. By 1999, there were more than 40,000 of these volunteers, mostly married women with children. Each volunteer monitored about fifty families.

- Family planning was integrated with primary healthcare. A rural health network was established with 17,000 clinics. Each clinic had three to four mobile units that provided family planning to 80 percent of the rural population. By 1997, rudimentary rural healthcare services were available to 85 percent of the population. Infant mortality rates dropped to 31 deaths per 1,000 live births, and mortality rates for children under five dropped to 36 deaths per 1,000 live births. Lower death rates for children resulted in lower pregnancy rates and smaller families. Healthcare centers vaccinated children, took care of the basic needs of the whole family, and also distributed contraceptives. As a result, there was no stigma attached to visiting a clinic for a (married) woman.

- The Sixth Parliament legalized abortion up to the fourth month of pregnancy if it threatened the life of the mother or the child. Abortion remained illegal in cases of rape or malformation of the fetus, despite attempts by the Sixth Parliament to legalize it in such instances. However, illegal abortions continued to take place in many hospitals and clinics, usually under a doctor's supervision.

- Infertility treatments became part of family planning, despite their prohibitive costs. This included artificial insemination (with the husband's semen). This policy generated much good will, since family planning was no longer equated solely with prevention of pregnancy.

- New family planning policies attempted to raise the awareness of both women and men regarding reproductive issues in general, rather than focusing solely on contraceptives. A massive nationwide campaign for family planning and modern sex education was begun. High-school students (both girls and boys) and factory workers received routine lectures and seminars on the subject. Engaged couples were required to attend family-planning classes before marriage, where they were taught about sex, including ways of obtaining and giving pleasure, and lectured on the benefits of smaller families. Iran became the only country in the region that required such classes before marriage. The same center conducted exams on venereal disease and drug abuse before marriage, and required those marrying close kin to undergo genetic tests to prevent hereditary diseases. Married couples were advised to delay pregnancy, and women were told to bear children between the ages of twenty and thirty-five.

- The state involved many clerics, including low-level ones, in the campaign for birth control. Since clerics have traditionally provided people with advice on sexual matters, their inclusion in the new policy was not as unusual as it may seem. Medieval Muslim literature had discussed birth control, and the government republished some of these texts in order to prove that birth control had long been acceptable under Islam. On television programs and in Friday prayers, clerics, including the Supreme Leader Khamenei, assured the public that contraceptives were religiously sanctioned.[8]
- The Basij organization, including the Basiji Sisters, was mobilized for health projects. From time to time, close to half a million Basijis were sent out on a national immunization campaign against polio and other infectious diseases. Vaccination rates for childhood diseases exceeded 95 percent, all of which was paid for by the state. On one occasion, according to the UN, more than eight million children under five were vaccinated in a single day (Howard 2002, 106).
- Journalists received incentives, such as free vacations, to give more coverage to family planning. By 1996, 93 percent of urban homes and 70 percent of rural ones had television sets, which advertised the social, economic, and health advantages of a smaller family. The media openly addressed the side effects of various contraceptive methods and suggested that husbands and wives should seek assistance from their clinic advisors in making their choice.
- The state instituted a broader social security and pension program for retirees, thereby reducing the need for large families as security for old age.
- Family planning was tied to the environmental and ecological concerns of Third World countries. Hence, birth control was presented as a form of political struggle for better living conditions in Iran and in the developing world (Fig. 11.5).[9]

Citizens complied with these policies to a remarkable degree, but in some cases, such as age of marriage, ignored the state's attempts to lower it. A subsequent study showed that the increase in a husband and wife's level of education had also contributed to the success of the program (Tehrani *et al.* 2001). While more girls than boys continued to die before their first birthday, there has been no evidence so far that substantial numbers of

---

[8] Milani 1999, 1.
[9] The above information is based on Hoodfar 1994; 1998; Hoodfar and Assadpour 2000; Roudi 1999; Dungus 2000; Howard 2002; Mirzazadeh 2004; Aghajanian and Mehryar 1999; Wright 2001; UNICEF 2007; recent issues of the journal *Behdasht-e Khanevadeh* (Family Health, Tehran); and interview with Muhammad Alizadeh, Tehran, April 2005.

Figure 11.5 Birth-control poster

baby girls were abandoned (as in China) or aborted (as in India) so that parents could have boys. Traditionally, Iranian society has valued sons over daughters. Moreover, since polygamy and repudiation were still male prerogatives, wives without sons would be expected to have been in a more precarious situation – but this has not proved to be the case, so far at least. Indeed, after a decade of revolution and war, families seemed to place greater value on having daughters than before.[10]

---

[10] For example, in a study that explored the attitudes of teenage girls in the province of Semnan toward puberty and marriage, 97 percent of the girls expressed the desire to have

Friedl writes that in rural areas and small towns in and around the province of Kohgiluge/Boir Ahmad in southwest Iran, fathers and brothers realized the economic significance of education. They pushed college girls to enter more lucrative fields like engineering, medicine, or pharmacy and discouraged them from the humanities and the social sciences, even when the girls wanted to study such fields. In contrast, boys were sometimes discouraged from advanced education and sent into business where returns are often higher. Fathers and brothers also welcomed financial assistance to the parents by daughters. The number of unmarried women who financially supported their parents rapidly increased. This process improved relations between fathers and daughters and reduced the financial burden on brothers, who have traditionally been the major source of support for older parents. As a result, sisters felt they were entitled to a larger share of their father's estate and some in Boir Ahmad went to court to challenge their brothers over inheritance rights (Friedl 2009).

An international study similarly suggested that men's attitudes toward women had changed. In a comparative study of Iran, Jordan, and Egypt, Mansoor Moaddel and Taghi Azadarmaki found that 76 percent of Iranians agreed that two or less was the ideal number of children in a family, 40 percent felt that a woman's employment did not interfere with her intimacy with her children, and only 45 percent felt that a woman needed to have children to feel satisfied. All of these numbers were substantially lower than those in Egypt and Jordan (Moaddel and Azadarmaki 2002).

Iran's birth-control campaign showed that the state was willing to articulate a more liberal discourse on sexuality when it suited its purposes, in this case population control. Even so, child marriage, violence against women, repudiation, polygamy, lack of community property, and unequal inheritance rights persisted. On the latter issues, the regime followed a patriarchal and often misogynistic reading of Islam, and refused to adopt a more liberal and tolerant interpretation that would have empowered women in their personal lives.

Women's empowerment was hardly the goal of the Islamist state. Moreover, whenever birth control came in conflict with men's access to sexual pleasure, the state refused to support the former. For the purposes of population control and women's health, doctors in the Ministry of Health recommended that women not have children until after the age of twenty ("Miyangin" 2005, 76). But the state continued to keep the legal age of marriage low in order to serve men's sexual interests. Finally, during the reformist Sixth Parliament, the state agreed to raise the legal marriage

one or two children, and most wanted at least one girl (Malekafzali *et al.* 1998, 8). Many points in the above paragraphs were suggested by Shahla Ezazi, Saeid Madani-Ghahfarokhi, and Houchang Chehabi.

age from nine to thirteen. Nonetheless, there was still a ten-year discrepancy between the legal age of marriage and the higher mean age of marriage.

Likewise, temporary marriage and polygamy remained legal, though both practices contributed to prostitution and venereal disease. The state continued to follow a dichotomous policy, on the one hand intervening in the sexual conduct of citizens to encourage smaller families and to assure men's unrestricted access to sex, and on the other denying women greater control in other areas of their lives. This was the secret of the Islamist state's sexual economy.

Once in office, Ahmadinejad tried to reverse the fertility trend and revive the pronatalist trends concomitant with Ayatollah Khomeini's jihadist policies of the early 1980s, even though Khomeini had supported population control by the time of his death in 1989. Ahmadinejad

Figure 11.6 President Mahmoud Ahmadinejad became the subject of numerous international cartoons after stating in February 2007 that Iran would not retreat on its nuclear program, which he compared to a train without brakes

declared that a stronger Iran, with a nuclear capability, needed to be more populous and recommended more part-time rather than full-time employment for women (Fig. 11.6). Even before he assumed power, the state attempted to restrict abortions. However, the president's comments alarmed the public and even many in the government, who saw them as yet another sign of his bellicose foreign and domestic policies ("Iran's President" 2006).

Sexual awakening: rural and town marriages and the dilemma of unmarried girls

Companionate, monogamous marriages, in which individuals have a strong voice in choosing a spouse, had become an accepted norm among the educated urban middle classes by the 1970s. But in poorer rural communities, parents continued to arrange their children's marriages, and girls were married at a very young age, often around puberty or before. With the nearly universal adoption of birth control, more health and sex education in the 1990s, and expanding access to a broader range of media, marriage practices evolved in rural communities as well. By 2000, people in poor rural communities of southwest Iran no longer viewed marriage as only an institution for procreation. Young people looked for psychological and social compatibility, mutual intimacy, and affection, better earning potential of their mate, and insisted on choosing their partner (Fig. 11.7). Some fathers granted their daughters more autonomy because they wanted them happy and because times had changed and it "would be futile to fight against the spirit of the times" (Friedl 2009). Relations between fathers and children had undergone a profound shift. In the province of Boir Ahmad the old autocratic fathers of yesterday who provided for the family but maintained their distance were now disparagingly called "shahs." The new father was expected to be a friend, *doust*. However, young people remained financially dependent on their fathers because of high unemployment. Meanwhile, state laws that granted fathers extensive power over children, especially daughters, made it complicated for fathers to remain *doust* (Friedl 2009).

Despite continued resistance by more conservative sectors of society, birth-control and sex-education classes became mandatory for prospective couples after 1993. Participants received contraceptives and advice on intimate sexual matters. Offered in about 5,000 health centers, these classes lasted over an hour, with separate sessions for men and women. Class content varied somewhat according to the cultural diversity of the nation, from the more liberal northern province of Gilan to the much

Figure 11.7 Courting

more conservative southeastern province of Sistan-Baluchestan. Generally, participants watched a film explaining the body's erogenous zones, and the sexual needs of men and women. The emphasis seemed to be on male sexual gratification and ways in which wives could keep their husbands satisfied and content (Mahdavi 2007b). Female sexuality was discussed. Many women were surprised by what they learned in this class. Shohreh, a twenty-year-old sociology student, who attended the classes before marrying her fiancé, declared:

I felt ashamed … that I'm twenty years old but I still know nothing about sex. I ask myself why I've never read any books about it. Before I watched this film, I thought that an orgasm was something only men have. I didn't know that women could have such a feeling. (Cited in Zangeneh 2005)

Many couples returned for individual counseling after marriage. This meant that young couples no longer had to exclusively rely on in-laws to resolve marital conflicts and had access to other sources of authority.

Medical doctors had reported marital rape on the wedding night for over a century. In an effort to reduce sexual and psychological trauma for young women who might be virgins until their wedding, doctors now advised a couple to wait until both were mentally and physically prepared and reminded them of the importance and impact of the first sexual encounter, especially on women. As Dr. Aminian points out:

If, for example, a couple is suffering from stress, or is physically tired, or one of the partners really doesn't feel like having sex, then they shouldn't force it just because it is the wedding night … We even tell the couples that it can take two or three weeks before the situation is right to have sex for the first time. (Cited in Zangeneh 2005)

The young couple is also advised to delay pregnancy until they have adjusted to their new life.

Other shifts in social and economic trends, including greater urbanization, contributed to these dramatic changes in gender relations and sexual mores. Hundreds of thousands of male and female university students shared same-sex apartments in cities. This furnished greater opportunities for dating, free of the watchful eyes of parents and neighbors. As parental authority substantially weakened in Tehran and other urban communities, a decline in arranged marriages and an increase in "marriages based on free choice" was observed (Kian-Thiébaut 2005, 52). Marriages within kinship groups also decreased. Slightly more than 20 percent of couples were first cousins, and around the same number were distant relatives. The lowest numbers of kin marriages were found in the culturally liberal northern province of Gilan, and the highest in the culturally conservative southeastern province of Sistan-Baluchestan, where the mean age of women at first marriage was sixteen (Bahramitash and Kazemipour 2006, 124).

Growing numbers of urban and rural women never married. They insisted that men had unfair expectations of women, even when the women were employed and contributing to the family income. Women were expected to do all the housework, to prepare elaborate meals and entertain guests, and to routinely visit in-laws and relatives (Friedl 2002). A "proper" wife still deferred to her husband's authority and respected the wishes of her in-laws. Many men promised to help with chores and childcare, to give their wives time to study and work outside the home, to be kind and understanding, but, as in so many other parts of the world, husbands often failed to fulfill these promises. Accounts of such occurrences influenced younger sisters and cousins, who sometimes chose not to marry at all (Kian-Thiébaut 2005).

Despite significant changes in the 1990s, great differences continued to exist between urban and rural communities, and between different regions. In increasingly urbanized northern villages, and those around Shiraz and Isfahan, educated girls, including doctors and dentists who earned substantial incomes, became desirable marriage partners. High-school teachers were even more sought after because their summers off gave them more free time in which to raise a family. Young women's expectations in marriage had also increased. Their ideal husband was a man who was "good to talk to, pleasant to look at, reasonable and good-tempered, [had] a good income, and [helped] with housework" (Friedl 2003, 166). Marriage ceremonies and the requisite gifts had also become more extravagant. A woman's family regarded an expensive wedding ceremony and a large *mahriyeh* as the best forms of insurance against repudiation (Friedl 2002, 113).

In villages surrounding Shiraz, young boys might decide whom they wanted to marry, and girls might refuse the husband their parents had chosen for them. Mary Hegland reports:

As a newly married couple moves to its own home, the older generation loses influence over their lives. Brides and daughters-in-law no longer have to work under the direction of their mothers-in-law and defer to their wishes. Brides run their own homes and kitchens, and do not want their mothers-in-law to tell them what to do. Twenty-five years ago, married couples barely spoke to each other in public ... Now married couples can be openly affectionate physically with each other in front of others ... Engaged couples go visiting together to the homes of relatives. They even go into Shiraz together. They visit in each other's homes, and may even stay overnight. (Hegland 2005)

Thus, a gradual process of individuation was taking place in rural communities as well. At the same time, the increase in the age of marriage for women and the reduced popularity of arranged marriages and kinship marriages had led to the appearance of an unprecedented social category, "the unmarried female teenager who lives at home" (Friedl 2002, 113). In villages and small urban communities this phenomenon was so new that

no culturally and socially acceptable and meaningful way of living has yet developed for these young women. While their teenage brothers have the run of their village or town, the young women cannot go out unchaperoned without risking their reputation; they have no income and are therefore entirely dependent on the generosity of their father and brothers; they have very little to do at home because housework is shared among all female family members; their social circle is extremely limited; and outside work is not to be had. Most of them simply sit, bored, in front of the television. They "sit at home waiting for a good suitor," people say. And as the days of early, arranged marriages are over in most families, this "waiting for a suitor" is more dependent on chance than ever before. (Friedl 2002, 113)

In more culturally conservative parts of the country, such as the southwestern province of Sistan-Baluchestan, the southern province of Khuzestan, the western province of Kurdistan, the northeastern provinces of Khorasan, or the central province of Yazd, where arranged marriages were still the norm, girls with college or even high-school diplomas were threatening to some men and their families. Here, young women found out that "their higher education, which they hoped would improve their marriage prospects, now 'overqualifies' them with most Iranian men" (Shavarini 2006, 208). From an early sample of more than 500 women in Yazd who had married and given birth before the age of fifteen, Soraya Tremayne concludes that girls who left school after the primary level married more easily and gained status by virtue of their marriage and children. Those who enrolled in university and moved away from home might find partners at the university. The problem, Tremayne reports, resided with the large middle group of girls who stayed in their villages, continued into secondary school, but neither attended college nor found employment. These young women missed out on both jobs and husbands, and were subject to much stricter paternal control. Their recreation seemed limited to intrafamilial activities, such as going out for pizza, watching television, visiting the extended family, or occasionally going on pilgrimage with them (Tremayne 2006, 80).

These young women were not ignorant of sexual matters, however. Religious teachers at school and on local television stations lectured on Shi'i regulations of sexuality. *Bazaaris* and itinerant vendors sold condoms alongside candy and cigarettes. Satellite television, present in a significant number of urban and rural homes, provided Western representations of sexuality in popular programs ranging from *Baywatch* and *Sex in the City* to more sober and educational ones, such as the *Oprah Winfrey Show*, where sex and sexuality were common themes.

Ahmadinejad knew well that such households comprised his political base. Rather than expanding employment for women, Ahmadinejad's central policy with regard to the family was facilitating marriage through various loans and subsidies, advocating pronatalist policies, encouraging polygamy, and promoting part-time employment. In 2007, Tehran's mayor, Muhammad Baqer Qalibaf, complained that he could not continue the marriage-loan program, which his predecessor Ahmadinejad had instituted as mayor, because it would bankrupt the city's treasury. At the same time, Ahmadinejad viewed marriage loans as integral to his campaign strategy and battled with the Seventh Parliament to institute similar loans for the whole nation. In 2006 he requested the sum of 1.3 billion dollars to provide cash subsidies for housing for newlyweds from low-income families, and established the Imam Reza Love Fund (Sandoq-e Mehr-e Imam Reza) for this purpose. When the Parliament refused to approve the fund, Ahmadinejad created an alternative venue, including conservative NGOs, that were not responsible to the Parliament and could distribute the funds independently. This provoked a major conflict between the president and the Parliament that spilled into other areas. The marriage crisis, coupled with high unemployment rates and a series of other social problems, could not be resolved with stopgap measures. Still, these measures were meant to enhance Ahmadinejad's populist credentials.[11]

A radical discourse on gay/lesbian rights

The new discourse on sexuality has not been limited to heterosexual relations, dating practices, or traditional marriage issues. In addition, it has cautiously touched upon the nation's small gay subculture. The Iranian Queer Organization (formerly known as the Persian Gay and Lesbian Organization or PGLO) was founded in 2004. Its headquarters are in Toronto, Canada, but the group has many branches in Europe and the US, as well as an underground office in Iran (Fig. 11.8).

In December 2004, *MAHA: The First Iranian GLBT e-Magazine* began publication from an anonymous site inside the country, with the support of diaspora GLBT activists in England. Like other journals of its kind, *MAHA* interviewed international gay activists, published articles and letters about the experience of being closeted, addressed the trauma of hiding one's sexuality in both the family and the workplace, and

Figure 11.8 Logos of Iran's GLBT community

---

[11] For more details see "Ruzaneh" 2007; "Dowreh-ye Tazeh" 2006; "Manba' Afzayesh" 2006. Special thanks to Meir Javadanfar for additional information.

celebrated coming out and rejoicing in one's sexuality. Additionally, it contained advice columns responding to readers' concerns about sexual problems, including HIV/AIDS.

The journal included glossy, provocative photographs, though it avoided illustrations with frontal nudity. It had regular features on the history of homosexuality. Articles about Oscar Wilde, Sigmund Freud, and Alfred Kinsey, as well as essays on sexuality under Stalinism and Nazism, appeared alongside discussions of homosexuality in Iranian history, including brief biographies of prominent artists such as Sadeq Hedayat and Fereydoun Farrokhzad.[12]

Efforts to redefine homosexuality and encourage a more modern gay culture extended to the domain of language itself. Instead of the term *hamjens baz* (roughly translated as "faggot") the journal used the more respectable term *hamjens gara* "homosexual orientationt". Many articles tried to explain the difference between the two terms. Jahangir Shirazi defined a *hamjens gara* as one who fights for his/her rights as a homosexual. A *hamjens gara* "does not try to trick or blackmail his partner" in order to exploit him sexually, as a *hamjens baz* does. Instead, a *hamjens gara* "wants a mutual and conscious relationship based on choice" (Shirazi 2005, 27). He also suggested caution in the appropriation of Western GLBT tactics in the linguistic domain. The queer movement in the West (re)claimed outrageously contemptuous terms with pride, but Shirazi argued that the Iranian struggle for homosexual rights, which was calling for basic recognition of human rights, could not do the same:

Today we had better avoid extremes and follow a gradual path of sexual enlightenment, depending on the appropriate time and place, and leave it to the next generation to define their feelings and emotions with whatever terms they wish. (Shirazi 2005, 28)

What made the journal such a groundbreaking publication was its discussion of homosexual relations within contemporary Iranian society and of the many ways in which closeted homosexuality also affected heterosexual marriages. *MAHA* was fearless in challenging the state's prohibition against homosexuality, writing, for example, that many religious texts recognized the right of a man to have sex with a little girl, but not the right to consensual homosexual relations among adults: "We belong to a society where pedophilia is legal and justified according to the *shariʿa*, yet a free and voluntary sexual relationship,

---

[12] See for example "Gerayesh-e Jensi" 2005, 18; and "Mosahebeh ba Babak" 2005, 8–9.

between two homosexual adults, is considered a crime" (Jamshid 2005, 27).[13]

Like many advocates of women's rights, *MAHA* was critical of the new religious thinkers for their silence concerning sexuality and gender. Religious reformers such as Abdolkarim Soroush and Mohsen Kadivar, who spoke of "Protestantization of Islam," closed their eyes to the sexual concerns of the nation and ignored

thousands upon thousands (if not millions) of Muslim homosexuals, who attend mosques, including homosexual clerics. The truth is that these individuals form a significant social, cultural, and religious foundation out of which the [reformist] religious thinkers have emerged. The silence of the theoreticians of Islamic Protestantization about the social and cultural rights of homosexuals, especially Muslim homosexuals, is the missing link in the discourse of our religious thinkers. ("Halqeh-ye Gomshodeh" 2004, 11–12)

MAHA proposed a more tolerant reading of the Qur'an. Pressing a believer into choosing between his "religious and conscientious beliefs" and his "sexual and inner inclinations," was akin to condemning him/her to a life of hell. It was not man but God who rendered this type of judgment in the afterlife ("Halqeh-ye Gomshodeh" 2004, 11–12). If Islam was a religion of equality, then believers should not be divided on the basis of their sexual orientation, "where homosexual believers become 'second class citizens' and non-homosexual ones are deemed closer to God. No one can claim to own God and the Qur'an, and no one can be forced out of a religion" ("Hamjensgarayan-e Mosalman" 2005, 16).

Critically appropriating the Aristotelian–Islamic definition of rational happiness, which calls for moderation as a prerequisite to contentment, *MAHA* argued for a "rational moderation" between one's religious beliefs and sexual desires, without clerical mediation between God and human beings. Every person should be the judge of his/her ethical conduct. Since homosexuals of "the two other Abrahamic religions [Judaism and Christianity] have reached a consensus between their religious beliefs and their sexual inclinations," Muslims should be able to do the same and continue "the path laid out by Jewish and Christian religious thinkers" ("Hamjensgarayan-e Mosalman" 2005, 17–18). This new reading of the Qur'an, *MAHA* advised, ought to begin with a reinterpretation of the story of Sodom and Gomorrah. "The story of the people of Lot suggests that homosexuality has been part of human society from its beginning and, contrary to what orthodox clerics claim, is not an imported Western product." Also, in the Qur'anic or biblical accounts "there is no single

---

[13] This article first appeared in www.taktaz.com.

reference to female homosexuality. So why is female homosexuality (*mosa-heqeh*) not free and recognized in Muslim societies?" ("Hamjensgarayan-e Mosalman" 2005, 16).

MAHA criticized secular Iranian intellectuals and artists who dared not speak out in defense of homosexuality: "If an artist or anyone else is sent to jail for the 'crime' of homosexuality, would Iranian artists and leftists speak out in his/her defense? We can definitely say no! This is the legacy of Islam and Stalinism! Though we must admit that in Europe, too, homosexuality is still viewed as only a tolerable 'perversion'" (Jamshid 2005, 27).

MAHA was critical of the persistent culture of status-defined homosexuality that maintained rigid active (*faʿel*) and passive (*mafʿul*) identities, and regarded only the latter as *hamjens baz*. The journal suggested that the gay and lesbian communities of Iran adopt a more flexible gender identity. The majority of the articles in *MAHA* were aimed at constructing a modern and humanistic gay culture in Iranian society, one that broke free from the remnants of status-defined homosexuality, with its roots in Greco-Roman and Middle Eastern traditions. *MAHA* insisted that homosexual relationships, like heterosexual ones, were based on emotional and sexual needs. They reflected our desire for "exchanging love and affection, for kindness and warmth, for friendship and unity, for the sharing of one's feelings and emotions, in a word, the need for becoming more complete, or the very same thing that takes place in a physical-sexual heterosexual relationship" ("Hamjensgarayan-e Mosalman" 2005, 16).

Through columns and letters, we learn that many "active" partners remained in denial of their sexual identity and treated their "passive" partners with contempt. In an analysis that continued the work of feminist thinkers in the West, *MAHA* linked this disdain for the "passive" partner to scorn for women:

There are homosexuals in our nation who, in their own words, are only *doers*. These people not only do not identify as homosexuals, but they also spend more time than others berating homosexuality and joking about it. People who think this way only show their backwardness and traditionalism. Because in our society, and quite unjustly, men have been given more rights, and women have been valued less, many homosexuals regard the "passive" [homosexual] as a woman, and hence have disdain for him. If we start adopting a more humane vision, we will not have such problems. ("Harfha-ye Shoma" 2005, 5)

The butch gays, those who identified themselves solely as "active," refused to recognize the problems of Iran's homosexuals as "their own problem," since they did not view themselves as homosexuals. But there was a second problem as well. The fem gays, those who identified themselves as "passive," put on feminine clothing and makeup, and even tried to have sex-change operations, when in reality they were not transvestites. Iranian culture assumed that "if a man is interested in another man, then he is not a man, but a woman" ("Gay Budan" 2005, 16).

Clerics (including Ayatollah Khomeini) approved of sex-change operations, reasoning that surgery would end gender ambiguity (Harrison 2005). Muhammad Mehdi Kariminia, a university professor and cleric in Qom who wrote his doctoral thesis on Iranian transsexuals, illustrates the mindset of those who encourage such operations. He believes that "transsexuals are sick because they are not happy with their sexuality and so should be cured" through operations, while "homosexuality is considered a deviant act" and punishable by law (Fathi 2007, 5). These operations are often unsuccessful in resolving a person's sexual ambiguity and might lead to depression and suicide (Ireland 2007). However, the state's recognition of transsexuality as a medical condition that can be "cured" has created new spaces for living a transgendered life. Gays and lesbians who pass as transsexuals receive a medical certificate that protects them from legal persecution. Many go through such ruses, claiming that they are waiting for an operation at some unspecified future time (Fig. 11.9).

The rigid gender division between "active" and "passive" partners is not limited to gay men, but has also defined many lesbian relations in Iran. Delaram, a lesbian columnist of *MAHA*, complained:

Unfortunately in our country, and among lesbians, a situation has developed where they avoid calling themselves passive (*maf'ul*) or even versatile. This is a term of ill repute for them. They even argue among themselves about who is more active (*fa'el*). Each tries to speak with a lower voice, or act as a *luti* [physically strong, even gangsterish male homosexual] and adopt such mannerisms ... Many refuse to perform so-called feminine chores. For example, they never want to cook ... It is as if they view themselves as distinct from women. So should they be called transsexuals when scientifically they have none of the symptoms that would qualify them for a sex-change operation? ... How could you be a homosexual and not be a feminist? How could you want a woman as your partner, but not demand equal rights for yourself and for your partner? (Delaram 2005a, 14–15)

Compulsory heterosexuality remains a significant problem in contemporary Iranian society, since family members continue to view homosexuality as a transitional stage to adult heterosexuality and therefore pressure homosexual relatives to marry a member of the opposite sex ("Hamjensgarayan va Mo'zal" 2005, 7). In addition, the state, the media, and the society as a whole place a great deal of pressure on unmarried people to wed. Delaram noted:

In our country, many homosexuals are forced to marry a member of the opposite sex and must suppress their feelings as a result of family pressure ... Most continue

Figure 11.9 Sex-change operations in Iran: cover of *Zanan*, 2005

to have same-sex relations in secret, and of course more men succeed in doing so than women. (Delaram 2005b, 26)

Parents often blame the mandatory sex-segregated policies of the state for their children's homosexuality, and pressure them to seek medical advice. Doctors adopt various approaches with homosexual clients. They sometimes prescribe antidepressants and spend most of the therapy sessions (often paid for by the parents) discussing other issues in the lives of their clients. More enlightened doctors tell their clients that nothing can be done to "cure" their homosexuality. A significant number of homosexuals end up marrying a member of the opposite sex, hoping to shed their sexual inclinations, or just to have a family. A modern solution (which replicates some premodern patterns of sexuality) is an arranged marriage between a lesbian and a gay man. The couple would have a "perfunctory marriage and look like a husband and wife," but in reality each would pursue his/her own lifestyle ("Hamjensgarayan va Mo'zal" 2005, 7).

A much older practice is to arrange the marriage of one's same-sex beloved with a sibling or cousin. For example, a young man might arrange the marriage of his sister to his male lover. He would then marry another woman himself. In this way, the two male lovers (who are now both married) become brothers-in-law and would be able to continue the relationship under the guise of family connections ("Seh Nameh" 2005, 25–26). But *MAHA* rejected the idea of marrying an unsuspecting partner and suggested that such marriages exploited other people (Delaram 2005b, 26):

> Do we really solve our pains and problems as gays and lesbians by getting married? Have we not sacrificed another human being, along with ourselves, in this marriage? Doesn't the person we marry have hopes, wishes, and dreams as we do? Does s/he not need an honest (and not forced) love and affection? Have we been honest with the person we are marrying for a lifetime? Why should we selfishly sentence such a person and ourselves to a life of misery without love and honesty? ("Hamjensgarayan va Mo'zal" 2005, 7)

The desire to have children was important, but did not justify marrying an unsuspecting heterosexual partner:

> Yes, some homosexuals want to have children. However, we cannot ethically or responsibly use marriage with a non-homosexual to reach our goal. More than anything else, marriage should be based on love, attraction, and affection, the desire for the union of two people, not the desire to have children. ("Hamjensgarayan va Mo'zal" 2005, 11)

MAHA claimed that among various NGOs and dissident political groups of Iran, there was greater tolerance for modern gay rights. In the 2005 presidential elections, several (unsuccessful) candidates, such as Mostafa Moin, included the slogan "respect for different lifestyles," a euphemism for gay and lesbian rights, in their political platforms.[14] But *MAHA*, which was distributed electronically in portable document format (.pdf) and managed to elude the Islamic Republic's censorship laws for two years, was forced to discontinue publication in 2006 under fear of arrest and execution of its contributors. Through its courageous reporting, *MAHA* showed that the demands of the Iranian gay/lesbian community are very similar to those of women in heterosexual communities; these include more companionate unions and the right to live in dignity and

---

[14] Private correspondence with editors of *MAHA*, December 2, 2005.

respect outside the matrimonial unit. Other publications such as *Cheraq* and the Iranian Queer Organization (formerly PGLO), led by Arsham Parsi in Canada, continue this work from the diaspora with covert input from the queer community inside Iran (Salami 2007).

State persecution of sexual transgression

Discussions surrounding marriage, fidelity, and sexual orientation continued, even in a persistent atmosphere of fear and intimidation, when the regime's persecution of openly gay men and transgressive heterosexual women increased after 2005. Mindful of its international image and reputation, the state sometimes replaced the stoning of women with public executions. In August 2004, ʿAtefeh Rajabi, a feisty sixteen-year-old, was hanged from a crane in the main public square of the town of Neka for no greater crime than having had sex with a man to whom she was not married. By contrast, her male partner's crime did not merit the death penalty in the eyes of the law. This discrepancy is based on the notion that a woman's sexual transgression is a much bigger offense than a man's. Neka was also the city where several members of the government and security forces were arrested a few months later for setting up brothels and organizing child prostitution rings ("Child Prostitution Ring" 2005).

The war against homosexuality and an openly gay lifestyle escalated almost immediately after Ahmadinejad was elected to the presidency. In July 2005, the world was horrified by the torture and execution of two teenage boys in Mashhad: Ayaz Marhoni, eighteen, and Mahmoud Asgari, who was either sixteen or seventeen according to press reports. The authorities initially accused them of sodomy (*lavat*) but later charged them with rape of a younger boy. However, three independent gay sources inside Iran confirmed that "the teens were well-known in the city's underground gay community as lovers who lived together, and the rape charge was fabricated" (Ireland 2005). This was followed by the torture and execution of several other men charged with pedophilia and various sexual transgressions, whose sole "crime" was consensual sex.[15]

Under Ahmadinejad, the state gave additional responsibilities to the Basijis, who began to function as sexual *agents provocateurs*. Undercover Basiji agents entrapped gay men through ads in Internet chat rooms. Once the unsuspecting young men arrived at the designated meeting place, they were apprehended by the Basijis and tortured. Meanwhile, in the same culturally conservative provinces where girls lived under harsh patriarchal

---

[15] Details can be read on veteran journalist Doug Ireland's web-log at http://direland. typepad.com/direland/.

fathers, male homosexuals risked death at the hands of the security forces, or even members of their own families, who justified the murder of a "deviant" relative as a matter of honor.

While the *shariʿa* requires either the actual confession of the accused or four witnesses who observed a homosexual act *in flagrante delicto*, today's authorities sometimes look only for medical evidence of penetration in homosexual relationships. Upon finding such evidence, they punish the men. Because execution of men on charges of homosexuality has prompted international outrage, the state has tended to compound these charges with others, such as rape and pedophilia. Continual use of these tactics has traumatized Iran's gay community and attenuated public sympathy for them. Meanwhile, many Iranians believe that pedophilia is rampant in the religious cities of Qom and Mashhad, including in the seminaries, where temporary marriage and prostitution are also pervasive practices.

Conclusion: Toward a new Muslim-Iranian sexuality for the twenty-first century

The lives of Iranian women changed substantially from the mid-nineteenth to the early twenty-first century. By 2007, the mean age at first marriage for women had gone up to 24 (from 19.7 in 1976), and more than 78 percent married after the age of 20. Literacy rates among girls and boys exceeded 95 percent, a majority of college students were women, the fertility rate had dropped to 2.0, and the infant mortality rate was 28 per 1,000 live births.

Although young men and women continued to consult and negotiate with parents about prospective partners, marriage increasingly became a prerogative of individual choice. Urban and rural youth formed friendships in public areas, universities, and workplaces despite Islamist prohibitions against the mingling of unrelated men and women. Cyberspace became a sphere where women dared speak about their intimate concerns, including sexual ones, often writing under pseudonyms. Among the more cosmopolitan middle classes, virginity was no longer crucial. Greater access to automobiles afforded more privacy, allowing more women to become sexually active before marriage. In some instances, young women negotiated to have premarital sex that maintained virginity or had access to safe but expensive hymenoplasty. Many parents in middle-class families accepted these facts, but more for sons than daughters.

No longer seen as mainly an institution for procreation, marriage now offered women possibilities for companionship, including emotional and sexual intimacy. Love was celebrated loudly and passionately. Valentine's Day became a major celebration and couples took ads in popular journals, expressing their eternal devotion for one another. Contraceptives became widely available, and condoms were sold by vendors in the *bazaar* and neighborhood stores. While parents still helped their sons and daughters with wedding preparations and costs, young people played an active role in choosing their spouses. Despite its illegality, even cohabitation among romantically involved but unmarried young people had gained a degree of social acceptance in more cosmopolitan urban areas. Iranian society also had become far less accepting of covert male bisexuality, while at the same time it was not ready to accept a modern gay lifestyle. Still, within small circles in Tehran and other cities, a small, clandestine gay subculture had emerged. Thus many elements of a sexual revolution were already in place in Iran.

Risky sex, unhappy marriages, and divorce

However, other social indicators suggested a grimmer picture, with exceedingly high rates of unprotected sex, marital unhappiness, unemployment, prostitution, drug addiction, and suicide. Although premarital sex was becoming more common among urban youth, this change impacted young women and men very differently. Young women had neither adequate legal protection from sexual molestation and rape, nor were they exposed to strong feminist frameworks healthy that would have allowed them to develop a sense of personal autonomy. As Norma Moruzzi and Fatemeh Sadeghi point out, this was an "Iranian sexual liberation on masculine terms":

Rejecting the traditional Islamic conception of patriarchal authority (and its corollary obligation of the man to respect the honor of the woman), but without an indigenous modern conception of feminine power (i.e., feminism), these young women find themselves free to experience the insidious double standard of their own and their society's masculinist orientation. This is the recognizably modern version of gender inequality: the right of the woman to be held accountable for her own relative lack of power. (Moruzzi and Sadeghi 2006, 28)

A similar situation prevailed within marriage. As women became more convinced of the importance of their emotional and sexual needs, and found themselves seldom satisfied in marriages still marked by blatant gender inequality, they searched desperately for a way out. Greater longevity and better health actually contributed to this increase in relative unhappiness. By 2005, general life expectancy was seventy, which meant that marriages might last fifty years or longer. Despite laws that made female-initiated divorce extremely difficult, urban divorce rates gradually increased. Marital conflicts also contributed to high levels of mental disorder among women. In 2002, the first extensive study of mental health in Iran concluded that nearly 26 percent of women, compared to 15 percent of men, suffered from mental illnesses (Madani-Ghahfarokhi 2004, 82–86; "Jozveh-ye Hoquqi" 2006).

According to Saeid Madani-Ghahfarokhi, editor-in-chief of the Tehran-based *Social Welfare Quarterly* (*Faslnameh-ye Refah-e Ejtema'i*), the average national rate of divorce was 120 per 1,000 marriages, while that in Tehran was more than 200 per 1,000, or one in every five marriages. At a national level, some 50 percent of divorces took place during the first year of marriage. Also nearly half of all divorces stemmed from

تو مرا دوست نــــداری

Figure 12.1 Woman chasing man: "You don't love me!," 2007

sexual problems and incompatibilities.[1] At the 2005 annual meeting of the Iranian Sociological Association, Dr. Hussein Aghajani reported that, given the opportunity, 50 percent of Iranian women would file for divorce. He attributed this change to increased levels of education, the decreasing influence of the extended family, smaller numbers of children, and the growing desire for intimacy and companionship in marriage (Fig. 12.1). Of course, to become a reality, such inclinations toward divorce would require a host of favorable concomitant circumstances, such as women's steady employment, financial security, and the ability to gain custody of their children ("Taghyir-e Sabk-e Zendegi" 2005, 77–78; Ezazi 1998, 48–51).

In the absence of adequate employment opportunities for women, even among the more educated urban middle classes, women desirous of both financial security and emotional and sexual compatibility sometimes resorted to a rebellious and dangerous marital strategy in order to have both. A young woman from an urban middle-class family with low

---

[1] Special thanks to Madani-Ghahfarokhi for information on this subject and other statistics discussed in this chapter via numerous e-mails in 2007–2008. See also Madani-Ghahfarokhi 2004, 81; Madani-Ghahfarokhi et al. in press; "Ellat-e 'Panjah Darsad'" 2008; "Talaq dar Iran" 2008.

Figure 12.2 "Love for husband or for *mahriyeh*?," 2006

prospects would accept the marriage offer of her wealthiest (and usually most conventional and oldest) suitor, and would negotiate a huge *mahriyeh*. But, a month after the wedding, she would sue for her *mahriyeh*. In the Islamic Republic, a woman's right to her *mahriyeh* remains one of her few rights in marriage, though a husband cannot be imprisoned for nonpayment (Mir-Hosseini 1993, 83). Often he paid a portion of it and the marriage unraveled, though seldom without violence. Then the young woman married another man, someone who was perhaps less well off, but who had more in common with her (Fig. 12.2).

In the industrialized world, more educated women who had found steady employment and financial security were opting out of dysfunctional marriages by the late twentieth century (Coontz 2005, 252–262). Social statistics seemed to confirm a similar trend for Iran. In 2001, more women (nearly 40 percent) than men (35 percent) initiated petitions for divorce (Madani-Ghahfarokhi 2004, 82–86). By 2008, twice as many women as men were petitioning for divorce ("Talaq dar Iran" 2008). However, since well-paid jobs for women were very difficult to find, and Iranian society as a whole remained intolerant of young divorcées, many women felt they had no choice but to remain in unhappy and even violent marriages.

Child marriages had substantially decreased but not disappeared. In rural southeastern province of Baluchestan and Sistan, parents still arranged temporary marriages before puberty for their sons or daughters.

In 2008, the number of such marriages was estimated at around 30,000 nationwide ("Amar-e Bala-ye Ezdevaj" 2008).

Unemployment and emigration

In the first decade of the twenty-first century, unemployment rates for both men and women were escalating. The percentage of women in the paid labor force remained exceedingly low, 13 percent, compared to other Muslim nations such as Turkey (over 25 percent) or Indonesia (over 38 percent), although Iranian women continued to participate in the mostly unpaid rural and nomadic agriculture. According to the Ministry of Planning and Policy Affairs, 43 percent of women between the ages of fifteen and twenty-two who had joined the paid labor force remained jobless ("Iran Official: Unemployment" 2003; Roudi-Fahimi and Moghadam 2006).

Pervasive unemployment pushed many young educated men to emigrate abroad, which decreased the number of socially and financially qualified men available for marriage. Iran had one of the highest "brain drains" in the world in the early twenty-first century. Each year, between 100,000 and 250,000 educated young people left the country, and many chose not to return. The state encouraged emigration to ease unemployment (Amuzegar 2004). High oil prices allowed the government to spend more on domestic social programs, but these expenditures did not contribute very much to economic development, let alone job creation. Instead, they served to increase inflation. Favoritism and government corruption continued unabated. The state awarded large contracts to members of the Pasdaran and Basij in exchange for their political backing. At the same time, growing internal consumption and aging production facilities limited Iran's capacity to export oil (Mouawad 2007; "Iran: Ahmadi-Nejad's" 2007, 11). During Ahmadinejad's presidency, which coincided with the second term of George W. Bush (2004–2008), political relations with the West steadily deteriorated, a situation that led to increased sanctions against Iran and worsened the economy.

Runaway girls, prostitutes, drug addicts, and suicide

The confluence of high unemployment, inflation, emigration, and idealistic expectations about marriage led to an increase in risky behaviors, especially among young women, significant numbers of whom fell into prostitution, drug addiction, or suicide. Since the year 2000, more than 11,000 girls have annually run away from home. Many left their families, hoping to find a companionate marriage. Instead, alone and destitute, they became prostitutes and drug addicts and joined the growing sex industry in the large cities and the Persian Gulf emirates (Sapa-DPA 2002; Madani-Ghahfarokhi *et al.* in press).

Prostitution became a regulated activity, involving adult women, girls, and boys. Nearly a quarter of those entering prostitution had contracted a temporary marriage. Despite this, in 2007 the Judiciary submitted new legislation to the Seventh Parliament that further facilitated temporary marriage. (International Campaign 2008, 10). Often state authorities were complicit in promoting prostitution. General Reza Zarei, Tehran's Chief of Police and a strong enforcer of morality regulations on the streets, was himself a client of prostitutes. In 2008, he was found in a brothel with six sex workers whom he had asked to pray naked before him and was subsequently arrested (Sigarchi 2008). Some government officials directly benefited from the sex trade and several police raids on brothels revealed the involvement of local officials and security officers (Hughes 2004; "Child Prostitution Ring" 2005).

Newspapers and tabloid periodicals published sensational accounts of girls sold into brothels across the border into Pakistan, Afghanistan, Dubai, and elsewhere. Other runaways became sex workers in the religious centers of Qom, Najaf, and Karbala, usually operating under the guise of *sigheh* marriage partners. In press interviews, the girls reported that they left home to escape strict parents who refused to accept modern gender norms, or because they were attracted by the allure of city life ("A Shocking Report" 2002). The Iranian public, however, saw the runaway phenomenon as a product of the breakdown of the patriarchal family structure, widespread unemployment, and the easy availability of drugs.

Illegal narcotics had become big business, with domestic annual sales figures estimated at $10 billion for 2005 alone. Drug traffickers used Iran as a transit point between Afghanistan and Europe and the Persian Gulf. In 2005, Iran had the highest rate of drug abuse in the world, with 2.8 percent of the population over fifteen years of age involved with illicit drug use.[2] Many Iranians were convinced that the state was deliberately addicting the youth in order to divert their anger, frustration, and energy away from the shortcomings of the society. For their part, young people claimed they used illicit drugs due to boredom and the lack of entertainment (Vick 2005; "Iran Tops World Addiction-Rate List" 2005).

Both prostitution and intravenous drug use had contributed to an increase in the rates of HIV/AIDS. Attempts to curb the spread of the

---

[2] Only two other countries passed the 2 percent rate, Mauritius and Kyrgyzstan.

Figure 12.3 AIDS poster at Tehran's Mehrabad Airport, 2005

virus were inefficient because the state refused to adopt measures that might interfere with men's sexual pleasure. According to the country's top AIDS specialist, Dr. Hamid Ahmadi, the government reached out to the intravenous drug users but "piously ignored the danger posed by a recent rise in prostitution and casual sex" including temporary marriage (Bellaigue 2005). Married women contracted the HIV virus from their husbands, but the state did not publicize this fact, athough it did advocate use of condoms (Meisami 2007; Marashi 2007) (Fig. 12.3).

The growing rate of female suicide constituted another grim indicator of the marriage crisis in Iran. In 2000, the average rate of suicide stood at 25–30 per 100,000 people ("Mental Health" 2007). Most were rural, married women in violent or otherwise unhappy marriages. Research on other parts of the world has shown that women attempt suicide more often, while men are more successful in their attempts to kill themselves. However, rural Iranian women who took their lives chose the method of self-immolation. Not only was it often fatal, but even if not, it caused serious injury and permanent disfiguration. Manijeh Zibaʻi, a member of a rural council in the western, Kurdish-speaking province of Ilam, where some 350 women set themselves on fire in 2001 alone, reported that the new generation's "awareness of their social and human needs and the depression they feel due to the unattainable nature of these desires," combined with excessive poverty, contributed to the frequency with which Ilami women were committing suicide. A community doctor suggested that women chose self-immolation to ensure that their cries of desperation were at least heard in death if not in life (Amiri 2001, 11).

Companionate marriages and divorce

In much of the West the trend toward more companionate marriages in the nineteenth and twentieth centuries was accompanied by legal changes that granted women more rights in marriage, and established equal inheritance, community property, and rights to employment and divorce, as well as child custody. Initially, the new emphasis on marital love may have increased women's emotional dependence on marriage. But by the late nineteenth century, a growing women's rights movement began to demand rights for women both inside and outside marriage, enabling women to leave marriage or to decline to enter it. In the twentieth century, the growing participation of Western women in the economy, and the wages they brought home, served to promote more egalitarian relations in marriage. This process also made marriage more optional and divorce more acceptable. The numbers of married couples continued to decrease, but those who remained married expressed greater satisfaction in their relationships. By 1980, the divorce rate stood at 50 percent in the United States, and at the beginning of the twenty-first century one in every three children was born to an unmarried woman, usually in a cohabiting relationship with a man.[3]

In Iran, the child-centered institution of marriage endured for the vast majority. Both fathers and mothers forfeited numerous pleasures, such as vacations and daily luxuries, in order for their children to receive a better education and to start married life with greater financial security. Many middle-class parents mortgaged their property to enable a son (and sometimes a daughter) to study abroad, knowing that their child might never return. Mothers and grandmothers remained the bedrock of Iranian

---

[3] Coontz 2005, 255, 264 and e-mail exchanges with her on April 3, 2007. Also Amato *et al.* 2007, 25–31.

society, and their sacrifices went beyond the call of duty. Wives stood up to husbands so that daughters could remain in school a little longer. Mothers encouraged daughters to study hard and repeatedly asked them to "make something of themselves" and not become just housewives. Working-class, middle-class, and even upper-class Iranian grandmothers took on extraordinary responsibilities to enable their married daughters to finish college and receive graduate degrees. They took care of their grand-children and watched over their homework. They shopped and cooked endlessly for their daughters' families and in-laws, thus allowing their daughters to comply with entertainment customs requiring elaborate home-cooked meals. Many women gained tremendous satisfaction through contributing to their children's accomplishments; however, they often resented their husbands and felt trapped in unhappy unions where men did not appreciate women's efforts, and had overwhelming legal advantages.

Women continued to have fewer personal legal rights than men, and their position in matrimony remained highly precarious. Fathers could still arrange marriages for their daughters before age thirteen, with court permission, and some still did so in isolated rural areas. Husbands still had veto power over their wives' occupations, could prevent them from visiting friends or traveling abroad, and could decide unilaterally on the couple's place of domicile. A woman still faced the possibility of sharing her husband with a second wife. Women experienced denial of child custody and destitution if divorced. In December 2008, the Eighth Parliament finally granted widows the right to inherit land from their deceased husbands. Still unequal inheritance laws, lack of community property in marriage, and horrific state punishments for female adulterers gave men significant advantages. In 2007, in response to angry husbands and their relatives, the judiciary introduced a new prenuptial agreement that conditioned the payment of *mahriyeh* upon men's financial ability, thus closing off one of the last favorable aspects of the *shari'a* for women ("Jozveh-ye Hoquqi" 2006). In 2008, despite vocal opposition by women's rights groups and liberal clerics such as Ayatollah Sana'i, Parliament gave its preliminary approval to a bill that encouraged polygamy by eliminating the right of the first wife to block her husband's second marriage. The Ahmadinejad government and the conservative Eighth Parliament extolled a greater resort to poly-gamy as a solution to pervasive female unemployment ("Layeheh" 2008).

Gender segregation and homosexuality

Gender-segregation rules continued to be observed, not only because of state enforcement but also because of deeply ingrained social and religious anxieties. In their campaigns around women's rights issues, even feminists seldom mentioned the *hijab* regulations. If they did, it was usually in relation to non-Muslim women, questioning why non-Muslims were forced to observe them ("Jozveh-ye Hoquqi" 2006). In the summer of 2008 sociologist Fatemeh Sadeghi broke this silence by publishing a powerful essay, "Why We Say No to Forced *Hijab*." Sadeghi talked about her own experience growing up in an Islamist family in the 1980s and wearing the *hijab* and the veil from a young age. What made the essay so remarkable was that Sadeghi was the daughter of Ayatollah Sadeq Khalkhali (d. 2003), the infamous Chief Justice of the Islamic Republic known in the early days of the revolution as the "hanging judge." Now his daughter declared that the veil "had nothing to do with morality and religion. It is all about power" (Sadeghi 2008, 10).

Concerns about ritual purity had not disappeared entirely. Many men continued to believe that sexual experience tainted a woman. It was as if the semen, once having entered her body, irrevocably marked her as impure. A married woman's sexual life was tolerated because it pleased her husband and produced legitimate children, but the sexual activities of single, divorced, or widowed women were constant sources of anxiety. The frequent use of terms such as *cleanliness* or *purity* (*paki*; *pakdamani*) with regard to women also indicated the persistence of such thinking within Iranian culture. Of course, Iranians were not unique in clinging to such views about sexual purity, which appeared in different guises in various religions and cultures. In some parts of the United States, legal prohibitions against miscegenation (interracial sex) had continued well into the era of the civil rights movement, while a substantial sector of public opinions remained opposed long after that.

In the West, the gradual adoption of normative heterosexuality was followed by the slow recognition of adult homosexuality. Even so, homosexuality remained controversial in the United States and influenced the election to the presidency of George W. Bush in 2000 and 2004, with decisive support from the religious right. In Iran, heterosexuality became the norm, but a gay lifestyle has yet to be recognized. Same-sex relations remained semi-covert, and some apparently heterosexual marriages remained, in effect, bisexual relationships. From time to time, the Islamist state hanged gay men, charging them with rape and pedophilia, thereby ensuring a lack of public sympathy for them.

One Million Signatures Compaign and state response

These sexual prejudices enjoyed wide support beyond rural areas of Iran. Many urban, intellectual men who campaigned for democracy and human rights were not yet ready to support equal rights for women in divorce, custody, inheritance, or property law; nor were they willing to recognize the rights of sexual minorities. Liberal theologians who campaigned against the Islamist orthodoxy were reluctant to challenge regulations involving public social interaction between men and women. Noted reform theologians such as Abdolkarim Soroush and Mohsen Kadivar, who boldly challenged the state's ideology, refused to shake hands with women, even at academic conferences and private gatherings abroad. Most also condemned a gay lifestyle. Thus, gender and sexuality remained highly contentious issues and continued as major focal points of modern Iranian politics.

One source of hope, however, was the country's educated urban and rural women, many of whom knew from experience that social activism could change things. Some had been budding feminists during the late Pahlavi era, some had joined the revolution as leftists or Islamists but were now increasingly conscious of women's rights issues, some were volunteer health providers in the rural areas who successfully promoted family-planning initiatives, and some were children of the revolution. The latter group comprised high-school and college students and graduates who had experienced a greater degree of autonomy in their private lives and who wished to close the enormous gap between the private and public realms.

When members of the security police violently attacked a peaceful women's rights demonstration on June 12, 2006, a small cluster of Iranian feminists in Tehran formed the Campaign for Equality and embarked on the grassroots One Million Signatures Campaign. Taking a page from Moroccan feminists, they blended traditional Middle Eastern practices of gathering petitions, the consciousness-raising techniques of American feminists in the 1970s, and contemporary methods of access to the Internet and electronic newsletters, in order to launch a movement to change laws restricting women's rights in marriage, divorce, and inheritance, among others.[4]

By March 2007, nearly 400 trained young women were going to private homes, doctors' offices, buses, trains, parks, restaurants, and elsewhere carrying petitions and asking for the signatures of ordinary women as well as men. Whether they signed or not, each person received a brochure explaining the legal inequalities facing women in plain language and with examples (Casey 2007). The movement did not call for the overthrow

[4] For the 1992 campaign of Moroccan women, see "Morocco" 2001; Keddie 2007, 144–148. For details on the Iranian campaign, I have relied on numerous e-mails and newsletters by Parvin Ardalan, Noushin Ahmad-Khorasani, Sussan Tahmasebi, and others in the campaign.

of the state, nor did it challenge the *shariʿa* directly. Noushin Ahmadi-Khorasani, one of the organizers, points out that, unlike secular feminists who opposed religion as a source for gender norms, and Islamic feminists who tried to fit feminism within an Islamic framework, this generation saw Islam, "whether one likes it or not," as a part of people's lives and accepted it as a reality. This generation also tried to read the religious texts strategically and to encourage the reinterpretation of orthodox and patriarchal readings of Islam in light of women's rights concerns ("Jozveh-ye Hoquqi" 2006).

In the summer of 2008, and in response to the One Million Signatures Campaign, the government of Ahmadinejad proposed a deceptively-worded bill which like the 1967/1975 law was called the "Family Protection Law." Three provisions of the 2008 bill increased men's privileged position in marriage and divorce. Article 53 would have abolished all components of the 1967/75 Family Protection Law not previously eliminated by the Islamic Republic. Article 23 would have eased polygamy by giving a wealthy man the right to take a second *ʿaqdi* without permission of his first wife, requiring only court approval. Article 25 would have taxed a woman's "excessive" *mahriyeh*. The tax on *mahriyeh* was an attempt to reduce a wife's bargaining position in marriage and during divorce proceedings.

The media reported that the bill would have taken away the right of a first wife to prevent a husband's second formal marriage. However, the bill was more harmful to women than reported in the media. The Iranian state has never given the first wife the right to block a second wife, not even during the Pahlavi era, when she gained only the right to sue for divorce rather than live in a polygamous formal marriage. In the Pahlavi era, a man was required to obtain his first *ʿaqdi*'s permission, and that of the court, for a second marriage. If she refused to give permission and he went ahead anyway, he might be jailed for six months to a year, but his second marriage was still valid. Thus, a first wife has never had an ironclad right to block or undo her husband's second marriage. All she could do was sue for divorce. Under the Islamic Republic, at least since 1984, the first wife with a properly executed prenuptial agreement can once again sue for divorce if her husband marries a second *ʿaqdi*. It remains unclear what the 2008 bill would do to this right of the first wife, if it were ultimately ratified.

In late August 2008, a coalition of prominent Iranian women, including Nobel Laureate Shirin Ebadi, the noted poet Simin Behbahani, former Reformist MP Elahee Koolaee, and the celebrated film director Rakhshan Bani E'temad joined together with progressive clerics and politicians to meet with Members of Parliament and protest the proposed new law. Feeling the pressure, the Parliamentary Judicial Committee agreed to drop the controversial articles, temporarily shelving what would have

Figure 12.4 Women's rights demonstration, the caption reads "Women's rights equals human rights," 2006

been a major setback for women. Many advocates of women's rights still feared that the bill would be reintroduced at some later point.

Despite these obstacles the Campaign for Equality continues to move ahead and has broken new ground on several levels. Activists have moved beyond the sectarian and ideological divides that hampered the women's movement for much of the twentieth century. They have made common cause with women from many different social, religious, and ideological backgrounds, established a genuine two-way conversation that has broken with both elitism and populism, and formulated demands that appeal to women of all social classes. They have also reclaimed a number of national and religious rituals and festivals, giving them new feminist interpretations (Tohidi 2008). Most of all, they have tried to change not just the law, but also the culture itself, and to articulate an independent feminist voice that demarcates "the women's movement from both the native Islamists and Western imperialist patriarchies" (Tohidi 2006). This last point is crucial. For too long, Western imperialist powers, most recently the United States, have opportunistically used the issue of the rights of Middle Eastern women for their strategic interests and abandoned it just as opportunistically when it no longer fit their purposes.

At the same time, the Iranian regime understands the power of the country's century-old women's movement and has used myriad strategies to stifle the Million Signatures Campaign. Activists are beaten, arrested, and thrown in jail, and then released; major newspapers are barred from covering the campaign or shut down outright; organizations that provide activists with a platform receive ominous warnings, and the cyberspace sites of the campaign are routinely shut down. By early 2009, the campaign was moving on slowly but defiantly, challenging a history of oppression and inequality, and seeking to change the position of Iranian women, one mind and one signature at a time (Fig. 12.4).

Glossary

adam-e tamkin	disobedience of a wife
amrad	adolescent boy in a same-sex relationship; a beardless adolescent
amrad khaneh	male house of prostitution
andaruni	inner compartment, occupied by wives, children, and female servants; women's quarters
anjomans	popular provincial councils
'aqdi	wife in a *nekah* (formal marriage)
bacheh	child who has not reached puberty
bacheh baz	pederast; an "active" lover
barda (also *bardeh*)	slave of either sex
biruni	outer compartment of a house where male guests were entertained and male servants lived
chador	shapeless and loose-fitting cloth that covers the entire body
concours	national entrance examination for universities
divan	collection of poems
erastes	adult lover in a homosexual relationship (Greek word)
fa'el	active; an "active" partner in a homosexual relationship
faqih	religious scholar
fatwa	religious edict
fiqh	jurisprudence
fitnah	serious trouble or even civil war; seductive behavior; chaos caused by sexuality or seduction
ghazal	form of poetry dedicated to love

ghilman (also *ghelman*)	Arabic plural of *gholam* used exclusively in Persian to refer to handsome youth in heaven promised to the faithful
gholam	male page, also male slave
gholam bacheh	page boy
ghosl	total immersion of the body (or the object) into a pool of still water for ritual purity, similar to the Jewish *miqveh*
hadith	stories attributed to the Prophet Muhammad
hijab	literally meaning "cover" in Arabic; a scarf or veil designed to cover the head and neck of a woman; religious covering; a modest attire and a headscarf
hodud	part of *shari'a* Islamic law that pertains to actions that transgress the limits/laws set by God
houris	beautiful, dark-eyed, virgin maidens promised to the faithful in heaven in the Qur'an; female angels
'idda	waiting period for a woman after divorce
jahiziyeh	trousseau, assets or goods a woman brings to her husband in marriage; dowry
kadkhoda	village elder
kaniz	female slave
khol'	method of divorce initiated by the wife in which a woman renounces her alimony and petitions a judge for divorce. Her husband's approval is needed.
kudak	child who has not yet reached puberty; a "passive" partner
lavat	Arabic *liwat*; sodomy; homosexual transgression
luti	dominant man in a homosexual relationship; also strongman; derived from the verb *lavatat*
ma'bun	adult man who has sought sexual submission; the receiver in a homosexual relationship
maf'ul	passive man; the receiver in a homosexual relationship

mahriyeh	marriage portion payable to the wife at any time after the marriage, but usually paid after divorce or death of the husband, with some similarities to alimony
majles	parliament
maktab	traditional religious schools
marjaʿ-e taqlid	religious source of imitation in Shiʿi tradition
mochul	snack; junior partner in a working-class homosexual relationship
mojtahed	jurisconsult, one who has received permission from senior clerics to interpret the laws of Shiʿi Islam
mosaheqeh	two women having sex, female homosexuality
muburat	divorce by mutual agreement
mukhannath	(pl.*mukhannathun*) effeminate man who was deemed very close to a woman in his malformation; a transgendered person
mutʿa	Arabic term for temporary marriage
nafaqeh	maintenance paid by husband to wife for daily necessities of life
najes	adjective: polluting, impure person or object, from a religious point of view
namus	a man's honor derived from the conduct of his women folk
nejasat	noun: impurity, uncleanliness, from a religious point of view
nekah	formal marriage; permanent marriage; contracted through civil law
now khatt	young man with a budding moustache; a "passive" man
paidika	adolescent boy in a homosexual relationship (Greek word)
pesar	boy
pesar baz	man inclined to relations with boys
rubandeh	long white face covering that reveals the eyes but disguises much of the face
seyyed	descendent of the Prophet
shahed	witness (to the faith); also male beloved; from the verb *shahadat*, to testify
shahedbaz	lover of boys

shahid	martyr, from the verb *shahadat*, to testify
shariʿa	Islamic law; rules and regulations that are derived in principle from the Qurʾan and traditions relating to the words and deeds of the Prophet; these rules govern the lives of Muslims
sigheh	verb: to utter the formula for any contract; to engage in temporary marriage in colloquial Persian
sigheh	noun: temporary marriage; a renewable contract of marriage for a defined duration from a few hours to ninety-nine years; a wife in such a marriage
sigheh-ye baradar khăndegi	brotherhood *sigheh*; a vow made in a male same-sex relationship
sigheh-ye khăhar khăndegi	sisterhood *sigheh*; a vow made in a female same-sex relationship
tabaq zadan	also *tabaq zani* or *sahaq*: lesbian sex, taking sisterhood vows
taharat	ritual purity
talaq	divorce initiated by a husband; repudiation
taʿziyeh	Shiʿi passion play
tefl	child between birth and puberty
tuman	unit of currency
ʿulama	clerics
umm walid	female slave who has given birth to a master's child
vali	guardian
vaqf	religious endowment; charitable contribution usually to religious schools and institutions, and other public welfare projects
zina	fornication; one of the actions that transgresses the *hodud* ordinances

Bibliography

NEWSPAPERS, JOURNALS, AND WEBSITES CONSULTED

Aeen
AftabNews
Ahangar
Al-Raida
American Ethnologist
Anjoman
Anthropological Quarterly
Azadi
Baba Shamal
Baztab
BBC News
BBCPersian.com
Behdasht-e Khanevadeh
British Journal of Middle Eastern Studies
Change 4 Equality
Cheragh
Comparative Sociology
Convergence
Critique: Critical Middle Eastern Studies
Culture, Health, and Sexuality
Danesh
Demography
Didar
Direland
Echo of Iran: Iran Almanac
Encyclopedia Iranica
Ettelaʿat (Tehran)
Family Practice
Feminist Review
The Feminist School
Ganjineh
Gay City News
Gay Iran News and Reports
Gender and History
GlobalSecurity.org
The Guardian
Gulf2000 Project

Hamjens-e Man
Harvard Journal of Law and Gender
Hasht-e Mars
Histoires d'Elles
Homan
Hoquq-e Zanan
HRW World Report 2001
ILGA Communications Media Committee
The Independent
International Crisis Group: Middle East Briefing
International Feminist Journal of Politics
International Institute for Strategic Studies
International Journal of Middle East Studies
International Journal of Middle Eastern Studies
International Journal of Sociology of the Family
Iran Daily Newspaper
Iran Emrooz
Iran Focus
Iran Nameh
Iran Press Service
Iran Source: Populi
IranDokht
Iran-e Now
The Iranian
Iranian.com
Iranian Studies
Iranshenasi
Iran Times
ISIM Review
Jawa Report
Journal of the American Oriental Society
Journal of Divorce and Marriage
Journal of the History of Sexuality
Journal of International Development
Journal of Marriage in the Family
Journal of Middle East Women's Studies
Journal of Women's History
Kaveh
Ketab-e Jom'eh
Keyhan (London)
Khanevadeh-ye Sabz
LA Weekly
MAHA: The First Iranian GLBT e-Magazine
Majles
Mehrnews.com
MERIP
Middle East Economic Survey

Middle East Report
Middle East Studies
Molla Nasreddin
Le Monde
Mozakerat-e Majles
Nameh-ye Zan: The Cultural Center of Women
Neda-ye Salamat
Negah-e Nou
The New York Review of Books
The New York Times
Nimeye Digar
OutRage!
Parcham
Payam-e Zan
Peyman
Peyvand.com
Piramoon
Population Studies
Population Today
Public Culture
Radical America
Radical Philosophy
Radio Zamaneh
Ruznameh-ye Rasmi-e Keshvar-e Shahanshahi
Shekufeh
Social Research
Studia Islamica
Studies in Family Planning
Sur-e Israfil
Swedish Lesbian/Gay Politics
Taghyir Bara-ye Barabari
Talash
The Times (London)
Towfiq
The Washington Post
WLUML Occasional Paper
Women in Iran
Women's Research: Journal of the Center for Women's Studies
World Health Organization: Country Reports and Charts
Zan: The Cultural Center of Women
Zanan
Zanestan
Zan-e Ruz

WORKS CITED

"A Shocking Report on the Sale of Iranian Girls." 2002. *Women in Iran*, September 2.

Abbott, Nabia. [1942] 1985. *Aishah the Beloved of Mohammed*. With a preface by Sarah Graham-Brown. London: Al Saqi Books.

'Abedini, Hasan. 1990. *Sad Sal Dastan Nevisi dar Iran*. Vol I. Tehran: Pagah Press.

Abrahamian, Ervand. 1982. *Iran Between Two Revolutions*. Princeton University Press.

 1989. *The Iranian Mojahedin*. New Haven and London: Yale University Press.

 1999. *Tortured Confessions: Prisons and Recantation in Modern Iran*. Berkeley and Los Angeles: University of California Press.

Abu-Lughod, Lila. 1998. *Remaking Women*. Princeton University Press.

Abu-Odeh, Lama. 1996. "Crimes of Honour and the Construction of Gender in Arab Societies." In *Feminism and Islam: Legal and Literary Perspectives*, ed. Mai Yamani, pp. 141–194. Reading: Ithaca Press.

"Activist Stunned by Swedish Embassy Report on Gays in Iran." 1996. *Swedish Lesbian/Gay Politics* 22 (July 13–August 15). A publication of the Swedish Federation for Gay and Lesbian Rights. Retrieved February 14, 2007 (www. Igirtf.org/newsletters/Fall96/FA96-15.html).

Adamiyat, Fereydoun and Homa Nategh. 1977. *Afkar-e Ejtema'i va Siyasi va Eqtesadi dar Asar-e Montasher Nashodeh-ye Dowran-e Qajar*. Tehran: Agah Publications.

Afary, Janet. 1989. "On the Origins of Feminism in Early Twentieth Century Iran." *Journal of Women's History* 1(2) (Fall): 65–87.

 1996. *The Iranian Constitutional Revolution of 1906–11: Grassroots Democracy, Social Democracy, and the Origins of Feminism*. New York: Columbia University Press.

 2001. "Portraits of Two Islamist Women: Escape from Freedom or Escape from Tradition?" *Critique: Journal for Critical Studies of the Middle East* 19 (Fall): 47–77.

Afary, Janet and Kevin B. Anderson. 2005. *Foucault and the Iranian Revolution: Gender and the Seductions of Islamism*. University of Chicago Press.

Afary, Parvin Mona. 1992. "In Search of an Identity: Cross-Cultural Study of Immigrant Iranian Women." Ph.D. Dissertation. Wright Institute of Graduate School of Psychology. Berkeley, CA.

Afghani, Ali Muhammad. 1962. *Showhar-e Ahu Khanom*. Tehran: Amir Kabir Press.

Afkhami, Gholamreza, ed. 2002. *Jame'eh, Dowlat, va Jonbesh-e Zanan-e Iran: Mosahebeh ba Mehrangiz Dowlatshahi*. Bethesda, MD: Foundation for Iranian Studies.

 ed. 2003. *Jame'eh, Dowlat, va Jonbesh-e Zanan-e Iran, 1342–1357: Mosahebeh ba Mahnaz Afkhami*. Bethesda, MD: Foundation for Iranian Studies.

Afkhami, Mahnaz. 1984. "A Future in the Past: The 'Prerevolutionary' Women's Movement." In *Sisterhood Is Global*, ed. Robin Morgan, pp. 330–338. New York: Anchor Books.

Afshar, Iraj, ed. 1992 *Ganjineh-ye Aksha-ye Iran be Hamrah-e Tarikhcheh-ye Vorud-e Akasi be Iran*. Tehran: Nashr-e Farhang-e Iran.

Afshari, Reza. 2001. *Human Rights in Iran: The Abuse of Cultural Relativism*. Philadelphia: University of Pennsylvania Press.

Aghajanian, Akbar. 1986. "Some Notes on Divorce in Iran." *Journal of Marriage and the Family* 48(4) (November): 749–755.

   1995. "A New Direction in Population Policy and Family Planning in the Islamic Republic of Iran." *Asia-Pacific Population Journal* 10(1) (March): 3–22.

Aghajanian, Akbar and Amir Mehryar. 1999. "Fa'aliyatha-ye Marbut be Barnameh-ye Barvari, Estefadeh az Vasa'il-e Pishgiri, va Tanzim-e Khanevadeh dar Jomhuri-ye Islami-ye Iran," trans. Natali Haqyerdiyan. *Behdasht-e Khanevadeh* 4(15) (Fall): 4–63.

   2005. "State Pragmatism versus Ideology: Family Planning in the Islamic Republic of Iran." *International Journal of Sociology of the Family* 31(1) (Spring): 58–67.

Aghajanian, Akbar and Ali Asghar Moghadas. 1998. "Correlation and Consequences of Divorce in an Iranian City." *Journal of Divorce and Remarriage* 28(3/4): 53–71.

Ahmadi-Khorasani, Noushin. 2002. "Gozareshha-ye Hasht-e' March." *Nameh-ye Zan: The Cultural Center of Women* 2–3 (Ordibehesht): 28–36.

   2007a. "Ba Motalebat-e Ma Moshkeli Nadarand, Bavar Konid!" *Zanestan*. Retrieved February 12, 2007 (http://herlandmag.net/weblog/07,02,12,05,14,20/).

   2007b. "Do Sal Zendegi-e Moshtarak dar Campain: Ba Hefz-e 'Hagh-e Talagh'." *Taghyir Bara-ye Barabari*. Retrieved January 27, 2007 (www.we-change.org/spip.php?article263).

Ahmadi-Khorasani, Noushin and Parvin Ardalan. 2003. *Senator*. Tehran: Tose'eh Press.

Ajami, Amir Ismail. 2005. "From Peasant to Farmer: A Study of Agrarian Transformation in an Iranian Village, 1967–2002." *International Journal of Middle East Studies* 37: 327–349.

Akhavi, Shahrough. 1980. *Religion and Politics in Contemporary Iran*. Albany: State University of New York Press.

   1988. "The Role of the Clergy in Iranian Politics, 1949–1954." In Bill and Louis 1988, pp. 91–117.

Akhtari, Shahla, Sediqeh Babran, and Fariba Ebtehaj-Shirazi. 1999a. "Imam Khomeini: Shayesteh Negari Bejay-e Tab'izha-ye Jensiyati." *Payam-e Zan* 8 (Shahrivar): 24–29.

   1999b. "Imam Khomeini: Shayesteh Negari Bejay-e Tab'izha-ye Jensiyati." *Payam-e Zan* 8(7) (Mehr): 154–159.

Akhundzadeh, Mirza Fath Ali. 1985. *Maktubat*. n.p.: Mard-e Emruz Press.

Alaedini, Pooya and Mohamad Reza Razavi. 2005. "Women's Participation and Employment in Iran: A Critical Examination." *Critique: Critical Middle Eastern Studies* 14(1) (Spring): 57–73.

'Alam, Asadollah. 2006. *Alam Diaries*. Washington, DC: Ibex Publishers.

Alamouti, Moustafa. 1990. *Iran dar 'Asr-e Pahlavi*. London: Book Press.

'Alavi, Bozorg. 1978a. "Namehha." In 'Alavi 1978d, pp. 1–44.

   1978b. "Yek Zan-e Khosh-bakht." In 'Alavi 1978d, pp. 95–112.

   1978c. *Cheshmhayash*. Tehran: Amir Kabir Press.

   1978d. *Namehha*. Tehran: Amir Kabir Press.

Al-e Ahmad, Jalal. [1963] 1994. *Gharbzadegi*. Tehran: Ferdows Press.

Algar, H. "Barda and Bardadari: VI. Regulations Governing Slavery in Islamic Jurisprudence." *Encyclopedia Iranica*. Retrieved January 16, 2007 (www.iranica.com/newsite).

Alizadeh, Parvin and Barry Harper. 1995. "Occupational Sex Segregation in Iran, 1976-86." *Journal of International Development* 7(4): 637–651.

Amanat, Abbas. 1989. *Resurrection and Renewal: The Making of the Babi Movement in Iran, 1844–1850*. Ithaca, NY: Cornell University Press.

1993. "The Changing World of Taj al-Saltanah." In Taj al-Saltana 1993, pp. 9–103.

1997. *Pivot of the Universe: Nasir al-Din Shah Qajar and the Iranian Monarchy, 1831–1896*. Berkeley and Los Angeles: University of California Press.

"Amar-e Bala-ye Ezdevaj-e Kamsalan dar Iran." 2007. *BBCPersian.com*, October 31. Retrieved on July 18, 2008 (www.bbc.co.uk/persian/iran/story/2007/10/07/1031).

Amato, Paul R., Alan Booth, David R. Johnson, and Stacy J. Rogers, eds. 2007. *Alone Together: How Marriage in America is Changing*. Cambridge, MA: Harvard University Press.

Amin, Camron Michael. 2008. "Globalizing Iranian Feminism, 1910–1950." *Journal of Middle East Women's Studies* 4(1) (Winter): 6–30.

Amin, Zohre. 2006. "Bara-ye man Kar az Kar Gozashteh, Bara-ye Dokhtaranam Emza Mikonam." *Taghyir Bara-ye Barabari*. Retrieved December 24, 2006 (www.we-change.org/spip.php?article129).

Amini, Mohammad. 2006. "Komiteh-e Sazman-e Ezdevaj." *BBCPersian.com*. Retrieved September 26, 2006 (www.bbc.co.uk/persian/buisness/story/2005/10/051030_ra-iran-marriage-loan.shtml).

Amir-Ebrahimi, Masserat. 2006. "Conquering Enclosed Public Spaces." *Cities: The International Journal of Urban Policy and Planning* 23(6) (December): 455–461.

Amiri, Fatimah. 2001. "Ilam Sarzamin-e Zanan-e Sho'lehvar." *Zanan* 77 (Tir): 10–16.

Amuzegar, Jahangir. "Iran's Unemployment Crisis." 2004. *Middle East Economic Survey* 47(41) (October 11). Retrieved December 14, 2005 (www.mees.com/postedarticles/oped/a47n41d01.htm).

Andrews, Walter G. and Mehmet Kalpakli. 2005. *The Age of Beloveds: Love and the Beloved in Early-Modern Ottoman and European Culture and Society*. Durham, NC: Duke University Press.

Anisi, Fariba. 1999. "Buy-e Madineh Midahad Chador-e Sabz-e Khaharam." *Payam-e Zan* 8(6) (Shahrivar): 24–29.

Arasteh, A. Reza. 1969. *Education and Social Awakening in Iran, 1850–1968*. Leiden: E.J. Brill.

Ardavan, Soudabeh. 2003. *Yadnegarehha-ye Zendan*. Laholm: Trydells Tryckeri AB.

Arjomand, Said Amir, ed. 1984. "Traditionalism in Twentieth-Century Iran." In *From Nationalism to Revolutionary Islam*, ed. Arjomand, pp. 195–232. Albany: State University of New York Press.

1988. *The Turban for the Crown: The Islamic Revolution in Iran*. Oxford University Press.

Armajani, Yahya. 1974. "Sam Jordan and the Evangelical Ethics in Iran." In *Religious Ferment in Asia*, ed. Robert J. Miller, pp. 23–26. Lawrence: University Press of Kansas.

'Asgar-Owladi, Habibollah. 1998. "Khaterat-e Habibollah 'Asgar-Owladi." *Keyhan* [London], December 17: 8.

Ashraf, Ahmad. 1995. "From the White Revolution to the Islamic Revolution." In *Iran after the Revolution: The Crisis of an Islamic State*, ed. Saeed Rahnema and Sohrab Behdad, pp. 22–44. London and New York: I.B. Tauris.

Ashraf, Ahmad and Ali Banuazizi. "Class System: Classes in the Qajar Period." *Encyclopedia Iranica*. www.Iranica.com

Asnad-e Enqelab-e Islami: E'lamiyeh-ha, Etela'iyeh-ha, Bayaniyeh-ha, Payam-ha, Telegraf-ha, Nameh-ha-ye Ayat-e 'Ozzam va Maraje'-ye Taqlid. 1995. Tehran: Markaz-e Enqelab-e Eslami.

Atabaki, Touraj. 1993. *Azerbaijan: Ethnicity and Autonomy in Twentieth-Century Iran*. London: I.B. Tauris.

'Attar, Farid al-Din. 1963. *Mantiq al-Tayr*, ed. Sadeq Goharin. Tehran: Bongah-e Tarjomeh va Nashr-e Ketab.

Aubin, Eugène. 1908. *La Perse d'aujourd'hui*. Paris: Armand Colin.

[1908] 1983. *Iran-e Emruz, 1906–1907*, trans. Ali Asghar Saidi from the original French above. Tehran: Zavvar Press.

'Ayn al-Saltaneh, Qahraman Mirza. 1995. *Ruznameh-ye Khaterat-e 'Ayn al-Saltaneh*. Vol. I, ed. Massoud Salur and Iraj Afshar. Tehran: Asatir Press.

1997. *Ruznameh-ye Khaterat-e 'Ayn al-Saltaneh*. Vol. II, ed. Massoud Salur and Iraj Afshar. Tehran: Asatir Press.

1998a. *Ruznameh-ye Khaterat-e 'Ayn al-Saltaneh*. Vol. III, ed. Massoud Salur and Iraj Afshar. Tehran: Asatir Press.

1998b. *Ruznameh-ye Khaterat-e 'Ayn al-Saltaneh*. Vol. V, ed. Massoud Salur and Iraj Afshar. Tehran: Asatir Press.

1999. *Ruznameh-ye Khaterat-e 'Ayn al-Saltaneh*. Vol. VI, ed. Massoud Salur and Iraj Afshar. Tehran: Asatir Press.

2001. *Ruznameh-ye Khaterat-e 'Ayn al-Saltaneh*. Vol. X, ed. Massoud Salur and Iraj Afshar. Tehran: Asatir Press.

Ayramlu, Taj al-Muluk. 2001. *Khaterat-e Malekeh Pahlavi*. Tehran: Beh Afarin Press.

Azad, Hasan. 1985. *Posht-e Pardehha-ye Haramsara*. Second edition. Urumiyeh: Anzali Press.

Azadeh, Masoudeh. 1999. "Az Tajrobeh-ha Biamuzim." In Matin-Daftari 1999, pp. 121–134.

'Azimi, Fakhreddin. 1999. "Entekhabat-e Bedun-e Haqq-e Entekhab? Entekhabat-e Parlemani va Tadavom-e Farhang-e Siyasi dar Iran." *Negah-e Nou* 42 (Fall): 13–46.

Babaie, Sussan, Kathryn Babayan, Ina Baghdiantz-McCabe, and Massumeh Farhad. 2004. *Slaves of the Shah: New Elites of Safavid Iran*. London and New York: I.B. Tauris.

Babayan, Kathryn. 1998. "The 'Aqa'id al-Nisa': A Glimpse at Safavid Women in Local Isfahani Culture." In *Women in the Medieval Islamic World: Power, Patronage, and Piety*, ed. Gavin R.G. Hambly, pp. 349–382. New York: St. Martin's Press.

2002. *Mystics, Monarchs, and Messiahs: Cultural Landscapes of Early Modern Iran.* Cambridge, MA and London: Harvard Middle Eastern Monographs.

2003. "Safavid Iran: Sixteenth to Mid-Eighteenth Century." In Joseph 2003, pp. 86–94.

Badran, Margot. 1995. *Feminists, Islam, and the Nation: Gender and the Making of Modern Egypt.* Princeton University Press.

Bagley, F.R.C. 1971. "The Iranian Family Protection Law of 1967: A Milestone in the Advance of Women's Rights." In *Iran and Islam*, ed. C.E. Bosworth, pp. 47–64. Edinburgh University Press.

Bahramitash, Roksana and Shahla Kazemipour. 2006. "Myths and Realities of the Impact of Islam on Women: Changing Marital Status in Iran." *Critique: Critical Middle Eastern Studies* 15(2) (Summer): 111–128.

Bahramitash, Roksana and Hadi Salehi-Esfahani, "Nimble Fingers No Longer! Women's Employment in Iran" December 2007. Unpublished.

Bakhtiari-Asl, Fariborz. 1996. *Zanan-e Namdar-e Tarikh-e Iran: Mahd-e 'Olya Madar-e Naser al-Din Shah.* Tehran: Zavvar Press.

Ball, Jennifer. 2005. "The Twilight of the Era of Hush and Pretend: Contraception, Public Mores, and Police Power in Connecticut, 1940–1965." Ph.D. Dissertation. Purdue University, Department of History.

Balta, Paul. 1979. "Le gouvernement tente d'enrayer la montée des exigences de l'extrême gauche." *Le Monde*, February 17.

Bamdad, Badr al-Muluk. 1977. *From Darkness into Light: Women's Emancipation in Iran*, trans. and ed. F.R. Bagley. Hicksville, NY: Exposition Press.

Bamdad, Veria. 2001. *Jomhuri-ye Zendanha.* Frankfurt: P. Iran CO.

Banani, Amin. 1961. *The Modernization of Iran 1921–1941.* Stanford University Press.

Baraheni, Reza. 1977. *The Crowned Cannibals: Writings on Repression in Iran.* Introduction by E.L. Doctorow. New York: Vintage.

Bartky, Sandra Lee. 1988. "Foucault, Femininity, and the Modernization of Patriarchal Power." In *Feminism and Foucault: Reflections on Resistance*, ed. Irene Diamond and Lee Quinby, pp. 61–86. Boston: Northeastern University Press.

Bashir, Shahzad. In press. *Bodies of God's Friends: Sufism and Society in Medieval Islam* New York: Columbia University Press.

Basiri, Nasrin. 1999. "Ma Ziba Budim." In Matin-Daftari 1999, pp. 135–154.

Bauer, Janet L. 1985. "Sexuality and the Moral 'Construction' of Women in an Islamic Society." *Anthropological Quarterly* 58(3) (July): 120–129.

Bayat, Mangol. 1982. *Mysticism and Dissent: Socioreligious Thought in Qajar Iran.* Syracuse University Press.

Bayat-Philipp, Mangol. 1978. "Women and Revolution in Iran, 1905–11." In Beck and Keddie 1978, pp. 295–308.

Beauvoir, Simone de. [1953] 1974. *The Second Sex*, trans. and ed. H.M. Parshley. New York: Vintage Books.

[1979] 2005. "Speech by Simone de Beauvoir." In Afary and Anderson 2005, pp. 246–247.

Beck, Lois. 1978. "Women Among Qashqa'i Nomadic Pastoralists in Iran." In Beck and Keddie 1978, pp. 351–373.

Beck, Lois and Nikki R. Keddie, eds. 1978. *Women in the Muslim World.* Cambridge, MA: Harvard University Press.

Beck, Lois and Guity Nashat, eds. 2004. *Women in Iran: From 1800 to the Islamic Republic.* Urbana: University of Illinois Press.

Behdad, Sohrab. 1994. "A Disputed Utopia: Islamic Economics in Revolutioniary Iran." *Comparative Studies in Society and History* 36(4) (October): 743–774.

1997. "Islamic Utopia in Pre-Revolutionary Iran: Navvab Safavi and the Fada'ine Eslam." *Middle Eastern Studies* 33(1) (January): 40–65.

Behfar, Mehri. 2000a. "Gozari bar Gozaran-e 'Elmi-Ejtema'e-ye Doktor Fatimah Sayyah: Sayyah, Naqd va Adabiyat-e Now." *Hoquq-e Zanan* 2(13) (Day/Bahman): 58–66.

2000b. "Gozari bar Gozaran-e 'Elmi-Ejtema'e-ye Doktor Fatimah Sayyah: Sayyah, Jonbesha-e Zanan-e Iran." *Hoquq-e Zanan* 14 (Farvardin): 56–60.

Behnam, Mariam. 1994. *Zelzelah: A Woman Before Her Time.* Dubai: Motivate Publishing.

Behrooz, Maziar. 2000. *Rebels with a Cause: The Failure of the Left in Iran.* London: I.B. Tauris.

Bell, Gertrude. 1928. *Persian Pictures.* With a Preface by Sir E. Denison Ross. New York: Boni and Liveright.

Bellaigue, Christopher de. 2005. "New Man in Iran." *The New York Review of Books,* August 11: 19–22.

Benjamin, S.G.W. 1887. *Persia and the Persians.* London: John Murray.

Berberian, Houri. 2001. *Armenians and the Iranian Constitutional Revolution of 1905–1911: "The Love for Freedom Has No Fatherland."* Boulder, CO: Westview Press.

Beyza'i, Ne'matollah Zaka'i. [1966] 1996. "Tazkareh-ye Sho'ara-ye Qarn-e Avval-e Baha'i." Selections in *Nimeye Digar* 3 (Winter): 159–161.

Bharier, Julian. 1968. "A Note on the Population of Iran, 1900–1966." *Population Studies* 22(2) (July): 273–279.

1971. *Economic Development in Iran 1900–1970.* Oxford University Press.

Bill, James A. and William Roger Louis, eds. 1988. *Musaddiq, Iranian Nationalism and Oil.* Austin: University of Texas Press.

Blücher, Wipert von. 1949. *Zeitenwende in Iran: Erlebnisse und Beobachtungen von Wipert v. Blücher, ehemaligem deutschen Gesandten in Tehran.* Biberach an der Riss: Koehler and Voigtländer Verlag.

Boaz, Shoshan. 2000. *Discourse on Gender/Gendered Discourse in the Middle East.* London: Praeger.

Bojnurdi, Ayatollah Mousavi Bojnurdi. 2002. "In Madeh-ye Qanuni Irad Darad." *Zanan* 87 (Ordibehesht): 11.

Bonakdarian, Mansour. 2006. *Britain and the Iranian Constitutional Revolution of 1906–1911: Foreign Policy, Imperialism, and Dissent.* Syracuse University Press.

Bordo, Susan. 1988. "Anorexia Nervosa: Psychopathology as the Crystallization of Culture." In Diamond and Quinby 1988, pp. 87–118.

Bosworth, C.E., E. van Donzel, B. Lewis and Ch. Pellat. 1986. *The Encyclopaedia of Islam.* New edition. Vol. V. Leiden: E.J. Brill.

Bouhdiba, Abdelwahab. [1975] 1985. *Sexuality in Islam,* trans. Alan Sheridan. London: Routledge and Kegan Paul.

Bozorg Omid, Abolhassan. 1957. *Az Mast ke Bar Mast: Mohtavi-ye Khaterat va Moshahedat-e Abolhassan Bozorg Omid.* Tehran: Piruz Press.

Brookshaw, Dominic Parviz. 2005. "Odes of a Poet-Princess: The *Ghazals* of Jahan-Malik Khatun." *Iran* (London: British Institute of Persian Studies) 43: 173–195.

Brosius, Maria. 1996. *Women in Ancient Persia (559–331 BC).* Oxford University Press.

Browne, Edward G. 1910. *The Persian Revolution, 1905–1909.* Cambridge University Press.

1914. *The Press and Poetry of Modern Persia.* Cambridge University Press.

Burgess, Ernest W. and Paul Wallin, with Gladys Denny Shultz. 1954. *Courtship, Engagement and Marriage.* Philadelphia and New York: J.B. Lippincott Company.

Burkett, Elinor. 1999. *The Right Women: A Journey Through the Heart of Conservative America.* New York: Simon and Schuster.

Casey, Maura J. 2007. "Challenging the Mullahs, One Signature at a Time." *The New York Times,* February 7. Retrieved February 7, 2007 (www.nytimes.com/2007/02/07/opinion/07observer.html).

Chafiq, Chahla. 2006. *Totalitarism-e Islami: Pendar ya Vaqe'iyat.* Paris: Khavaran Press.

Chancer, Lynn S. 2000. "Fromm, Sadomasochism, and Contemporary American Crime." In *Erich Fromm and Critical Criminology: Beyond the Punitive Society,* ed. Kevin B. Anderson and Richard Quinney, pp. 31–58. Urbana: University of Illinois Press.

Chardin, Jean, Sir. 1811. *Voyages du chevalier Chardin en Perse, et autres lieux de l'Orient, enrichis d'un grand nombre de belles figures en taille-douce, représentant les antiquités et les choses remarquables du pays.* Vols. IV and VI. Nouv. éd., soigneusement conférée sur les 3 éditions originales, augm. d'une notice de la Perse, depuis les temps les plus reculés jusqu'à ce jour, de notes, etc., par L. Langlès. Paris: Le Normant, Imprimeur-Libraire.

Charrad, Mounira M. 2001. *States and Women's Rights: The Making of Postcolonial Tunisia, Algeria, and Morocco.* Berkeley: University of California Press.

Chauncey, George. 1994. *Gay New York: Gender, Urban Culture, and the Making of the Gay Male World 1890–1940.* New York: Basic Books.

Chehabi, Houchang E. 1990. *Iranian Politics and Religious Modernism: The Liberation Movement of Iran under the Shah and Khomeini.* London: I.B. Tauris.

1993. "Staging the Emperor's New Clothes: Dress Codes and Nation-Building Under Reza Shah." *Iranian Studies* 26(3–4): 209–229.

2000. "Voices Unveiled: Women Singers in Iran." In *Iran and Beyond: Essays in Middle Eastern History in Honor of Nikki R. Keddie,* ed. Rudi Matthee and Beth Baron, pp. 151–166. Costa Mesa, CA: Mazda Publishers.

2003. "The Banning of the Veil and its Consequences." In *The Making of Modern Iran: State and Society under Riza Shah, 921–1941,* ed. Stephanie Cronin, pp. 193–210. London: Routledge Curzon.

2004. "Dress Codes for Men in Turkey and Iran." In *Men of Order: Authoritarian Modernization under Atatürk and Reza Shah,* ed. Touraj Atabaki and Erik J. Zürcher, pp. 209–237. London: I.B. Tauris.

Chelkowski, Peter and Hamid Dabashi. 1999. *Staging a Revolution: The Art of Persuasion in the Islamic Republic of Iran*. New York University Press.

"Chera Dokhtaran Az Jensiyat-e Khod Naraziyand?" 2005. *Piramun* 4(68) (Shahrivar): 7.

"Child Prostitution Ring Run by Revolutionary Guards Officers Uncovered in Iran." 2005. *Iran Focus*. Retrieved March 13, 2007 (www.iranfocus.com/modules/news/article.php?storyid=1840).

Clawson, Patrick. 1993. "Knitting Iran Together: The Land Transport Revolution, 1920–1940." *Iranian Studies* 26(3–4): 235–250.

Cole, Juan. 1998. *Modernity and the Millennium: The Genesis of the Baha'i Faith in the Nineteenth-Century Middle East*. New York: Columbia University Press.

Collins, Patricia Hill. 2000. *Black Feminist Thought: Knowledge, Consciousness, and the Politics of Empowerment*. New York and London: Routledge.

Coontz, Stephanie. 2005. *Marriage, a History: From Obedience to Intimacy, or How Love Conquered Marriage*. New York: Viking Press.

Cottam, Richard. 1979. *Nationalism in Iran: Updated Through 1978*. University of Pittsburgh Press.

  1988a. "Nationalism in Twentieth-Century Iran and Dr. Muhammed Musaddiq." In Bill and Louis 1988, pp. 23–46.

  1988b. *Iran and the United States: A Cold War Case Study*. University of Pittsburgh Press.

Coulson, N.J. 1971. *Succession in the Muslim Family*. Cambridge University Press.

Cowen, Tyler. 2007. "Matrimony Has Its Benefits and Divorce Has a Lot to Do with That." *New York Times*, April 19.

Cronin, Stephanie. 1997. *The Army and the Creation of the Pahlavi State in Iran, 1910-1926*. London: Tauris Academic Studies.

Curzon, George N.H. [1892] 1966. 2 vols. *Persia and the Persian Question*. London: Frank Cass and Company Ltd.

Dabbagh, Marziyeh. 1995. "Khabar." *Payam-e Zan* 3(12) (Esfand): 26.

Dandamaev [also Dandamayev], Muhammad A. and Vladimir G. Lukonin. 1989. *The Culture and Social Institutions of Ancient Iran*, trans. Philip L. Kohl with D.J. Dadson. Cambridge University Press.

Danesh, Raf'at. 2006. "Afzayesh-e Talaq dar Jame'eh-ye Iran Padideh-ye Faragir." *Didar* 12 (Summer): 18–19.

Dehkhoda, 'Ali Akbar. 1908. "Charand Parand." *Sur-e Israfil* 31 (June 11): 7.

  1946–. *Loghatnameh*. Tehran University Press.

Delaram. 2005a. "Nasihati be Lezbiyanha." *MAHA* 9 (September): 14–15.

  2005b. "Valedayn-e Hamjensgara." *MAHA* 8 (August): 25–27.

Delfani, Mahmoud. 1996. *Farhang Setizi dar Dowran-e Reza Shah*. Tehran: Entesharat-e Sazeman-e Asnad-e Melli-ye Iran.

Delrish, Bashri. 1996. *Zan dar Dowreh-ye Qajar*. Tehran: Sazeman-e Tabliqat-e Islami.

D'Emilio, John and Estelle B. Freedman. 1997. *Intimate Matters: A History of Sexuality in America*. Second edition. University of Chicago Press.

Diamond, Irene and Lee Quinby, eds. 1988. *Feminism and Foucault: Reflections on Resistance*. Boston: Northeastern University Press.

Dieulafoy, Jane. 1887. *La Perse, la Chaldée et la Susiane, 1881–1882.* Paris: Hachette.

[1887] 1983. *Safarnameh-ye Dieulafoy dar Zaman-e Qajar,* trans. Farahvashi from the original French above. Tehran: Khayyam Press.

Djilas, Milovan. 1983. *The New Class: An Analysis of the Communist System.* New York: Harvest/Harcourt.

Dokouhaki, Parastu. 2005. "Hasht sal Kar Baray-e Zanan." *Zanan* 121 (Khordad): 15–21.

Douglas, Mary. [1966] 2002. *Purity and Danger: An Analysis of Concepts of Pollution and Taboo.* London and New York: Routledge.

Dover, Kenneth J. [1978] 1989. *Greek Homosexuality.* Cambridge, MA: Harvard University Press.

"Dowreh-ye Tazeh-ye Monasebat dar Ravabet-e Majles va Dowlat." 2006. *Baztab.* Retrieved September 26, 2006 (http://baztab.com/news/49123.php).

Drew, Paula E. 1997. "Iran." *The International Encyclopedia of Sexuality.* Vols. I–III, ed. Robert T. Francoeur. New York: The Continuum Publishing Company. Retrieved August 13, 2006 (www2.hu-berlin.de/sexology/IES/iran.html).

Dungus, Abubakar. 2000. "Iran's Other Revolution." *Iran Source: Populi* 27(2): 1–8.

Duran, Khalid. 1993. "Homosexuality and Islam." In *Homosexuality and World Religions,* ed. Arlene Swidler, pp. 181–197. Valley Forge, PA: Trinity Press International.

Dworkin, Andrea. 1983. *Right-Wing Women.* New York: Perigee Books.

Ebadi, Shirin. 2002. *Hoquq-e Zan dar Qavanin-e Jomhuri-ye Islami-ye Iran.* Tehran: Ketabkhaneh-ye Ganj-e Danesh.

2006. *Iran Awakening: A Memoir of Revolution and Hope.* Written in collaboration with Azadeh Moaveni. New York: Random House.

Ebrahimi, Zahra. 2001. "Porsesh az Zanan-e Nemayandeh-ye Majles-e Sheshom." *Zanan* 75 (Ordibehesht): 27–29.

2005. " 'Effat Shariati E'lam Kard: Mokhalefat-e Ba'zi Zanan-e Nemayandeh ba Tashkil-e Komisyon-e Zanan." *Zanan* 127 (Azar-Day): 20–24.

Ebrahimzadeh, Raziyeh. 1994. *Khaterat-e Yek Zan-e Tudeh'i.* Cologne: Mehr Publications.

Ehlers, Eckart and Willem Floor. 1993. "Urban Change in Iran, 1920–1941." *Iranian Studies* 26(3–4): 252–276.

Ehsani, Kaveh. 2006. "Rural Society and Agriculture Development in Post-Revolution Iran: The First Two Decades." *Critique: Critical Middle Eastern Studies* 15(1) (Spring): 79–96.

Eickelman, Dale and James Piscatori, eds. 1990. *Muslim Travellers: Pilgrimage, Migration, and the Religious Imagination.* Berkeley and Los Angeles: University of California Press.

"Ellat-e 'Panjah Darsad' Talaq-e Zowjha-ye Irani 'Masa'el-e Jensi E'lam Shod." 2008. *Iran Times* 38(1900) (April 11): 5.

El-Rouayheb, Khaled. 2005. *Before Homosexuality in the Arab–Islamic World, 1500–1800.* University of Chicago Press.

E'tesami, Parvin. 1985. *A Nightingale's Lament: Selections from the Poems and Fables of Parvin E'tesami (1904–41),* trans. Heshmat Moayyad and A. Margaret Arent Madelung. Lexington, KY: Mazdâ Publishers.

Ettehadiyeh, Mansoureh Nezam Mafi. 1982. *Peydayesh va Tahavvol-e Ahzab-e Siyasi-ye Mashrutiyat.* Tehran: Nashr-e Gostardeh.

Ezazi, Shahla. 1998. "Khoshunat-e Khanevadegi Baztab-e Sakhtar-e Ejtema." *Zanan* 50 (Bahman): 48–51.

"Ezdevaj-e Movaqqat Yeki az Rahha-ye Mahar-e Biband va Bari va Fesad." 1991. *Keyhan* (25 Shahrivar 1370): 4.

Faghfoory, Mohammad. 1993. "The Impact of Modernization on the Ulama in Iran, 1925–1941." *Iranian Studies* 26(3–4): 277–312.

Fakhra'i, Ebrahim. 1977. *Gilan dar Jonbesh-e Mashrutiyat.* Tehran: Ketabha-ye Jibi.

Farahani, Fataneh. 2007. "Diasporic Narratives of Sexuality: Identity Formation Among Iranian-Swedish Women." Ph.D. Dissertation. Stockholm University, Stockholm, Sweden.

Farman Farmaian, Sattareh and Dona Munker. 1993. *Daughter of Persia: A Woman's Journey from Her Father's Harem Through the Islamic Revolution.* New York: Anchor.

Farmer, Sharon and Carol Braun Pasternack, eds. 2003. *Gender and Difference in the Middle Ages.* Minneapolis: University of Minnesota Press.

Farrokhi, Abdollah. 1973. "Jam'iyat: Ghuli ke Donya-ye Farda ra Tahdid Mikonad." *Talash* 44 (Azar/Day): 25–29.

Farrokhzad, Forough. 1982. *Bride of Acacias: Selected Poems of Forugh Farrokhzad,* trans. Jascha Kessler with Amin Banani. With an introduction by Amin Banani and an Afterword by Farzaneh Milani. Delmar, NY: Caravan Books.

———. 2002. *Majmu'eh-ye Ash'ar-e Forough.* Tabriz: Aydin Press.

Fathi, Maryam. 2004. *Kanun-e Banuan.* Tehran: Mo'aseseh-ye Motale'at-e Tarikhi Mo'aser-e Iran.

Fathi, Nazila. 2004. "Iran Moves to Roll Back Rights Won by Women." *The New York Times,* September 19.

———. 2005. "A Revolutionary Channels His Inner Michael Moore." *The New York Times,* November 26: A 4.

———. 2007. "Despite President's Denials, Gays Insist They Exist, if Quietly, in Iran." *The New York Times,* September 30: A 5.

Feuvrier, J.B. 1899. *Trois ans à la cour de Perse.* Paris: F. Juven.

——— [1899] 1947. *Seh Sal dar Darbar-e Iran (1306–1309 AH),* trans. 'Abbas Eqbal from the original French above. Tehran: Ketabkhaneh-ye Ali Akbar 'Elmi va Shoraka'.

Filizadeh, Hussein. 2006. *Ruzi Ruzegari.* Tehran: Farhang-e Pazhuheshi-ye Chap va Nashr-e Nazar.

Fischer, Michael M.J. 1978. "On Changing the Concept and Position of Persian Women." In Beck and Keddie 1978, pp. 189–215.

Floor, Willem. "Barda and Bardadari: IV. From the Mongols to the Abolition of Slavery." *Encyclopedia Iranica.* Retrieved January 16, 2007 (www.iranica.com/newsite).

——— 1983. "The Revolutionary Character of the Ulama: Wishful Thinking or Reality?" In *Religion and Politics in Iran: Shi'ism From Quietism to Revolution,* ed. Nikki R. Keddie, pp. 73–100. New Haven: Yale University Press.

1987. *Jastarha'i az Tarikh-e Ejtema'i-ye Iran dar 'Asr-e Qajar*, trans. A. Serri. Tehran: Tus Publications.

2003. *Agriculture in Qajar Iran*. Washington, DC: Mage Publishers.

2004. *Public Health in Qajar Iran*. Washington, DC: Mage Publishers.

2008. *A Social History of Sexual Relations in Iran*. Washington, DC: Mage Press.

Forbes, Simon. 2006. "Iran – The State-Sponsored Torture and Murder of Lesbians and Gay Men." *OutRage!* Retrieved March 26 (www.petertatchell.net/international/iranstatemurder.htm).

Foucault, Michel. [1975] 1977. *Discipline and Punish: The Birth of the Prison*, trans. Alan Sheridan. New York: Pantheon Books.

[1976] 1980. *The History of Sexuality*, vol. I: *An Introduction*, trans. Robert Hurley. New York: Vintage Books.

[1979] 2005. "A Powder Keg Called Islam." In Afary and Anderson 2005, pp. 239–241.

[1984] 1985. *The History of Sexuality*, vol. II: *The Uses of Pleasure*, trans. Robert Hurley. New York: Pantheon Books.

Freud, Sigmund. [1910] 1957. "The Taboo of Virginity: Contributions to the Psychology of Love III." In *The Standard Edition of the Complete Psychological Works of Sigmund Freud Vol. XI: Five Lectures on Psycho-Analysis, Leonardo da Vinci and Other Works*, trans. James Strachey, pp. 193–208. London: The Hogarth Press.

Friedl, Erika. 1991. "The Dynamics of Women's Spheres of Action in Rural Iran." In Keddie and Baron 1991, pp. 195–214.

2002. "A Thorny Side of Marriage in Iran." In *Everyday Life in the Muslim Middle East*, ed. Donna Lee Bowen and Evelyn A. Early. Second edition, pp. 111–120. Bloomington: Indiana University Press.

2003. "Tribal Enterprises and Marriage Issues in Twentieth-Century Iran." In *Family History in the Middle East*, ed. Beshara Doumani, pp. 151–170. Albany: State University of New York Press.

2009. "New Friends: Gender Relations within the Family." *Iranian Studies* 42(1) (February).

Fromm, Erich. [1941] 1994. *Escape from Freedom*. New York: Henry Holt.

1955. *The Sane Society*. Greenwich, CT: Fawcett.

1973. *The Anatomy of Human Destructiveness*. New York: Holt, Rinehart, and Winston.

Garmrudi, Mirza Fattah Khan. 1969. *Safarnameh-ye Mirza Fattah Khan Garmrudi be Urupa dar Zaman-e Muhammad Shah Qajar*, ed. Fath al-Din Fattahi. Tehran: Bank-e Bazargani-ye Iran.

Gasiorowski, Mark J. 1987. "The 1953 Coup d'État in Iran." *International Journal of Middle East Studies* 19(3): 261–286.

"Gay Budan Ya'ni Cheh?" 2005. *MAHA* 8 (August): 15–18.

Gazargahi, Kamal al-Din Hussein. [1502] 1996. *Majales al-ushshaq*, ed. Q.T. Majd. Tehran: Qiyam Press.

"Gerayesh-e Jensi-ye Sadeq-e Hedayat." 2005. *MAHA* 3 (February): 18–23.

Ghaffari-Fard, 'Abbas Qoli. 2005. *Zan dar Tarikh Negari-ye Safaviyeh*. Tehran: Amir Kabir Press.

Ghanoonparvar, M.R. 1993. "Chand Tasvir az Zanan dar Dastanha-y Sadeq Chubak." *Iranshenasi* 5(2) (Summer): 268–275.

Ghazzali, Abu Hamid Muhammad. 1954. *Kimiya-ye Sa'adat*. Tehran: Markazi Publications.

Ghazzali, Ahmad. 1979. *Majmu'eh-ye Asar-e Farsi-ye Ahmad Ghazzali*. Tehran University Publications.

Gheissari, Ali and Vali Nasr. 2005. "The Conservative Consolidation in Iran." *International Institute for Strategic Studies* 47(2) (Summer): 175–190.

Giviyan, 'Esmat. 1992. "Payam-e Sargozasht." *Payam-e Zan* 1(11) (Bahman): 21–34, 74–75.

    1993a. "Goftogu ba Khanom Fereshteh Erabi." *Payam-e Zan* 2(3) (Khordad): 14–18.

    1993b. "Goftogu ba Khanom Simin Ahmadi." *Payam-e Zan* 2(5) (Mordad): 16–55.

    1993c. "Payam-e Sargozasht." *Payam-e Zan* 1(11) (Bahman): 21–34, 74–75.

    1993d. "Payam-e Sargozasht." *Payam-e Zan* 2(3) (Khordad): 6–13.

    1994a. "Goftogu ba Zahra Rahnavard." *Payam-e Zan* 3(5) (Mordad): 4–11.

    1994b. "Goftogu ba Zahra Rahnavard." *Payam-e Zan* 3(6) (Shahrivar): 4–11.

    1994c. "Goftogu ba Zahra Rahnavard." *Payam-e Zan* 3(7) (Mehr): 6–11.

    1994d. "Goftogu ba Khanom Mohtaram Jamali." *Payam-e Zan* 3(10) (Azar): 23–26.

    1999. "Zan Jame'eh-ye Madani ra dar Khaneh Payrizi Mikonad." *Payam-e Zan* 7(11) (Bahman): 5–9.

Gordon, Linda. 1990. *Woman's Body, Woman's Right: Birth Control in America*. Revised edition. New York: Penguin Books.

Gozaresh-e Eqtesadi va Taraznameh-ye Sal-e 1356. 1977. Tehran: Bank-e Markazi-ye Iran.

Gueyras, Jean. 1979. "Les formations de gauche déconseillent aux femmes la poursuite des manifestations de rue." *Le Monde*, March 14.

Haeri, Shahla. 1989. *Law of Desire: Temporary Marriage in Shi'i Iran*. Syracuse University Press.

Hafez-e Shirazi, Shams al-Din Muhammad. 1994. *Divan-e Khwajeh Shams al-Din Muhammad Shirazi*. Based on the edition corrected by Alameh Qazvini and Qasem Ghani. Tehran: Muhammad Press.

Halper, Louise. 2005. "Law and Women's Agency in Post-Revolutionary Iran." *Harvard Journal of Law and Gender* 28(1) (Winter): 85–142.

"Halqeh-ye Gomshodeh." 2004. *MAHA* 1 (December): 11–12.

"Hamjensgarayan va Mo'zal-e Ezdevavj." 2005. *MAHA* 9 (September): 7–13.

"Hamjensgarayan-e Mosalman." 2005. *MAHA* 2 (January): 15–18.

Hamraz, Sepideh. 2002. "Fahsha, Aineh-ye Tamam Nama-ye Setam bar Zan dar Jomhori-e Islami." *Hasht-e Mars* 6 (Fall): 4–9.

"Harfha-ye Shoma." 2005. *MAHA* 2 (January): 4–5.

Harrison, Frances. 2005. "Iran's Sex-Change Operations." *BBC News*, January 5.

Hashemizadeh, Iraj. 2007. "Dar Masir-e Enqelab pa be pay-e Ruznameh-ye 'Nameh-ye Mardom': Part 5." *Keyhan* [London], March 7: 14.

Hatem, Mervat F. 1997. "The Professionalization of Health and the Control of Women's Bodies as Modern Governmentalities in Nineteenth-Century Egypt." In Zilfi 1997, pp. 66–80.

Healey, Dan. 2001. *Homosexual Desire in Revolutionary Russia*. University of Chicago Press.

Hedayat, Sadeq. [1933] 1959. *ʿAlaviyeh Khanom va Velengari*. Tehran: Chapkhaneh-ye Bank-e Bazargani.

[1936] 1957. *The Blind Owl*, trans. D.P. Costello. New York: Grove Press.

1979. *Sadeq Hedayat: An Anthology*, ed. Eshan Yarshater. Boulder, CO: Westview Press.

1993. *Majmuʿeh-ye as Asar-e Sadeq-e Hedayat*, ed. Muhammad Baharlu. Tehran: Tarh-e Now Press.

2002. *Sadeq Hedayat: Hashtad va do Nameh be Hasan Shahid-nuraʾi*. Second edition, ed. Nasser Pakdaman. Paris: Cesmandaz.

Hegland, Mary Elaine. 2005. "Aliabad of Shiraz: Transformation from Village to Suburb." Middle East Studies Association Annual Meeting, Washington DC, November.

2009. "Educating Young Women: Culture, Conflict, and New Identities in an Iranian Village." *Iranian Studies* 42(1) (February).

Hejazi, Banafsheh. 2002. *Zaʿifeh: Barrasi-ye Jaygah-e Zan-e Irani*. Tehran: Qasidehsara Press.

Hesabha-ye Melli-ye Iran, 1338–56. 1981. Tehran: Bank-e Markazi-ye Iran.

al-Hilli al-Muhaqqiq al-Awwal, Jaʿfar Ibn al-Hasan. 1974. *Tarjomeh-ye Farsi-ye Sharaye' al-Islam*. Tehran University Press.

Hillmann, Michael C., ed. 1978. *Hedayat's "The Blind Owl" Forty Years Later*. Austin: University of Texas at Austin.

Hiro, Dilip. 1990. *The Longest War: The Iran–Iraq Military Conflict*. New York: Routledge.

Hodgson, Marshall G.S. 1974. *The Venture of Islam: The Classical Age of Islam*. Vol. I. University of Chicago Press.

The Holy Quran. 1991. Columbus, OH: Holy Quran Publishing Project.

Hoodfar, Homa. 1994. "Devices and Desires: Population Policy and Gender Roles in the Islamic Republic." *Middle East Report* (September–October): 11–17.

1998. "Volunteer Health Workers in Iran as Social Activists: Can 'Governmental Non-Governmental Organizations' be Agents of Democratisation?" *WLUML Occasional Paper* 10 (December): 1–30.

Hoodfar, Homa and Samad Assadpour. 2000. "The Politics of Population Policy in the Islamic Republic of Iran." *Studies in Family Planning* 31(1) (March): 19–34.

Hooglund, Eric J. 1982. *Land and Revolution in Iran, 1960–1980*. Austin: University of Texas Press.

Hourcade, Bernard. 2006. "In the Heart of Iran: The Electorate of Mahmoud Ahmadinejad." *Middle East Report* 241 (Winter): 10–11.

Howard, Jane. 2002. *Inside Iran: Women's Lives*. Washington, DC: Mage Publishers.

Hughes, Donna M. 2004. "Islamic Republic's Sex Scandal." *Iran Press Service*, June 11. Retrieved October 15, 2006.

Ibrahimi, Zahra. 2004a. "Dar Naharkhori-ye Majles Dowr-e Zanan Pardeh Keshidand." *Zanan* 111 (Mordad): 26–31.

2004b. "Davazdah Zan-e Majles-e Haftom: Qodrat Bedun-e Eqtedar." *Zanan* 110 (Tir): 33–39.

2004c. "Zanan, Tahasson, Este'fa." *Zanan* 106 (Bahman): 2–10.

International Campaign for Human Rights in Iran. 2008. "Equal Rights Denied: The Systematic Repression of the Women's Rights Movement in Iran." Retrieved July 21 (www.iranhumanrights.org/themes/womens-rights.html).

Iraj Mirza, Jalal al-Malek. 1972. *Divan-e Iraj Mirza*. Tehran: Mozaffari Press.

Iran: A Country Study. 2004. Whitefish, MT: Kessinger Publishing.

"Iran: Ahmadi-Nejad's Tumultuous Presidency." 2007. *International Crisis Group: Middle East Briefing No. 21*, February 6: 1–27. Retrieved March 18 (www.crisisgroup.org).

"Iran Asked to End Executions of Homosexuals." 1997. *ILGA Communications Media Committee*, August 4. Retrieved February 14, 2007 (www.qrd.org/qrd/world/asia/iran/ILGA.asks.end.execution.of.homosexuals-08.06.97).

"Iran: Foreign Area Handbook." 2002. *Gulf2000 Project*. Columbia University. Retrieved March 20, 2007 (http://gulf2000.columbia.edu).

"Iran–Iraq War." 2004. *Microsoft Encarta Online Encyclopedia*. Retrieved March 15, 2005 (http://encarta.msn.com).

"Iran 'Killer of Rapist' Reprieved." 2004. *BBC News*, July 27.

"Iran Official: Unemployment Rampant Among Youth, Women." 2003. *Iran Daily Newspaper*, July 1. Retrieved December 15, 2005 (www.payvand.com/news/03/jul/1001.html).

"Iran's President Urges Higher Birth Rate." 2006. *The Washington Post*, October 23.

"Iran Tops World Addiction-Rate List." 2005. *Iran Focus*, September 24. Retrieved March 21, 2007.

"Iranian Leader Bars Reforms' Press Bill." 2000. *The New York Times*, August 7.

Ireland, Doug. 2005. "Shame on Iran: US Remains Silent on Gay Hangings." *LA Weekly*, September 2–8. Retrieved March 20, 2007 (www.laweekly.com/ink/05/41/news-ireland.php).

2006a. "Iran's Brutal Assault Yesterday on Women Celebrating International Women's Day." *Direland*. Retrieved on March 13, 2007 (http://direland.typepad.com/direland/2006/03/irans_brutal_as.html).

2006b. "Iran Hacks Web Sites to Bury Anti-Gay Pogrom." *Direland*. Retrieved April 26, 2006 (http://direland.typepad.com).

2007. "Change Sex or Die." *Gay City News*. Retrieved May 27, 2007 (www.gaycitynews.com/site/news.cfm?newsid=18324930&BRD=2729&PAG=461&dept_id=569346&rfi=6).

Ja'fari, Morteza, Soghra Esma'ilzadeh, and Ma'sumeh Farshchi. 1992. *Vaqe'eh-ye Kashf-e Hijab*. Tehran: Entesharat-e Sazeman-e Madarek-e Farhangi-ye Enqelab-e Islami.

Ja'fariyan, Rasul. 2001. *Rasa'il-e Hijabiyeh: Shast Sal Talash-e 'Elmi dar Barabar-e Bad'at-e Kashf-e Hejab*. 2 vols. Qom: Dalil-e Ma Press.

Jain, Anrudh K. 1981. "The Effect of Female Education on Fertility: A Simple Explanation." *Demography* 18(4) (November): 577–595.

Jamalzadeh, Muhammad Ali. 1947. *Sahra-ye Mahshar*. Tehran: Khorrami Press.

James, Lionel. 1909. *Side-Tracks and Bridle-Paths*. Edinburgh and London: William Blackwood and Sons.

Jami, 'Abd al-Rahman. 1987. *Baharestan*, ed. A'la Khan Afsahzad. Moscow: Tajikistan Academy of Sciences, Oriental Institute.

Jami, Nur al-Din. 1958. *Masnavi-ye Haft Owrang*, ed. M.M. Gilani. Tehran: Sa'di Publications.

Jamshid. 2005. "Hamjensgara'i: Darkha va Bardashtha." *MAHA* 2 (January): 21–27.

Javadi, Hasan, Manijeh Marashi, and Simin Shekarloo, eds. 1992. *Ta'dib al-Nisvan va Ma'ayeb al-Rejal*. General editor, Janet Afary. Chicago: Historical Studies of Iranian Women.

Jayegah-e Zan dar Qanun. 1995. Tehran: Daftar-e Omur-e Zanan dar Nahad-e Riyasat-e Jomhuri va Vezarat-e Farhang va Ershad-e Islami.

Jazayery, Mohammad Ali. 1973. "Ahmad Kasravi and the Controversy over Persian Poetry: 1. Kasravi's Analysis of Persian Poetry." *International Journal of Middle Eastern Studies* 4: 190–203.

— 1978. "Kasrawi Tabrizi," *Encyclopedia of Islam*, vol. IV. Second edition, ed. E. van Donzel, B. Lewis, and Ch. Pellat. Leiden: Brill.

— 1981. "Ahmad Kasravi and the Controversy over Persian Poetry: 2. The Debate on Persian Poetry between Kasravi and His Opponents." *International Journal of Middle Eastern Studies* 13: 311–327.

Joseph, Suad, ed. 2003. *Encyclopedia of Women and Islamic Cultures*. Vol. I. Leiden and Boston: Brill.

— 2005. *Encyclopedia of Women and Islamic Cultures*. Vol. II. Leiden and Boston: Brill.

"Jozveh-ye Hoquqi: Ta'sir-e Qavanin bar Zendegi-ye Zanan." 2006. *Taghyir Bara-ye Barabari*. Retrieved December 24, 2006 (www.we-change.org/spip.php?article48).

Kamguyan, Azam. 2001. *Jonbesh-e Barabari Talabi-ye Zanan dar Iran*. Stockholm: Nasim Press.

Kandiyoti, Deniz. 1991. "Islam and Patriarchy: A Comparative Perspective." In Keddie and Baron 1991, pp. 23–44.

Kanun-e Nevisandegan-e Iran. 1979. "Kanun-e Nevisandegan-e Iran be Dowlat Hoshdar Midahad." *Ettela'at*, 10 Esfand 1357/March 1: 8.

Kar, Mehrangiz. 1999a. *Raf'-e Tab'iz az Zanan. Moqayeseh-ye Konvansiyon-e Raf'-e Tab'iz az Zanan ba Qavanin-e Dakheli-ye Iran*. Tehran: Nashr-e Qatreh.

— 1999b. *Sakhtar-e Hoquqi-ye Nezam-e Khanevadeh dar Iran*. Tehran: Entesharat-e Roshangaran va Motale'at-e Zanan.

— 2000a. *Zanan dar Bazar-e Kar-e Iran*. Tehran: Rowshangaran Press va Motale'at-e Zanan.

— 2000b. *Pazuheshi dar bareh-ye Khoshunat 'Aleyhe-e Zanan dar Iran*. Tehran: Entesharat-e Roshangaran va Motale'at-e Zanan.

— 2003. "The Invasion of the Private Sphere in Iran." *Social Research* 70(3) (Fall): 829–836.

Karachi, Ruhangiz. 2004. "Forough: Bayan-e Jonun Amiz-e Zananegi." *Zanan* 107 (March): 74–79.

"Karnameh-ye Hasht Saleh-ye Sepah-e Danesh." 1971. *Talash* 29 (Tir/Mordad): 73–75.

Kashani, Abu al-Qasem. 1983. *Majmu'eh-ye az Maktubat, Sokhanraniha va Payamha*, ed. M. Dehnavi. Tehran: Chapakhsh Press. 3 vols.

Kashani-Sabet, Firoozeh. 2005. "Patriotic Womanhood: The Culture of Feminism in Modern Iran, 1900–1941." *British Journal of Middle Eastern Studies* 32(1): 29–46.

2006. "The Politics of Reproduction: Maternalism and Women's Hygiene in Iran, 1896–1941." *International Journal of Middle East Studies* 38: 1–29.

Kasravi, Ahmad. 1974. *Khăharan va Dokhtaran-e Ma.* Tehran: n.p.

[1944] 1977. *Dar Piramun-e Adabiyat.* Tehran: Roshdiyeh Press.

1984. *Tarikh-e Mashruth-ye Iran.* Tehran: Amir Kabir Press.

Katouzian, Homa. 1991. *Sadeq Hedayat: The Life and Legend of an Iranian Writer.* London: I.B. Tauris.

2002. "Kasravi va Adabiyyat." *Iran Nameh* 20(2–3) (Spring/Summer): 171–193.

Kaviyanpour, Maryam. 1993. "Goftogu ba Khanom-e Tayebeh Soltani." *Payam-e Zan* 2(5) (Mordad): 20–33.

Kaykavus Ibn Iskandar. 1951. *A Mirror for Princes: The Qabus Nama*, trans. Reuben Levy. London: Cresset Press.

Kazemi, Farhad. 1999. "Feda'ian-e Eslam." In *Encyclopaedia Iranica.* Vol. IX, pp. 470–474. New York: Bibliotheca Press.

Keddie, Nikki R. 1981. *Roots of Revolution: An Interpretive History of Modern Iran.* With a section by Yann Richard. New Haven: Yale University Press.

1991. "Introduction: Deciphering Middle Eastern Women's History." In Keddie and Baron 1991, pp. 1–22.

2003. *Modern Iran: Roots and Results of Revolution.* New Haven: Yale University Press.

2007. *Women in the Middle East, Past and Present.* Princeton University Press.

Keddie, Nikki R. and Beth Baron, eds. 1991. *Women in Middle Eastern History: Shifting Boundaries in Sex and Gender.* New Haven: Yale University Press.

Kermani, Mirza Aqa Khan. 2006. *Sad Khetabeh*, ed. Muhammad Ja'far Mahjoub. Los Angeles: Ketab Corporation.

Keyvani, Mehdi. 1982. *Artisans and Guild Life in the Later Safavid Period: Contributions to the Socio-Economic History of Persia.* Berlin: Klaus Schwarz.

"Khanevadeh-ye Shohada." 2005. *Khanevadeh-ye Sabz* 7(141) (Mehr 1): 57.

Khomeini, Ruhollah. [1943] 1984. *Kashf al-Asrar.* n.p.

1947. *Resaleh-ye Towzih al-Masa'el.* Qom: Ruh Press.

1999. *Sahifeh-ye Imam* [Collected Lectures, Interviews, and Fatwas]. Tehran: Mo'aseseh-ye Tanzim va Chap-e Asar-e Imam Khomeini. 22 vols.

2005. *Jayegah-e Zan dar Andisheh-ye Imam Khomeini.* Tehran: Tanzim va Nashr-e Asar-e Imam Khomeini.

Khosrokhavar, Farhad. 1995. *L'Islamisme et la mort: Le martyre révolutionnaire en Iran.* Paris: Éditions L'Harmattan.

Khănsari, Molla Jamal. 1999. *Kolsum Naneh*, ed. Bahram Chubineh. Cologne: Ghassedek Press.

Kian-Thiébaut, Azadeh. 2005. "From Motherhood to Equal Rights Advocates." *Iranian Studies* 38(1): 45–66.

Kiani-Haftlang, Kianoush. 2007. *Tasvirha-ye Iran.* Tehran: Sazeman-e Asnad va Ketabkhaneh-ye Melli Iran.

Kinzer, Stephen. 2003. *All the Shah's Men: An American Coup and the Roots of Middle East Terror.* Hoboken, NJ: John Wiley and Sons.

Koolaee, Elaheh. 2006. "Majles-e Sheshom va Hoquq-e Zanan." *Aeen* (December 2006).

Kuniholm, Bruce Robellet. 1980. *The Origins of the Cold War in the Near East: Great Power Conflict and Diplomacy in Iran, Turkey, Greece.* Princeton University Press.

Ladjevardi, Habib. 1985. *Labor Unions and Autocracy in Iran.* Syracuse University Press.

"Layeheh-ye 'Zed-e Khanevadeh' dar Showr Avval va Bedun-e Taghyir dar Komissyon-e Majles Tasvib Shod!" 2008. *Change4Equality,* 24 Tir 1387. Retrieved July 22, 2008 (www.change4equality.info/spip.php?article2373).

Lewis, Franklin D. 2001. *Rumi: Past and Present, East and West: The Life, Teaching and Poetry of Jalâl al-Din Rumi.* New York: Oneworld Publications.

"Liwat." 1986. *The Encyclopedia of Islam.* Leiden: Brill: 776–779.

Madani-Ghahfarokhi, Saeid. 2004. "Gendered Impacts of Declining Social Capital." *Women's Research: Journal of the Center for Women's Studies* 1(1) (June): 75–88.
    2005. *Kudak Azari dar Iran.* Tehran: Aknun Press.

Madani-Ghahfarokhi, Saeid, Jaleh Shaditalab, and Fariborz Raeisdana. Forthcoming. *Arzyabi-ye Sariʿ-e Ruspigari dar Shahr-e Tehran.* Tehran: United Nations Population Fund (UNFPA).

Mahdavi, Pardis. 2007a. "Meeting, Mating, and Cheating on Him in Iran." *Isim Review* 19 (Spring): 18.
    2007b "Passionate Uprisings: Young People, Sexuality and Politics in Post-Revolutionary Iran." *Culture, Health and Sexuality* 9(5) (September–October): 445–457.

Mahdavi, Shireen. 1987. "Taj al-Saltaneh, an Emancipated Qajar Princess." *Middle Eastern Studies* 23(2): 188–193.
    2004. "Reflections in the Mirror – How Each Saw the Other: Women in the Nineteenth Century." In Beck and Nashat 2004, pp. 63–84.

Mahvash. 1957. *Raz-e Kamyabi-ye Jensi.* Tehran: n.p.

Majd Ziya'i, Habibollah. 1945. "Mohtava-ye Dorus-e Madares-e Dokhtaran." *Ruznameh-ye Rasmi-ye Keshvar-e Shahanshahi.* Bahman 1323/1945 [Fourteenth Parliament, 1945–1947], Session 94.

Majlesi, Mohammad Baqir. 1983. *Helliyat al-Motaqqin.* Tehran: Taheri Press.

Malcolm, Sir John. 1829. *History of Persia.* London: John Murray. 2 vols.

Malekafzali, Hussein, Muhammad Zareʿ, and Jaʿfar Jandoqi. 1998. "Taʿyin-e Niyazha-y Amuzeshi-ye Dokhtaran-e Semnani dar Ertebat ba Behdasht-e Boluq va Taʿin-e Estrateji-ye Monaseb barayi ta'min-e An." *Behdasht-e Khanevadeh* 3(9) (Spring): 3–11.

Maleki, G. 1996. "Zanan dar Majles: Az Ebetda ta Konun." *Payam-e Zan* 5(3) (Khordad): 30–35.

Malekzadeh, Elham. 2006. "The Effect of the Constitutional Revolution on Charitable Deeds in Tehran." Presented at the Centenary Conference of the Iranian Constitutional Revolution, Oxford University. August.

Malijak, Aziz al-Sultan. 1997. *Ruznameh-ye Khaterat-e Aziz al-Saltaneh. Malijek-e Sani.* Vol. I. Tehran: Zaryab Press.

Malikzadeh, Mahdi. 1992. *Tarikh-e Enqelab-e Mashrutiyat-e Iran.* Tehran: ʿElmi Press. 7 vols.

"Manba'-ye Afzayesh-e Budjeh-ye Mehr-e Reza Kojast?" 2006. *AftabNews*. Retrieved November 10, 2006 (www.aftabnews.ir/vdcdjj0ytk0fk.html).

Maqsudi, Morad. 2005. *Haq al-Zahme-ye Khanehdar-ye Zanan*. Ilam: Entesharat-e Gouyesh.

Marashi, Simin. 2007. "Mobarezeh ba HIV/AIDS Bedun-e Barabari-ye Jensiyati-Tabaqati Emkan Pazir Nakhahad Bud." *Zanestan* 20 (Winter). Retrieved March 18, 2007 (http://herlandmag.net/issue20/07,02,04,03,09,00/).

Marcuse, Herbert. [1963] 1989. "The Obsolesence of the Freudian Concept of Man." In *Critical Theory and Society: A Reader*, ed. Stephen Eric Bronner and Douglas MacKay Kellner, pp. 233–246. New York and London: Routledge.

Marmon, Shaun. E, ed. 1999. *Slavery in the Islamic Middle East*. Princeton: Markus Wiener Publishers.

Marsot, Aff Lutfi al-Sayyid. 1978. "The Revolutionary Gentlewomen in Egypt." In Beck and Keddie 1978, pp. 261–276.

Martin, Vanessa. 2005. *The Qajar Pact: Bargaining, Protest, and the State in Nineteenth-Century Persia*. London: I.B. Tauris.

Massell, Gregory J. 1974. *The Surrogate Proletariat: Moslem Women and Revolutionary Strategies in Soviet Central Asia, 1919–1929*. Princeton University Press.

Mathers, E. Powys. 1927. *Eastern Love: The Book of Women and Education of Wives*. Vol. III. London: John Rodker.

Matin-Daftari, Maryam. 1990. "Ruz-e Jahani-ye Zan." *Azadi* 2(7–8) (Mehr–Esfand): 36–39.

  ed. 1999. *Bazbini-ye Tajrobeh: Ettehad-e Melli-ye Zanan*. Berkeley, CA: Noqteh Press.

  2001. "Cheshm Andaz-e Vaz'iyat-e Zanan-e Irani ba Negahi be Tajrobiyyat-e Gozashteh." In *Barrasi-ye Motale'at va Mobarezat-e Feministi-ye Zanan-e Iran dar Do Daheh-ye Akhir va Cheshmandaz-e Ayandeh*. Berkeley: Proceedings of the 15th Conference of Bonyad-e Pazuheshha-ye Zanan-e Iran.

Matthee, Rudi. 1993. "Transforming Dangerous Nomads into Useful Artisans, Technicians, Agriculturalists: Education in the Reza Shah Period." *Iranian Studies* 26(3–4): 313–336.

  2000. "Prostitutes, Courtesans, and Dancing Girls: Women Entertainers in Safavid Iran." In *Iran and Beyond: Essays in Middle Eastern History in Honor of Nikki R. Keddie*, ed. Rudi Matthee and Beth Baron, pp. 121–150. Los Angeles: Mazda Publishers.

  2005. *The Pursuit of Pleasure: Drugs and Stimulants in Iranian History, 1500–1900*. Princeton: Princeton University Press and Mage Press.

Mattson, Ingrid. 2003. "Law: Family Law: Seventh–Late Eighteenth Centuries." In Joseph 2005, pp. 450–457.

Mbembe, Achille. 2003. "Necropolitics." *Public Culture* 15(1) (Winter): 11–40.

Meghdadi, Bahram and Leo Hamalian. 1978. "Oedipus and the Owl." In Hillmann 1978, pp. 142–152.

Mehdevi, Anne Sinclair. 1953. *Persian Adventure*. New York: Alfred A. Knopf.

Mehran, Golnar. 1991. "The Creation of the New Muslim Woman: Female Education in the Islamic Republic of Iran." *Convergence* 23 (November 4): 42–52.

Mehrpour, Hussein. 2000. *Mabahesi az Hoquq-e Zan az Manzar-e Hoquq-e Dakheli, Mabani-ye Feqhi, va Mavazin-e Beyn al-Melali*. Tehran: Ettela'at Press.

Meisami, Julie Scott. 1987. *Medieval Persian Court Poetry*. Princeton University Press.

Meisami, Parisa. 2007. "Zanan-e Irani az Showhareshan AIDS Migirand." *Zanestan*. Retrieved February 7, 2007 (http://herlandmag.net/issure20/07,02,04,03,02,00/).

Menashri, David. 1992. *Education and the Making of Modern Iran*. Ithaca, NY: Cornell University Press.

"Mental Health." 2007. *World Health Organization: Country Reports and Charts*. Retrieved February 22, 2007 (www.who.int/mental_health/prevention/suicide).

Mernissi, Fatima. 1987. *Beyond the Veil: Male–Female Dynamics in Modern Muslim Society*. Second edition. Bloomington: Indiana University Press.

Messkoub, Mahmood. 2006. "Social Policy in Iran in the Twentieth Century." *Iranian Studies* 39(2) (June): 227–252.

Milani, Farzaneh. 1982. "Forugh Farrokhzad: A Feminist Perspective." In Farrokhzad 1982, pp. 141–147.

1992. *Veils and Words: The Emerging Voices of Iranian Women Writers*. Syracuse University Press.

1994. "Neotraditionalism in the Poetry of Simin Behbahani." In *Reconstructing Gender in the Middle East*, ed. Fatma Müge Göçek and Shiva Balaghi, pp. 30–39. New York: Columbia University Press.

Milani, Houriyeh Shamshiri. 1999. *Neda-ye Salamat* 4: 1–2.

Millett, Kate. 1982. *Going to Iran*. With photographs by Sophie Keir. New York: Coward, McCann and Geoghegan.

Minorsky, V. 1980. *Tadhkirat al-Muluk: A Manual of Safavid Administration*. Second edition. Cambridge: Gibb Memorial Trust.

Mir-Hosseini, Ziba. 1993. *Marriage on Trial: A Study of Islamic Family Law: Iran and Morocco Compared*. London: I.B. Tauris.

1999. *Islam and Gender: The Religious Debate in Contemporary Iran*. Princeton University Press.

2004. "Sexuality, Rights, and Islam: Competing Gender Discourses in Post-Revolutionary Iran." In Beck and Nashat 2004, pp. 204–217.

Mirza Saleh, Qolamhussein. 1993. *Reza Shah: Khaterat-e Soleyman Behboudi, Shams Pahlavi, Ali Yazdi*. Tehran: Tarh-e Now.

Mirzai, Behnaz A. 2004. "Slavery, the Abolition of the Slave Trade and the Emancipation of Slaves in Iran, 1828–1928." Ph.D. Dissertation. York University, North York, Ontario.

Mirzazadeh, Shirin. 2004. "Qanuni Baray-e Nabudan." *Zanan* 106 (Bahman): 44–53.

"Miyangin-e Sen-e Ezdevaj-e Zanan dar Iran 3.9 darsad Ezafeh yaft." 2005. *Zanan* 119 (Farvardin): 76.

Moaddel, Mansoor. 2008. "Religious Regimes and Prospects for Liberal Politics: Futures of Iran, Iraq, and Saudi Arabia." In *Population Studies Center Research Report*, pp. 1–23. Ann Arbor: Population Studies Center, University of Michigan Institute for Social Research.

Moaddel, Mansoor and Taghi Azadarmaki. 2002. "The World Views of Islamic Publics: The Cases of Egypt, Iran, and Jordan." *Comparative Sociology* 1(3–4): 299–319.

Moallem, Minoo. 2005. *Between Warrior Brother and Veiled Sister: Islamic Fundamentalism and the Politics of Patriarchy in Iran*. Berkeley and Los Angeles: University of California Press.

Moaveni, Azadeh. 2005. *Lipstick Jihad: A Memoir of Growing Up Iranian in America and American in Iran*. New York: Public Affairs.

Moghadam, Fatemeh Etemad. 2009. "Undercounting Women's Work in Iran" *Iranian Studies* 42: 1 (February).

Moghadam, Valentine. 1991. "Islamist Movements and Women's Responses in the Middle East." *Gender and History* 3(3) (Autumn): 268–284.

Moghissi, Haideh. 1996. *Populism and Feminism in Iran*. New York: St. Martin's Press.

Mohammadi, Majid. 1999. "Jensiyat: Khat-e Qermez-e Roshanfekran-e Dini." *Zanan* 58 (Azar): 39–40.

Mohri, Homa. 2003. "Majles va Zanan." *Hoquq-e Zanan* 23 (Bahman): 28–35.

Moin, Baqer. 1999. *Khomeini: Life of the Ayatollah*. New York: St. Martin's Press.

Mojab, Shahrzad. 2001. "Conflicting Loyalties: Nationalism and Gender Relations in Kurdistan." In *Of Property and Propriety: The Role of Gender and Class in Imperialism and Nationalism*, ed. Himani Bannerji, Shahrzad Mojab, and Judy Whitehead, pp. 116–152. University of Toronto Press.

"Morocco: Action Urged on Legal Code Reform." 2001. *HRW World Report 2001: Women's Human Rights*. Retrieved March 12, 2007 (www.hrw.org/press/2001/03/morocco0320.htm).

Moruzzi, Norma Claire and Fatemeh Sadeghi. 2006. "Out of the Frying Pan, Into the Fire: Young Iranian Women Today." *MERIP* 241 (Winter): 22–28.

"Mosahebeh ba Babak: Az Faʿalan-e Sabeq-e Gorouh-e Houman." 2005. *MAHA* 8 (August): 8–9.

Moshfeq-Kazemi, Morteza. 1941/1942. *Tehran-e Makhowf*. Tehran: Parvin Publications.

Motahhari, Morteza. [1974] 1988. *Nezam-e Hoquq-e Zan dar Islam*. Tehran: Sadra Publications.

    1982. *Dah Goftar*. Tehran: Sadra Press.

    [1989] 1997. *Majmuʿeh Asar (Collected Works)*. Tehran: Sadra Press. 11 vols.

Mottahedeh, Negar. 2002. "Karbala Drag Kings and Queens." Paper presented at the Society for Iranian Studies Biannual Meeting. Bethesda, MD (May).

Mouawad, Jad. 2007. "West Adds to Strains on Iran's Lifeline." *The New York Times*. February 13: C 1–4.

Musallam, B.F. 1983. *Sex and Society in Islam: Birth Control Before the Nineteenth Century*. Cambridge University Press.

Naficy, Hamid. 2001. "Veiled Voice and Vision in Iranian Cinema: The Evolution of Rakhshan Banietemad's Films." In *Ladies and Gentlemen, Boys and Girls: Gender in Film at the End of the Twentieth Century*, ed. Murray Pomerance, pp. 36–53. New York: SUNY Press.

In press. *Cinema and National Identity: A Social History of a Century of Iranian Cinema*. Durham, NC: Duke University Press.

Nafisi, Azar. 2003. *Reading Lolita in Tehran*. New York: Random House.

Nafisi, Said. 1966. *Tarikh-e Moʿaser-e Iran*. Tehran: Foroughi Press.

Naghibi, Nima. 2007. *Rethinking Global Sisterhood: Western Feminism and Iran*. Minneapolis: University of Minnesota Press.

Nahan, Sima. 2006. "Don't Cry for me, Oriana." *Iranian.com*. Retrieved February 5, 2007 (www.iranian.com/Nahan/Iran/4.html).

Nahid, Abdulhussein. 1981. *Zanan-e Iran dar Jonbesh-e Mashruteh*. Tehran: n.p.

Najmabadi, Afsaneh. 1993. "Zanha-ye Millat: Women or Wives of Nation?" *Iranian Studies* 26(1–2) (Winter–Spring): 51–71.

   1996. *Bibi Khanom Astarabadi va Afzal Vaziri*. Chicago: Midland Press.

   1998a. "Crafting an Educated Housewife in Iran." In Abu-Lughod 1998, pp. 91–125.

   1998b. *The Story of the Daughters of Quchan: Gender and National Memory in Iranian History*. Syracuse University Press.

   2005. *Women with Mustaches and Men Without Beards: Gender and Sexual Anxieties of Iranian Modernity*. Berkeley and Los Angeles: University of California Press.

Nashat, Guity. 2004. "Marriage in the Qajar Period." In Beck and Nashat 2004, pp. 37–62.

Nasr, Seyyed Hossein. 1977. *Sufi Essays*. New York: Schocken Books.

Nasser, Ladane. "Religion and Love." 2006. *IranDokht*. Retrieved February 15, 2006 (www.irandokht.com/news/readnews.php?newsID=16733).

Nategh, Homa. 1979. "Negahi be Barkhi Neveshteh-ha va Mobarezat-e Zan dar Dowran-e Mashrutiyat." *Kitab-e Jomeh* 30: 45–54.

   2006. "Naser al-Din Shah-e Palid, Seyyed Jamal al-Din va Malkom Khan." *Negah-e Nou* 70 (Mordad): 34–39.

Navaei, Abdulhusain. 1995–1996. "Ruzegar Ast, Anke Gah Ezzat Dahad, Gah Khăr Darad." *Ganjineh* 5(3–4) (Fall–Winter): 51–55.

Navaei, Abdulhusain and Elham Malekzadeh. 2005. *Ruznameh-ye Khaterat-e Nasir al-Din Shah (1306 AH/1888 CE)*. Tehran: Sazeman-e Asnad va Ketabkhaneh-ye Melli-ye Jomhuri-ye Islami-ye Iran.

Nejat-Hosseini, Mohsen. 2000. *Bar Faraz-e Khalij. Khaterat-e Mohsen Nejat-Hosseini Ozv-e Sabeq-e Sazman-e Mojahedeen Khalq Iran (1354–1346 A.H.)*. Tehran: Nashr-e Ney.

"Nerkh-e Tavarrom." 2007. *BBCPersian.com*, April 11. Retrieved April 11, 2007 (BBCPersian.com)

Neuhaus, Jessamyn. 2000. "The Importance of Being Orgasmic: Sexuality, Gender, and Marital Sex Manuals in the United States, 1920–1963." *Journal of the History of Sexuality* 9: 447–473.

Nichols, Jack. 1997. "Saviz Shafaie: An Iranian Gay Activist Leader: Interview." *Gay Iran News and Reports*, May 27. Retrieved February 14, 2007 (www.globalgayz.com/iran-news.html).

Nikbakht, Faryar. 2002. "As with Moses in Egypt: Alliance Israélite Universelle Schools in Iran." In Sarshar 2002, pp. 197–236.

Nikkhah-Qamsari, Narges. 2005. *Tahavvol-e Negaresh Nesbat be Zan va Ta'sir-e an dar Enqelab-e Islami*. Tehran: Pajuheshkadeh-ye Imam Khomeini va Enqelab-e Islami.

"Niruyeh Moghavemat Basij: Mobilization Resistance Force." 2006. Retrieved on February 5, 2007 (www.globalsecurity.org/intell/world/iran/basij.htm).

Nizam al-Molk. 1962. *Siyar al-Moluk (Siyasat Nameh)*, ed. Hubert Darke. Tehran: Entesharat-e Bongah-e Tarjomeh va Nashr-e Ketab.

"Nokat va Molahezat." 1920. *Kaveh* 5(46) (November 13): 2.

Nomani, Farhad and Sohrab Behdad. 2006. *Class and Labor in Iran: Did the Revolution Matter?* Syracuse University Press.

Novin, Parviz and Abbas Khăjeh Piri. 1999. *Hoquq-e Madani*. Vol. VIII. Tehran: Ketabkhaneh-ye Ganj-e Danesh.

Omid, Homa. 1994. *Islam and the Post-Revolutionary State in Iran*. New York: St. Martin's Press.

Ong, Aihwa. 1990. "State Versus Islam: Malay Families, Women's Bodies, and the Body Politics in Malaysia." *American Ethnologist* 17(2) (May): 195–216.

Ono, Morio. 1998. *Kheir-Abad Nameh*, trans. Hashem Rajabzadeh. Tehran University Publications.

Ostadmalek, Fatemeh. 1988. *Hijab va Kashf-e Hijab dar Iran*. Tehran: Ata'i Press.

Paidar, Parvin. 1995. *Women and the Political Process in Twentieth-Century Iran*. Cambridge University Press.

Pakdaman, Nasser. 2001. *Qatl-e Kasravi*. Second edition. Cologne: Forough Publications.

Papan-Matin, Firoozeh. 2005. *The Love Poems of Ahmad Shamlu*. Poems trans. F. Papan-Matin and Arthur Lane. Bethesda, MD: Ibex Publishers.

Parsipour, Shahrnoosh. 1996. *Khaterat-e Zendan*. Stockholm: Baran Press.

"Pasdaran." 2007. *Global Security.org*. Retrieved February 5, 2007 (www. globalsecurity.org/military/world/iran/pasdaran.htm).

Patai, Raphael. 1998 *Jadid Al-Islam: The Jewish "New Muslims" of Meshhed*. Detroit: Wayne State University.

Peirce, Leslie P. 1993. *Imperial Harem: Women and Sovereignty in the Ottoman Empire*. Oxford University Press.

Petry, Carl F. 1991. "Class Solidarity versus Gender Gain: Women as Custodians of Property in Later Medieval Egypt." In Keddie and Baron 1991, pp. 122–142.

Pharr, Suzanne. 2001. "Homophobia as a Weapon of Sexism." In *Race, Class, and Gender in the United States*, ed. Paula S. Rothenberg, pp. 143–163. New York: Worth Publishers.

Pirnazar, Jaleh. 1995. "Chehreh-ye Yahud dar Asar-e Seh Nevisandeh-ye Motejaded-e Irani." *Iran Nameh* 13(4): 483–501.

    2002. "The Anusim of Mashhad." In Sarshar 2002, pp. 117–136.

Pirnia, Mansore. 1992. *Safarnameh-ye Shahbanu*. Rockville, MD: Mehr Iran Publishing Company.

    2007. *Khanom-e Vazir: Khaterat va Dastneveshtehha-ye Farrokhrou Parsay*. Potomac, MD: Mehr Iran Publishing.

Plato. 1961. *The Collected Dialogues of Plato*, ed. Edith Hamilton and Huntington Cairns. With Introduction and Prefatory Notes. Princeton University Press.

Polak, Jakob Eduard. [1861] 1982. "Prostitution in Persia." In *Jahrbuch 1982 des Verbandes Iranischer Akademiker in der Bundesrepublik Deutschland und Berlin-West.* Vol. II, pp. 36–44. Hildesheim, Zürich, and New York: Georg Olms Verlag.

[1865] 1976. *Persien, das Land und seine Bewohner: Ethnographische Schilderungen.* Hildesheim and New York: Georg Olms Verlag. 2 vols.

Postel, Danny. 2006. *Reading Legitimation Crisis in Tehran: Iran and the Future of Liberalism.* Chicago: Prickly Paradigm Press.

Poya, Maryam. 1999. *Women, Work and Islamism: Ideology and Resistance in Iran.* London and New York: Zed Press.

Price, Massoume. 2002. "Chaman Andam: Slavery in Early Twentieth Century Iran." *The Iranian.com.* Retrieved January 16, 2007 (www.iranian.comMassoumePrice/2002/October/Slavery).

"Qanun-e Eslah-e Moqararat-e Marbut-e be Talaq." 1992. *Ruznameh-ye Rasmi,* 13914(19 Azar 1371).

Qavimi, Fakhri. 1973. *Karnameh-ye Zanan-e Mashhur-e Iran.* Tehran: Vezarat-e Amuzesh va Parvarish Press.

Qazi, Ne'matollah Shakib. 1993. *Elal-e Soqut-e Hokumat-e Reza Shah.* Tehran: Nashr-e Asar.

Rahnavard, Zahra. 1987. *Safar be Diyar-e Zanan-e Botparast.* Tehran: Soroush Publications.

Rajabi, Muhammad Hasan. 1995. *Mashahir-e Zanan-e Irani va Parsiguy: Az Aghaz ta Mashruteh.* Tehran: Soroush Publications.

Ramazani, Rouhollah K. 1966. *The Foreign Policy of Iran, 1500–1941: A Developing Nation in World Affairs.* Charlottesville: University Press of Virginia.

Ravandi, Morteza. 1984. *Tarikh-e Ejtema'i-ye Iran.* Tehran: Amir Kabir Press. 7 vols.

1989. *Tarikh-e Ejtema'i-ye Iran.* Vols. VI and VII. Tehran: Fajr Islam.

Reeves, Minou. 1989. *Female Warriors of Allah: Women and the Islamic Revolution.* New York: E.P. Dutton.

Resaleh-ye Towzih al-Masa'el Motabeq ba Fatva-ye Maraje'-ye Mo'zam-e Taqlid. 1993. Qom: Balaghat Publications.

Rice, Clara Colliver. 1923. *Persian Women and Their Ways.* London: Seeley, Service and Co. Ltd.

Rice, Cyprian. 1964. *The Persian Sufis.* London: George Allen and Unwin.

Richard, Yann. 2003. "Contemporary Shi'i Thought." In Keddie 2003, pp. 188–212.

Ricks, Thomas M. 1989. "Slaves and Slave Traders in the Persian Gulf, Eighteenth and Nineteenth Centuries: An Assessment." In *The Economics of the Indian Ocean Slave Trade in the Nineteenth Century,* ed. William Gervase Clarence-Smith, pp. 60–70. London: Frank Cass.

2002. "Slaves and Slave Trading in Shi'i Iran, AD 1500–1900." In *Conceptualizing/Re-Conceptualizing Africa: The Construction of African Historical Identity,* ed. Maghan Keita, pp. 77–88. Leiden, Boston, and Cologne: Brill.

Ringer, Monica. 2001. *Education, Religion and the Discourse of Cultural Reform in Qajar Iran.* Costa Mesa: Mazda Press.

Rostam-Kolayi, Jasmin. 2002. "Foreign Education, the Women's Press, and the Discourse of Scientific Domesticity in Early-Twentieth-Century Iran." In *Iran and the Surrounding World: Interactions in Culture and Cultural Politics*, ed. Nikki R. Keddie and Rudolph Matthee, pp. 182–202. Seattle: University of Washington Press.

Roudi, Farzaneh. 1999. "Iran's Revolutionary Approach to Family Planning." *Population Today* (July/August): 4–5.

Roudi-Fahimi, Farzaneh and Valentine M. Moghadam. 2006. "Empowering Women, Developing Society: Female Education in the Middle East and North Africa." *Al-Raʿidah* 23 and 24 (114 and 115) (Summer–Fall): 4–10.

Rowson, Everett K. 1991a. "The Categorization of Gender and Sexual Irregularity in Medieval Arabic Vice Lists." In *Body Guards: The Cultural Politics of Gender Ambiguity*, ed. Julia Epstein and Kristina Straub, pp. 50–79. New York: Routledge.

1991b. "The Effeminates of Early Medina." *Journal of the American Oriental Society* 3(3–4): 671–693.

2003. "Gender Irregularity as Entertainment: Institutionalized Transvestism at the Caliphal Court in Medieval Baghdad." In Farmer and Pasternack 2003, pp. 45–72.

Forthcoming. *Homoeroticism in Medieval Islamic Societies.*

"Rowzeh Khāni va Madreseh-ye Dokhtaran." 1920. *Kaveh* 5(43) (August 16): 3.

Rumi, Mowlana Jalal al-Din Muhammad. 1995. *Koliyat-e Shams-e Tabrizi*. Based on the edition corrected by Badiʿ al-Zaman Foruzanfar. Tehran: Bustan Books.

1996. *Masnavi-ye Maʿnavi*, ed. Badiʿ al-Zaman Foruzanfar. Based on the edition corrected by Reynold A. Nicholson. Tehran: Safi Ali Shah.

"Ruzaneh 2000 Nafar Bara-ye Daryaft-e Vam Sabt-e-Nam Mikonand." 2007. *Mehrnews.com*. Retrieved February 13, 2007 (http://mehrnews.com/fa/NewsDetail.aspx?NewsID=434804).

Sabahi, Farian. 2002. "Gender and the Army of Knowledge in Pahlavi Iran, 1968–1979." In *Women, Religion and Culture in Iran*, ed. Sarah Ansari and Vanessa Martin, pp. 99–126. Richmond, Surrey: Curzon Press.

Sabbah, Fatna. A. 1984. *Woman in the Muslim Unconscious*, trans. Mary Jo Lakeland. New York: Pergamon Press.

Saber, M.A. 1992. *Hop Hop Nameh*. Baku: Sharq-Qarb Nashriyati.

Sadeghi, Fatemeh. 2008. "Chera be Hijab-e Ejbari 'Nah' Migu'im?" *Radio Zamaaneh*, 11 Tir 1387. Retrieved July 22, 2008 (http://radiozamaaneh.com/humanrights/2008/05/print_post_245.html).

Saʿdi, Abu al-Qasem. 1996. *Koliyat-e Saʿdi*, ed. M.A. Foroughi. Tehran: Tolu' Publications.

Saheb al-Zamani, Naser al-Din. [1964] 1999. *Ansu-ye Chehreha*. Tehran: Zaryab Press.

Sahim, Haideh. 2002. "Clothing and Makeup." In *Esther's Children: A Portrait of Iranian Jews*, ed. Houman Sarshar, pp. 175–196. Los Angeles and Philadelphia: Center for Iranian Jewish Oral History and the Jewish Publication Society.

Sakurai, Keiko. 2004. "University Entrance Examination and the Making of an Islamic Society in Iran: A Study of the Post-Revolutionary Iranian Approach to 'Konkur.'" *Iranian Studies* 37(3): 385–406.

Salami, Mahmaz. 2007. "Unveiling the Iranian Queer Organization: An Interview with Arsham Parsi." Retrieved November 26, 2007 (www.gozaar.org/template.print_en.php?id=461).

Salami, Qolamreza and Afsaneh Najmabadi, eds. 2005. *Nehzat-e Nesvan-e Sharq.* Tehran: Shirazeh Press.

Salehi-Isfahani, Djavad. 2000. "Demographic Factors in Iran's Economic Development." *Social Research.* Retrieved February 14, 2007 (www.findarticles.com/p/articles/mi_m2267/is_2_67/ai_63787345/print).

Salnameh-ye Amari 1352 Keshvar. 1973–1974. Tehran: Sazeman-e Barnameh va Budjeh-ye Markaz – Amar-e Iran. 394.

Sanasarian, Eliz. 1982. *The Women's Rights Movement in Iran: Mutiny, Appeasement, and Repression from 1900 to Khomeini.* New York: Praeger.

2000. *Religious Minorities in Iran.* Cambridge University Press.

San'ati, Mahin and Afsaneh Najmabadi, eds. 1998. *Sedigheh Dowlatabadi.* Chicago: Midland Press. 3 vols.

Sapa-DPA. 2002. "Iran Faces Taboo Topic of Prostitution." *The Independent,* December 13. www.uri.edu/artsci/wms/hughes/taboo_topic.

Sarshar, Houman, ed. 2002. *Esther's Children: A Portrait of Iranian Jews.* Beverly Hills, CA: The Center for Iranian Jewish Oral History.

Schayegh, Cyrus. 2004. "Hygiene, Eugenics, Genetics, and the Perception of Demographic Crisis in Iran, 1910s–1940s." *Critique: Critical Middle Eastern Studies* 13(3) (Fall): 335–361.

Schimmel, Annemarie. 1975. *Mystical Dimensions of Islam.* Chapel Hill: University of North Carolina Press.

Scholz, Piotr O. 2001. *Eunuchs and Castrati: A Cultural History.* Princeton: Markus Wiener Publishers.

Sciolino, Elaine. 2005. *Persian Mirrors: The Elusive Face of Iran.* New York: Free Press.

Scott, James C. 1985. *Weapons of the Weak: Everyday Forms of Peasant Resistance.* New Haven: Yale University Press.

Sebbar, Leila. 1979. "En Iran, le tchador glisse, à Paris, il brûle." *Histoires d'Elles* 11 (April).

Sedghi, Hamideh. 2007. *Women and Politics in Iran: Veiling, Unveiling, and Reveiling.* Cambridge University Press.

Segal, Ronald. 2001. *Islam's Black Slaves: The Other Black Diaspora.* New York: Farrar, Straus and Giroux.

"Seh Nameh az Khanandegan va Yek Javab az MAHA." 2005. *MAHA* 8 (Tir): 22–29.

"Seminar-e Masa'el-e Javanan." [1964] 1999. In Sahib al-Zamani [1964] 1999, pp. 273–281.

Serena, Carla. 1883. *Hommes et choses en Perse.* Paris: G. Charpentier.

[1883] 1983. *Safarnameh-ye Madam Karla Serena (1877–1878),* trans. Ali Asghar Saidi from the original French above. Tehran: Zavvar Press.

Sha'bani, Reza and Gholam Hossein Zargarinejad. 1992. *Vaqaye'-ye Kashf-e Hijab.* Tehran: Sazeman-e Madarek-e Farhangi-ye Enqelab-e Islami.

Shabastari, Mojtahed. 1999. "Zanan, Ketab, va Sonnat." *Zanan* 57 (Aban): 19–22.
Shaditalab, Jaleh. 2002a. "Doganehgi Miyan-e Zanan-e Nokhbeh va Tudeh-ye Zanan: Gozaresh-e az Vaz'iyat-e Zanan pish az Enqelab-e Islami. *Zanan* 84 (Bahman): 42–45.
  2002b. "Moqe'iyat-e Zanan pas as Enqelab-e Eslami: Part II." *Zanan* 86 (Farvardin): 26–31.
Shahidian, Hammed. 1994. "The Iranian Left and the 'Woman Question' in the Revolution of 1978–79." *International Journal of Middle East Studies* 26(2) (May): 223–247.
Shahri, Ja'far. 1968. *Shekar-e Talkh*. Tehran: Rooz Chap.
  1990. *Tarikh-e Ejtema'i-ye Tehran dar Qarn-e Sizdahom*. Tehran: Rasa Publications. 6 vols.
  1991. *Gusheh-ye az Tarikh-e Ejtema'i-ye Tehran-e Qadim*. Vol. I. Tehran: Mo'in Press.
Shahvar, Soli. 2008 *The Forgotten Schools: The Baha'is and Modern Education in Iran, 1899–1934*. London: I.B. Tauris.
Shakeri, Shokoufeh and Sahereh Labriz. 1992. "Mard: Sharik ya Ra'is?" *Zanan* 2 (Esfand): 26–32.
Shakerifar, Elhum. 2006. "Temporary Marriage in Modern Iran." Paper presented at the Sixth Biennial Conference of the International Society for Iranian Studies, London.
Shaki, Mansour. 1971. "The Sassanian Matrimonial Relations." *Archiv Orientalni* 39: 322–345.
Shakiba, Parvin. 1998. *Az Rabe'eh ta Parvin: Zanan-e Sha'er-e Farsi Zaban*. Champaign, IL: Kiyumars Books Press.
Shamisa, Sirus. 2002. *Shahedbazi dar Adabiyat-e Farsi*. Tehran: Ferdows Press.
Shariati, Ali. [1971–1976] 1990. *Collected Works of Ali Shariati*, vol. XXI: *Zan* [Women]. Tehran: Bonyad-e Farhangi-ye Doctor Ali Shariati.
Sharif-Kashani, Muhammad Mahdi. 1983. *Vaqe'at-e Ettefaqiyeh dar Rouzegar*. Tehran: Nashr-e Tarikh-e Iran. 3 vols.
Shavarini, Mitra K. 2006. "Wearing the Veil to College: The Paradox of Higher Education in the Lives of Iranian Women." *International Journal of Middle East Studies* 38: 189–211.
Shaygan, Ali. 1979. "Iran Nemitavanad be Sadr-e Islam Bazgardad." *Ettela'at* (6 Esfand 1357/25 February): 8.
Shaykh Rezaei, Ensiya and Shahla Azari [1885–1888] 1999. *Gozareshha-ye Nazmiyeh az Mahallat-e Tehran, 1303–1305 AH*. Tehran: Sazman-e Asnad-e Melli-ye Iran. 2 vols.
Sheikh al-Islami, Ali. 1925. "Adab-e Qadimi-ye 'Arusi." *Omid* 295 (Aban 17): 1–3.
Sheikh al-Islami, Pari. 1972. *Zanan-e Ruznameh-nigar va Andishmandi-e Iran*. Tehran: Maz Graphics Press.
Sheil, Mary (Lady). [1856] 1973. *Glimpses of Life and Manners in Persia*. New York: Arno Press.
Sherkat, Shahla. 1998. "*Zanan* dar Dadgah." *Zanan* 43 (Khordad): 2–4.
Shirazi, Faegheh. 2001. *The Veil Unveiled: The Hijab in Modern Culture*. University Press of Florida.

Shirazi, Fariba. 1977. "Qavanin-e Ta'min-e Ejtema'i dar Mored-e Zanan Bayad Eslah Shavad." *Payam-e Zan* 6(2) (Ordibehesht): 5–31.

Shirazi, Jahangir. 2005. "Chera man 'Hamjensbaz' Nistam, Vali 'Hamjensgara' Hastam?" *MAHA* 6 (June): 25–30.

Sigarchi, Arash. 2008. "Hashtad Shaki-ye Sardar Zare'i." *News.gooya.com.* Ordibehesht 1387.

Smith, Margaret. 1928. *Rabi'a the Mystic and Her Fellow Saints in Islam.* Cambridge University Press.

Smith, William Robertson. 1903. *Kinship and Marriage in Early Arabia.* London: Adam and Charles Black.

Soraya, Malekeh. 2003. *Khaterat-e Malekeh Soraya.* Tehran: Afrasiyab Press.

Soroush, Abdolkarim. 1999. "Qabz va Bast-e Hoquq-e Zanan." *Zanan*, 59 (Day): 32–37.

Southgate, Horatio. 1840. *Narrative of a Tour Through Armenia, Kurdistan, Persia and Mesopotamia*, vol. II. New York: D. Appleton and Company.

Southgate, Minoo S. 1984. "Men, Women, and Boys: Love and Sex in the Works of Sa'di." *Iranian Studies* 16(4) (Autumn): 43–452.

Spellberg, D.A. 1994. *Politics, Gender, and the Islamic Past: The Legacy of A'isha Bint Abi Bakr.* New York: Columbia University Press.

Stern, Gertrude H. 1939. *Marriage in Early Islam.* London: The Royal Asiatic Society.

Stites, Richard. 1978. *The Women's Liberation Movement in Russia: Feminism, Nihilism, and Bolshevism, 1860–1930.* Princeton University Press.

Stowasser, Barbara Freyer. 1994. *Women in the Qur'an, Traditions, and Interpretation.* Oxford University Press.

Surieu, Robert. 1967. *Sarv-e Naz: An Essay on Love and the Representation of Erotic Themes in Ancient Iran*, trans. James Hogarth. Geneva: Nagel Publishers.

Sykes, Ella Constance. 1898. *Through Persia on a Side-Saddle.* Philadelphia: J.B. Lippincott Company.

[1910] 2005. *Persia and Its People.* London: Elibron Classics.

Tabari, Azar. 1984. "Chronology." *Nimeye Digar* 1 (Spring 1984): 104–107.

Tabari, Azar and Nahid Yeganeh, eds. 1982. *In the Shadow of Islam: The Women's Movement in Iran.* London: Zed Press.

Tabrizi, Shams al-Din. 1990. *Maqalat-e Shams-e Tabrizi*, ed. Mohammad Ali Movahed. Tehran: Khãrazmi Press.

"Taghyir-e Sabk-e Zendegi Mohemtarin 'Amel-e Talaq dar Iran Ast." 2005. *Zanan* 125 (Mehr): 77–78.

Tait, Robert. 2007. "Iranian Minister Backs Temporary Marriage to Relieve Lust of Youth." *The Guardian.* Retrieved June 4, 2007 (www.guardian.co.uk/iran/story/0,,2094767,00.html).

Taj al-Saltana. [1914] 1982. *Khaterat-e Taj al-Saltaneh*, ed. Mansureh Ettehadieh (Nezam Mafi) and Cyrus Sa'duniyan. Tehran: Nashr-e Tarikh-e Iran.

1993. *Crowning Anguish: Memoirs of a Persian Princess from the Harem to Modernity, 1884–1914*, ed. Abbas Amanat. Washington, DC: Mage Publishers.

"Talaq dar Iran va Ekhtelaf dar Amarha." 2008. *BBCPersian.com*, March 3 Retrieved July 22, 2008 (www.bbc.co.uk/persian/iran/story/2008/03/080302_bd-divorce.shtml).

Talattof, Kamran. 1997. "Iranian Women's Literature: From Pre-Revolutionary Social Discourse to Post-Revolutionary Feminism." *International Journal of Middle East Studies* 29: 531–558.

Tapper, Nancy. 1978. "The Women's Subsociety Among the Shahsevan Nomads of Iran." In Beck and Keddie 1978, pp. 374–398.

1990. "Ziyaret: Gender, Movement, and Exchange in a Turkish Community." In Eickelman and Piscatori 1990, pp. 236–255.

Tapper, Richard, ed. 2002. *The New Iranian Cinema: Politics, Representation and Identity*. London: I.B. Tauris.

Taqizadeh, Hasan. 1920. "Dowreh-ye Jadid." *Kaveh* 5(36) (January 22): 2.

Tariqi, Noushin. 2004. "Yek Eshtebah-e Qanuni." *Zanan* 112 (Shahrivar): 2–6.

Tatchell, Peter. 2007. "Tehran's Heroic Women: Despite Violent Repression, the Iranian Women's Movement is Defiant." *The Guardian*, March 7.

Tavakoli-Targhi, Mohamad. 1993. "Imagining Western Women: Occidentalism and Euro-Eroticism." *Radical America* 24(3): 73–85.

2001a. *Refashioning Iran: Orientalism, Occidentalism, and Historiography*. New York: Palgrave.

2001b. "Tajaddod-e Ekhtera'i, Tamaddon-e 'Ariyati, va Enqelabi Rowhani." *Iran Nameh* 20(2–3): 195–236.

Tehrani, F., F. Farahani and M. Hashemi. 2001. "Factors Influencing Contraceptive Use in Tehran." *Family Practice* 18(2) (April): 204–208.

Tezcur, Gunes Murat, Taghi Azadarmaki, and Mehri Bahar. 2006. "Religious Participation Among Muslims: Iranian Exceptionalism." *Critique: Critical Middle Eastern Studies* 15(3) (Fall): 217–232.

Tohidi, Nayareh. 1991. "Gender and Islamic Fundamentalism: Feminist Perspectives in Iran." In *Third World Women and the Politics of Feminism*, ed. Chandra Talpade Mohanty, Ann Russo, and Lourdes Torres, pp. 251–260. Bloomington: Indiana University Press.

1996. *Feminizm, Demokrasi va Islamgara-ye*. Los Angeles: n.p.

2006. "Iran's Women's Rights Movement and the One Million Signatures Campaign." Retrieved December 17, 2006 (www.peyvand.com/news/06/dec/1174.html).

2008. "Taghyir-e 'Qavanin-e Khanevadeh' Akharin Marhaleh az Farayand-e Sekularizasion?" *The Feminist School*, 28 Khordad 1387. Retrieved July 22, 2008 (http://feministschool.info/spip.php?article804).

Touba, Jacquiline Rudolph. 1987. "The Widowed in Iran." In *Widows: The Middle East, Asia, and the Pacific*, ed. Helena Z. Lopata, pp. 106–132. Durham, NC: Duke University Press.

Tremayne, Soraya. 2006. "Modernity and Early Marriage in Iran: A View from Within." *Journal of Middle East Women's Studies* 2(1) (Winter): 65–94.

Tucker, Judith E. 1998. *In the House of the Law: Gender and Islamic Law in Ottoman Syria and Palestine*. Berkeley: University of California.

UNICEF. 2005. "At a Glance." (www.unicef.org/infobycountry/iran_statistics.htm).

2007. "At a Glance: Iran (Islamic Republic of)." Retrieved February 12, 2007 (www.tsunamigeneration.com/infobycountry/iran.html).

Vahdati, Soheila. 2005. "Az Evin ke Azad Shodam, Showharam Besheddat Ma Ra Kotak Mizad: Vajiheh Reza'i dar Goftegu ba Soheila Vahdati." Retrieved March 7, 2007 (http://zanan.iran-emrooz.net/index.php?/zanan/more/5791/).

Vatandoust, Reza. 1985. "The Status of Iranian Women During the Pahlavi Regime." In *Women and the Family in Iran*, ed. Asghar Fathi, pp. 107–130. Leiden: E.J. Brill.

Vick, Karl. 2005. "Opiates of the Iranian People." Washingtonpost.com, September 23. Retrieved March 21, 2007.

Vieille, Paul. 1975. *La féodalité et l'état en Iran*. Paris: Éditions Anthropos.

——— 1978. "Iranian Women in Family Alliance and Sexual Politics." In Beck and Keddie 1978, pp. 451–472.

Vieille, Paul and Morteza Kotobi. 1966. "Familles et unions de familles en Iran." *Cahiers Internationaux de Sociologie* (December): 93–103.

Wagner, Moritz. 1856. *Travels in Persia, Georgia and Koordistan*. Vol. III. London: Hurst and Blackett.

Wakin, Jeanette. "Family Law: II. In Islam." *Encyclopedia Iranica*. Retrieved January 16, 2007 (www.iranica.com/newsite).

Westenholz, Joan Goodnick. 1989. "Tamar, Qedesa, Qadistu, and Sacred Prostitution in Mesopotamia." *Harvard Theological Review* 82(3) (July): 245–265.

Wishard, John, G. 1908. *Twenty Years in Persia: A Narrative of Life Under the Last Three Shahs*. New York and Chicago: Fleming H. Revell Company.

"Women's Rights in Persia: Appeal for the Suffrage in the Mejliss." 1911a. *The Times*, August 22: 3.

"Women's Rights in Persia." 1911b. *The Times*, August 28: 3.

Woodsmall, Ruth Frances. 1936. *Moslem Women Enter a New World*. New York: Round Table Press, Inc.

Wright, Robin. 2001. *The Last Great Revolution: Turmoil and Transformation in Iran*. New York: Vintage Books.

Yadgar-Azadi, Mina. 1992a. "Qezavat-e Zan." *Zanan* 4 (Ordibehesht): 20–26.

——— 1992b. "Qezavat-e Zan." *Zanan* 5 (Khordad-tir): 17–25.

Yarshater, Ehsan. 1960. "The Theme of Wine-Drinking and the Concept of the Beloved in Early Persian Poetry." *Studia Islamica* 13: 43–53.

Yavari, M. 1981. *Naqsh-e Rowhaniyat dar Tarikh-e Mo'aser-e Iran*. Los Angeles: Ketab Corporation.

Yeganeh, Nahid. 1993. "Women, Nationalism, and Islam in Contemporary Political Discourse in Iran." *Feminist Review* 44 (Summer): 3–18.

Yonan, Rev. Isaac Malek. 1898. *Persian Women*. Nashville: Cumberland Presbyterian Publishing House.

Zahedi, Ashraf. 2006. "State Ideology and the Status of Iranian War Widows." *International Feminist Journal of Politics* 8(2) (June): 267–286.

"Zahra Rahnavard." 1999. *Zanan* 51 (Farvardin): 9.

Zakani, 'Obeyd. 1964. *Koliyat-e 'Obeyd-e Zakani*, ed. Parviz Atabaki. Tehran: Zavvar Press.

Zamani, Afsaneh. 2000. "Amalkard-e Majles-e Panjom dar Mored-e Zan va Khanevadeh." *Hoquq-e Zanan* (13 Day-Bahman): 6–10.

Zangeneh, Hamid. 2003. "The Iranian Economy and the Globalization Process." In *Iran Encountering Globalization: Problems and Prospects*, ed. Ali Mohammadi, pp. 107–133. London and New York: Routledge Curzon.

Zangeneh, Roshanak. 2005. "Sexuality in Iran No Longer a Taboo." December 2. Retrieved March 12, 2007 (www.irandokht.com/editorial/index4.php?area= par&sectionID=25&editorialID=1056).

Zargarinezhad, Gholam Hussein. 1995. *Rasaʿel-e Mashrutiyat*. Tehran: Kavir Press.

Ze'evi, Dror. 2006. *Producing Desire: Changing Sexual Discourse in the Ottoman Middle East, 1500–1900*. Berkeley: University of California Press.

Zerang, Muhammad. 2002. *Tahavvol-e Nezam-e Qaza'i-ye Iran: Az Mashruteh ta Soqut-e Reza Shah*. Tehran: Markaz-e Asnad-e Enqelab-e Islami. 2 vols.

Zilfi, Madeline C., ed. 1997. *Women in the Ottoman Empire: Middle Eastern Women in the Early Modern Era*. Leiden and New York: Brill.

Index